T0339998

DATA, METHODS AND THEORY IN THE ORGANIZATIONAL SCIENCES

Data, Methods and Theory in the Organizational Sciences explores the long-term evolution and changing relationships between data, methods, and theory in the organizational sciences. In the last 50 years, theory has come to dominate research and scholarship in these fields, yet the emergence of big data, as well as the increasing use of archival data sets and meta-analytic methods to test empirical hypotheses, has upset this order. This volume examines the evolving relationship between data, methods, and theory and suggests new ways of thinking about the role of each in the development and presentation of research in organizations.

This volume utilizes the latest thinking from experts in a wide range of fields on the topics of data, methods, and theory and uses this knowledge to explore the ways in which behavior in organizations has been studied. This volume also argues that the current focus on theory is both unhealthy for the field and unsustainable and it provides more successful ways theory can be used to support and structure research and demonstrates the most effective techniques for analyzing and making sense of data.

This is an essential resource for researchers, professionals, and educators who are looking to rethink their current approaches to research, and who are interested in creating more useful and more interpretable research in the organizational sciences.

Kevin R. Murphy is Professor Emeritus at the University of Limerick, Ireland. He is a former SIOP President and Editor of the *Journal of Applied Psychology*, and has been published in areas ranging from performance appraisal and psychometrics to honesty in the workplace.

SIOP Organizational Frontiers Series

Series Editors

The Organizational Frontiers Series is sponsored by the Society for Industrial and Organizational Psychology (SIOP). Launched in 1983 to make scientific contributions accessible to the field, the series publishes books addressing emerging theoretical developments, fundamental and translational research, and theory-driven practice in the field of Industrial-Organizational Psychology and related organizational science disciplines including organizational behavior, human resource management, and labor and industrial relations.

Books in this series aim to inform readers of significant advances in research; challenge the research and practice community to develop and adapt new ideas; and promote the use of scientific knowledge in the solution of public policy issues and increased organizational effectiveness.

The Series originated in the hope that it would facilitate continuous learning and spur research curiosity about organizational phenomena on the part of both scientists and practitioners.

The Society for Industrial and Organizational Psychology is an international professional association with an annual membership of more than 8,000 industrial-organizational (I-O) psychologists who study and apply scientific principles to the workplace. I-O psychologists serve as trusted partners to business, offering strategically focused and scientifically rigorous solutions for a number of workplace issues. SIOP's mission is to enhance human well-being and performance in organizational and work settings by promoting the science, practice, and teaching of I-O psychology. For more information about SIOP, please visit www.siop.org.

For more information about this series, please visit www.routledge.com/
SIOP-Organizational-Frontiers-Series/book-series/SIOP

DATA, METHODS AND THEORY IN THE ORGANIZATIONAL SCIENCES

A New Synthesis

Edited by Kevin R. Murphy

Routledge
Taylor & Francis Group

NEW YORK AND LONDON

SOCIETY for
INDUSTRIAL and
ORGANIZATIONAL
PSYCHOLOGY

ORGANIZATIONAL FRONTIERS SERIES

Cover image: © Getty Images

First published 2022
by Routledge
605 Third Avenue, New York, NY 10158

and by Routledge
4 Park Square, Milton Park, Abingdon, Oxon, OX14 4RN

Routledge is an imprint of the Taylor & Francis Group, an informa business

Library of Congress Cataloging-in-Publication Data
Names: Murphy, Kevin R., 1952- editor.
Title: Data, methods, and theory in the organizational sciences : a new synthesis / edited by Kevin R Murphy.
Description: First Edition. | New York, NY : Routledge, 2022. |
Series: Siop organizational frontiers series | Includes bibliographical references and index. |
Identifiers: LCCN 2021047167 (print) | LCCN 2021047168 (ebook) |
ISBN 9780367857707 (hardback) | ISBN 9780367857646 (paperback) |
ISBN 9781003015000 (ebook)
Subjects: LCSH: Organizational behavior. | Human-computer interaction. |
Organizational sociology--Research.
Classification: LCC HD58.7 .D3558 2022 (print) | LCC HD58.7 (ebook) |
DDC 302.3/5--dc23/eng/20211112
LC record available at https://lccn.loc.gov/2021047167
LC ebook record available at https://lccn.loc.gov/2021047168

ISBN: 9780367857707 (hbk)
ISBN: 9780367857646 (pbk)
ISBN: 9781003015000 (ebk)

DOI: 10.4324/9781003015000

Typeset in Bembo
by KnowledgeWorks Global Ltd.

CONTENTS

FIGURES

TABLES

PREFACE

In the last 20 years, there has been a substantial change in the types of data that can be used to study behavior in organizations, and the increased availability of big data, archival datasets and simulation is changing the relationships between data, methods, and theory. These changes, while disorienting for some, represent only the most recent iteration of the changing set of relationships between data, methods, and theory. When viewed from a long-term perspective, these changes represent a continuation of the long evolution of our field.

The early history of I/O psychology placed a strong emphasis on using data to solve practical problems, with relatively little emphasis on theory and virtually none on contributions to theory. If you scan the major journals covering our field in the early part of the 20th century, what you will see are short empirical papers with few citations and often no mention of theory at all. For example, the first two empirical papers published in *Journal of Applied Psychology* dealt with using ability tests to select policemen and firemen (Terman et al., 1917) and the legibility of telephone directories (Baird, 1917). As Cucina and Nester note in this volume (Chapter 13), I/O psychology retained its highly empirical character well into the 20th century, and our current emphasis on theory-first articles is a recent phenomenon.

There is still a strong empirical emphasis in the field of Industrial and Organizational Psychology, as evidenced by a recent issue of *Journal of Applied Psychology* (Volume 105, Issue 1, 2021), which includes five articles devoted to understanding work and employment in the COVID-19 pandemic in which theory development plays a minor role. However, I/O psychologists who wish to publish in journals with the highest status rankings[1] will find it rough going unless their papers make some clear contribution to theory. Papers that do not make an identifiable contribution to theory will be desk-rejected at many journals, and even those that are sent out for review are likely to be criticized by reviewers if they fail to put theory first.

Hambrick (2007) argues that the devotion to theory in management research (and increasingly in other organizational sciences) is in part a reaction to criticisms of business education in the 1950s and 1960s. By the 1970s, leading management journals emphasized the importance of theoretical contributions, and over time, this emphasis grew into an absolute requirement that every article published in this journal must contribute to theory. At that time, research in I/O Psychology was still strongly empirical, but the data of data-first "dustbowl empiricism" were clearly coming to an end, and theory was becoming more important across the organizational sciences.

It did not take long for an emphasis on theory in management research to turn into a near obsession. As Hambrick (2007) noted, in management research, empirical tests of the key contributions of a theory were not thought of as worthwhile contributions, and a paper that did little more that test a theory, no matter how compelling the test, was unlikely to be even sent out for review. Over the years, this emphasis on theory has spread from management journals to journals I/O psychology journals.

In the last 10 years, the data landscape has changed, and organizational scientists are increasingly taking advantage of big data, simulations, archival data, secondary analyses and meta-analyses to address important research questions, and this change in the types of data used and the sources of data has had important implications for the relationship between data, methods and theory. Theory is still very important, but our field is already seeing movement away from theory-first research toward research that is informed but not driven by theory. If you take a long view of the progression of our field, you might suspect that I/O psychology is returning to its roots, in which both theory and data are important tools for answering questions about behavior in organizations, and in which neither necessarily takes precedence. The aim of this volume is not to denigrate or degrade theory, but rather to help the field move back toward a healthy and sustainable relationship between theory, methods and data. Over the last 50 years, we have often lost sight of Lewin's maxim that "there is nothing as practical as a good theory" (McCain, 2015); it is time for I/O psychologists to stop worshiping theory and start using it.

The first four chapters of this book look at the types of data that are becoming available to organizational researchers and the implications of using data that are often collected by others for purposes that may have little to do with the questions pursued by the researcher who uses these data. Studies in which individual researchers choose and administer a set of measures designed to test specific predictions of a theory or to measure constructs that are central to that theory are still an important part of research in the organizational sciences, but they are being displaced by studies that rely on big data, archival data, meta analyses and the like, and one consequence of this change in data is that research is increasingly likely to become opportunistic – i.e., pursuing specific questions because the data are available rather than pursuing them because your theoretical orientation suggests that they are important.

Chapters 5–7 concentrate on the methods we use to create and to make sense of data. One of the running themes of this section is that as data become more complex, the methods used to make sense of the data are likely to become simpler, with more emphasis on good descriptions of data and less on inferential statistics and significance tests.

Chapters 8–10 describe the ways theories develop and decline, the way they are used by researchers and the type of course correction that is likely as the absolute primacy of theory declines. Chapters 11 and 12 examine the opportunities and challenges in the rapidly changing research environment, as well as the implications of these changes for the training of organizational scientists. The final chapter proposes that the scientific method can serve as a roadmap for rebuilding the relationships between data, methods, and theory.

A book like this is the work of many hands, and I want to recognize the contributions of my Series co-Editor, Angelo DeNisi, and of the Editorial Board of the Society for Industrial and Organizational Psychology's *Organizational Frontiers* series. The focus and structure of this book emerged over a series of discussions, proposals and feedback that contributed immensely to the success of this project. I was lucky to attract a distinguished and accomplished set of authors, and they delivered what I hope will be book that stimulates thinking and debate on the ongoing relationship between data, methods, and theory in the organizational sciences.

Kevin R. Murphy
Professor Emeritus and Kemmy Chair of Work
and Employment Studies, University of Limerick

Note

1 It is routine for Business Schools to maintain lists of "A", "B" etc. journals and for them to require a certain number of "A" publications to qualify for tenure and promotion. Many psychology departments have moved in this direction.

References

Baird, J. W. (1917). The legibility of a telephone directory. *Journal of Applied Psychology, 1,* 30–37.

Hambrick, D. J. (2007). The field of management's devotion to theory: Too much of a good thing? *Academy of Management Journal, 50,* 1346–1352.

Mael, F. A., & Hirsch, A. C. (1993). Rainforest empiricism and quasi-rationality: Two approaches to objective biodata. *Personnel Psychology, 46,* 719–738.

McCain, K. W. (2015), "Nothing as practical as a good theory" Does Lewin's Maxim still have salience in the applied social sciences?. *Proceedings of the Association for Information Science Technology, 52,* 1–4.

Terman, L. M., Otis, A. S., Dickson, V., Hubbard, O. S., Norton, J. K., Howard, L., Flanders, J. K., & Cassingham, C. C. (1917). A trial of mental and pedagogical tests in a civil service examination for policemen and firemen. *Journal of Applied Psychology, 1,* 17–29.

SERIES FOREWORD

Human resource information systems and other systems for collecting Big Data in organizations are increasingly important sources of information in the organizational sciences. The increasing use of this type of data, as well as archival data and data from meta-analytic reviews is changing the relationships among data, methods, and theory. For the last 40–50 years, the relationships among these three components has often been tenuous at best. In many cases, scholarly research (and scholarly journals) focused on proposing new theories rather than how we might test existing theories, and so data was more of an afterthought. Also, as new, and more sophisticated methods were being developed, methodology often became its own goal, rather than being viewed as a way of analyzing data to answer important theoretical questions. Overall, the relationships between theory, data and the methods used to collect and make sense of data are evolving rapidly, and the field of I/O Psychology is on the cusp of a revolution in the way we use theory and data to help understand behavior in organization.

Murphy has gathered a distinguished set of contributors who raise important questions about the state of our science (e.g., should journals that propose theories but refuse to publish tests of those theories remain at the top of the priority list?), about the methods used to analyze data (e.g., should descriptive statistics get more emphasis?) and about the way theories develop and fade (e.g., do theories outlive their creators?). It examines the way organizations collect and use data, the way data are shared and preserved, the design of studies and the analysis of data emerging from those studies, the development and evolution of theories, the research environment and ways of rebuilding relationships among data methods and theories.

The goal of the Organizational Frontiers Series is to publish books that help to define and advance the frontiers of our knowledge about behavior in organizations and stimulate future research and applications. *Data, Methods and Theory* advances these goals and provides a roadmap for future progress in our field.

Angelo S. DeNisi
Series Co-Editor

CONTRIBUTORS

Frank A. Bosco, *Virginia Commonwealth University, USA*

Georgia T. Chao, *University of South Florida, USA*

Karyssa A. Courney, *Rice University, USA*

Jeffrey M. Cucina, *U.S. Customs and Border Protection, USA*

James G. Field, *West Virginia University, USA*

Alexis A. Fink, *Facebook, USA*

Martin Götz, *University of Zurich, Switzerland*

Rick Guzzo, *Mercer and Workforce Sciences Institute, USA*

Louis Hickman, *University of Pennsylvania, USA*

Wayne Hochwarter, *Florida State University, USA*

Samantha L. Jordan, *University of North Texas, USA*

Steve W.J. Kozlowski, *University of South Florida, USA*

Keith McNulty, *McKinsey, UK*

Kevin R. Murphy, *University of Limerick, Ireland*

Mary Anne Nester, *Logos, USA*

Frederick L. Oswald, *Rice University, USA*

Christopher C. Rosen, *University of Arkansas, USA*

Craig J. Russell, *University of Oklahoma, USA*

Chelsea Song, *Purdue University, USA*

Sang Eun Woo, *Purdue University, USA*

Felix Y. Wu, *Rice University, USA*

Heng Xu, *American University, USA*

Nan Zhang, *American University, USA*

Le Zhou, *University of Minnesota, USA*

PART 1
Data

1

ORGANIZATIONAL DATA AND ITS IMPLICATIONS FOR RESEARCH AND THEORY

Richard A. Guzzo

Never has the potential for change in the organizational sciences been greater. Data makes it so. There is a continuing expansion of scientifically valuable data – superabundant, easily accessed, remarkably varied, cumulative – that will fundamentally impact the character of organizational research. This proliferation of data about employees, work behaviors, workplaces, management practices, and organizations' attributes generically referred to here as "big data," has a multitude of consequences for the organizational sciences. It will impact methods of statistical analysis by stimulating new ones and by drawing in analytic techniques developed in other domains. It increases the range of topics open to rigorous investigation, in particular making it more feasible to address complex and consequential issues. Big data in organizations raises the prospects of better (e.g., more thorough, more reliable) quantification of abstract ideas and constructs. It accelerates progress in making management practices more thoroughly evidence-based. It will influence the interdisciplinarity of the organizational sciences because such data is open to researchers of varying professional backgrounds and amenable to interpretation from differing perspectives. And, especially important for science practice disciplines, the data available in organizations today holds the potential to significantly influence how theories are created, tested, improved, and made more useful. In other words, big data provides a path to maximizing rigor and relevance simultaneously.

This chapter focuses on the nature and use of data relevant to the organizational sciences, specifically data that are constantly produced and stored through typically routine processes and technologies in organizations. This data is complementary to that which is intentionally generated by researchers, such as data coming from wearable sensors introduced into a workplace in a study of social

DOI: 10.4324/9781003015000-2

interactions and from instruments requiring employee responses, such as tests, questionnaires, and diaries. The chapter begins by describing, with examples and illustrations, the sorts and sources of the naturally occurring data in focus here. It concludes by examining implications of this ever-growing mass of data for four core research issues: construct measurement, reproducibility of findings, causation and theory building, and the simultaneous pursuit of research rigor and relevance.

Sources and Types of Data

HRIS Data

A singularly important source of relevant data is the Human Resource Information System (HRIS) database. This is an employing organization's go-to system of record for facts about employees, work, and workplaces. It is enormously useful for research purposes. Because an organization relies on this database for management reporting and decision-making, there is little tolerance for errors, thus the quality of data in HRIS databases is generally high. Another valuable feature of HRIS databases is that they provide census rather than sample data. That is, data about all employees – populations – is recorded, including those no longer with the organization, up to the date of their departure. The scope and detail of HRIS databases make them cornerstones of any integrated "big data platform" created to support workforce analytics broadly, as described by Ryan and Herleman (2016). Given their importance, it is worth taking a tour of their key features.

Table 1.1 illustrates the types of data found in employers' HRIS systems, showing sample field names and descriptions of each variable. While there is a great deal of commonality across organizations, every such system has customization as to which of the many possible fields are actually populated and maintained, how values are coded, and rules of operation (e.g., who can enter or change data). To illustrate, every HRIS system records the date an individual's employment is terminated, yet systems will differ markedly in who has permission to record the event and how reasons for terminations are recorded. Some systems offer a lengthy menu of "action-reason codes" (a partial listing of action-reason codes might include retirement, dual-career relocation, excessive absenteeism, poor job performance, better opportunity elsewhere, health, and job elimination) while other systems offer just a few alternatives. Discretion exists in the use of these codes. The amount of discretion in their use and the meaning of the codes can be essential concerns to organizational researchers, such as codes that provide the basis for distinguishing between voluntary (employee-initiated) and involuntary (employer-initiated) turnover. When researchers rely on HRIS systems as the source of turnover data care needs to be taken to properly categorize coded

TABLE 1.1 Typical variables in HRIS systems

Sample field names	Descriptions and possible values
EmpID	Unique employee identifier
EffD	Effective date of data download
Birth	Date of birth
Gender	Gender code
Ethnicity (US only)	Example: A = Asian; B = Black or African American; H = Hispanic, etc.
EmpStatus	Example: A = Active; L = On paid leave; U= On unpaid leave; T = Terminated
FLSA (US only)	E = Exempt; N = Nonexempt
EeoJobCd (US only)	EEO-1 job code – Executive/Senior Level Officials and Managers, First/Mid-Level Officials and Managers, Professionals, Service Workers, etc.
OrigHire	Original hire date
MRHire	Most recent hire date (if the employee was rehired)
TermDate	Termination date
TermType	Termination reason code
TermReason	Termination reason description
ServiceDt	Date field for calculating the overall length of time an employee has worked for the organization, taking into account breaks in service
PdLeavAmt	Amount of paid leave
PdLeavReas	Reason for most recent paid leave
UnpdLeavAmt	Amount of unpaid leave during snapshot week in #days or other unit
UnpdLeavReas	Reason for most recent unpaid leave
AbsentAmt	Amount of absenteeism
JobCode	Job code
JobTitle	Job title for the above job code
JobDt	Date entered current job
JobFamily	Job family (or job function) code
JobFamDesc	Description associated with job family (or job function) code
EmpType	Employee type – regular, temporary, etc.
EmpClass	Employee classification, if applicable
FullPart	Work schedule code – e.g., full time or part time
StdHrs	Number of standard hours employee per work week
FTE	Full-time equivalent percentage – e.g., decimal between 0 and 1
Grade	Salary grade code
GradePlan	Salary grade plan code, if multiple grade plans are in use
GradeDt	Salary grade date – date entered current grade
SupID	Supervisor ID – the EmpID of the individual the employee reports to
OrgCd1	Often multiple fields, OrgCd1 … OrgCdn; indicating organization structure
OrgDesc1	Description/name of OrgCd1 … OrgCdn
HomeCity	Home address city
HomeState	Home address state (US)
HomePostal	Home address postal code

(Continued)

TABLE 1.1 Typical variables in HRIS systems *(Continued)*

Sample field names	Descriptions and possible values
LocCode	Work location code
LocName	Work location name
LocCity	Work location city
LocState	Work location state (US)
LocPostal	Work location postal code
Rating	Annual performance rating
RatingDt	Date of performance rating
RatingPlan	Performance rating plan associated with rating if >1 plan
PayType	Employee pay type (e.g., salary, hourly, commission)
AnnPayRate	Annual 12-month base pay rate
HrPayRate	Hourly base pay rate
MidPayRate	The midpoint base pay rate for the employee's salary grade/band
BasePay	Base pay received
BonusElig	Eligibility for bonus pay (y/n)
BonusPay	Amount of bonus payment received
Overtime	Amount of overtime hours worked
TotalHours	Total hours worked
TrainType1	Type of training employee completed; multiple fields are possible
TrainType1Req	Mandatory/elective
TrainType1Hrs	Hours completed for training type
RetPlan	Retirement plan participation (y/n)
BenPlan	Health plan participation (y/n)
BenPlanType	Type of employer-sponsored plan, if multiple plans are available
PTO	Amount of paid time off available
PTOUse	Amount of paid time off used
BeneCd1	Other employee benefit code #1; often multiple codes
BeneDes1	Description of BenCd1, etc.

reasons into those two categories, which sometimes is not so straightforward a task, as when discretion or an organization's normative practices influence coding. "Better opportunity elsewhere" may seem like a clearly recorded reason for voluntary departure and often it is authentically so. But for some employers it may also be used as a default or catchall reason, or one that sometimes represents a mutual employer-employee agreement that the individual should take their talents elsewhere due to a lack of person-organization fit, or the choice of the current employer not to match a competing employment offer. Or that code may be used to avoid the censure that an involuntary termination code would communicate to an individual's potential new employer if that next employer makes an inquiry about the reason why the individual's prior employment ended. The point here is not to dwell deeply on turnover reason codes and categories per se but to make the point that, however, ubiquitous HRIS data is, when using it for research purposes there remains the need to understand where the data comes from to ensure that, in that organization, it can be used to validly represent constructs of interest.

The data fields illustrated in Table 1.1 often provide the direct measures of variables core to research interests. A researcher interested in understanding relationships between age and job performance, for example, can use measures of these two variables taken straight from an HRIS database, age because date of birth is in all HRIS systems and a common performance metric recorded in them is an annual performance rating. That performance score usually is a single summary rating but some organizations preserve ratings made on multiple dimensions of performance, such as innovativeness or collaboration. Having multiple dimensions certainly expands research possibilities.

Another of the strengths of HRIS data is that, because so many variables are recorded in one place, there is the immediate opportunity to deploy some of them as control variables when analyzing relationships of interest. Age-performance relationships, for example, might be investigated while controlling for important other variables taken from the same source database, such as time in job or the job training recently completed. Indeed, the abundance of HRIS variables raises the risk of their misuse as control variables. Becker (2005) offers suggestions for using them well when seeking to rule out alternative explanations. Control variables also serve other objectives, such as reducing statistical error terms and avoiding faulty assumptions about the ignorability of variables known to be present in the organizational context being studied. Thoughtful use of control variables should carry the day.

The wealth of data in HRIS databases also allows for testing conditionals, factors that can be expected to moderate relationships of interest. Consider the hypothesis that the relationship between an individual's age and one specific aspect of their performance, collaboration, depends on the similarity between the employee's age and that of their coworkers. Age similarity might be operationalized as the absolute value of the difference between an employee's age and the average of their coworkers, which would require knowing who the coworkers are. HRIS databases typically make that easy. For example, they include information about reporting relationships – that is, who reports to whom. Thus, a researcher might define coworkers as those other individuals who report to the same manager. A more elaborate operational definition might be created by defining coworkers as those individuals performing like jobs (as indicated by a job code or job family code) and who work in the same location (work address) and who report to the same manager, all of which could be read directly from one HRIS database.

Root HRIS data can be used to calculate many things. Time and rate calculations (e.g., individuals' time in current job or rate of promotion over a career with the employer) highlight another valuable feature of HRIS data: it is cumulative. HRIS databases are repositories of the sequenced documentation of events, behaviors, changes in situations, and more. Thus, HRIS databases readily enable longitudinal analyses. To use the age-performance illustration once more, an HRIS database could be the single source of data relied on to investigate the relationship between employee age and collaborativeness as the ages of employees' coworkers change over time with the naturally occurring arrivals and departures of fellow employees, all while accounting for the influence of potentially confounding factors such as an employee's time in current job. This example hints at another of the powers of HRIS data: it makes it possible to investigate a number of related issues in a single effort, potentially generating findings that might otherwise be attained only through several separate bite-sized studies.

In addition to providing data about individuals and work groups, their experiences, events in and characteristics of their workplaces HRIS databases yield ample insights into organizational structures and practices. Structural features of organizations observable through HRIS data include such things as work unit size, spans of control, and the steepness of hierarchies. Organizational practices, too, can be inferred and evaluated from HRIS data. Assessments of the fairness of practices – such as those related to promotions, performance evaluations, job assignments, and pay – use data straight out of HRIS databases to answer the question of whether such practices unjustifiably favor one demographic group of employees over another, after accounting for (statistically speaking) other factors that legitimately can be expected to influence the outcomes of interest. If there is one must-have tool in the researcher's toolbox, the HRIS database is it.

Other Employee Databases

Numerous other common databases are sources of data for researchers. Apart from value in their own right, they enhance the value of an HRIS database by linking to it. The gateway fields for linking most often are individual-level identifiers, such as an assigned employee ID, indicators of job or occupation performed, and location, like work or home address.

Case Study 1 illustrates the integration of HRIS with multiple other databases to address sales effectiveness. Performed by an in-house data analytics team, the case was one of the first examples of this style of applied big data research in this organization. The work thus required some "socializing" to gain acceptance of data use and analytic approach to pave the way for successful buy-in of findings and their action implications.

Case Study 1: Sales Effectiveness[1]

Situation: The CEO of a global provider of B2B products and services challenged the company's divisional leadership to better identify the attributes of successful sales representatives and the management practices that most contribute to their success. Meeting the challenge fell to the organization's analytics function.

Data and Analyses: The analytics team focused its research on the quarterly performance of sales reps for the most recent 4-year period. Data was drawn from six databases. Two HRIS systems (one was the legacy system of an acquired business) provided extensive facts about sales employee attributes and experience and four other databases provided supplemental data about sales employees, their lines of business, and their performance. Performance was measured as the percentage change in quarterly sales. Because this was one of the first major analytic efforts of its type in the organization, extensive effort was required to reconcile (clean, verify, integrate) data from the different sources to be able to create a unified analysis-ready dataset. Part of that effort also required validating the data and analytic approach with internal stakeholders not just to ensure the accuracy of the data but also to lay the foundation for acceptance of the findings. Analyses involved time series regression with numerous control variables for employee demographics, time of year, organizational attributes, location, and other performance-relevant factors.

Findings: While the full research report remains proprietary, several key findings can be shared. Individual-level differences among sales reps, such as their time in job and extent of prior work experience, were significantly, positively related to performance. The single most powerful predictor of quarterly growth in sales, however, was the number of one-on-one meetings between a sales rep and his or her regional sales manager during the prior quarter. Sales reps who met with their regional leaders three times a quarter experienced a statistically significant 70% higher rate of sales growth in the next quarter relative to those who met with that leader only once. The impact on sales of the frequency of meetings between sales reps and their immediate supervisors also was positive but was overwhelmed in magnitude by the impact attributable to meetings with regional managers, who were themselves two or more hierarchical levels above that of sales reps. The results demonstrated the value of higher-level leaders staying closely connected with frontline employees and of the coaching those higher-level leaders provided.

Implications: The breadth of the findings informed a number of actions, such as refining the hiring profile to place greater emphasis on the value of prior work experience. But the major intervention that followed from the results, not surprisingly, concerned requirements for regular meetings between sales reps and regional leaders. Checklists were created to support the substance of the discussions, for example, and tracking mechanisms were put in place to ensure that the meetings took place with the desired frequency. Beyond the practical importance of the research findings for this organization, the case is one of the rare empirical demonstrations of the impact of one-on-one coaching and mentoring on business results.

In many organizations, the HR department is the custodian of several additional databases that can be linked to the HRIS. Performance review processes overseen by the HR function often generate text descriptions of employees' strengths and developmental needs, sometimes with reference to an existing competency model, as well as goal statements regarding future job performance and career aspirations. Such text data tends not to be stored in core HRIS databases but rather in ancillary databases that are the responsibility of the function. Analyzing that text data can serve a wide variety of research interests including but not limited to leadership style, attributes of feedback, employee career orientations, and fair treatment. Data about an employee's high-potential status may be found in an HRIS system or in a separate source; an employee's place in a succession plan often is maintained separately from the master HRIS database. In a company with global operations HR will often maintain a distinct database regarding the (potentially expansive) terms of employment and remuneration for individuals working abroad as expatriates. Some employee-centric databases valuable for research are limited-access because of the sensitivity of the information they contain or simply because they are atypical sources of behavioral data. Research into harassment and other dysfunctional behaviors at work can be well informed by accessing databases that contain records of employee relations incidents. When an employee makes a claim of an incident of dysfunctional or harmful behavior – such as another's violation of employer policies, misconduct, shirking, harassment, or retaliation – a record is created that documents important details about the nature of the event, the verification of relevant facts, the employee alleging its occurrence, the alleged violator or violators, circumstances, and the claim's ultimate resolution (e.g., reassignment of an employee, reprimand, dismissal, a training requirement, no action). The facts recorded in these databases guide the resolution of each individual case as it is adjudicated by, say, the legal or HR functions. A database of such claims can be linked to HRIS data for research into personal and situational determinants of dysfunctional behaviors. For example, in the author's experience working with a client organization, HRIS and employee relations databases were joined to identify such determinants. Statistical models revealed that, all else equal, age at hire was a significant predictor of dysfunctional workplace behavior. Specifically, employees hired at mid-career age ranges were more likely to engage in dysfunctional behaviors at higher than statistically expected frequencies. The client organization, which was characterized by a strong and idiosyncratic culture, interpreted the findings as indicating that mid-career hires did not acculturate as quickly as younger hires because their more extensive prior work experience elsewhere interfered with their learning and internalizing the organization's culture. Other factors, such as organizational unit size, also influenced the occurrence of dysfunctional behaviors. A further example of databases that are perhaps less utilized for research purposes are those related to business travel records and reimbursements to employees for the out-of-pocket costs of their business travel. A researcher interested in work-life balance might find such databases useful.

One employer in the author's experience, for example, analyzed travel records and found that 41% of all business flights taken by employees had departure times during nonwork hours. This data point in conjunction with other relevant data – namely, engagement survey responses indicating a felt lack of work-life balance and records of employees' hours spent on premise – led the employer to set new policies to achieve a more optimal work-life balance for its employees.

Organizational communication data, which amasses swiftly, also is a good source of data for research. Consider emails as communication events. Emails leave electronic traces that identify senders and recipients, have content (subject line, body, attachments) that can be analyzed for sentiment and substance, and come with markers (metadata) such as time stamps and server identity that may be useful in research. Making email communication data ready for analysis usually requires an investment in data preparation. For example, if the interest is in using email traffic to study interpersonal networks of relationships then broadcast emails, which might be defined as those with a number of recipients above some threshold (e.g., 12), may be deemed nuisance events and removed to create a less contaminated database for analysis. If the focus is not on content but on patterns of interaction, emails' subject lines, body, and attachments may be stripped out for privacy (individual and organizational) before analyzing. Identities of recipients who are not employees of an organization also may be excluded for reasons of their privacy. Communications from SMS messaging and apps that support team collaboration face similar requirements of data preparation.

Communication databases can become gold mines of insight when joined with HRIS and other data. Brass and Borgatti (2020) provide a compendium of reviews of research using network analysis to study such things as team dynamics in the workplace, performance, affect, turnover, and career advancement. HRIS information can be relied on as a source of extensive data about the attributes of network nodes (e.g., a node could be an individual, a team, or a location). As an illustration of joining HRIS performance and demographic data with email data consider the following example from the author's experience. In a large professional services organization, a network analysis was made of intraorganizational emails. Placing another employee in the "To" or "Cc" field of an email – or not – is a clear act of inclusion/exclusion. Analyses in this organization showed that high-performing individuals, as indicated by their most recent annual performance rating, tended to occupy positions of high centrality. Compared to less highly rated individuals they were substantially more likely to be included as email recipients, and in network analysis centrality is indicative of personal influence and impact. High performers' centrality, and thus influence and impact, was a finding favorably regarded by the organization. Less favorably regarded was the further finding that the centrality effect of performance was true for White employees but not for Black and Latino employees. That is, an unwanted marginalization of high-performing Black and Latino employees was occurring. Networked relationships also can be constructed from data sources other than communication databases, such as electronic calendars to identify links among individuals based on participation in the same scheduled events and databases that record joint presence on project teams, work crews, or shifts.

Operational Databases

Operational databases that are created for normal business purposes, such as monitoring production processes, tracking customer behavior, financial management, and quality control also are potentially valuable sources of research data. Often they are the best source of performance measures. While an HRIS database may contain subjective evaluations of performance (e.g., managers' ratings), objective performance measures often are found elsewhere, such as in operational databases. As Case Study 1 illustrates, operational databases supporting the sales function were the sources of measures of the critical dependent variable, growth in revenue per sales employee. In a customer service center, the average time spent resolving customer calls is a commonly kept measure and can be used as a performance indicator in research. When the performance of a work unit is the interest, operational databases are the go-to source of performance data. Examples of unit-level measures of performance include sales by department in retail stores and shrinkage (unexplained loss) of goods from inventory, output in tons by mining crews, percent of restaurant orders served within 15 minutes by a fast-casual restaurant, patient satisfaction ratings and number of postoperative infections in a hospital unit, hours of downtime as a percent of total time for a manufacturing line, and in branch banks rates of client retention and numbers of referred new customers. All are examples of performance data obtainable from common operational databases in their respective organizations.

In addition to their value as sources of performance measures, operational databases also are a good source of data on control variables. Facilities management functions, for example, often maintain a bevy of such data points. The facilities management function of a company in the hospitality industry, for example, maintains data on such things as time since a hotel was last refurbished, a potentially important influence on guest satisfaction ratings which a researcher may want to control for when analyzing the impact of management practices or employees' behavior on guest experiences. The marketing function of a retail business can be the source of control variables important to store performance, such as the intensity of competition in a local market as measured by the number and types of competitor establishments within a specified distance of each of its own establishments. Additionally, operational databases are a source of variables about features of workplaces that may be hypothesized to be moderators of relationships.

Sensor-Generated Data

Sensor-based data is rather familiar through everyday use of smart phones, fitness trackers, navigation systems, home security systems and so on. Organizations routinely collect such sensor-based data for a variety of workforce and operational reasons. Often that data serves industrial engineering purposes, such as when employees on the production line wear sensors to track their steps for the purpose of identifying and removing unnecessary movements so as to lay out more efficient work stations. Video data is a source of insight into speed of production processes in a manufacturing setting and a source of workplace safety data, as when placed in ride-sharing vehicles to help protect drivers from abusive customers. Video surveillance and other forms of automated oversight, such as tracking internet use, time spent on emails, and frequency of scheduled meetings, are used to monitor performance and provide feedback. Interestingly, while automated monitoring may be a good source of performance measurements, evidence indicates that supervisors are preferred as the source of performance feedback over its automated delivery (Adler & Ambrose, 2005; Bhave, 2014). Sensor data also often is used to closely surveil and control worker behavior in real time. Employers in the business of delivering goods for Amazon, for example, may be alerted automatically if a driver in their employ stops their delivery vehicle for more than three minutes, which in turn can prompt a dispatcher-to-driver call (Sainato, 2021).

Whatever the business objectives are of implementing sensors in work settings, they can produce voluminous data. And like almost any data source, sensor data can have quality limitations important to researchers. Data from key cards that unlock office doors and thus record an employee's entrance to or exit from a workplace has errors it in when an employee passes through a door opened by another's card; cameras may not have full fields of vision. While the general research-ready quality of passively-collected sensor data in organizations seemingly has not been assessed, the quality of sensing technologies introduced into workplaces by researchers has been, such as data generated by wearable sensors utilizing Bluetooth technology (Matusik et al., 2019). Potentially instructive with regard to the use of sensor data from all sources, Matusik et al. offer numerous recommendations and caveats regarding best use of that one type of sensor-generated data.

Vendor-Held Databases

Other relevant data that can be linked to in-house databases is held by service providers to organizations. Applicant tracking systems (ATS) manage steps and data in the hiring process. Most often an ATS is provided by a vendor and that vendor maintains the collected descriptive and evaluative data based on biographical markers, prior employment histories, scores on tests and other screening measures. When joined with HRIS data ATS data can become useful inputs into research involving those applicants who become employees. An organization's engagement survey data may be held by its provider of survey services; data about employees' utilization of health benefits and wellness programs often reside with vendors. Payroll service providers accumulate data on such things as earnings, hours worked, and schedule variability., Learning management systems, often maintained by vendors, are sources of data on training and development activities completed by employees. Researchers interested in employee financial well-being or retirement-relevant behaviors might link HRIS data to employees' choices to participate in and contribute to retirement savings plans using data that is typically maintained by an outside vendor. Employee-linked data residing outside the employing organization are accessible to the organization on request (with restrictions that limit the disclosure to employers of some aspects of employee health data or restrictions contractually agreed to by organizations and their vendors).

Case Study 2 illustrates an example of a research project that joins HRIS data with health data about employees. Health data was maintained by an external service provider in this case, the administrator of the employer's health insurance benefits programs.

Case Study 2: Employee Health and Performance[2]

Situation: Motivated by an interest in understanding how employee health benefit programs can best support the workforce, an executive responsible for those programs in a global consumer products company sponsored a study of employee health and workforce dynamics, such as performance, retention, and career success. An outside consulting firm conducted the research.

Data and Analyses: Analyses, involving several thousand employees per year over a 6-year period, predicted next year outcomes based on prior year variables. Two databases were joined for the work, the company's HRIS database and a health benefits database maintained by a vendor. The HRIS database provided employee-level data on demographics, jobs, how jobs are situated in the organization (e.g., level of responsibility, product line), attributes of the managers employees report to, the composition of employees' work groups, career-related events, such as changes of job, promotions, and turnover, and individual performance (annual ratings). Seasonality and location were control variables. Employee-level health variables included the dollar value of annual health insurance claims and health risk scores calculated by the vendor. Analyses involved a mix of logistic and OLS modeling.

Findings: It was expected, and analyses confirmed, that employee demographics of age and gender are important determinants of employee health benefits claims. Well-known patterns were evident in this case, such as higher health expenses among all employees age 60 and above and health expenses lowest among young males. These relationships were controlled for when assessing other work and health relationships. Analyses of the impact of health on work revealed relatively modest relationships. For example, employee health status as indicated by the magnitude of prior year's claims or health risk scores were not predictive of future promotions, although employees with the highest health risk scores in one year were significantly more likely to quit in the next year. In contrast, findings about the impact of work on health were more extensive and robust. For example, employees who experienced lateral moves – changes from one job to another without a coincident promotion – were significantly more likely to have lower health costs and lower risk scores in the year following the job change. Social influences in the workplace also were prominent, illustrated by the finding that women's health status was significantly better when they worked in groups composed of proportionally more women relative to women working in largely male groups. Also, while current employee health status did not predict future performance (as measured by annual ratings), poorer current job performance was significantly predictive of poorer health in the following year.

Implications: Evidence regarding the power of workplace – work group composition, job changes, and performance – to predict subsequent health status is rich with theoretical import regarding why such relationships occur. The findings also provided a basis for changing workforce management practices to maximize health and performance, such as with regard to job changes and work group composition. However, the road from research results to management practices sometimes is not easily traveled. This organization struggled to act on the research results due to "turf" or divisions of responsibilities (for health benefits versus for workforce management) that created obstacles to unified executive action based on the research results.

Publicly Available Data

Organizationally held and vendor-maintained data also can be linked to a plethora of publicly available, often free, data. When it comes to government-sponsored databases, the link to such data frequently is made through a location or occupational variable. Location variables can be used to link to data on a variety of local economic and community characteristics, such as household income, unemployment, and population demographics. Commercially available mapping tools combine geospatial information with data from numerous other sources, including some that are publicly-available, such as periodic census data and continually refreshed community characteristics [e.g., American Community Survey (ACS)] as well as some that are proprietary in origin (e.g., a marketing firm's data on consumer behavior). Extensive job- and occupational-level data is available in libraries, such as O*NET (see onetonline.org). O*NET catalogs over 900 jobs in the US economy and is a source of extensive data on such things as the knowledge, skills, abilities, and technology-related requirements of jobs as well as data on competency profiles, specific tasks and activities required by a job, and typical interest profiles of job incumbents. It also links to other sources of data, such as the Bureau of Labor Statistics for additional job-relevant data, such as wages. Counterparts to O*NET include Canada's National Occupational Classification, International Standard Classification of Occupations, and European, Skills, Competencies, qualifications and Occupations databases, the latter of which has nearly 3,000 occupations in it. Linking data from these sources to an organization's HRIS data can be exceptionally useful for research on matters of job analysis and job design, the automatability of activities, the transportability of skills, competencies, career paths, and other topics.

It is worth noting briefly that plenty of research in the organizational sciences gets accomplished using databases that exist independently of any one employer. Sociologists and labor and organizational economists rely heavily on publicly available survey-based databases, such as the National Longitudinal Survey of Youth (by the US Bureau of Labor Statistics), the ACS (by the US Census Bureau), and the Panel Survey of Income Dynamics from the University of Michigan. A study of job satisfaction reported by Hernandez, Newman, and Jeon (2016) illustrates the use of such databases. The researchers extracted twitter data by location (city), content coded tweets to create measures of expressed job satisfaction, and then tested relationships of those measures to other same city variables, such as absenteeism from work and home-to-work travel time. Absenteeism and travel time measures came from the Integrated Public Use Microdata Series database, itself a compilation of data from surveys such as the ACS.

In summary, there is an enormous volume and variety of naturally occurring "big data" constantly being created and stored through typical practices and technologies in organizations. Fortunately for researchers, that data is very accessible and often easily augmented with data from other sources. Not only does such data has great scientific value on its own but also potentially even greater value when joined up with researcher-driven methods of data collection.

Implications of Big Data: Challenges and Opportunities

Addressed here, at a high-level, are implications of big data for core considerations in organizational research, framed as opportunities to be taken advantage of and challenges to be mastered. The issues considered are:

- Construct measurement
- Replication and reproducibility
- Establishing causation and theory building
- Rigor, relevance, and reporting

Construct Measurement

Accessing organizations' vaults of big data creates opportunities to measure theoretical constructs in new ways. Ideally – that is, not trading off fidelity for easy data access – these opportunities can decrease uncertainty and errors in the quantification of abstract concepts and increase the ability of empirical investigations to yield more specific insights into factors influencing, and influenced by, those constructs. There are seemingly countless constructs in the organizational sciences and one, job performance, is considered here for purposes of illustration.

Job performance can be quantified as a single overall score or as multiple scores, one for each of several separate dimensions of performance. Either way, scores can be created through subjective or objective means. One of the things that organizational big data does, for many jobs and for many aspects of performance but by no means equally for all, is to radically expand measurement possibilities by virtue of the accessibility of performance-relevant data constantly being generated and stored by organizational technologies and practices. This is a sea change for researchers. To illustrate, consider Ng and Feldman's (2008) review of 380 empirical studies of age and job performance relationships. The reviewed studies contained 438 samples, an average of 1.15 per study, and collectively measured ten dimensions of job performance (viz., core task performance, creativity, training performance, organizational citizenship behaviors directed at four different targets, safety, counterproductive work behaviors, workplace aggression, workplace substance abuse, tardiness, and three types of absenteeism). Tallying from their Table 1.1, the studies reported 648 total measures of performance, an average of 1.71 per study. Of the 648 measures 80% were classified as subjective (i.e., ratings) and 20% as objective.[3] The date of Ng and Feldman's publication and thus the dates of the studies reviewed precede the "era of big data." But how might a body of research on job performance look different in the current era of big data, using prior studies as a baseline?

One major change we might expect is a drastic rebalancing of the 80/20 split of subjective and objective performance measures. Operational and sensor data, as previously described, can be convenient sources of objective measures of core task performance for many jobs; technologies that routinely collect customer behavior data likewise provide objective measures of performance for many frontline workers. Other dimensions of performance that had been measured only subjectively, such as workplace aggression, may now be complemented, or replaced, by objective measures taken from sources such as employee relations databases that record verified incidents of aggression, stored electronic messages that can be content coded for hostile language, or video files for analyses of antagonistic or belligerent acts. Another major change to expect is an increase in the number of performance measures per study to well above the 1.71 figure from the Ng and Feldman (2008) review. Big data presents the opportunity to measure performance in multiple dimensions concurrently. This will benefit future studies and speed up the growth of knowledge about how distinct dimensions of performance move together or independently, something not so easily achieved with only 1.71 measures per study. These more expansive big data measurements of performance can lead to refined theoretical insights into how aspects of job performance as a dependent variable are and are not responsive to events and interventions (e.g., training, job redesigns, and organizational restructurings). When investigated as an independent variable, discoveries become more attainable about such things as which aspects of performance most influence personal consequences for employees such as their relationships with coworkers and their career advancement. Features of performance per se, such as the persistence of performance levels and the distinction between typical and peak performance, also can be powerfully addressed from a big data perspective. Not unrelated to the increased research value, the practical value of multiple, big data-driven performance measures for coaching and performance improvement also can rise. Performance is but one example of how the measurement of, theories about, and practical uses of a core construct can be transformed by research that takes advantage of what is now routinely available organizational data.

Not all construct measurement will be so aided. Specifically, one of the challenges of big data is its use for enhancing the measurement of psychological states and processes typically assessed via self-report. Some internal states, such as preferences and interests, can be assessed subjectively through self-reports as well as inferred from objectively recorded choices and behaviors, such as indicators of developmental interests expressed by participation in elective training programs as recorded in learning management systems and health-related behaviors and preferences as recorded in health benefits databases. However, the general usefulness of the sorts of big data discussed here for direct or indirect measurement of attitudes, affect, cognitive processes and other intrapersonal processes and states is yet to be established.

Case Study 3 provides an example of using data to identify the emergent construct of "collaborative friction" within an organization. The construct is informed by intentionally-designed measures (e.g., an employee survey) as well as by a technology specific to that organization which captures the running record of collaborative acts among employees.

Case Study 3: Supporting Fast Growth in a Technology Company[4]

Situation: The CEO of a fast-growing tech company charged his CHRO with identifying what its employees want – and need – to drive successful business results. The People Analytics function, partnering with a consulting firm, took the lead in diagnoses and action recommendations.

Data and Analysis: *Data was consolidated from:*

1. *Focus groups and employee engagement surveys, including a onetime conjoint analysis of employees' reward preferences and a k-means cluster analysis to identify workforce segments defined by shared preferences,*
2. *Visualizations of the flows of hired, promoted, and separated employees by career levels, and*
3. *Statistical modeling of causes of five workforce outcomes: regretted turnover, employee engagement, promotion, total compensation, and pay growth.*

Data sources included three years of information from five systems: HRIS, employee surveys, applicant tracking, learning management, and a customized system recording the initiation and receipt of collaborative acts by employees.

Findings: Two major patterns emerged. The first, labeled "collaborative friction," concerned the inability to work effectively across business lines, despite collaboration being an espoused core value of the company. Employee surveys documented frustration with collaboration and statistical modeling showed that employees at the 75th percentile with regard to initiating collaborative acts across business lines were no more likely to be rewarded for it via promotions or pay than employees at the 50th percentile. On the other hand, employees who were at the 75th percentile of frequency of receiving collaborative efforts initiated by others were, relative to those at the 50th percentile, more likely to be promoted and to receive higher pay increases. Simply put, the incentives for initiating collaboration were not aligned with the espoused company value. Second, career advancement was a multifaceted problem. Surveys documented employees' lack of clarity about promotions and deep dissatisfaction with advancement opportunities; talent flow analyses showed that the high rates of new hires at senior levels were obstructing promotion from within opportunities for those who had joined the company early in their careers and who experienced rapid rises into middle management; one in five employees experienced a change of their manager each year, an event that did not affect their promotion chances but that significantly raised those employees' likelihoods of becoming a regretted talent loss in the following year; and both qualitative and quantitative analyses indicated that the company was over-rewarding people managers relative to individual contributors.

Implications: Executives rallied around the findings and committed to developing ways of reducing collaborative friction and improving career advancement practices. For example, promotion policies were adopted that, when filling senior-level position vacancies, required slates of internal candidates that included individuals from business lines other than that of the position vacancy. Business unit leaders were made accountable for removing sources of collaborative friction and for creating greater clarity regarding advancement opportunities, supported by coaching about ways to achieve these objectives. The HR function designed clearer career paths for advancement by employees in individual contributor roles. HR business partners were supplied with *guidance on how to review, size, and prioritize pay increases to better align financial rewards with desired behaviors. Further, the research findings were shared with all employees with three calls to action: (1) alleviate collaborative friction, (2) engage in quarterly career conversations focusing on skills to hone and develop, and (3) people managers were asked to publicly communicate reasons for an employee's promotion and the heightened expectations that would accompany the new role. Checklists, training materials, communication campaigns, and other resources supported the calls to action.*

Replication and Reproducibility

The larger the organization, the greater the number of accessible variables, observations of people, and situations to study. Consequently, in larger organizations there is greater opportunity to incorporate multiple tests of replicability and reproducibility into research, although organizations of even modest size present opportunities for the same. Repeated testing of relationships across multiple segments of a workforce, workplaces, and other circumstances in the same study or with varying methods all within a single study serves two major objectives:

1. It helps sort out reliable, durable relationships from those that are ephemeral, due to chance, or artifactual, and
2. It accelerates the development of theories "to account for more relevant factors and to become more complex, specific, and nuanced – and ideally more accurate and useful as a result" (Guzzo, 2016, p. 348).

Prevailing discourse on the topic of repeated testing of research results involves a mix of somewhat overlapping terminology. For example, Bettis, Helfat, and Shaver (2016) distinguish "narrow" from "quasi" replications, the distinction being the number of parameters that differ between a prior study and its later reconstitution. Köhler and Cortina (2021) emphasize the perceived degree of constructiveness of a replication, the extent to which a follow-on study's features are judged to have improved upon those of a predecessor. Crandall and Sherman (2015) more simply distinguish between "direct" (also known as "exact") and "conceptual" replications, the latter defined as studies that address previously observed relationships and theoretical interpretations but do so by varying one or more aspects of research design, measurement, setting, sample, etc. They make clear the value of conceptual replications for serving the second of the two major objectives, theory development. That is, conceptual replications disperse opportunities to fail to replicate over samples, settings, measures, and methods. Thus, compared to "exact" or "narrow" replications, conceptual replications' failures to reproduce prior findings are more informative as to reasons why those failures occur and force researchers to become more articulate and specific about when, where, and for whom theoretical propositions hold true. These resulting gains in specificity and nuance increase a theory's accuracy and usefulness.

An important opportunity for the organizational sciences, then, is to perform multiple conceptual replications as part of a single big data research project. Considerable latitude exists in how best to do that. With ample longitudinal data a researcher may elect to test hypothesized relationships at earlier and later time periods. With HRIS data on employee populations, replications can be conducted across workforce segments. Tests can be made in separate places, such as when an organization operates in multiple cities or regions. In large enough organizations, multiple approaches are possible concurrently. In short, big data makes it very efficient to conduct and learn from within-study replications.

A related challenge for the organizational sciences is clarifying standards for what "good" looks like with regard to conducting and reporting such within-study conceptual replications. Mini-replications, such as the use of holdout samples to test models developed on training samples, are relevant but not germane to the larger issue, which is about how best to consolidate what can be heterogeneous findings into coherent wholes. For example, McShane and Böckenholt (2017) describe a single-study meta-analysis approach potentially applicable to integrating findings of multiple within-study replications, although their approach does have limitations described by the authors.

Causation and Theory-Building

The experiment is a favored method for testing causation yet, while designed experiments in the workplace are possible (Eden, 2017), they cannot be relied on as a primary method of establishing causal relationships in the organizational sciences. Too many practical and ethical barriers exist to randomly assigning people to treatment conditions at work and too many important variables of interest cannot be directly manipulated. Fortunately, big data opens the door to powerful alternatives to experiments as ways of establishing cause-and-effect relationships.

Naturally occurring data in organizations often has the essential ingredients. It permits the necessary temporal ordering of hypothesized causes and consequences. There is a veritable bounty of variables, preexisting or able to be computed, to use as converging, multiple measurements and thus remove noise and error and when establishing empirical regularities. As mentioned previously, there is an abundance of useful control variables available to de-confound and isolate causal influences. Multiple alternative causal pathways can be tested against each other. Statistical power runs high. And, as just discussed, the built-in capacity of big data research to replicate and reproduce analyses within a single study support the testing and development of explanations (theories) regarding the conditions under which a causal effect does and does not occur.

Statistical modeling methods rather than experimentation are core to using big data to draw causal statements. Fortunately, there is a growing sophistication regarding how best to infer causality from nonexperimental data, which Pearl and Mackenzie (2018) refer to as "the causal revolution" (p. 9).

The revolution is not a reveal of heretofore undiscovered secrets but rather greater ingenuity and discipline in stating causal assertions and testing them empirically. The basics of plausible causation still hold, of course, such as temporal ordering and reliable nonzero associations between A's and B's before one can be said to be said to cause the other. Organizational big data is especially useful for verifying such associations when A and B are low-frequency events, when the interval between them is long, and when the A–B relationship is heavily influenced by third variables. Also, the constant recording of temporally ordered data in organizations provide documentation of events that constitute "natural experiments" of all kinds – of changes in practices, acts of leadership, new workplace experiences and so on along with their potential consequences. Testable statements about causes and consequences could be straightforward deductions from preexisting theories or they could be novel and grounded in the particulars of an organizational context. Whatever their source, such statements, according to Pearl and Mackenzie (2018), are best expressed visually in what they call "structural causal models" with each path in a model an "implication."[5] Visualizing pathways permits them to be assessed in orderly ways guided by sets of logical rules regarding tests of such things as directionality and reverse causation, conditioning variables, confounders, and mediated relationships, all of which can be assessed in a single big data study. The essence of the approach is not to make overall goodness-of-fit tests of a model to a dataset but rather to parse and test specific causal connections in formal ways, with the sum of such tests providing empirically verified, rejected, or refined sets of causal statements.

The repeated moving back-and-forth between causal proposition and its test, as described by Pearl (Pearl & Mackenzie, 2018; Pearl, Glynmour & Jewell, 2016), is a form of theory-building through abduction. Guzzo, Schneider, and Nalbantian (in press) describe abduction as a process for reaching "best explanations" based on multistage analyses and multivariate fact patterns (e.g., also see Douven, 2017, and Haig, 2005). As an inferential process it is starkly different from traditional hypothetico-deductive testing of propositions, an approach that can be straightjacketed by the limitations of preexisting theory. In a big data world preexisting theories often are inadequate because they are silent about – that is, they were neither intended to nor required to anticipate – the multitude and nuances of potentially observable relationships in a big data environment (Guzzo, Schneider & Nalbantian, in press). Abduction is thus a much-needed addition to familiar hypothetico-deductive methods. Authors such as Behfar and Okhuysen (2018) speak directly to the value of engaging in both forms of inference-making in organizational research (also see Prosperi et al., 2019).

For many researchable issues nonexperimental methods are equal to or more powerful than experimental research for understanding causality in organizations. In this regard there is an apt analogy between the organizational and biomedical sciences. Biomedical research shares several characteristics of the style of organizational research described here: voluminous observations, many variables, longitudinal investigations, extensive use of control variables, causal modeling and so on. Biomedical research also heavily relies on experiments, or randomized control trials (RCTs). For example, RCTs are regarded as the "gold standard" for judging whether a new drug or vaccine is producing its intended effects and thus whether it can be made available for general use. However, there is no guarantee that the results of RCTs hold up after the experiments end. After learning of favorable findings from research on the early use of his company's COVID-19 vaccine with the general public, Dr. Phil R. Dormitzer, Pfizer's chief scientific officer for viral vaccines, said, "You're never quite sure, after a controlled trial, will it really look like this in the real world?" (New York Times, Feb. 24, 2021). Similarly, Dr. John Segreti, a medical college director of infection control, commented, "Often the real-world results are worse than the trial results … real-world data are often different" (WebMD, April 2, 2021). There are many reasons real-world results can differ from those of RCTs: the greater statistical power of big data to spot risks or unintended consequences, longer time periods for analyzing the permanency of effects, the ability to assess efficacy over changing circumstances (e.g., the evolution of viral variants), opportunity to study populations excluded from RCTs (e.g., polypharmacy individuals), and the ability to detect moderating factors and interactions that are not realistically testable in an RCT. Consequently, a drug can be removed from the market when subsequent research empirically verifies undesired effects or waning impact. If an RCT is the "gold standard" for introducing a drug or vaccine for use then real-world, multivariate, nonexperimental, longitudinal, big data research is the authoritative "platinum standard" with final say in whether it remains in use.

Rigor, Relevance, and Reporting

I recall (perhaps inexactly) on Day One of my first semester graduate-level research methods course seeing a hand-drawn version of Figure 1.1, a version with only one line, the line labeled "traditional research." That was not the label back then; it was simply "research." The point of the drawing was to prompt consideration of commonly encountered trade-offs between conducting research that conforms to scientific standards of rigor and excellence and that which serves the practical, perhaps pressing interests of a host organization. Back then big data was not a thing. It is now and so I have added the second line to visualize the point that big data changes things.

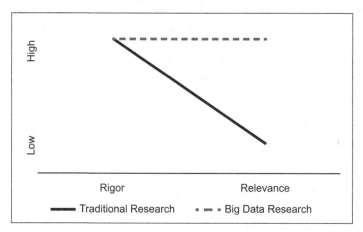

FIGURE 1.1   Rigor and relevance.

In fairness, in the pre-big data era it was possible to do rigorous applied research in organizations. Thus, the trade-offs were never absolute. But compromises often were real, depending on research topic and circumstances. Where rigor might call for longitudinal research designs, the urgency of an organization's needs may rule them out; where rigor might call for multiple measures or multiple tests, an organization's available resources might not support them. Also in fairness, big data does not fully alleviate rigor-relevance trade-offs for all research issues, as Figure 1.1 implies. Nonetheless, rigor and relevance are very much simultaneously attainable in big data organizational research.

The case studies featured here are examples of rigorous research that served practical interests. Case Studies 1 and 3 successfully moved from research results to changes in practices; Case Study 2 is a reminder of the hazards that "organizational politics" can present when trying to convert research-based knowledge into action. Collectively the cases represent research into important issues using large numbers of variables and observations drawn from numerous sources of data and analyzed with an emphasis on causal interpretation. Findings from cases like these are of interest not only to the host organizations. Findings regarding the impact of coaching on job performance (Case Study 1), links between work on health (Case Study 2), and practices that affect collaborative behavior in the workplace (Case Study 3) are relevant to existing research literatures and to many interest groups within the organizational sciences. While only three in number here, these cases are the tip of an iceberg and represent a large body of similarly conducted research on other issues and in other organizations.

Unfortunately, at present relatively few such studies will enter into the public domain in the form of journal articles, book chapters, and other publications in mainstream organizational sciences literature. The barriers to such publication are many. Organizationally-based researchers may have little incentive or opportunity to produce scientific research reports for public consumption; organizations' competitive interests may deter publicly sharing findings; and publishers of scientific papers may impose conditions (e.g., data sharing, full disclosure) meant to serve open science objectives but which cannot be met for reasons of protecting employee privacy and proprietary business interests. A detailed discussion of such barriers, and of potential ways of overcoming them, are found in Guzzo, Schneider, and Nalbantian (in press). They present tactics for meeting open science objectives while minimizing the risks to organizations and employees that are inherent in data sharing and disclosure as well as suggesting broader actions to foster a science culture that values big data organizational research. Getting rigorous, relevant, big data research results into the public domain is a looming challenge for the organizational sciences.

Notes

1 Adapted from Hirsch and Sachs (2016).
2 Adapted from Nalbantian (2018).
3 For one performance dimension, tardiness, the seven measures in the analysis were described as "rated by supervisor or objective" (Ng & Feldman, 2008, Table 1, p. 401) and were classified as objective for this calculation.
4 Thanks to Min Park for contributing this case.
5 Pearl and Mackenzie (2018, pp. 85–86) acknowledge that they are updating what 1960s social science referred to as path diagrams and path analysis. They lament that path analysis in sociology became structural equation modeling (SEM), calling it a rote method of analysis more concerned with matters of statistical estimation than causality, and that in economics path analysis fell into disuse as the field overemphasized simultaneous equation models and matrix algebra.

References

Adler, G. S., & Ambrose, M. L. (2005). An examination of the effect of computerized performance monitoring feedback on monitoring fairness, performance, and satisfaction. *Organizational Behavior and Human Decision Processes, 97*, 161–177. https://doi.org/10.1016/j.obhdp.2005.03.003

Becker, T. E. (2005). Potential problems in the statistical control of variables in organizational research: A qualitative analysis with recommendations. *Organizational Research Methods, 8*(3), 274–289. https://doi.org/10.1177/1094428105278021

Behfar, K., & Okhuysen, G. A. (2018). Discovery within validation logic: Deliberately surfacing, complementing, and substituting abductive reasoning in hypothetico-deductive inquiry. *Organization Science, 29*(2), 323–340. https://doi.org/10.1287/orsc.2017.1193

Bettis, R. A., Helfat, C. E., & Shaver, J. M. (2016). The necessity, logic, and forms of replication. *Strategic Management Journal, Special Issue: Replication in Strategic Management, 37*, 2193–2203. https://doi.org/10.1002/smj.2580

Bhave, D. P. (2014). The invisible eye? Electronic performance monitoring and employee job performance. *Personnel Psychology, 67*, 605–635. https://doi.org/10.1111/peps.12046

Brass, D. J., & Borgatti, S. P. (2020). *Social networks at work.* New York: Routledge.

Crandall, C. S., & Sherman, J. W. (2015). On the scientific superiority of conceptual replications for scientific progress. *Journal of Experimental Social Psychology, 66*, 93–99. http://dx.doi.org/10.1016/j.jesp.2015.10.002

Douven, I. (2017). Abduction. In E. N. Zalta (Ed.), *The Stanford Encyclopedia of Philosophy* (Summer 2017 Edition). https://plato.stanford.edu/archives/sum2017/entries/abduction/

Eden, D. (2017). Field experiments in organizations. *Annual Review of Organizational Psychology and Organizational Behavior, 4*, 91–122. https://doi.org/10.1146/annurev-orgpsych-041015-064400

Guzzo, R. A. (2011). The universe of evidence-based I-O psychology is expanding. *Industrial and Organizational Psychology, 4*, 65–67.

Guzzo, R. A. (2016). How big data matters. In S. Tonidandel, E. King, & J. Cortina (Eds.), *Big data at work: The data science revolution and organizational psychology.* New York: Routledge, 336–349.

Guzzo, R. A., Schneider, B., & Nalbantian, H. R. (in press). Open science, closed doors: The perils and potential of open science for research-in-practice. *Industrial and Organizational Psychology.*

Haig, B. D. (2005). An abductive theory of scientific method. *Psychological Methods, 10*(4), 371–388. https://doi.org/10.1037/1082-989X.10.4.371

Hernandez, I., Newman, D. A., & Jeon, G. (2016). Twitter analysis: Methods for data management and a word count dictionary to measure city-level job satisfaction. In S. Tonidandel, E. King, & J. Cortina (Eds.), *Big data at work: The data science revolution and organizational psychology.* New York: Routledge, 64–114.

Hirsch, W., & Sachs, D. (2016). Driving sales success: Measuring and quantifying talent predictors. Paper presented at the Northwestern University Third Annual Leadership Roundtable on Talent Analytics, Evanston, IL, November.

King, G., & Persily, N. (2019). A new mode for industry-academic partnership. *PS: Political Science and Politics.* https://doi.org/10.1017/S1049096519000102l

Köhler T., & Cortina, J. M. (2021). Play it again, Sam! An analysis of constructive replication in the organizational sciences. *Journal of Management, 47*(2), 488–518. https://doi.org/10.1177/0149206319843985

Matusik, J. G., Heidl, R., Hollenbeck, J. R., Yu, A., Lee. H. W., & Howe, M. (2019). Wearable Bluetooth sensors for capturing relational variables and temporal variability in relationships: A construct validation study. *Journal of Applied Psychology, 104*(3), 357–387. http://dx.doi.org/10.1037/apl0000334

McShane, B. B., & Böckenholt, U. (2017). Single-paper meta-analysis: Benefits for study summary, theory testing, and replicability. *Journal of Consumer Research, 43*(6), 1048–1063. https://doi.org/10.1093/jcr/ucw085

Nalbantian, H. R. (2018). Measuring the workforce and business impact of employer investments in employee health and well-being. Paper presented at the OECD Well Being at Work Conference, Paris, France, October.

New York Times (2021, Feb. 24). The Pfizer vaccine's initial success holds up in wider use, a study finds. https://www.nytimes.com/live/2021/02/24/world/covid-19-coronavirus

Ng, T. W., & Feldman, D. C. (2008). The relationship of age to ten dimensions of job performance. *Journal of Applied Psychology, 93*(2), 392. https://doi.org/10.1037/0021-9010.93.2.392

Pearl, J., Glynmour, M., & Jewell, N. P. (2016). *Causal inference in statistics: A primer.* New York: Wiley.

Pearl, J., & Mackenzie, D. (2018). *The book of why: The new science of cause and effect.* New York: Basic Books.

Prosperi, M., Bian, J., Buchan, I. E., Koopman, J. S., Sperrin, M., & Wang, M. (2019). Raiders of the lost HARK: A reproducible inference framework for big data science. *Palgrave Communications, 5*(125). https://doi.org/10.1057/s41599-019-0340-8

Ryan, J., & Herleman, H. (2016). A big data platform for workforce analytics. In S. Tonidandel, E. King, & J. Cortina (Eds.), *Big data at work: The data science revolution and organizational psychology.* New York: Routledge, 19–42.

Sainato, M. (2021). 14-hour days and no bathroom breaks: Amazon's overworked delivery drivers. *The Guardian*, March 11. https://www.theguardian.com/technology/2021/mar/11/amazon-delivery-drivers-bathroom-breaks-unions

WebMD (2021, April 2). Pfizer COVID-19 vaccine protects for 6 months or more. https://www.webmd.com/vaccines/covid-19-vaccine/news/20210402/pfizer-covid-vaccine-protects-for-6-months-or-more

2

USING OTHER PEOPLES' DATA

Implications of Reliance on Meta-Analysis and Archival Data

Frank A. Bosco and James G. Field

> *It is easier to say something new than to reconcile things that have already been said.*
> Luc de Clapiers Vauvenarques, 1715–1747

Although the value of synthesizing research areas was recognized more than a hundred years ago (Pearson, 1904), some degree of consensus regarding how to best assimilate information from independent studies was not reached until relatively recently. The advent of meta-analysis provided researchers with the means to integrate results from existing studies – even imperfect, small-sample studies (Rubin, 1990) – to reveal patterns between relations, the establishment of which could serve as general principles and cumulative knowledge (Glass, 1976; Schmidt & Hunter, 1977; Smith & Glass, 1977). Simply put, meta-analysis introduced a way for researchers to use other peoples' data to provide the best available empirically-based answers to questions of scientific and practical interest – a way for researchers to address some of the challenges introduced by the existence of multiple, often contradictory, answers to a given question (Rosenthal & DiMatteo, 2001; Schmidt, 2010). Indeed, meta-analysts helped to identify and overcome flawed procedures previously used for achieving cumulative knowledge (e.g., qualitative or narrative literature reviews that failed to reconcile the conflicting findings) and have been relied upon in many domains for a variety of purposes.

In terms of aiding research, meta-analysis has been used in a variety of fields – including applied psychology (e.g., Howard, Cogswell & Smith, 2020), law (e.g., Papalia et al., 2020), strategic management (e.g., Combs & Ketchen, 2003), education (e.g., Richardson, Abraham & Bond, 2012), medicine (Berlin & Colditz, 1990; Laureano-Phillips et al., 2019), and policy formulation (Reynolds et al., 2020) – to provide

DOI: 10.4324/9781003015000-3

us with an overview of where a given research domain has been, summarize, and integrate its extant scientific findings and suggests new directions for future inquiry. Indeed, by virtue of its ability to extract relatively clear answers from an existing literature, meta-analysis provides a foundation for theory development (Schmidt & Hunter, 2015). For example, Barrick and Mount's summary of more than 35 years of personality research concluded that the five-factor model "provides a meaningful framework for formulating and testing hypotheses relating individual differences in personality to a wide range of criteria in personnel psychology" (1991, p. 23). Although meta-analysis itself does not directly generate or develop theory (Guzzo, Jackson & Katzell, 1987), one can hardly deny the role played by Barrick and Mount's (1991) meta-analytic findings in serving as the building blocks for theory in subsequent studies, especially in the subfields of personnel selection, performance appraisal, and training and development (at the time of writing this chapter, their paper had 3,848 citations). Indeed, the assertion that meta-analytic findings serve as guideposts for future theory and inquiry is not reserved for Barrick and Mount's (1991) review of personality research and can likely be extended to many other studies that employ meta-analysis (e.g., see Griffeth, Hom & Gaertner, 2000; Iaffaldano & Muchinsky, 1985; Judge & Bono, 2001; Loher et al., 1985)

Despite its utility for guiding future research, over the years scientists have felt the need to expand the meta-analysis toolbox – perhaps in an attempt to overcome criticism that meta-analysis is atheoretical and does not help to advance theory (e.g., Chow, 1987; Eysenck, 1984). As such, it can be argued that meta-analysis has evolved over time, diversifying from a method of summary that simply examines the nature of bivariate relations to a method that examines a variety of effects (e.g., moderator, mediator, and multilevel) and even help to test hypotheses derived from complex models. For example, Bennett, Bakker, and Field (2018) used traditional meta-analytic procedures to summarize relations between work-related antecedents (e.g., hindrance demands) and recovery experiences (e.g., psychological detachment), but also used recently developed meta-analytic tools (i.e., meta-analytic structural equation modeling) to test hypotheses derived from job demands-resources theory. Their approach illustrates that one-way meta-analysis has evolved to permit stronger causal statements. Yet, ironically, their approach also illustrates how meta-analysis – a tool that was developed to circumvent problems associated with statistical significance testing (Schmidt & Hunter, 1997) – has evolved to allow for inferences on the basis of null hypothesis significance testing (NHST). Indeed, NHST and meta-analysis are routinely used together in modern meta-analysis for a variety of purposes (e.g., testing for homogeneity among different levels in multilevel meta-analysis, model comparisons using likelihood ratio tests, tests for direct versus indirect mediation, and the like).

It is worth noting that meta-analysis has evolved in many other ways and today is much more than just a method of summary. An informative, modern meta-analysis is expected to provide – at the minimum – estimates of mean effects and their dispersion (i.e., descriptive statistics). However, perhaps most interesting meta-analytic outcomes involve higher-order inferences. Tests for the significance of moderating or mediating effects and meta-analytic structural equations model comparisons are cases in point. Furthermore, statistical procedures for these approaches have evolved to, for example, accommodate effects corrected for unreliability (Aguinis & Pierce, 1998). Still, the procedures are not universally agreed upon and without issue. Indeed, Köhler et al.'s (2015) findings indicate that pairs of reliability values are nonindependent (i.e., correlated), meaning that correcting for both predictor and criterion reliability is, to some degree, an act of *double-dipping* that leads to inflation of the disattenuated effect size.

Furthermore, meta-analysis has also become a tool used to study non–substantive questions. Across various fields, meta-analysis is used to examine: (a) the prevalence of questionable research practices (e.g., O'Boyle, Banks & Gonzalez-Mulé, 2017), (b) effect size benchmarks for interpreting scientific findings and progress (Bosco et al., 2015), (c) the explanatory power of cultural theoretical perspectives (Field et al., 2021), (d) the relative importance of antecedents of given outcomes (e.g., Miao, Humphrey & Qian, 2017), (e) potential construct and empirical redundancy (i.e., jingle-jangle issues; Banks et al., 2021), and (f) methodological and substantive moderating effects that cannot be assessed using a single primary study (e.g., Park & Shaw, 2013).

Practitioners often rely on meta-analytic results to guide evidence-based practice (Rousseau & McCarthy, 2007). For example, meta-analytic results can serve as input to utility analyses, which can help practitioners to ascertain the economic and productivity costs/benefits associated with organizational decisions (e.g., see Hancock et al., 2013; Schmidt et al., 1979). Indeed, greater meaning is given to meta-analytic findings and they have broader use when translated into common parlance understood by practitioners. Additionally, meta-analysis plays an important role in guiding education practices. Notwithstanding the many "how to" textbooks on meta-analysis that are typically used at the graduate levels (e.g., Borenstein et al., 2009; Cooper, 2015; Hedges & Olkin, 1985; Lipsey & Wilson, 2000; Schmidt & Hunter, 2015), it is common for undergraduate industrial-organizational (IO) psychology textbooks to cite meta-analytic findings to support proposed conceptualizations of organizational phenomena. Finally, meta-analysis can be used to inform policy decisions (e.g., environmental, public, and education) and, thus, can help to direct resources to potentially good programs and away from bad ones. For example, Tanner-Smith, Wilson, and Lipsey's (2013) meta-analysis on outpatient treatments for adolescent substance abuse revealed that family therapy programs tended to be more effective than comparison programs (e.g., motivational enhancement therapy). Their evidence-based policy recommendations are now being used in hundreds of juvenile drug courts across the United States. Similarly, meta-analysis revealed that the "Scared Straight" program, which was intended to expose youth to realistic depictions of life behind bars in an attempt to discourage them from breaking the law, provoked rather than prevented teenage delinquency (Petrosino, Petrosino & Buehler, 2005). Consequently, the program was abolished.

Up to this point, we have provided the reader with some of the historical context and a sample of use cases pertinent to meta-analysis from the last half century. Looking ahead to the next 50 years, a period during which global scientific publication output may grow up to 400% (Bornmann & Mutz, 2015), it is likely that meta-analysis' role in guiding future research, practice, education, and policy may become even more important. Thus, it is a good time for a critical evaluation of meta-analysis and discussion of how it may evolve in the future as IO psychology and other research areas embrace the era of big data. The remainder of this chapter provides a sample of meta-analysis topics. Similar to previous reviews in this area (e.g., Oswald et al., 2015), ours covers a selection of the major landmarks and bypasses some others in order to provide a nontechnical description of the overall landscape. We start by describing the benefits of meta-analysis for overcoming certain shortcomings associated with primary research. Next, we highlight a number of limitations associated with meta-analysis as well as potential user errors that affect its application potential. We conclude our tour by outlining a number of broad implications that can be delineated from research that relies on other people's data, including archival data and repositories that store vast corpora of scientific findings (e.g., metaBUS; Bosco et al., 2020). Taken together, our goal is simple – to improve the reader's understanding of meta-analysis, its limitations, and its potential for tackling "big data" questions in future research.

Benefits of Meta-Analysis

Meta-analysis is an "analysis of analyses" (Glass, 1976, p. 3). Put differently, it is a statistical tool used for estimating the mean and variance of an underlying population effect from a collection of effect sizes that ostensibly examine the same phenomenon. Indeed, by incorporating data from more than one primary study, meta-analytic reviews typically have larger sample sizes and, thus, greater statistical power that primary studies. The Hedges and Olkin (1985) and Schmidt and Hunter (2015) approaches to meta-analysis are most commonly used to summarize research literatures (for a comparison of both approaches, see Kepes et al., 2013) – the latter being the most popular approach in IO research and related research areas (e.g., organizational behavior, management) because of its ability to correct for unreliability and other sources of artifactual variance. In the following sections, we briefly describe a sample of statistical artifacts (i.e., sampling error, measurement error, and range restriction) that meta-analysis can correct for[1]. By dint of being able to correct for such distorting effects, meta-analysis allows researchers to arrive at conclusions that are more stable and credible than what can be reported in a single primary study and/or in a nonquantitative, systematic review.

Sampling error causes observed (i.e., primary study) effects to misestimate true score estimates. At the level of the individual study, it is impossible to correct for sampling error because it is random, which is why observed effect sizes can be potentially inaccurate and untrustworthy. However, at the level of meta-analysis, when multiple effect sizes are being analyzed, sampling error can be estimated and corrected for.

Random measurement error in the independent and dependent variables have a systematic multiplicative effect on the effect size, which attenuates meta-analytic mean effect size estimates (Schmidt & Hunter, 2015); others (Murphy & DeShon, 2000) have argued that nonrandom measurement error can strengthen or weaken observed effects. The correction for measurement error is made by dividing the observed effect size by the square root of the product of the reliability coefficients. Such corrections can be made at the level of individual studies when reliability information is available for both variables. However, reliability information is not always reported in primary studies. Even under these conditions, meta-analysis can estimate the attenuation by pooling reliability estimates from a number of existing studies. Thus, even in the presence of missing data, meta-analysis can be an effective tool for estimating the true population effect size.

Another artifact commonly corrected for in IO meta-analyses is range restriction, which is a special case of biased sampling (Schmidt & Hunter, 2015). Similar to the measurement error, the effect of range restriction is systematic and attenuates the meta-analytic mean effect size. To illustrate this artifact, imagine that only the top performers on an entrance exam are admitted to a graduate program. Under this condition, a researcher interested in estimating the validity of the entrance exam will have data from a restricted population (i.e., only those who were admitted), but be expected to make inferences that generalize to an unrestricted population (i.e., all exam takers). To correct for range restriction, the meta-analyst needs to be able to estimate the ratio of the SD in the restricted population to the SD in the unrestricted population. If the latter statistic is available, then range restriction can be corrected for. However, the needed statistics, oftentimes the observed SD in the unrestricted population, are not always available and, thus, the correction for range restriction cannot always be made. Taken together, range restriction is not a simple artifact; it can occur directly or indirectly in both the independent and dependent variables and corrections are often applied erroneously (Hunter, Schmidt & Le, 2006).

Finally, meta-analysts have the means to examine research questions that cannot be addressed by any of the primary studies being summarized. For example,

Park and Shaw (2013) included an assessment of context- (e.g., industry) and methods-related (e.g., cross-sectional versus panel data structures) moderators to explore possible differences in the relation between turnover rates and organizational performance. Indeed, none of the 110 studies included in their meta-analysis could explore boundary conditions in this way. As such, meta-analysis is advantageous because it creates new opportunities for discovery, which could help to guide future research and practice.

Limitations of Meta-Analysis

Like all methodologies, meta-analysis is not without its limitations. One relatively well-documented limitation is publication bias, which occurs when studies that are available in the published literature are unrepresentative of the population of completed studies (Rothstein, Sutton & Borenstein, 2005). Indeed, when this occurs, the meta-analyst will violate a primary assumption underlying meta-analysis, which holds that the population – or, at least, an unbiased sample – of effect sizes must be analyzed in order to produce the best true score estimate. Given that small sample studies with statistically nonsignificant results tend to be missing from the available literature (Rothstein, Sutton & Borenstein, 2005), publication bias typically inflates the magnitude of meta-analytic mean effect size estimates. (Inflation can also arise from nonindependence of results over time; that is, existing, established findings [e.g., positive, medium correlation between general mental ability (GMA) and role performance] might prevent future null effects from reaching print.)

Publication bias has been detected in several literatures (e.g., Field, Bosco & Kepes, 2021), which naturally brings into question the trustworthiness of our cumulative knowledge. However, there is a lack of empirically-based interpretation guidelines to help consumers of science quantify the extent to which publication bias may threaten meta-analytic results and conclusions. For example, one approach to quantifying the magnitude of publication bias is Kepes and McDaniel's (2015) percentage-based comparison, which examines the relative difference between a meta-analytic mean effect size and a meta-analytic mean estimate that has been adjusted for the effect of publication bias. According to their guidelines, a meta-analytic mean estimate of .05 is severely misestimated if a publication bias detection technique (e.g., trim-and-fill model; Duval & Tweedie, 2000) produced an adjusted effect size of .02 ($|\Delta| = .03$ or 60%, a "large" degree of bias). In contrast, comparing an adjusted effect size of $r = .30$ against a meta-analytic mean effect size of .27, also an absolute difference of .03, would be labeled a "negligible" difference as the corresponding relative difference is just 10%. One potential issue with this approach is that the observed difference (i.e., delta) is not independent from the magnitude of the effect size. Thus, one may overstate the magnitude of publication bias when dealing with small effect sizes, and underestimate the magnitude for relatively large effect sizes.

Furthermore, the exact conditions (e.g., degree of heterogeneity, number of effect sizes in the meta-analytic distribution) under which publication bias detection techniques perform best is unknown (van Assen, van Aert & Wicherts, 2015). For example, Stanley (2017) observed that the precision-effect test and precision-effect estimate with standard errors performed poorly under certain conditions. Likewise, simulations conducted by Terrin et al. (2003; Carter et al., 2019) revealed that the trim-and-fill model's performance may be threatened when the meta-analytic database is made up of heterogeneous effect sizes. Furthermore, weighted distribution approaches (i.e., selection models) to detecting potential bias often require large sample sizes and are based on strict assumptions (McShane, Böckenholt & Hansen, 2016). Taken together, any threat to the robustness of meta-analytic estimates should be worrisome. Yet, consensus regarding how to best assess the trustworthiness of meta-analytic results has not been reached, which is surprising given how important they are for guiding research, practice, education, and policy. As surprising as this may be, it may be even more surprising that greater attention has not been given to addressing some of the other limitations of meta-analysis.

Temporal Trends

Given that meta-analysis is an arduous and time-consuming task, several years may pass before meta-analytic studies are updated to include recent primary research findings. If the effects' magnitudes are changing over time, then a given meta-analytic summary should provide diminishing return for guiding research, practice, education, and policy as time passes. The shelf life of meta-analytic findings may be especially threatened if evidence from newly published primary research is sensitive to an event that transpired after the meta-analysis appeared in the literature. For example, Jiang and Lavaysse (2018) reported that affective job insecurity had stronger relations with most outcomes and correlates (e.g., turnover intention and organizational commitment) than did cognitive job insecurity. However, we do not know if the pattern of findings will be the same in the aftermath of the COVID-19 pandemic. That is, the post-pandemic world could create serious hazards for application of meta-analytic evidence. (This is likely especially true of constructs, such as autonomy.) Furthermore, in its current form, meta-analysis does not help us to discern when the detection of such temporal trends will be revealed. Taken together, whether meta-analytic results should have an "evidentiary statute of limitations" (Greene, Prasad & Cifu, 2019, p. 1356) has not been determined, which is worrisome given that even recently published meta-analyses may be outdated. Indeed, meta-analyses in medicine appear to have an average shelf life of 5.5 years, and 7% expire between the manuscript acceptance and publication dates (Shojania et al., 2007). Thus, meta-analyses – especially those relying on (now) decades-old primary studies – might poorly reflect the phenomenon as it unfolds now.

Given that cumulative evidence is not static and tends to evolve over time as new primary research appears in the published literature, it is important to understand the extent to which temporal variation in effect sizes may exist. In addition, it is important to understand what may be driving such variations (e.g., real temporal change or heterogeneity from other sources). Temporal trends in effect sizes typically manifest as decline effects (i.e., a decrease in the magnitude of the effect size with publication year; Koricheva, Jennions & Lau, 2013; Protzko & Schooler, 2017). Indeed, temporal instability of the evidence base can threaten the robustness of meta-analytic results and conclusions (Koricheva & Kulinskaya, 2019), causes the observed meta-analytic mean effect size estimate to lose statistical or practical significance (e.g., Johnsen & Friborg, 2015), or even changes the directionality of the effect size (Ioannidis & Trikalinos, 2005).

Various factors may help to explain why the magnitude of effect sizes for a given bivariate relation diminish over time. For example, the Proteus effect, which occurs when larger effects are published quicker because they are more interesting and provocative (Trikalinos & Ioannidis, 2005), is one plausible cause for temporal instability of observed effect sizes. However, temporal trends might be confounded with heterogeneity in the effect sizes. Put differently, if effect sizes are smaller or larger under certain conditions (e.g., a moderator effect), a temporal trend may be detected if studies in one condition are published more often over time than studies in any other condition (Koricheva & Kulinskaya, 2019). Likewise, changes in research methods over time may produce temporal trends, especially if the effect sizes associated with newly developed methods differ from those produced by older methods. Taken together, temporal trend analyses may reveal patterns of evidence reversal or sources of heterogeneity that may go undetected if temporal trends are not examined in the first place. In either case, a meta-analysis will likely produce results that overestimate the magnitude of a given bivariate relation. Although temporal trends have been observed in several areas of the medical sciences (e.g., Foo et al., 2017; Rødgaard et al., 2019), it is rarely studied by IO meta-analysts (Banks, Kepes & McDaniel, 2012; for some recent exceptions, see Eisenberger et al., 2019; Gong & Jiao, 2019; Pietschnig et al., 2019). Thus, in general, we do not know whether noticeable changes in the magnitude or even direction of IO research findings have been observed over time. Indeed, this is surprising because several methods for the detection of temporal instability are available to IO meta-analysts. What follows is a brief description of graphical and statistical methods that would aid IO meta-analysts in this endeavor.

Perhaps the easiest way to ascertain if a potential temporal tend is present in a meta-analytic dataset is to produce a scatterplot that displays effect sizes and their corresponding publication year. In the absence of temporal change, the effect sizes will be uniformly distributed. In contrast, a decline effect is observed if the plot displays a downward scatter. Another graphical technique that can be used to examine temporal change is the cumulative meta-analysis (CMA). To conduct a CMA, the researcher must first arrange the effect sizes in a meta-analytic distribution by their publication year. Following this, iterative meta-analyses are conducted by adding one additional effect size. When arranged by publication year, the earliest available effect size is entered into the analysis first, followed by next available, and so on, until the most recent effect size has been added. This process results in a series of cumulative point estimates which can be plotted in a forest plot and examined for "drift" (Borenstein et al., 2009). Drift occurs when cumulative means derived from early iterations in the CMA differ in magnitude from later ones. Therefore, a negative drift indicates that the magnitude of the mean effect size decreases following each iteration and suggests evidence reversal is observed because older effect sizes are larger than newer ones.

Although graphical tools are useful, they only provide a rudimentary inspection of the data because, as the body of earlier evidence increases, a new temporal trend becomes more difficult to assess using these existing methods. Furthermore, given that tools like scatterplots and CMA forest plots do not come with clear interpretation guidelines, they are subject to misinterpretation. Therefore, as with all visual methods, those used to assess temporal instability in effect sizes should be supplemented with formal statistical methods. One approach available to researchers is to examine whether the first available effect size is statistically different from the average of all subsequent effect sizes (see Fanshawe, Shaw & Spence, 2017). This mean difference should be evaluated relative to the square root of the sum of the corresponding variances (similar to a t-test). It is worth noting that this approach works only for effect sizes that follow an approximate normal distribution and, thus, is most apt for Fisher z-transformed correlations, log response ratios, and log odds ratios. Meta-analysts can also conduct a nonparametric test that compares the number of iterations in a CMA by publication year with positive and negative drift (see Trikalinos & Ioannidis, 2005). In the absence of temporal change, the number of iterations in the CMA that present with positive drift will equal the number of iterations with negative drift. However, this approach offers a coarse assessment of potential temporal change because it examines the direction, but not the magnitude, of effect size change after each iteration of the CMA. As such, its results should be interpreted with caution.

The temporal stability of effect sizes in a meta-analytic dataset can also be assessed by indicators of sufficiency and stability (see Mullen, Muellerleile & Bryant, 2001). Together, the indicators of sufficiency and stability may help meta-analysts identify the point in a research literature's history where additional tests of a specific hypothesis amount to "flogging a dead horse" (Mullen, Muellerleile & Bryant, 2001, p. 1460). Sufficiency is estimated using the fail-safe ratio, which indicates whether the fail-safe number for a given iteration of a CMA exceeds Rosenthal's (1979) 5k + 10 benchmark[2]. If the fail-safe ratio is greater than 1, the current iteration of the CMA has exceeded the benchmark of 5k + 10, and it can be claimed that the cumulative weight of evidence appears to be sufficiently tolerant of future null results. Mullen, Muellerleile, and Bryant (2001) suggested that stability can be inferred by calculating the "cumulative slope," which is identical to a CMA with one alteration; instead of iteratively estimating the meta-analytic mean effect size estimate, each effect size is presented at each iteration. Under this approach, the earliest available effect size is displayed at the first iteration. Following this, the earliest available effect size and the next available effect size is displayed at the second iteration, and so on until all effect sizes are presented at the final iteration. A regression line is fitted to the CMA database and its slope can be used to infer the magnitude of temporal change. Stability is achieved when the slope approaches zero, indicating that adding another effect size will not affect the cumulative effect size. It is worth noting that both approaches introduced by Mullen, Muellerleile, and Bryant (2001) have limitations. For example, the shortcomings of fail-safe number are well-documented (e.g., Becker, 2005) and the significance of the cumulative slope cannot be formally tested because of multiple testing.

Meta-analysts can also conduct a linear weighted regression analysis that assesses the relationship between publication year and effect size (Fanshawe, Shaw & Spence, 2017; Gehr, Weiss & Porzsolt, 2006). Indeed, this approach works well if the temporal change is linear (e.g., consistently decreases over time). However, given that shifts in effect size are not always uniform (e.g., sometimes they are small, large, or even in the opposite direction), the linearity assumption that underlying the general linear model is often violated when assessing the temporal stability of effect sizes. If it is suspected that the relationship between effect size and publication year is nonlinear, sophisticated techniques like fractional polynomial regression and spline regression can be employed (Bagnardi et al., 2004), which rely on a likelihood ratio test to test for nonlinearity by comparing the nonlinear and linear models.

Quality control and cumulative sum chart methodologies developed for industrial applications of statistics were originally used to ascertain if variations in production processes were random or attributable to particular causes. They have since been adapted to assess the significance of effects and detect trends over time in CMA (Kulinskaya & Koricheva, 2010). These methods rely on control limits around a target level of effect size (e.g., ± 5 SDs; see Fanshawe, Shaw & Spence, 2017). Temporal stability is observed when each iteration of the CMA falls within the established control limit. However, the process is considered "out of control" (i.e., control limits) and, thus, temporal instability in the effect sizes is observed when either a single iteration or a run of iterations falls outside of the control limit.

Finally, meta-regression is another tool available to IO meta-analysts for estimating the temporal stability of effect sizes. Meta-regression is conceptually similar to traditional linear regression analysis, but studies are the unit of analysis rather than individuals. Typically, the dependent variable in a meta-regression is the effect size from each study and the independent variables are the corresponding study characteristics. These study-level covariates may be numerical or categorical. Thus, publication year can be included as a potential moderator of effect size magnitude in a meta-regression (e.g., see Bosco et al., 2016; Eisenberger et al., 2019; Rockstuhl et al., 2020). In such cases, the observed coefficient represents the extent to which publication year explains variance in effect size. Put differently, the observed coefficient quantifies how much effect sizes change year after year. (Once many first-order meta-analyses have been accumulated, second-order meta-analysis [Schmidt & Oh, 2013] might be used for the same purpose.)

Meta-Analytic Reporting and Citation Plasticity

Perhaps one of the greatest threats to relying on existing cumulative evidence (i.e., meta-analytic summaries) is seen in how the results are digested, communicated, and applied. Two reviews of meta-analytic information citation have appeared (i.e., Carlson & Ji, 2011; DeSimone, Köhler & Schoen, 2019), both of which reveal that meta-analytic citation tends to be relatively cursory in nature. That is, most citations of meta-analytic evidence do so at the expense of nuance by, for example, only referencing the existence of a bivariate relation without its boundary conditions or other important details.

Consider the flexibility with which one is faced when citing meta-analytic evidence. One may choose to cite an omnibus estimate that lumps together findings from the lab and field; this is the most common usage. Alternatively, one may reference specific moderator levels (e.g., subjective versus objective measures of performance) to add nuance when conducting new studies or developing hypotheses (DeSimone, Köhler & Schoen, 2019). However, the accommodational plasticity (cf. Hitchcock & Sober, 2004) provided by the variety of meta-analytic estimates can also cause confusion and facilitate questionable research practices (e.g., preference for larger, omnibus estimates to influence a priori power analysis). Furthermore, while the use of omnibus estimates may seem reasonable for purposes of testing theoretical models, they are usually less well suited for application to organizational contexts. Indeed, if one's goal is to infer from the cumulative evidence expected utility (e.g., of a selection device; Highhouse et al., 2017), we should not be shocked that practitioners might insist on the exclusion of lab studies' findings – especially if they present with a different mean magnitude.

Related to the problem above, another striking feature of meta-analytic reporting is their tendency to test moderators sequentially rather than simultaneously.

That is, a meta-analyst might begin with 100 effects and then place them into buckets (e.g., lab versus field). Next, they're reassembled into one large pile and again placed into new buckets (e.g., objective versus subjective performance). If researchers in any of the social sciences were to conduct regression analyses in this way, they would be rightly criticized because such an approach ignores possible covariance among the predictors. If, instead, researchers were to use meta-regression or similar approaches (Cheung, 2015) to arrive at slope coefficients for each predictor, it would become possible to arrive at an expected effect more precisely for a combination of factors.

Further complicating citation problems is a lack of a common language and reporting standards among scientists. Indeed, to our knowledge, there exists no official, consensus-based classification system for organizational research constructs, resulting in meta-analyses with incommensurable moderator levels. For example, some meta-analysts include absenteeism in measures of counterproductive work behavior (Marcus et al., 2016), and others do not (Dalal, 2005). Similarly, some meta-analysts include training performance as measures of job performance, and others do not. Thus, when referring to existing meta-analytic summaries, conflicting conclusions may be reached. This becomes problematic, to some degree, for second-order meta-analysts. However, this sort of apples and oranges problem would likely be sorted out with effort. However, the greater threat is likely miscommunication with nontechnical audiences (e.g., practicing managers), who might not appreciate the taxonomic distinctions.

Indeed, imagine that GMA predicted 10 training performance effects with, say, mean $r = .40$ and 10 role performance effects with $r = .30$. If the two were grouped together into a *performance* category, the relation between GMA and *performance* might be $r = .35$. However, imagine a different meta-analysis on the same general topic that grouped 10 extra-role performance effects (mean $r = .20$) and the same 10 role performance effects (mean $r = .30$) into a *performance* category; that summary effect might be $r = .25$. To complicate matters further, imagine role performance was simply reported more frequently (i.e., role performance $k = 100$, $r = .30$; extra-role performance $k = 10$, $r = .20$) – now, the summary effect might be $r = .29$! There exists a great deal of flexibility – perhaps too much – in how meta-analytic inputs are grouped. Until some form of standardization for naming constructs is adopted, this additional noise will remain.

In many cases, an additional complication arises from the variety of psychometric corrections available. For example, meta-analytic summaries may be reported as corrected only for sampling error (i.e., mean r), after correction for attenuation due to unreliability, direct or indirect range restriction, and the like. Operational validities are corrected for unreliability in the criterion *and* indirect or direct range restriction in the predictor. Thus, to make an apples-to-apples comparison of, say, two selection devices, each summary would have to encompass roughly the same criterion space and employ the same artifact corrections. We suspect that this level of commensurability exists with relatively low frequency, often leading to misleading comparisons. For example, Phillips's (2020) *Strategic Staffing* text reports the "average validity" of cognitive ability tests as ".51" and structured interviews as ".51–.63" (Table 9-3, p. 352). The former estimate is reported as taken from Schmidt and Hunter (1998), and the latter from McDaniel et al. (1994) and Wiesner and Cronshaw (1988). Students, after reading this text chapter, would come away thinking that cognitive ability tests perform at the lower end of structured interviews which, for many or most job contexts, simply cannot be. Indeed, the most recent operational validity estimate for structured interviews of which we are aware is $\rho = .41$ (Oh, Postlethwaite & Schmidt, 2013), and cognitive ability outperforms that figure with, in most cases, $\rho = .50$ or higher (Schmidt, Shaffer & Oh, 2008). Although textbooks are often limited in detail by design, we find it perfectly reasonable to insist upon the provision of uncorrected summary estimates (i.e., "bare-bones" meta-analytic estimates) alongside corrected effects in most – if not all – cases.

A Brief Appraisal and Possible Steps Forward

Ultimately, how valuable are existing meta-analytic summaries? Certainly, their value exceeds that of the typical primary study. However, after using and reusing existing primary study data for several decades, can we be certain that meta-analysis (as currently employed) will continue to provide similar levels of return on investment? Where might it fail? What might be better? We suspect that the existing meta-analytic evidence has a rather short shelf life. However, to be clear, our concern is not with the equations underlying meta-analysis, per se. Rather, our primary concerns involve a rapidly changing workplace and processes involved in systematic review including data collection and curation for later use.

As noted above, meta-analyses are snapshots in time that are updated rather infrequently – with luck, once per decade. They often include findings aged several decades without concomitant tests for temporal trends. However, looking back from 2021, quite a lot has changed in just the last 20 years. Consider that the percentage of U.S. households with a computer and Internet access passed 50% for the first time 20 years ago (Day, Janus & Davis, 2005) and the number carrying similar technology in their pockets (i.e., smartphones) first passed 50% roughly 10 years ago (Pew Research Center, 2021). Furthermore, just within the last few years, an increasing number of individuals have considered alternatives to traditional college education, and organizations, such as Google, have begun providing low-cost options for job-ready skills training. Most obviously, however, consider the potential massive shift toward work-from-home arrangements that will likely arise in the wake of the COVID-19 pandemic. In the future, hypothetical taxonomy of work, the very first branch – the most important distinction, perhaps – might be *remote versus in-person*, and this distinction could have wide-ranging implications for job satisfaction, work-life balance, personal wealth, freedom to live where one wishes, and the like. In fact, it might be unsurprising if we begin to see decreases in job satisfaction of traditional, in-person professional roles, such as many medical professions for these very reasons.

In our view, these changes in our world are substantial enough to cast doubt on much of the cumulative evidence in organizational research, depending on topic, until more recent evidence is accumulated. Indeed, the workplace of the future – especially for many technologies or business jobs – might involve much less interpersonal contact – especially informal communication. Furthermore, the workforce of the future might rely more heavily on objective measures of performance by dint of improved technology and desire to reduce biases, such as email response latencies or rework as indicated by file modifications and their timestamps. In this potential future, will practitioners be drawn to the many existing meta-analyses summarizing coworker incivility or supervisory ratings? Perhaps not so much.

So, how might meta-analysis retool to handle volatility and better serve stakeholders in the future? One approach is to focus effort on the development of living databases of scientific information. In fact, such community-augmented meta-analyses are being built already in a growing number of fields, such as cognitive development (e.g., infant language learning; Bergmann, Tsuji & Cristia, 2017; Burgard, Bošnjak & Studtrucker, 2021). In organizational research, the metaBUS project (Bosco et al, 2020) maintains the largest database of manually classified findings in the social sciences (presently more than 1.1 million correlations), each tagged to a branching taxonomy (i.e., ontology) of topics studied in the scientific space. The database has been used to address a variety of meta-science questions (e.g., large-scale tests of relations between effect sizes and response rates [Bosco et al., 2014], grant funding status [Field et al., 2015], sample types [Field, Bosco & Pierce, 2013]) and substantive questions in organizational research (e.g., comparing variance explained by five popular cross-cultural models for 136 bivariate relations; Field et al., 2021). (For a review of research finding database leverage in organizational research, see Bosco [2022]).

There are several benefits of taking such bottom-up approaches to curating scientific information. First, as described above, a constant tracking of evidence will allow detection of trends in real-time (e.g., out of control limits), which would allow researchers to better understand changes in the experience of work. Second, open, massive databases allow large-scale assessments of various research aberrations (e.g., publication bias), which would be much more effective than publishing a series of papers each time a new publication bias detection algorithm emerges.

The reliance on other peoples' data now has a long history in IO research. Such efforts have provided many important insights to scientists and practitioners alike.

However, our research landscape – and the nature of work itself – is in a rapid state of change. For such insight to continue, our findings – existing and yet to be published – must be more effectively curated. Platforms like metaBUS offer a potential solution. However, it is not yet known whether IO psychologists are willing to come together to contribute to such efforts without obvious, immediate reward.

Notes

1 Although Schmidt and Hunter identified 10 study design artifacts that can alter meta-analytic results (2015; see Chapter 3), they claimed that they were unaware of any study that could correct for each. Thus, we chose to describe the three artifacts that are corrected for most frequently in IO meta-analyses.

2 Rosenthal's failsafe N takes as input a meta-analytic distribution's number of effects and mean effect size and provides as output the number of null findings (e.g., $r = .00$) that would need to be added to the distribution to change the summary estimate's p-value from significant to nonsignificant. Rosenthal's approach considers robust those distributions whose failsafe N is at least $5k + 10$ (e.g., for a summary with $k = 10$ independent effects, failsafe N should be at least 60 to indicate tolerance to future or suppressed null results).

References

Aguinis, H., & Pierce, C. A. (1998). Testing moderator variable hypotheses meta-analytically. *Journal of Management, 24*(5), 577–592.

Bagnardi, V., Zambon, A., Quatto, P., & Corrao, G. (2004). Flexible meta-regression functions for modeling aggregate dose-response data, with an application to alcohol and mortality. *American Journal of Epidemiology, 159*(11), 1077–1086. https://doi.org/10.1093/aje/kwh142

Banks, G. C., Fischer, T., Gooty, J., & Stock, G. (2021). Ethical leadership: Mapping the terrain for concept cleanup and a future research agenda. *The Leadership Quarterly.* https://doi.org/10.1016/j.leaqua.2020.101471

Banks, G. C., Kepes, S., & McDaniel, M. A. (2012). Publication bias: A call for improved meta-analytic practice in the organizational sciences. *International Journal of Selection and Assessment, 20*(2), 182–196. https://doi.org/10.1111/j.1468-2389.2012.00591.x

Barrick, M. R., & Mount, M. K. (1991). The big five personality dimensions and job performance: A meta-analysis. *Personnel Psychology, 44*(1), 1–26. https://doi.org/10.1111/j.1744-6570.1991.tb00688.x

Becker, B. J. (2005). The failsafe N or file-drawer number. In H. R. Rothstein, A. J. Sutton, & M. Borenstein (Eds.), *Publication bias in meta-analysis: Prevention, assessment, and adjustments* (pp. 111–126). West Sussex, UK: Wiley.

Bennett, A. A., Bakker, A. B., & Field, J. G. (2018). Recovery from work-related effort: A meta-analysis. *Journal of Organizational Behavior, 39*(3), 262–275. https://doi.org/10.1002/job.2217

Bergmann, C., Tsuji, S., & Cristia, A. (2017). Top-down versus bottom-up theories of phonological acquisition: A big data approach. In *Proceedings of Interspeech 2017*, pp. 2013–2016. https://doi.org/10.21437/Interspeech.2017-1443

Berlin, J. A., & Colditz, G. A. (1990). A meta-analysis of physical activity in the prevention of coronary heart disease. *American Journal of Epidemiology*, *132*(4), 612–628. https://doi. org/10.1093/oxfordjournals.aje.a115704

Borenstein, M., Hedges, L. V., Higgins, J. P., & Rothstein, H. R. (2009). *Introduction to meta-analysis*. West Sussex, UK: Wiley.

Bornmann, L., & Mutz, R. (2015). Growth rates of modern science: A bibliometric analysis based on the number of publications and cited references. *Journal of the Association for Information Science and Technology*, *66*(11), 2215–2222. https://doi.org/10.1002/asi. 23329

Bosco, F. A. (2022). Accumulating Knowledge in the Organizational Sciences. *Annual Review of Organizational Psychology and Organizational Behavior*, *9*(1) https://doi.org/10.1146/ annurev-orgpsych-012420-090657.

Bosco, F. A., Aguinis, H., Field, J. G., Pierce, C. A., & Dalton, D. R. (2016). HARKing's threat to organizational research: Evidence from primary and meta-analytic sources. *Personnel Psychology*, *69*(3), 709–750. https://doi.org/10.1111/peps.12111

Bosco, F. A., Aguinis, H., Kepes, S., Gabriel, A. S., & Field, J. G. (2014, August). Assessing the impact of nonresponse bias: A "big science" approach. In F. Bosco & P. Steel (Chairs), The "big science" revolution in management: Possibilities, technology, and applications. Symposium conducted at the meeting of the Academy of Management, Philadelphia, PA.

Bosco, F. A., Aguinis, H., Singh, K., Field, J. G., & Pierce, C. A. (2015). Correlational effect size benchmarks. *Journal of Applied Psychology*, *100*(2), 431–449. https://doi.org/10.1037/ a0038047

Bosco, F. A., Field, J. G., Larsen, K., Chang, Y., & Uggerslev, K. L. (2020). Advancing meta-analysis with knowledge management platforms: Using metaBUS in psychology. *Advances in Methods and Practices in Psychological Science*, *3*(1), 124–137.

Bosco, F. A., Uggerslev, K. L., & Steel, P. (2017). MetaBUS as a vehicle for facilitating meta-analysis. *Human Resource Management Review*, *27*(1), 237–254. https://doi.org/10.1016/j. hrmr.2016.09.013

Burgard, T., Bošnjak, M., & Studtrucker, R. (2021). Community-Augmented Meta-Analyses (CAMAs) in Psychology. *Zeitschrift für Psychologie 229*(1), 15–23. http://dx.doi. org/10.1027/2151-2604/a000431.

Carlson, K. D., & Ji, F. X. (2011). Citing and building on meta-analytic findings: A review and recommendations. *Organizational Research Methods*, *14*(4), 696–717.

Carter, E. C., Schönbrodt, F. D., Gervais, W. M., & Hilgard, J. (2019). Correcting for bias in psychology: A comparison of meta-analytic methods. *Advances in Methods and Practices in Psychological Science*, *2*(2), 115–144. https://doi.org/10.1177/2515245919847196

Cheung, M. W. L. (2015). metaSEM: An R package for meta-analysis using structural equation modeling. *Frontiers in Psychology*, *5*, 1521.

Chow, S. L. (1987). Meta-analysis of pragmatic and theoretical research: A critique. *The Journal of Psychology*, *121*(3), 259–271. https://doi.org/10.1080/00223980.1987.9712666

Combs, J. G., & Ketchen Jr, D. J. (2003). Why do firms use franchising as an entrepreneurial strategy?: A meta-analysis. *Journal of Management*, *29*(3), 443–465. https://doi.org/ 10.1016/S0149-2063_03_00019-9

Cooper, H. M. (2015). *Research synthesis and meta-analysis: A step-by-step guide* (5th ed.). Thousand Oaks, CA: Sage.

Dalal, R. S. (2005). A meta-analysis of the relationship between organizational citizenship behavior and counterproductive work behavior. *Journal of Applied Psychology*, *90*(6), 1241.

Day, J. C., Janus, A., & Davis, J. (2005). Computer and Internet Use in the United States: 2003. U.S. Census Bureau Current Population Reports, P23–208. Retrieved from https://www.census.gov/prod/2005pubs/p23-208.pdf

DeSimone, J. A., Köhler, T., & Schoen, J. L. (2019). If it were only that easy: The use of meta-analytic research by organizational scholars. *Organizational Research Methods, 22*(4), 867–891.

Duval, S., & Tweedie, R. (2000). A nonparametric "trim and fill" method of accounting for publication bias in meta-analysis. *Journal of the American Statistical Association, 95*(449), 89–98. https://doi.org/10.1080/01621459.2000.10473905

Eisenberger, R., Rockstuhl, T., Shoss, M. K., Wen, X., & Dulebohn, J. (2019). Is the employee–organization relationship dying or thriving? A temporal meta-analysis. *Journal of Applied Psychology, 104*(8), 1036–1057. https://doi.org/10.1037/apl0000390

Eysenck, H. J. (1984). Meta-analysis: An abuse of research integration. *The Journal of Special Education, 18*(1), 41–59. https://doi.org/10.1177/002246698401800106

Fanshawe, T. R., Shaw, L. F., & Spence, G. T. (2017). A large-scale assessment of temporal trends in meta-analyses using systematic review reports from the Cochrane Library. *Research Synthesis Methods, 8*(4), 404–415. https://doi.org/10.1002/jrsm.1238

Field, J. G., Bosco, F. A., & Kepes, S. (2021). How robust is our cumulative knowledge on turnover? *Journal of Business and Psychology, 36,* 349–365. https://doi.org/10.1007/s10869-020-09687-3

Field, J. G., Bosco, F. A., Kraichy, D., Uggerslev, K. L., & Geiger, M. K. (2021). More alike than different? A comparison of variance explained by cross-cultural models. *Journal of International Business Studies, 5*(1), 1–21.

Field, J. G., Bosco, F. A., & Pierce, C. A. (2013, August). Variability in effect-size magnitude as a function of sample type. In C. Wiese & J. Marcus (Co-Chairs), *Investigating understudied moderators in meta-analysis.* Symposium conducted at the meeting of the Academy of Management, Orlando, FL.

Field, J. G., Mihm, D. C., O' Boyle, E. H., Bosco, F. A., Uggerslev, K. L., & Steel, P. (2015, August). An examination of the funding-finding relation in the field of management. Paper presented at the meeting of the Academy of Management, Vancouver, BC.

Foo, Y. Z., Nakagawa, S., Rhodes, G., & Simmons, L. W. (2017). The effects of sex hormones on immune function: A meta-analysis. *Biological Reviews, 92*(1), 551–571. https://doi.org/10.1111/brv.12243

Gehr, B. T., Weiss, C., and Porzsolt, F. (2006). The fading of reported effectiveness. A meta-analysis of randomized controlled trials. *BMC Medical Research Methodology, 6,* 25. https://doi.org/10.1186/1471-2288-6-25

Glass, G. V. (1976). Primary, secondary, and meta-analysis of research. *Educational Researcher, 5*(10), 3–8. https://doi.org/10.3102/0013189X005010003

Gong, Z., & Jiao, X. (2019). Are effect sizes in emotional intelligence field declining? A meta-meta analysis. *Frontiers in Psychology, 10,* 1655. https://doi.org/10.3389/fpsyg.2019.01655

Greene, P., Prasad, V., & Cifu, A. (2019). Should evidence come with an expiration date? *Journal of General Internal Medicine, 34*(7), 1356–1357. https://doi.org/10.1007/s11606-019-05032-4

Griffeth, R. W., Hom, P. W., & Gaertner, S. (2000). A meta-analysis of antecedents and correlates of employee turnover: Update, moderator tests, and research implications for the next millennium. *Journal of Management, 26*(3), 463–488. https://doi.org/10.1177/014920630002600305

Guzzo, R. A., Jackson, S. E., & Katzell, R. A. (1987). Meta-analysis analysis. In L. L. Cummings & B. M. Staw (Eds.), *Research in Organizational Behavior, 9*. Greenwich, CT: JAI Press.

Hancock, J. I., Allen, D. G., Bosco, F. A., McDaniel, K. R., & Pierce, C. A. (2013). Meta-analytic review of employee turnover as a predictor of firm performance. *Journal of Management, 39*(3), 573–603. https://doi.org/10.1177/0149206311424943

Hedges, L. V., & Olkin, I. (1985). *Statistical methods for meta-analysis.* San Diego, CA: Academic Press.

Highhouse, S., Brooks, M. E., Nesnidol, S., & Sim, S. (2017). Is a .51 validity coefficient good? Value sensitivity for interview validity. *International Journal of Selection and Assessment, 25*(4), 383–389.

Hitchcock, C., & Sober, E. (2004). Prediction versus accommodation and the risk of overfitting. *The British Journal for the Philosophy of Science, 55*(1), 1–34.

Howard, M. C., Cogswell, J. E., & Smith, M. B. (2020). The antecedents and outcomes of workplace ostracism: A meta-analysis. *Journal of Applied Psychology, 105*(6), 577–596. https://doi.org/10.1037/apl0000453

Hunter, J. E., Schmidt, F. L., & Le, H. (2006). Implications of direct and indirect range restriction for meta-analysis methods and findings. *Journal of Applied Psychology, 91*(3), 594–612. https://doi.org/10.1037/0021-9010.91.3.594

Iaffaldano, M. T., & Muchinsky, P. M. (1985). Job satisfaction and job performance: A meta-analysis. *Psychological Bulletin, 97*(2), 251–273. https://doi.org/10.1037/0033-2909.97.2.251

Ioannidis, J. P., & Trikalinos, T. A. (2005). Early extreme contradictory estimates may appear in published research: The Proteus phenomenon in molecular genetics research and randomized trials. *Journal of Clinical Epidemiology, 58*(6), 543–549. https://doi.org/10.1016/j.jclinepi.2004.10.019

Jiang, L., & Lavaysse, L. M. (2018). Cognitive and affective job insecurity: A meta-analysis and a primary study. *Journal of Management, 44*(6), 2307–2342. https://doi.org/10.1177/0149206318773853

Johnsen, T. J., & Friborg, O. (2015). The effects of cognitive behavioral therapy as an anti-depressive treatment is falling: A meta-analysis. *Psychological Bulletin, 141*(4), 747–768. https://doi.org/10.1037/bul0000015

Judge, T. A., & Bono, J. E. (2001). Relationship of core self-evaluations traits—self-esteem, generalized self-efficacy, locus of control, and emotional stability—with job satisfaction and job performance: A meta-analysis. *Journal of Applied Psychology, 86*(1), 80–92. https://doi.org/10.1037/0021-9010.86.1.80

Kepes, S., & McDaniel, M. A. (2015). The validity of conscientiousness is overestimated in the prediction of job performance. *PLoS One, 10*(10), e0141468. https://doi.org/10.1371/journal.pone.0141468

Kepes, S., McDaniel, M. A., Brannick, M. T., & Banks, G. C. (2013). Meta-analytic reviews in the organizational sciences: Two meta-analytic schools on the way to MARS (the Meta-Analytic Reporting Standards). *Journal of Business and Psychology, 28*(2), 123–143. https://doi.org/10.1007/s10869-013-9300-2

Köhler, T., Cortina, J. M., Kurtessis, J. N., & Gölz, M. (2015). Are we correcting correctly? Interdependence of reliabilities in meta-analysis. *Organizational Research Methods, 18*(3), 355–428.

Koricheva, J., Jennions, M. D., & Lau, J. (2013). Temporal trends in effect sizes: causes, detection, and implications. *Handbook of Meta-analysis in Ecology and Evolution*, 237–254. https://doi.org/10.1016/j.tree.2019.05.006

Koricheva, J., & Kulinskaya, E. (2019). Temporal instability of evidence base: A threat to policy making? *Trends in Ecology & Evolution, 34*(10), 895–902. https://doi.org/10.1016/j.tree.2019.05.006

Kulinskaya, E., & Koricheva, J. (2010). Use of quality control charts for detection of outliers and temporal trends in cumulative meta-analysis. *Research Synthesis Methods, 1*(3–4), 297–307. https://doi.org/10.1002/jrsm.29

Laureano-Phillips, J., Robinson, R. D., Aryal, S., Blair, S., Wilson, D., Boyd, K., & Wang, H. (2019). HEART score risk stratification of low-risk chest pain patients in the emergency department: A systematic review and meta-analysis. *Annals of Emergency Medicine, 74*(2), 187–203. https://doi.org/10.1016/j.annemergmed.2018.12.010

Lipsey, M. W., & Wilson, D. B. (2000). *Practical meta-analysis.* Thousand Oaks, CA: Sage.

Loher, B. T., Noe, R. A., Moeller, N. L., & Fitzgerald, M. P. (1985). A meta-analysis of the relation of job characteristics to job satisfaction. *Journal of Applied Psychology, 70*(2), 280–289. https://doi.org/10.1037/0021-9010.70.2.280

Marcus, B., Taylor, O. A., Hastings, S. E., Sturm, A., & Weigelt, O. (2016). The structure of counterproductive work behavior: A review, a structural meta-analysis, and a primary study. *Journal of Management, 42*(1), 203–233.

McDaniel, M. A., Whetzel, D. L., Schmidt, F. L., & Mauer, S. D. (1994). The validity of employment interviews: A comprehensive review and meta-analysis. *Journal of Applied Psychology, 79,* 599–616.

McShane, B., Böckenholt, U., & Hansen, K. T. (2016). Adjusting for publication bias in meta-analysis: An evaluation of selection methods and some cautionary notes. *Perspectives on Psychological Science, 11*(5), 730–749. https://doi.org/10.1177/1745691616662243

Miao, C., Humphrey, R. H., & Qian, S. (2017). A meta-analysis of emotional intelligence and work attitudes. *Journal of Occupational and Organizational Psychology, 90*(2), 177–202. https://doi.org/10.1111/joop.12167

Mullen, B., Muellerleile, P., & Bryant, B. (2001). Cumulative meta-analysis: A consideration of indicators of sufficiency and stability. *Personality and Social Psychology Bulletin, 27*(11), 1450–1462. https://doi.org/10.1177/01461672012711006

Murphy, K., & DeShon, R. (2000). Inter-rater correlations do not estimate the reliability of job performance ratings. *Personnel Psychology, 53,* 873–900.

O'Boyle, E. H., Banks, G. C., & Gonzalez-Mulé, E. (2017). The chrysalis effect: How ugly initial results metamorphosize into beautiful articles. *Journal of Management, 43*(2), 376–399. https://doi.org/10.1177/0149206314527133

Oh, I.-S., Postlethwaite, B. E., & Schmidt, F. L. (2013). Rethinking the validity of interviews for employment decision making: Implications of recent developments in meta-analysis. In D. J. Svyantek & K. Mahoney (Eds.), *Received wisdom, kernels of truth, and boundary conditions in organizational studies.* Charlotte, NC: Information Age Publishing. Chapter 12, pp. 297–329.

Oswald, F. L., Putka, D. J., Tonidandel, S., King, E., & Cortina, J. (2015). Statistical methods for big data. *Big data at work: The data science revolution and organizational psychology.* New York, NY: Routledge.

Papalia, N., Spivak, B., Daffern, M., & Ogloff, J. R. (2020). Are psychological treatments for adults with histories of violent offending associated with change in dynamic risk factors? A meta-analysis of intermediate treatment outcomes. *Criminal Justice and Behavior, 47*(12), 1585–1608. https://doi.org/10.1177/0093854820956377

Park, T. Y., & Shaw, J. D. (2013). Turnover rates and organizational performance: A meta-analysis. *Journal of Applied Psychology*, *98*(2), 268–309. https://doi.org/10.1037/a0030723

Pearson, K. (1904). Antityphoid inoculation. *British Medical Journal*, *2*(2294), 1667–1668. https://doi.org/10.1136/bmj.2.2294.1667

Petrosino, A., Petrosino, C. T., & Buehler, J. (2005). "Scared Straight" and other juvenile awareness programs for preventing juvenile delinquency. *Campbell Systematic Reviews*, *1*(1), 1–62. https://doi.org/10.4073/csr.2004.2

Pew Research Center (2021). Retrieved April 8, 2021. https://www.pewresearch.org/internet/fact-sheet/mobile/

Phillips, J. (2020). *Strategic Staffing* (4th ed.). Chicago Business Press.

Pietschnig, J., Siegel, M., Eder, J. S. N., & Gittler, G. (2019). Effect declines are systematic, strong, and ubiquitous: A meta-meta-analysis of the decline effect in intelligence research. *Frontiers in Psychology*, *10*, 2874. https://doi.org/10.3389/fpsyg.2019.02874

Protzko, J., & Schooler, J. W. (2017). Decline effects: Types, mechanisms, and personal reflections. In S. O. Lilienfeld & I. D. Waldman (Eds.), *Psychological science under scrutiny: Recent challenges and proposed solutions* (p. 85–107). Wiley Blackwell. https://doi.org/10.1002/9781119095910.ch6

Reynolds, J. P., Stautz, K., Pilling, M., van der Linden, S., & Marteau, T. M. (2020). Communicating the effectiveness and ineffectiveness of government policies and their impact on public support: A systematic review with meta-analysis. *Royal Society Open Science*, *7*(1), 190522. https://doi.org/10.1098/rsos.190522

Richardson, M., Abraham, C., & Bond, R. (2012). Psychological correlates of university students' academic performance: A systematic review and meta-analysis. *Psychological Bulletin*, *138*(2), 353–387. https://doi.org/10.1037/a0026838

Rockstuhl, T., Eisenberger, R., Shore, L. M., Kurtessis, J. N., Ford, M. T., Buffardi, L. C., & Mesdaghinia, S. (2020). Perceived organizational support (POS) across 54 nations: A cross-cultural meta-analysis of POS effects. *Journal of International Business Studies*, *51*, 933–962. https://doi.org/10.1057/s41267-020-00311-3

Rødgaard, E. M., Jensen, K., Vergnes, J. N., Soulières, I., & Mottron, L. (2019). Temporal changes in effect sizes of studies comparing individuals with and without autism: A meta-analysis. *JAMA Psychiatry*, *76*(11), 1124–1132. https://doi.org/10.1001/jamapsychiatry.2019.1956

Rosenthal, R. (1979). The file drawer problem and tolerance for null results. *Psychological Bulletin*, *86*(3), 638–641. https://doi.org/10.1037/0033-2909.86.3.638

Rosenthal, R., & DiMatteo, M. R. (2001). Meta-analysis: Recent developments in quantitative methods for literature reviews. *Annual Review of Psychology*, 52, 59–82. https://doi.org/10.1146/annurev.psych.52.1.59

Rousseau, D. M., & McCarthy, S. (2007). Educating managers from an evidence-based perspective. *Academy of Management Learning & Education*, *6*(1), 84–101. https://doi.org/10.5465/amle.2007.24401705

Rothstein, H. R., Sutton, A. J., & Borenstein, M. (2005). Publication bias in meta-analyses. In H. R. Rothstein, A. J. Sutton, & M. Borenstein (Eds.), *Publication bias in meta-analysis: Prevention, assessment, and adjustments* (pp. 1–7). West Sussex, UK: Wiley.

Rubin, D. B. (1990). Comment: Neyman (1923) and causal inference in experiments and observational studies. *Statistical Science*, *5*(4), 472–480. https://doi.org/10.1214/ss/1177012032

Schmidt, F. (2010). Detecting and correcting the lies that data tell. *Perspectives on Psychological Science, 5*(3), 233–242. https://doi.org/10.1177/1745691610369339

Schmidt, F. L., & Hunter, J. E. (2015). *Methods of meta-analysis: Correcting error and bias in research findings* (3rd ed.). Newbury Park, CA: Sage.

Schmidt, F. L., & Hunter, J. E. (1998). The validity and utility of selection methods in personnel psychology: Practical and theoretical implications of 85 years of research findings. *Psychological Bulletin, 124*(2), 262.

Schmidt, F. L., & Hunter, J. E. (1997). Eight common but false objections to the discontinuation of significance testing in the analysis of research data. In L. Harlow, S. Muliak, & J. Steiger (Eds.), *What if there were no significance tests?* (pp. 37–64). Mahwah, NJ: Lawrence Erlbaum.

Schmidt, F. L., & Hunter, J. E. (1977). Development of a general solution to the problem of validity generalization. *Journal of Applied Psychology, 62*(5), 529–540. https://doi.org/10.1037/0021-9010.62.5.529

Schmidt, F. L., Hunter, J. E., McKenzie, R. C., & Muldrow, T. W. (1979). Impact of valid selection procedures on work-force productivity. *Journal of Applied Psychology, 64*(6), 609–626. https://doi.org/10.1037/0021-9010.64.6.609

Schmidt, F. L., & Oh, I. S. (2013). Methods for second order meta-analysis and illustrative applications. *Organizational Behavior and Human Decision Processes, 121*(2), 204–218.

Schmidt, F. L., Shaffer, J. A., & Oh, I.-S. (2008). Increased accuracy of range restriction corrections: Implications for the role of personality and general mental ability in job and training performance. *Personnel Psychology, 61*, 827–868.

Shojania, K. G., Sampson, M., Ansari, M. T., Ji, J., Doucette, S., & Moher, D. (2007). How quickly do systematic reviews go out of date? A survival analysis. *Annals of Internal Medicine, 147*(4), 224–233.

Smith, M. L., & Glass, G. V. (1977). Meta-analysis of psychotherapy outcome studies. *American Psychologist, 32*(9), 752–760. https://doi.org/10.1037/0003-066X.32.9.752

Stanley, T. D. (2017). Limitations of PET-PEESE and other meta-analysis methods. *Social Psychological and Personality Science, 8*(5), 581–591. https://doi.org/10.1177/1948550617693062

Tanner-Smith, E. E., Wilson, S. J., & Lipsey, M. W. (2013). The comparative effectiveness of outpatient treatment for adolescent substance abuse: A meta-analysis. *Journal of Substance Abuse Treatment, 44*(2), 145–158. https://doi.org/10.1016/j.jsat.2012.05.006

Terrin, N., Schmid, C. H., Lau, J., & Olkin, I. (2003). Adjusting for publication bias in the presence of heterogeneity. *Statistics in Medicine, 22*(13), 2113–2126. https://doi.org/10.1002/sim.1461

Trikalinos, T. A., & Ioannidis, J. P. A. (2005). Assessing the evolution of effect sizes over time. In H. R. Rothstein, A. J. Sutton, & M. Borenstein (Eds.), *Publication bias in meta-analysis: Prevention, assessment and adjustments* (pp. 241–259). Chichester, UK: Wiley

van Assen, M. A. L. M., van Aert, R. C. M., & Wicherts, J. M. (2015). Meta-analysis using effect size distributions of only statistically significant studies. *Psychological Methods, 20*(3), 293–309. https://doi.org/10.1037/met0000025

Wiesner, W. H., & Cronshaw, S. F. (1988). A meta-analytic investigation of the impact of interview format and degree of structure on the validity of the employment interview. *Journal of Occupational Psychology, 61*(4), 275–290.

3

DATA SHARING AND DATA INTEGRITY

Martin Götz and James G. Field

"We do not call the rain that follows a long drought a water crisis."

(Nelson et al., 2018, p. 512)

Data are the cornerstone of research. Without them, problems cannot be solved. The events that immediately followed the announcement of a global pandemic that started to twirl the world in early 2020 help to illustrate these claims. Ten days after a pneumonia-like illness was first reported in China, researchers released the genetic sequence of a new coronavirus (i.e., SARS-CoV-2) to an open access online repository (Johnson, 2020). As the virus began to ravage the world medically, socially, and economically, researchers from all over the world began to study the virus' characteristics. What followed this unprecedented global collaboration? Researchers proposed adequate countermeasures and developed promising vaccines (Collins, 2021; see also London & Kimmelman, 2020). Large-scale international trials were conducted in record time, resulting in a global vaccination effort that promises to – at the very least – contain the pandemic (see McKenna, 2021; Oliu-Barton et al., 2021). Indeed, these accomplishments would not have been achieved so quickly without data sharing and research transparency, if at all.

As vividly as the foregoing example illustrates the value of open data for science and society in general, the availability and usability of data are currently not the norm among researchers (Martone et al., 2018). The current state of affairs stands in stark contrast to early calls for a mandate to share research data openly (Ceci & Walker, 1983), as well as the readily available modern infrastructure to permit data sharing via online repositories (e.g., Hartgerink & Van Zelst, 2018; Nosek et al., 2015). As such, we are left to only dream about what other grand

DOI: 10.4324/9781003015000-4

challenges (e.g., Banks et al., 2016) could be conquered if data sharing was the norm rather than the exception.

Such aspirations are particularly salient for psychological researchers, given that their scientific spaces are currently experiencing an alleged credibility crisis[1]. Indeed, several replication projects (e.g., Ebersole et al., 2020; Moshontz et al., 2018; Open Science Collaboration, 2015) have brought into question the integrity of scientific findings in a variety of fields. Replication, defined as "the ability of an independent researcher, collecting new data under sufficiently similar conditions as in the original study, to reach similar conclusions" (Artner et al., 2021, p. 2), is the sine qua non of what makes an empirical finding a scientific finding (e.g., Asendorpf et al., 2013; Chambers, 2017; Nosek et al., 2022). Yet, it is estimated that only around 1% of articles published in psychology journals since 1900 are direct replications (Makel et al., 2012). Likewise, reproducibility, defined as "the ability [of a reported statistical result] to be verified by an independent researcher through the act of identification and execution of the underlying (often deterministic) calculation(s) on the same dataset" (Artner et al., 2021, p. 2), should be the most basic feature of any scientific result. However, reproducibility efforts typically produce success rates well below 70%, and these reproducibility rates only apply to the scientific claims for which authors actually provided data, analysis scripts, and rather often specific guidance (e.g., Artner et al., 2021; Hardwicke et al., 2018; Obels et al., 2020). Indeed, these observations should be worrisome for researchers and practitioners because without the verification of an observed phenomenon, knowledge cannot be separated from circumstance and, thus, credibility cannot be calibrated (Schmidt, 2009).

Although there is no single cause of the credibility crisis, evidence is mounting that suggests a continuum of data integrity issues have contributed to it (e.g., incorrect or inexistent documentation of the data, inconsistencies in selection of variables and/or cases, issues with the version of statistical software; Artner et al., 2021; Epskamp, 2019; Obels et al., 2020). Moreover, it is a common practice to keep research materials under lock and key (e.g., design protocols, analytic scripts; Munafò et al., 2017; Nosek & Bar-Anan, 2012; Nosek et al., 2012), making it difficult to detect and rectify these underlying causes. The advent of sophisticated methodologies, such as artificial intelligence and machine learning, has ushered in a new frontier in psychological research (Oswald et al., 2020). However, whether or not these rapidly evolving tools mitigate or amplify some of the data integrity issues that have beset I-O research is yet to be determined.

Up to this point, we have illustrated some of the challenges that psychological scientists face in their quest to motivate future discovery and inform evidence-based practice. Indeed, looking ahead, their efforts will be complicated as analytic techniques increase in complexity and automated data collection tools are augmented (e.g., web-based surveys, web scraping). We argue that it is a good time to illustrate the importance of data integrity to the scientific enterprise, and how it can be improved in future I-O research. The remainder of this chapter is organized as follows. First, we provide context by summarizing common definitions of data – the primary ingredient in any empirical study. Following this, we describe a variety of threats to data integrity, which can have major ramifications for research credibility and, thus, evidence-based practice returns. Next, we describe a grassroots initiative – the open science movement – that aims to increase transparency throughout the research cycle. Finally, we briefly describe the diversity of tools available to researchers that can mitigate data integrity concerns and present an alternative scientific model that may be ubiquitous in future I-O research. Taken together, the goal of this chapter is to increase awareness of the consequences that may be brought about by a lack of data integrity, and to illustrate ways that the veracity of I-O inquiry can be improved.

What Are Data?

Precisely defining data is a cumbersome task because almost anything can be included in dataset. As Borgman wrote in her book on data in the modern academic world: "The concept of data is itself worthy of book-length explication" (2015, p. 19). The most pragmatic approach appears to define data by examples and/or their characteristics. In this spirit, and at the most general level, the Consultative Committee for Space Data Systems (CCSDS[2]) defined data as "a reinterpretable representation of information in a formalized manner suitable for communication, interpretation, or processing. Examples of data include a sequence of bits, a table of numbers, the characters on a page, the recording of sounds made by a person speaking, or a moon rock specimen" (2012, p. 10). Focusing on the (psychological) academic setting, Martone, Garcia-Castro, and VandenBos defined data as "the measurements, observations or facts taken or assembled *for* analysis as part of a study and upon which the results and conclusions of the study are based" (2018, p. 111). In other words, data can be anything from exact numbers regarding a person's height, numeric representations of their perception of a coworker's counterproductive work behaviors, or their qualitative answers to open-ended questions.

A more fine-grained, yet also somewhat fuzzy distinction is generally made between *big data, long-tail data,* and *dark data* (e.g., Borgman, 2015; Martone et al., 2018). *Big data* might be defined as extremely large datasets that are characterized by the four Vs – volume, velocity, variety, and veracity (Oswald et al., 2020). Big data could refer to a large collection of effect sizes and their corresponding metadata (e.g., Bosco et al., 2017), as well as a corpus of data generated by social media platforms, such as Facebook or Twitter (e.g., Kosinski et al., 2016). For example, Obschonka et al. (2020) analyzed 1.5 billion tweets by 5.25 million users to estimate the Big Five personality traits and an entrepreneurial personality profile for 1,772 US counties (see also Harlow & Oswald, 2016). In contrast, *long-tail data*[3] can be defined as "small, granular datasets, collected by individual laboratories in the course of day-to-day research" (Ferguson et al., 2014). In other words, long-tail data refer to the diverse and heterogeneous datasets that are typically collected by I-O researchers (e.g., Martone et al., 2018). For example, Götz et al. (2020) investigated the indirect effect of leader-member exchange on performance via organizational identification in a set of four studies using independent datasets comprised of roughly a few hundred employees each. Finally, *dark data* are "unpublished data that includes results from failed experiments and records that are viewed as ancillary to published studies" (Ferguson et al., 2014, p. 1443). Here, one could instantly think of the so-called grey literature that meta-analysts typically attempt to include in their analyses to synthesize all available empirical evidence regarding particular relationships between constructs of interest (Giustini, 2019)[4].

Taken together, data are the bedrock on which knowledge is built. As Borgman put it, their "value lies in their use" (2015, p. 3). In the psychological sciences, quantitative long-tail data are typically used in that researchers numerically operationalize relevant psychological constructs to address their respective research questions statistically. For example, a researcher might collect data from one or multiple sources (e.g., self- or other-report, archival, objective) over the course of one or more measurement points (e.g., cross-sectional, time-lagged, longitudinal, intensive longitudinal) to operationalize (e.g., survey scale, experimental manipulation, task) relevant psychological constructs. The collected data are then typically subjected to data quality assessments (e.g., screening for careless effort responding), which are followed by tailored statistical analyses (e.g., structural equation modeling, multilevel modeling, time-series analysis) in order to allow for inferences to be drawn from the data in response to the specified research questions.

Data Integrity Issues that Threaten Evidence-Based Practice Recommendations

The self-ascribed goal of I-O psychology research is to scientifically derive "principles of individual, group and organizational behavior and [apply] this knowledge to the solution of problems at work" (American Psychological Association [APA], 2008; see also Society for Industrial and Organizational Psychology [SIOP], 2021). To this end, I-O researchers typically subject quantitative[5] data to statistical analyses. Yet, inferences derived from such analyses are only as good as the data that inform them. As such, data integrity is an essential part of any data management plan (e.g., Research Connections, 2017; Wilkinson et al., 2016) and a prerequisite for "good" science (e.g., Levenstein & Lyle, 2018).

Data integrity broadly refers to the overall accuracy, completeness, and consistency of data. It is typically governed by certain rules or standards that guide study/data collection designs. Research Connections (2017) outlined specific issues that need to be addressed to assure data integrity, namely: (1) how will data be input or captured, (2) in which format data are going to be stored (e.g., numeric or character), (3) which measures are going to be put in place to identify invalid cases/values or inconsistent responses, and (4) which measures are going to be taken to manage data versions throughout the data life cycle (e.g., data entry, cleaning, and analysis). Addressing these issues before collecting data, aids both the use, and the reuse of research data (Wilkinson et al., 2016).

In psychological research, specific threats to data integrity have been discussed as part of the ongoing debate on the credibility crisis (e.g., Banks et al., 2018; Flake & Fried, 2020; O'Boyle & Götz, 2020). Threats commonly discussed in the literature include: (1) validity and reliability of measurements, (2) construct proliferation, (3) common method bias (CMB), (4) generalizability concerns, (5) questionable research practices (QRPs), and (6) data handling and storage. In the following sections, we briefly describe each of these threats to data integrity.

Given that I-O scientists typically collect data on unobservable, latent constructs, measurement instruments play a critical role in I-O research. Therefore, the psychometric properties of these instruments, specifically their validity and reliability[6], are critically important. As the physicist Walter H. G. Lewin put it, "the accuracy is the *only* [original emphasis] thing that matters, and a measurement that doesn't also indicate its degree of accuracy is meaningless" (2011, p. 8; see also Hand, 2016). As such, when selecting what measures should be used in a study, I-O researchers should give thorough consideration to how well they are calibrated. Indeed, measurement error assessment is a critical aspect of any scientific discipline as it reveals how reliable measures and, thus, research findings may be (for a related discussion, see Murphy & Deshon, 2000; Schmidt et al., 2000). Yet, as evidenced by Viswesvaran et al. (1996) estimate of .52 for the reliability of performance ratings, which indicates that almost half of the variance in performance ratings may be due to random measurement error, I-O psychology researchers may be doing a relatively poor job at measuring substantive constructs. Alternatively, it could be argued that this estimate may indicate that it is potentially irresponsible to use performance ratings as a criterion in I-O research. Such observations led Flake and Fried (2020) to introduce the hyperbolical term *measurement schmeasurement* to illustrate a laissez-faire attitude to measurement that is far too common among researchers and their willingness to adopt measures that are used by convention rather than selecting the ones that are most appropriate for examining the phenomenon under investigation. They go on to define questionable measurement practices as "decisions researchers make that raise doubts about the validity of the measures used in a study, and ultimately the validity of the final conclusion" (p. 458). To improve transparency as well as measurement validity and reliability, Flake and Fried (2020) provided researchers with a set of exemplary issues to address when designing to measure psychological constructs.

Second, and closely related, is the phenomenon of construct proliferation, which refers to the notion that "constructs may lack discriminant validity relative to other constructs; that is, they may be redundant with existing constructs" (Le et al., 2010, p. 112). Because constructs are the verbal descriptions of what data represent (Shadish, 2002), it is critically important that they are not mislabeled as to avoid a clogged and frittering body of knowledge. Here, the *jingle-jangle fallacy*, originally described by Kelley (1927), comes to mind. A *jangle fallacy* describes labeling two measures differently, despite them assessing the same construct. A *jingle fallacy*, on the other hand, refers to using the same label for constructs that actually each assess something different. There is plenty of evidence to suggest that constructs have proliferated in I-O research (e.g., Cole et al., 2012; Götz et al., 2019; Shaffer et al., 2016). Indeed, this is much more than just a concern about semantics. Construct proliferation impedes science, as the use of two constructs that measure the same phenomena makes it more difficult to reconcile the respective nomological net and complicates how data can be reused (e.g., for meta-analyses; Bosco et al., 2017).

Third, CMB, defined as "variance that is attributable to the measurement method rather than to the constructs the measures represent" (Podsakoff et al., 2003, p. 879), is another threat to the efficacy of data (e.g., Lance et al., 2010). If one or more variables in a particular dataset are measured using the same method (e.g., self-report survey), "[i]t is widely believed that relationships between variables measured with the same method will be inflated due to the action of common method variance" (Spector, 2006, p. 221). These inflated correlations, in turn, can be considered spurious as they could lead to inaccurate inferences (e.g., evidence-based practice recommendations) to be drawn from the data (Lance et al., 2010; Spector, 2006). Such spurious relations might help to explain what Meehl (1990) called the *crud factor*, namely the observation that, in a typical psychological dataset, everything correlates with everything else (see also Orben & Lakens, 2020). Against this background, to assure data integrity, it appears necessary to not only consider valid and reliable measures in psychological research but also to explicitly consider potential method factors in one's dataset – at the very least, the source of a respective measure should be explicitly documented.

Fourth, above and beyond considerations regarding the variables to collect, suboptimal generalizability also renders a threat to the integrity of data (e.g., Banks & O'Boyle, 2013). Here, generalizability means how well inferences can be made from observations in a particular sample to either a population or a particular theory of interest – as such, generalizability depends largely on the cases contained in a particular dataset (i.e., sampling; Tiokhin et al., 2019). In psychological research, samples are typically comprised by individuals from Western, educated, industrialized, rich and democratic (WEIRD; Peterson & Merunka, 2014) contexts, which may limit generalizations to non-WEIRD populations. Likewise, a growing amount of (experimental) research in psychology is being conducted using samples obtained from crowdsourcing platforms, such as MTurk (Aguinis et al., 2021). Yet, Stewart and colleagues (2015) suggested that studies that use this sampling procedure typically draw from an active MTurk population of about 7,300 individuals (for in-depth discussions; Chmielewski & Kucker, 2020; Robinson et al., 2019). Indeed, this may limit inferences to very specific populations. Moreover, this may imply nonindependence (i.e., MTurk research subjects in Study A may also participate in Studies B and C), which could threaten meta-analytic inferences and, thus, evidence-based practice recommendations. Note that similar concerns have been raised regarding the appropriateness of using nonemployee samples (e.g., college students; Gordon et al., 1986). Taken together, to address data integrity issues form a generalizability perspective, researchers should consider the following questions: "(1) who the sample should consist of;, (2) how credible or accurate this group is relative to the purpose of the test;, (3) what obstacles are likely to be encountered in acquiring the sample;, and (4) how might these obstacles be avoided or addressed" (Price, 2017, p. 173).

Fifth, QRPs pose an imminent threat to the validity of scientific findings (e.g., O'Boyle & Götz, 2020). These practices typically take place in the *grey zone* between proper scientific conduct and overt fraud and generally have the goal of improving the likelihood of a manuscript being accepted for publication by making the results appear to be more palatable (e.g., Lynöe et al., 1999)[7]. Specifically, QRPs center on – knowingly or unknowingly – using *researcher degrees of freedom* (Simmons et al., 2011) when collecting, handling, and analyzing data. Examples of QRPs in the realms of data integrity can be found when researchers, typically informed by peeking at the data: (1) decide to stop or prolong their data collection efforts in order to obtain "interesting" findings (e.g., $p < .05$), (2) alter their inclusion/exclusion criteria for cases, and/or (3) collapse experimental conditions (e.g., O'Boyle & Götz, 2020). If undisclosed, such behaviors are labeled as QRPs because they may lead to false positives (e.g., Simmons et al., 2011) and, thus, can threaten the respective inferences they produce in primary and secondary analyses. In sum, QRPs can be thought of as contributing to overall selection bias in research (i.e., publication bias, QRP); a fact, that ultimately entails a tainted and potentially misleading body of knowledge (e.g., Stanley et al., 2018).

Finally, although researchers and practitioners alike rely on scientific findings every day, they often lament that they are typically inaccessible. In general, the millions of findings appearing in scientific journals have not been extracted, categorized, and made available for ease of location and use (e.g., Bosco et al., 2017). Furthermore, the corresponding raw data and the analytic scripts used to inform these research findings are, for the most part, poorly maintained and stored (e.g., Artner et al., 2021; Hardwicke et al., 2018; Obels et al., 2020). Under these circumstances, it is incredibly difficult to detect and identify the severity of potential data integrity issues. Taken together, researchers have room for improvement in this regard – be it the formatting of data in a comprehensive and shareable format, the usage of proper repositories to protect against data loss, or the foresighted writing of respective analysis scripts to aid future usage of the data (for specific recommendations, see Buchanan et al., 2021; Epskamp, 2019; Wiebels & Moreau, 2021). Indeed, improved data handling and storage practices will reduce the risk of inputs needed for reproducibility and replication efforts and meta-analysis being mishandled in the short term and lost in the long term.

Open Science: A Self-Correction Mechanism for I-O Research

Science is supposed to be a cumulative and self-corrective enterprise to collectively discover knowledge (Popper, 1963). Indeed, until recently, there was relatively little concern regarding these assumptions (Klein et al., 2018a). However, a series of events (for a review, see Nelson et al., 2018) led to a chorus of claims that suggested a substantial proportion of our cumulative knowledge may consist of false or misleading results (e.g., Ioannidis, 2016). This motivated researchers to examine the replicability and credibility of scientific claims (Nosek et al., 2022). The results of these endeavors were not especially encouraging – statistical tests in primary studies appeared grossly underpowered and affected by QRPs (e.g., Götz et al., 2021; O'Boyle et al., 2019), replication rates for primary studies have ranged from 39% to 77% when using a criterion of $p > .05$ (Klein et al., 2018b; Open Science Collaboration, 2015), and the robustness of meta-analytic findings have been brought into question (e.g., Field et al., 2021; Harrison et al., 2017). Together, the accumulated evidence supported the notion that the psychological sciences are experiencing a "crisis of confidence" (De Boeck & Jeon, 2018), which has lead practitioners and the general public to question the utility of academic scholarship (Banks et al., 2016; Rynes, Colbert & O'Boyle, 2018; Tourish, 2019).

However, there may be a silver lining. Specifically, in response to these challenges, science has witnessed a shift toward openness, transparency, and reproducibility – a movement operating under the umbrella term "open science." In short order, the open science movement is transforming how I-O research is done, reported, and evaluated and, thus, may indicate that better days are ahead for all stakeholders in this scientific space (Nelson et al., 2018; Spellman, 2015; Vazire, 2018).

But what is open science? A recent systematic literature review concluded that open science can be defined as transparent and accessible knowledge that is shared and developed through collaborative networks (Vicente-Saez & Martinez-Fuentes, 2018). Although helpful, we argue that this definition does not fully capture the scope or intricacy of what open science is. We contend that open science is a thriving facet of the scientific ecosystem (Hardwicke et al., 2020), and is nurtured by a variety of concepts, ranging from scientific philosophies and cultural norms, to specific practices that operationalize these perspectives and help scholars to enact such norms (Nosek et al., 2015). As such, open science can be understood as a movement for the betterment of scientific integrity and communication for all scientific stakeholders (e.g., researchers, reviewers, journals, funding agencies, practitioners).

Examples of open science practices include: (1) sharing data and analytic files to improve the reproducibility of research (Martone et al., 2018; Nosek et al., 2015), (2) implementing new reward systems to improve the openness, accessibility, and persistence of data and materials that underlie scientific research (e.g., badges for data sharing; Kidwell et al., 2016), (3) explicitly justifying statistical significance thresholds and required sample sizes to allow for more trustworthy interpretations of research findings (Lakens, 2021), (4) preregistering studies and corresponding analytic plans to document important judgment calls made during the scientific process, which can help to distinguish between a priori and post hoc research (Banks et al., 2019), (5) encouraging replication studies to assess the stability and generalizability of research findings (Köhler & Cortina, 2021; Koole & Lakens, 2012), (6) removing potential reviewer bias by promoting alternate paths to journal publication (e.g., results-blind reviews; Kreamer & Rogelberg, 2020; Woznyj et al., 2018), (7) supporting and utilizing open access interfaces that promote research transparency (e.g., metaBUS, MetaSen, statcheck; Bosco et al., 2017; Field et al., 2021; Nuijten & Polanin, 2020), and (8) removing paywalls to increase access to scientific material (Nosek & Bar-Anan, 2012).

In the last decade, the volume and veracity of arguments in favor of open science has grown substantially. Indeed, the primary goal of this movement is to improve the openness, integrity, and reproducibility of research by pulling back on the curtain on scientific inquiry (i.e., preventing research misconduct or reducing questionable research and/or reporting practices; Chambers, 2017). In addition, the open science movement aims to foster a more inclusive environment – one in which practitioners and other scientific stakeholders (e.g., educators, policy makers) benefit from increased access to scholarly content (e.g., Hartgerink & Van Zelst, 2018). However, there are also pragmatic reasons for promoting open science. For instance, data transparency may facilitate greater communication between researchers with similar interests and eliminate the duplication of efforts, which could improve the rate of scientific discovery. Furthermore, in our own anecdotal experience, we have learned that data sharing is an excellent way to protect against data loss and can facilitate future research endeavors – in the past, our own requests for meta-analytic datasets were often denied because the corresponding author no longer had access to the original files (see also Artner et al., 2021; Hardwicke et al., 2018; Obels et al., 2020).

Although the recommendations in favor of open science practices can be very convincing (Nosek et al., 2015), their adoption rates remain relatively low

(Houtkoop et al., 2018; Washburn et al., 2018). Indeed, it is important to recognize that open science is not a *magic pill* and, thus, is not a panacea for the population of problems that scientists face. For example, open science alone does not fully address rigor or relevance issues (Vermeulen, 2005). Indeed, open science practices will not improve the quality of what appears in the literature if researchers continue to employ suboptimal methodology (e.g., biased sampling, inadequate statistical power, reliance on single-source data; Stanley et al., 2018). As Munafò and Smith put it, replication is a "laudable, but insufficient" (2018, p. 399) way to advance our body of knowledge – while replication efforts are an integral aspect of validating scientific findings, triangulation via the synthesis of multiple lines of research is needed to allow for progress.

On the potential folly of certain open science practices (e.g., study preregistration), it has been argued that increased transparency and rigor may come at the expense of serendipitous discovery (see Leavitt, 2013). Relatedly, mandates on data sharing may have unintended deleterious effects on certain scientific disciplines given that researchers may have valid reasons for not sharing their data. For example, requiring data sharing may deter members of sensitive populations (e.g., marginalized employees in the workplace) from participating in studies (Gabriel & Wessel, 2013). Concerns have also been raised regarding a potential "dark side" of open science (e.g., illegitimate use of open access data to publish in predatory journals; Pickler et al., 2015). Finally, we concede that the efficacy of open science should be evaluated based on its merits, not on its aesthetics. Thus, one important question that needs to be addressed is: Does open science work? Preliminary evidence suggests that open science practices yield generally positive returns (e.g., increased data sharing, lower positve results rates in registered reports; Rowhani-Farid et al., 2020; Scheel et al., 2021). However, we note that studies that adhere to certain open science practices may be perceived as being "messier" than traditional studies. For example, preregistered articles have corresponding documentation that should be reviewed by journal reviewers and readers. Such tasks may be viewed as being nonessential or even cumbersome, especially if the respective study does not present statistically significant results. Indeed, in such cases, the value added by findings facilitated by open science may questioned (e.g., "Does a study presenting exclusively nil findings provide value?"; Grand et al., 2018; Scheel et al., 2021)[8]. Admittedly, the movement is not mature enough to answer this question definitively. Although the prevailing sentiment seems to be that open science cannot fail, empirical evidence to support this claim is yet to be accumulated. In other words, despite its appeal, the jury is still out on open science.

Taken together, the 2010s revealed a painful truth – the "crisis" experienced across the psychological sciences could be traced back to decades of loyalism to indoctrinated systems (see Chambers, 2017; Giner-Sorolla, 2012). Simply put, broadly speaking, psychological scientists got lost in the excitement of novel discovery (see Tihanyi, 2020) and, in the process, ran the risk of losing their legitimacy (Bedeian et al., 2010). In the last 10 years, we have come to learn that many of the challenges facing psychological scientists are systemic and cultural (Munafò et al., 2017; Washburn et al., 2018), which means that they can likely be addressed through prudent intervention. Open science is one possible treatment for these problems, but its effectiveness is not guaranteed. The next 10 years may reveal that enthusiasm surrounding the open science movement was a precursor to an era of "revolution" (Spellman, 2015; Vazire, 2018) or "renaissance" (Nelson et al., 2018) in psychological science. Alternatively, future history books may reveal that open science was just another flash in the pan. However, given the increase in the number of tools tailored toward supporting open science, we are optimistic (and hopeful) that open science will become a staple of (I-O) research.

Highways and Byways: The Open Science Infrastructure

The rise of the open science movement has led to a proliferation of tools, services, and protocols aimed at improving research integrity. Although we agree that a greater diversity of resources is helpful, we concede that researchers may be faced with a "paradox of choice" (Klein et al., 2018a, p. 2) when attempting to engage in open science. Put differently, there is a risk that the open science infrastructure will become overly congested and, without proper navigation, scientific stakeholders will never reach a preferred state (e.g., scientific utopia; Nosek & Bar-Anan, 2012; Nosek, Spies & Motyl, 2012). In the following sections, we offer a guide to popular open science tools, which will likely become even more important as researchers continue to develop sophisticated analytic techniques (see Epskamp, 2019) and different scientific stakeholders, including world leaders (e.g., Group of Seven, 2021), continue to make calls for improved data sharing practices. We note that our guide is not exhaustive; it describes a sample of mainstream open science resources that we are most familiar with. Indeed, the open science movement is supported by many other, equally useful, resources that serve the same goal – to improve rigor and transparency in (I-O) research. What we present here is just the tip of the iceberg!

Open Science Guidelines

The Transparency and Openness Promotion (TOP) guidelines are becoming the most widely used tool for implementing open science practices in academic journals (see Nosek et al., 2015) – at the time of writing this chapter, more than 5,000 signatories, including the APA, have adopted the guidelines. The TOP guidelines are comprised of eight modular standards, each with three levels of rigor, and can be adopted by publishers singly or collectively as a means to move scientific communication toward great transparency (see Table 3.1). Indeed, the

TABLE 3.1 Summary of the transparency and openness promotion (TOP) guidelines

Standard	Not implemented	Level I	Level II	Level III
Citation standards	No mention of data citation.	Journal describes citation of data in guidelines to authors with clear rules and examples.	Article provides appropriate citation for data and materials used consistent with journal's author guidelines.	Article is not published until providing appropriate citation for data and materials following journal's author guidelines.
Data transparency	Journal encourages data sharing, or says nothing.	Article states whether data are available, and, if so, where to access them.	Data must be posted to a trusted repository. Exceptions must be identified at article submission.	Data must be posted to a trusted repository, and reported analyses will be reproduced independently prior to publication.
Analytic methods (code) transparency	Journal encourages code sharing, or says nothing.	Article states whether code is available, and, if so, where to access it.	Code must be posted to a trusted repository. Exceptions must be identified at article submission.	Code must be posted to a trusted repository, and reported analyses will be reproduced independently prior to publication.
Research materials transparency	Journal encourages materials sharing, or says nothing.	Article states whether materials are available, and, if so, where to access them.	Materials must be posted to a trusted repository. Exceptions must be identified at article submission.	Materials must be posted to a trusted repository, and reported analyses will be reproduced independently prior to publication.
Design and analysis transparency	Journal encourages design and analysis transparency, or says nothing.	Journal articulates design transparency standards.	Journal requires adherence to design transparency standards for review and publication.	Journal requires and enforces adherence to design transparency standards for review and publication.

(Continued)

TABLE 3.1 Summary of the transparency and openness promotion (TOP) guidelines *(Continued)*

Standard	Not implemented	Level I	Level II	Level III
Study preregistration	Journal says nothing.	Article states whether preregistration of study exists, and, if so, where to access it.	Article states whether preregistration of study exists, and, if so, allows journal access during peer review for verification.	Journal requires preregistration of studies and provides link and badge in article to meeting requirements.
Analysis plan preregistration	Journal says nothing.	Article states whether preregistration of study exists, and, if so, where to access it.	Article states whether preregistration with analysis plan exists, and, if so, allows journal access during peer review for verification.	Journal requires preregistration of studies with analysis plans and provides link and badge in article to meeting requirements.

Note: For each standard, level 0 illustrates the respective standard as not fulfilled, whereas levels 1 to 3 represent increasingly stringent requirements. From: "Promoting an open research culture" by Nosek et al. (2015), *Science, 348*(6242), 1422–1425. https://doi.org/10.1126/science.aab2374. Copyright © 2015, American Association for the Advancement of Science.

guidelines illustrate that the shift to open science will not happen overnight, but demonstrate how scientific stakeholders can improve research transparency incrementally over time. Virtually, all of the guidelines, in one way or another, are aimed at addressing data integrity issues. For example, at the most stringent level, the "Data Transparency" standard recommends that data are posted to a trusted repository, and reported analyses are reproduced independently prior to publication. Indeed, this practice would likely help to curtail QRPs (e.g., *p*-hacking) as the obtained results would have to be independently verified using the original data. The value of the TOP guidelines becomes even more apparent when the multiplicative effects of individual standards are considered. For instance, if implemented together, the "Data Transparency" and "Preregistration" standards would allow characteristics of the data (e.g., reliability and validity) to be assessed *and* provide an exhaustive report of the research that was carried out. Under this approach, researcher degrees of freedom (for a review, see Wicherts et al., 2016) that are typically hidden and contribute to QRPs could be disclosed and, thus, could be accounted for in future replication efforts.

We are also encouraged by steps taken by professional associations and specific journals to improve transparency. For example, in response to mounting concerns regarding transparency, the APA revised and expanded its reporting standards (Appelbaum et al., 2018). Likewise, recently SIOP formed the Committee for the Advancement of Professional Ethics (see https://www. siop.org/Career-Center/Professional-Ethics), which disseminates resources on research ethics to the association's members and those in the I-O profession. In addition, many flagship journals are now encouraging (and in some cases are requiring) researchers to engage in certain open science practices (e.g., Bergh & Oswald, 2020; Beugelsdijk et al., 2020). Overall, our view is that change is unfolding – albeit slowly (Banks et al., 2019). Indeed, this should come as no surprise as change takes time, especially when new protocols and policies must be developed. Still, we are encouraged by the progress being made and expect the (I-O) research landscape to continue to change in the years ahead.

Open Access Platforms

Multiple infrastructure platforms have emerged that facilitate open science practices, such as Open Science Framework (OSF) and *ResearchEquals* (see Herman et al., 2020). First, the OSF (https://osf.io/) has become a one-stop-shop for researchers interested in preregistering their studies, sharing their data, analytic scripts, and the like. Although similar, the suite of tools offered by service providers like Dropbox and Google are imperfect substitutes for OSF as they do not meet recommended standards (e.g., Klein et al., 2018a; Nosek et al., 2015; Wilkinson et al., 2016). Also, OSF provides users with globally unique and persistent identifiers (e.g., digital object identifiers [DOIs]) so that credit can be attributed to researchers who share their materials, allows for licenses to be posted that clarify how shared materials can be reused, and permits metadata descriptions (e.g., data dictionaries; Buchanan et al., 2021). However, perhaps more importantly, OSF is fairly easy to use (for a detailed tutorial on using the OSF to share research products, see Soderberg, 2018) and, thus, may empower more and more researchers to participate in open science.

Second, ResearchEquals (https://researchequals.com/) is somewhat more progressive than OSF in that it aims to create an entirely modular way of scholarly work and respective communication (Hartgerink, 2019; Hartgerink & Van Zelst, 2018). The overall goal is to make science accessible to and transparent for all, and to also break up the typical roles of researchers (e.g., author, reviewer, editor). Specifically, the classic paper format is broken down into research modules (e.g., theory, materials, data) that are communicated and linked with each other "as-you-go" instead of "after-the-fact." Built on the peer-to-peer web protocol Dat, ResearchEquals thereby creates a decentralized and immutable register of research modules that allows for content and data integrity (Hartgerink, 2019).

While essentially anyone can author a research module, anyone also can review a respective module and link his or her review to the respective module. In addition, ResearchEquals aims for a more transparent and broader assessment of researchers' contribution to the body of knowledge using social network analytics and goes beyond typical assessments, such as the impact factor of published works. For example, a researcher's value could be assessed via the number of modules created, the number of existing modules connected, the number of modules that were inspired by the researchers' work, and so on.

A variety of other open access platforms aiming at improving research integrity have also emerged in the last decade. For example, there are tools available that aid in: (1) supporting error detection and correction, such as *statcheck* (Nuijten & Polanin, 2020) and *Granularity Related Inconsistent Means* (Brown & Heathers, 2017), (2) enabling living and community-augmented meta-analyses (i.e., *metaBUS*; Bosco et al., 2017), (3) detecting publication bias and outliers in research syntheses (i.e., *Meta-Sen*; Field et al., 2021), and (4) locating instruments for measuring latent constructs (i.e., *Internomological Network*; Larsen & Bong, 2016). Although these tools are not omnipresent across scientific disciplines, their advent indicates that the open science movement is gaining traction. Moreover, the plethora of new tools aimed at improving rigor and transparency in research is encouraging because it suggests that scientists have responded positively to recent criticism regarding the credibility of their empirical findings.

Bringing It All Together: A Revised Scientific Model

By now it should be evident that many solutions have been proposed to mitigate data integrity concerns and improve research transparency. Collectively, these proposals may result in a scientific model that looks drastically different than the system currently used in I-O research. In its current form, the knowledge creation process can be characterized as a "closed loop" (Hambrick, 1994, p. 13) – one in which the *entire* scientific process is limited to a few paragraphs (e.g., a Methods section in journal article), anonymous peers evaluate the fruit of this labor, and many stakeholders cannot access its published version. What follows is a description of an alternative scientific model, one that leverages several recommended open science practices and has the potential to align scientific values and practices (cf. Woznyj et al., 2018) and may be ubiquitous in future I-O research.

In the first step of this alternative scientific model, researchers preregister their study. Study preregistration occurs when a researcher independently registers their research questions, hypotheses, design, and analysis plan via an independent organization (e.g., Center for Open Science; see https://www.cos.io/initiatives/prereg). Preregistration provides an opportunity for researchers to create and save a transparent, time-stamped plan of their intended project. Importantly, researchers are able to document deviations from the approved research plan if changes are required – after all, science can be a messy exercise. Such flexibility allows researchers to keep a record of how their study evolved over time and provides readers with the necessary information to evaluate the credibility of the corresponding inferences.

After successfully preregistering their study, the researcher conducts the approved study. The resulting manuscript, sans the results and discussion sections, is then submitted to a journal (i.e., results-blind review; Woznyj et al., 2018). The initial submission is evaluated based on the quality and rigor of the theoretical arguments and methods presented (Aguinis et al., 2017). Importantly, key aspects of the approved preregistration are included in the initial submission (e.g., analysis plan, anticipated statistical power, measurement information). Reviewers are able to reject, request revisions, or offer an in-principle acceptance to manuscripts. In the event of an in-principle acceptance, the complete manuscript is submitted and evaluated by the same set of reviewers. All subsequent revisions focus on whether the authors delivered on what they proposed and if the corresponding results are interpreted correctly. Although additional revisions can be requested, results that have been traditionally deemed as being not interesting (e.g., $p > .05$) are not grounds for rejection. Indeed, such a process protects against researcher and reviewer bias against papers that report certain results (Rosenthal, 1979). Not only will it help to improve transparency in research, but it will also benefit future efforts to synthesize research areas by making a greater diversity of research findings – not just the positive ones – available to meta-analysts who are interested in taking stock of our cumulative scientific knowledge.

Upon acceptance, the manuscript is sent to print, where it goes through traditional copyediting and quality assessment checks. However, similar to other disciplines, the post-peer review, pre-copyedit version of the manuscript is also made available on a relevant preprint server (e.g., PsyArXiv; see https://psyarxiv.com/) or personal website (relatedly, see London & Kimmelman, 2020; Moshontz et al., 2018). Such practice will provide access to scholarly content to those who do not have institutional access or the means to satisfy paywall requirements. We note that peer-reviewed *and* non-peer-reviewed manuscripts may be uploaded to preprint servers, which is why peer-reviewed papers should include an acknowledgement that the final authenticated version is available at the respective journal page. Importantly, all versions of the paper include a link to a project page that is hosted by an independent third party (e.g., OSF). The project page includes all research materials needed to verify and extend the observed findings, including the approved preregistration form, data collection instruments, anonymized data, and annotated analytic scripts that illustrate how analyses were performed.

The challenges of moving toward greater scientific transparency and integrity are solvable. The major question for scientific stakeholders is whether the problems are worth solving. If they are, how can we go about it? The aforementioned scientific model illustrates "what could be" in I-O research. We do not necessarily advocate its adoption. However, when compared to "what is" in I-O research currently, we argue that practices that promise to increase the integrity of psychological research need to increase in orders of magnitude.

Author Note

Both authors contributed to this chapter equally. We would like to thank Kevin R. Murphy for his constructive feedback on an earlier version of this chapter.

Notes

1 Many umbrella terms exist to refer to this crisis, such as replicability, reproducibility, dependability, credibility, confidence, or robustness (De Boeck & Jeon, 2018; O'Boyle & Götz, 2020). It is noteworthy that the social sciences are not the only scientific disciplines facing this crisis. For example, the validity of findings in chemistry and economics (e.g., Chang & Li, 2022; Mebane et al., 2019) have also been brought into question.

2 The CCSDS is a multi-national forum for governmental and quasi-governmental space agencies that discusses and develops standards for data and information systems for spaceflight (see Consultative Committee for Space Data Systems, 2012).

3 The term long-tail data was coined by Anderson (2006) who used the power law distribution to describe the commercial power of hit songs compared to so-called niche songs and the implications for the music industry. As such, roughly 15% of the curve cover its head (e.g., hit songs) and the remaining 85% cover its tails (e.g. niche songs). Applied to research data, a minority of researchers work with large data sets, whereas the majority works with small data sets – nonetheless, both types of data have their own merits.

4 Of course, attempts to include all available evidence into a research synthesis often fail for various reasons (e.g., unavailability/inaccessibility of data, non-response of corresponding authors, language barriers), resulting in an imperfect summary of the research literature (e.g., McAuley et al., 2000).

5 Of course, there is also qualitative research using the respective data in psychology in general, and IO specifically – yet, covering the challenges of qualitative data is beyond the scope of this chapter (for a review see Levitt et al., 2018).

6 Validity is defined as "the degree to which evidence and theory support the interpretations of test scores for proposed uses of tests" (American Educational Research Association, 2014, p. 14). Closely related, reliability is defined as "consistency of the scores across instances of the testing procedure, and the term reliability coefficient to refer to the reliability coefficients of classical test theory" (American Educational Research Association, 2014, p. 33).

7 Fabrication and falsification of data render the negative pole of this continuum. Because such acts must eventually be considered as death blows to data integrity, we do not focus on these practices as threats to data integrity here (e.g., Gross, 2016).

8 By no means do we want to give the impression that we discredit nil findings (relatedly, see Dienes, 2014; Landis et al., 2014; Romero & Sprenger, 2020). Yet, because we are currently accustomed to seeing statistically significant effects that we tend to interpret as substantive ones, interpreting nil findings correctly and extracting their value might appear as something *new* to most of us. In turn, an according question should be asked when seeing statistically significant results (i.e., "Does this study presenting statistically significant findings provide value?").

References

Aguinis, H., Cascio, W. F., & Ramani, R. S. (2017). Science's reproducibility and replicability crisis: International business is not immune. *Journal of International Business Studies, 48*, 653–663.

Aguinis, H., Villamor, I., & Ramani, R. S. (2021). MTurk research: Review and recommendations. *Journal of Management, 47*, 823–837.

American Educational Research Association. (2014). *Standards for educational and psychological testing*. American Educational Research Association.

American Psychological Association. (2008). Industrial and organizational psychology. Retrieved from https://www.apa.org/ed/graduate/specialize/industrial

Anderson, C. (2006). *The long tail: How endless choice is creating unlimited demand*. London, UK: Random House Business.

Appelbaum, M., Cooper, H., Kline, R. B., Mayo-Wilson, E., Nezu, A. M., & Rao, S. M. (2018). Journal article reporting standards for quantitative research in psychology: The APA publications and communications board task force report. *American Psychologist, 73*, 3–25.

Artner, R., Verliefde, T., Steegen, S., Gomes, S., Traets, F., Tuerlinckx, F., & Vanpaemel, W. (2021). The reproducibility of statistical results in psychological research: An investigation using unpublished raw data. *Psychological Methods, 26*(5), 527–546. https://doi.org/10.1037/met0000365

Asendorpf, J. B., Conner, M., De Fruyt, F., De Houwer, J., Denissen, J. J. A., Fiedler, K. Funder, D.C., Kleigel, R. Nosek, B.A., Perugini, M., Roberts, B.W., Schmitt, M., van Aken, M.A.G., Weber, H. & Wilkerts, J.M. (2013). Recommendations for increasing replicability in psychology. *European Journal of Personality, 27*, 108–119.

Banks, G. C., Field, J. G., Oswald, F. L., O'Boyle, E. H., Landis, R. S., Rupp, D. E. & Rogelberg, S.G. (2019). Answers to 18 questions about open science practices. *Journal of Business and Psychology, 34*, 257–270.

Banks, G. C., Gooty, J., Ross, R. L., Williams, C. E., & Harrington, N. T. (2018). Construct redundancy in leader behaviors: A review and agenda for the future. *The Leadership Quarterly, 29*, 236–251.

Banks, G. C., & O'Boyle, E. H. (2013). Why we need industrial–organizational psychology to fix industrial–organizational psychology. *Industrial and Organizational Psychology, 6*, 284–287.

Banks, G. C., Pollack, J. M., Bochantin, J. E., Kirkman, B. L., Whelpley, C. E., & O'Boyle, E. H. (2016). Management's science–practice gap: A grand challenge for all stakeholders. *Academy of Management Journal, 59*, 2205–2231.

Bedeian, A. G., Taylor, S. G., & Miller, A. N. (2010). Management science on the credibility bubble: Cardinal sins and various misdemeanors. *Academy of Management Learning & Education, 9*, 715–725.

Bergh, D. D., & Oswald, F. L. (2020). Fostering robust, reliable, and replicable research at the *Journal of Management*. *Journal of Management, 46*, 1302–1306.

Beugelsdijk, S., van Witteloostuijn, A., & Meyer, K. E. (2020). A new approach to data access and research transparency (DART. *Journal of International Business Studies, 51*, 887–905.

Borgman, C. L. (2015). *Big data, little data, no data: Scholarship in the networked world*. MIT Press.

Bosco, F. A., Uggerslev, K. L., & Steel, P. (2017). MetaBUS as a vehicle for facilitating meta-analysis. *Human Resource Management Review, 27*, 237–254.

Brown, N. J. L., & Heathers, J. A. J. (2017). The GRIM test: A simple technique detects numerous anomalies in the reporting of results in psychology. *Social Psychological and Personality Science, 8*, 363–369.

Buchanan, E. M., Crain, S. E., Cunningham, A. L., Johnson, H. R., Stash, H., Papadatou-Pastou, M. Isager, P.M., Carlsson, R. & Aczel, B. (2021). Getting started creating data dictionaries: How to create a shareable dataset. *Advances in Methods and Practices in Psychological Science*, 4, https://doi.org/10.1177/2515245920928007

C. C. S. D. S. (2012). *Reference model for an open archival information system (OAIS)*.

Ceci, S. J., & Walker, E. (1983). Private archives and public needs. *American Psychologist*, *38*, 414–423.

Chambers, C. D. (2017). *The seven deadly sins of psychology: A manifesto for reforming the culture of scientific practice*. Princeton University Press.

Chang, A. C., & Li, P. (2022). Is economics research replicable? Sixty published papers from thirteen journals say "often not". *Critical Finance Review*, *11*.

Chmielewski, M., & Kucker, S. C. (2020). An MTurk crisis? Shifts in data quality and the impact on study results. *Social Psychological and Personality Science*, *11*, 464–473.

Cole, M. S., Walter, F., Bedeian, A. G., & O'Boyle, E. H. (2012). Job burnout and employee engagement: A meta-analytic examination of construct proliferation. *Journal of Management*, *38*, 1550–1581.

Collins, F. S. (2021). COVID-19 lessons for research. *Science*, *371*, 1081–1081.

De Boeck, P., & Jeon, M. (2018). Perceived crisis and reforms: Issues, explanations, and remedies. *Psychological Bulletin*, *144*, 757–777.

Dienes, Z. (2014). Using Bayes to get the most out of non-significant results. *Frontiers in Psychology*, *5*.

Ebersole, C. R., Mathur, M. B., Baranski, E., Bart-Plange, D.-J., Buttrick, N. R., Chartier, C. R. Corker, K.S., Corley, M., Hartshorne, J.K., IJezerman, H., Lazarević, L.B., Rabagliati, H., Ropovik, I., Aczel, B., Aeschbach, A.F., Andrighetto, I., Arnel, J.D., Arrow, H., Babincak, P. ... Nosek, B.A. (2020). Many labs 5: Testing pre-data-collection Peer review as an intervention to increase replicability. *Advances in Methods and Practices in Psychological Science*, *3*, 309–331.

Epskamp, S. (2019). Reproducibility and replicability in a fast-paced methodological world. *Advances in Methods and Practices in Psychological Science*, *2*, 145–155.

Ferguson, A. R., Nielson, J. L., Cragin, M. H., Bandrowski, A. E., & Martone, M. E. (2014). Big data from small data: Data-sharing in the 'long tail' of neuroscience. *Nature Neuroscience*, *17*, 1442–1447.

Field, J. G., Bosco, F. A., & Kepes, S. (2021). How robust is our cumulative knowledge on turnover? *Journal of Business and Psychology*, *36*, 349–365.

Flake, J. K., & Fried, E. I. (2020). Measurement schmeasurement: Questionable measurement practices and how to avoid them. *Advances in Methods and Practices in Psychological Science*, *3*, 456–465.

Gabriel, A. S., & Wessel, J. L. (2013). A step too far? Why publishing raw datasets may hinder data collection. *Industrial and Organizational Psychology*, *6*, 287–290.

Giner-Sorolla, R. (2012). Science or art? How aesthetic standards grease the way through the publication bottleneck but undermine science. *Perspectives on Psychological Science*, *7*, 562–571.

Giustini, D. (2019). Retrieving grey literature, information, and data in the digital age. In H. M. Cooper, L.V. Hedges, & J. C. Valentine (Eds.), *The handbook of research synthesis and meta-analysis* (3rd ed., pp. 101–126). Russell Sage Foundation.

Gordon, M. E., Slade, L. A., & Schmitt, N. (1986). The "science of the sophomore" revisited: From conjecture to empiricism. *Academy of Management Review*, *11*, 191–207.

Götz, M., Bollmann, G., & O'Boyle, E. H. (2019). Contextual undertow of workplace deviance by and within units: A systematic review. *Small Group Research*, *50*, 39–80.

Götz, M., Donzallaz, M., & Jonas, K. (2020). Leader-member exchange fosters beneficial and prevents detrimental workplace behavior: Organizational identification as the linking pin. *Frontiers in Psychology, 11*, 1788–1788.

Götz, M., O'Boyle, E. H., Gonzalez-Mulé, E., Banks, G. C., & Bollmann, S. S. (2021). The "Goldilocks Zone": (Too) many confidence intervals in tests of mediation just exclude zero. *Psychological Bulletin, 147*, 95–114.

Grand, J. A., Rogelberg, S. G., Banks, G. C., Landis, R. S., & Tonidandel, S. (2018). From outcome to process focus: Fostering a more robust psychological science through registered reports and results-blind reviewing. *Perspectives on Psychological Science, 13*, 448–456.

Gross, C. (2016). Scientific misconduct. *Annual Review of Psychology, 67*, 693–711.

Group of Seven. (2021). G7 research compact.

Hambrick, D. C. (1994). What if the academy actually mattered? *Academy of Management Review, 19*, 11–16.

Hand, D. J. (2016). *Measurement: A very short introduction*. Oxford University Press.

Hardwicke, T. E., Mathur, M. B., MacDonald, K., Nilsonne, G., Banks, G. C., Kidwell, M. C. Mohr, A.H., Clayton, E., Yoon, E.J., Tessler, M.H., Lenne, R.L., Altman, S., Long, B. & Frank, M.C. (2018). Data availability, reusability, and analytic reproducibility: Evaluating the impact of a mandatory open data policy at the journal Cognition. *Royal Society Open Science, 5*, 180448.

Hardwicke, T. E., Serghiou, S., Janiaud, P., Danchev, V., Crüwell, S., Goodman, S. N. & Ioannidis, J.P.A. (2020). Calibrating the scientific ecosystem through meta-research. *Annual Review of Statistics and Its Application, 7*, 11–37.

Harlow, L. L., & Oswald, F. L. (2016). Big data in psychology: Introduction to the special issue. *Psychological Methods, 21*, 447–457.

Harrison, J. S., Banks, G. C., Pollack, J. M., O'Boyle, E. H., & Short, J. (2017). Publication bias in strategic management research. *Journal of Management, 43*, 400–425.

Hartgerink, C. (2019). Verified, shared, modular, and provenance based research communication with the dat protocol. *Publications, 7*, 40.

Hartgerink, C. H. J., & Van Zelst, M. (2018). "As-you-go" instead of "After-the-fact": A network approach to scholarly communication and evaluation. *Publications, 6*, 21.

Herman, E., Akeroyd, J., Bequet, G., Nicholas, D., & Watkinson, A. (2020). The changed – and changing – landscape of serials publishing: Review of the literature on emerging models. *Learned Publishing, 33*, 213–229.

Houtkoop, B. L., Chambers, C., Macleod, M., Bishop, D.V. M., Nichols, T. E., & Wagenmakers, E.-J. (2018). Data sharing in psychology: A survey on barriers and preconditions. *Advances in Methods and Practices in Psychological Science, 1*, 70–85.

Ioannidis, J. P. (2016). The mass production of redundant, misleading, and conflicted systematic reviews and meta-analyses. *The Milbank Quarterly, 94*, 485–514.

Johnson, C. Y. (2020, January 24). Scientists are unraveling the Chinese coronavirus with unprecedented speed and openness. *The Washington Post*.

Kelley, T. L. (1927). *Interpretation of educational measurements*. World Book Company.

Kidwell, M. C., Lazarević, L. B., Baranski, E., Hardwicke, T. E., Piechowski, S., Falkenberg, L.-S. Kennet, C., Slowik, A., Sonnleitner, C., Hess-Holden, C., Errington, T.M., Fiedler, S. & Nosek, B.A. (2016). Badges to acknowledge open practices: A simple, low-cost, effective method for increasing transparency. *PLOS Biology, 14*, e1002456.

Klein, O., Hardwicke, T. E., Aust, F., Breuer, J., Danielsson, H., Mohr, A. H. IJezerman, H., Nilsson, G., Vanpaemal, W. & Frank, M.C. (2018a). A practical guide for transparency in psychological science. *Collabra: Psychology, 4*.

Klein, R. A., Vianello, M., Hasselman, F., Adams, B. G., Adams, R. B., Alper, S. Aveyard, M., Axt, J.R., Babaola, M.T., Bahník, H., Batra, R., Berkics, M., Bernstein, M.J., Berry, D.R., Bialobrzeska, O., Binan, E.D., Bocian, K., Brandt, M.J. ... Nosek, B.A. (2018b). Many labs 2: Investigating variation in replicability across samples and settings. *Advances in Methods and Practices in Psychological Science, 1,* 443–490.

Köhler, T., & Cortina, J. M. (2021). Play it again, Sam! An analysis of constructive replication in the organizational sciences. *Journal of Management, 47,* 488–518.

Koole, S. L., & Lakens, D. (2012). Rewarding replications: A sure and simple way to improve psychological science. *Perspectives on Psychological Science, 7,* 608–614.

Kosinski, M., Wang, Y., Lakkaraju, H., & Leskovec, J. (2016). Mining big data to extract patterns and predict real-life outcomes. *Psychological Methods, 21,* 493–506.

Kreamer, L., & Rogelberg, S. G. (2020). Using results-blind reviewing to support the peer review competency framework. *Industrial and Organizational Psychology, 13,* 28–31.

Lakens, D. (2021). Sample size justification. *PsyArXiv.*

Lance, C. E., Dawson, B., Birkelbach, D., & Hoffman, B. J. (2010). Method effects, measurement error, and substantive conclusions. *Organizational Research Methods, 13,* 435–455.

Landis, R. S., James, L. R., Lance, C. E., Pierce, C. A., & Rogelberg, S. G. (2014). When is nothing something? Editorial for the null results special issue of journal of business and psychology. *Journal of Business and Psychology, 29,* 163–167.

Larsen, K. R., & Bong, C. H. (2016). A tool for addressing construct identity in literature reviews and meta-analyses. *MIS Q, 40,* 529–551.

Le, H., Schmidt, F. L., Harter, J. K., & Lauver, K. J. (2010). The problem of empirical redundancy of constructs in organizational research: An empirical investigation. *Organizational Behavior and Human Decision Processes, 112,* 112–125.

Leavitt, K. (2013). Publication bias might make us untrustworthy, but the solutions may be worse. *Industrial and Organizational Psychology, 6,* 290–295.

Levenstein, M. C., & Lyle, J. A. (2018). Data: Sharing is caring. *Advances in Methods and Practices in Psychological Science, 1,* 95–103.

Levitt, H. M., Bamberg, M., Creswell, J. W., Frost, D. M., Josselson, R., & Suárez-Orozco, C. (2018). Journal article reporting standards for qualitative primary, qualitative meta-analytic, and mixed methods research in psychology: The APA publications and communications board task force report. *American Psychologist, 73,* 26–46.

Lewin, W. H. G. (2011). *For the love of physics: From the end of the rainbow to the edge of time - a journey through the wonders of physics.* Free Press.

London, A. J., & Kimmelman, J. (2020). Against pandemic research exceptionalism. *Science, 368,* 476–477.

Lynöe, N., Jacobsson, L., & Lundgren, E. (1999). Fraud, misconduct or normal science in medical research–an empirical study of demarcation. *Journal of Medical Ethics, 25,* 501–506.

Makel, M. C., Plucker, J. A., & Hegarty, B. (2012). Replications in psychology research: How often do they really occur? *Perspectives on Psychological Science, 7,* 537–542.

Martone, M. E., Garcia-Castro, A., & VandenBos, G. R. (2018). Data sharing in psychology. *American Psychologist, 73,* 111–125.

McAuley, L., Pham, B., Tugwell, P., & Moher, D. (2000). Does the inclusion of grey literature influence estimates of intervention effectiveness reported in meta-analyses? *The Lancet, 356,* 1228–1231.

McKenna, S. (2021). Vaccines need not completely stop COVID transmission to curb the pandemic. *Scientific American.*

Mebane, C. A., Sumpter, J. P., Fairbrother, A., Augspurger, T. P., Canfield, T. J., Goodfellow, W. L. Guiney, P.D., LeHuray, A., Maltby, L., Mayfield, D.B., McLaughlin, M.J., Ortego, L.S., Schlekat, T., Scroggins, R. P. & Versylcke, T. A. (2019). Scientific integrity issues in environmental toxicology and chemistry: Improving research reproducibility, credibility, and transparency. *Integrated Environmental Assessment and Management, 15,* 320–344.

Meehl, P. E. (1990). Why summaries of research on psychological theories are often uninterpretable. *Psychological Reports, 66,* 195–244.

Moshontz, H., Campbell, L., Ebersole, C. R., IJzerman, H., Urry, H. L., Forscher, P. S. Grahe,J.E., McCarthy, R.J., Musser, E.D., Antfolk, J., Castille, C.M., Evans, T.R., Fiedler, S., Flake, J.K.,Forero, D.A. Janssen, S.M.J., Keene, J.R., Protzko, J., Aczel, B. ... Chartier, C.R. (2018). The psychological science accelerator: Advancing psychology through a distributed collaborative network. *Advances in Methods and Practices in Psychological Science, 1,* 501–515.

Munafò, M. R., Nosek, B. A., Bishop, D.V. M., Button, K. S., Chambers, C. D., Percie du Sert, N. Simonsohn, U., Wagenmakers, E., Warre, J.J. & Iaonnidis, J.P.A. (2017). A manifesto for reproducible science. *Nature Human Behaviour, 1,* 0021.

Munafò, M. R., & Smith, G. D. (2018). Robust research needs many lines of evidence. *Nature, 553,* 399–401.

Murphy, K. R., & Deshon, R. (2000). Interrater correlations do not estimate the reliability of job performance ratings. *Personnel Psychology, 53,* 873–900.

Nelson, L. D., Simmons, J., & Simonsohn, U. (2018). Psychology's renaissance. *Annual Review of Psychology, 69,* 511–534.

Nosek, B. A., Alter, G., Banks, G. C., Borsboom, D., Bowman, S. D., Breckler, S. J. Buck, S., Chambers, C.D., Chin, G., Christensen, G., Contestabile, M., Dafoe, A., Eich, E., Freese, J., Glennerster, R., Goroff, D., Green, D.P., Hesse, B., Humphreys, M. ... Yarkoni, T. (2015). Promoting an open research culture. *Science, 348,* 1422.

Nosek, B.A., & Bar-Anan, Y. (2012). Scientific utopia I: Opening scientific communication. *Psychological Inquiry, 23,* 217–243.

Nosek, B. A., Hardwicke, T. E., Moshontz, H., Allard, A., Corker, K. S., Dreber, A. Almberg, A.D., Fidler, F., Hilgard, J., Struhl, M.K., Nuijten, M.B., Rohrer, J.M., Romero, F., Scheel, A.M., Scherer, L., Schönbrodt, F. & Vazire, S. (2022). Replicability, Robustness, and Reproducibility in Psychological Science. *Annual Review of Psychology 73,* 719–748.

Nosek, B.A., Spies, J. R., & Motyl, M. (2012). Scientific utopia: II. Restructuring incentives and practices to promote truth over publishability. *Perspectives on Psychological Science, 7,* 615–631.

Nuijten, M. B., & Polanin, J. R. (2020). "statcheck": Automatically detect statistical reporting inconsistencies to increase reproducibility of meta-analyses. *Research Synthesis Methods, 11,* 574–579.

O'Boyle, E., Banks, G. C., Carter, K., Walter, S., & Yuan, Z. (2019). A 20-year review of outcome reporting bias in moderated multiple regression. *Journal of Business and Psychology, 34,* 19–37.

O'Boyle, E. H., & Götz, M. (2020). Questionable research practices. In L. Jussim, J.A. Krosnick, & S. T. Stevens (Eds.), *Research integrity in the behavioral sciences.* Oxford University Press.

Obels, P., Lakens, D., Coles, N. A., Gottfried, J., & Green, S. A. (2020). Analysis of open data and computational reproducibility in registered reports in psychology. *Advances in Methods and Practices in Psychological Science, 3,* 229–237.

Obschonka, M., Lee, N., Rodríguez-Pose, A., Eichstaedt, J. C., & Ebert, T. (2020). Big data methods, social media, and the psychology of entrepreneurial regions: Capturing cross-county personality traits and their impact on entrepreneurship in the USA. *Small Business Economics, 55,* 567–588.

Oliu-Barton, M., Pradelski, B. S. R., Aghion, P., Artus, P., Kickbusch, I., Lazarus, J. V. Sridhar, D. & Vanderslott, S. (2021). SARS-CoV-2 elimination, not mitigation, creates best outcomes for health, the economy, and civil liberties. *The Lancet, 397*, 2234–2236.

Open Science Collaboration. (2015). Estimating the reproducibility of psychological science. *Science, 6251.*

Orben, A., & Lakens, D. (2020). Crud (re)defined. *Advances in Methods and Practices in Psychological Science, 3*, 238–247.

Oswald, F. L., Behrend, T. S., Putka, D. J., & Sinar, E. (2020). Big data in industrial-organizational psychology and human resource management: Forward progress for organizational research and practice. *Annual Review of Organizational Psychology and Organizational Behavior, 7*, 505–533.

Peterson, R. A., & Merunka, D. R. (2014). Convenience samples of college students and research reproducibility. *Journal of Business Research, 67*, 1035–1041.

Pickler, R., Noyes, J., Perry, L., Roe, B., Watson, R., & Hayter, M. (2015). Authors and readers beware the dark side of open access. *Journal of Advanced Nursing, 71*, 2221–2223.

Podsakoff, P. M., MacKenzie, S. B., Lee, J.-Y., & Podsakoff, N. P. (2003). Common method biases in behavioral research: A critical review of the literature and recommended remedies. *Journal of Applied Psychology, 88*(5), 879–903. https://doi.org/10.1037/0021-9010.88.5.879

Popper, K. (1963). *Conjectures and refutations: The growth of scientific knowledge.* Routledge and Kegan Paul.

Price, L. R. (2017). *Psychometric methods: Theory into practice.* Guilford Press.

Research Connections. (2017). Guide to archiving data with research connections: Considerations throughout the research life cycle.

Robinson, J., Rosenzweig, C., Moss, A. J., & Litman, L. (2019). Tapped out or barely tapped? Recommendations for how to harness the vast and largely unused potential of the mechanical Turk participant Pool. *PLOS ONE, 14*, e0226394.

Romero, F., & Sprenger, J. (2020). Scientific self-correction: The Bayesian way. *Synthese.*

Rosenthal, R. (1979). The file drawer problem and tolerance for null results. *Psychological Bulletin, 86*, 638–641.

Rowhani-Farid, A., Aldcroft, A., & Barnett, A. G. (2020). Did awarding badges increase data sharing in *BMJ Open*? A randomized controlled trial. *Royal Society Open Science, 7*, 191818.

Rynes, S. L., Colbert, A. E., & O'Boyle, E. H. (2018). When the "Best Available Evidence" doesn't win: How doubts about science and scientists threaten the future of evidence-based management. *Journal of Management, 44*, 2995–3010.

Scheel, A. M., Schijen, M. R. M. J., & Lakens, D. (2021). An excess of positive results: Comparing the standard psychology literature with registered reports. *Advances in Methods and Practices in Psychological Science, 4*. https://doi.org/10.1177/25152459211007467

Schmidt, F. L., Viswesvaran, C., & Ones, D. S. (2000). Reliability is not validity and validity is not reliability. *Personnel Psychology, 53*, 901–912.

Schmidt, S. (2009). Shall we really do it again? The powerful concept of replication is neglected in the social sciences. *Review of General Psychology, 13*, 90–100.

Shadish, W. R. (2002). *Experimental and quasi-experimental designs for generalized causal inference.* Houghton Mifflin.

Shaffer, J. A., DeGeest, D., & Li, A. (2016). Tackling the problem of construct proliferation: A guide to assessing the discriminant validity of conceptually related constructs. *Organizational Research Methods, 19*, 80–110.

Simmons, J. P., Nelson, L. D., & Simonsohn, U. (2011). False-positive psychology: Undisclosed flexibility in data collection and analysis allows presenting anything as significant. *Psychological Science, 22*, 1359–1366.

Society for Industrial and Organizational Psychology. (2021). SIOP vision, mission, values, and goals. Retrieved from https://www.siop.org/About-SIOP/Mission

Soderberg, C. K. (2018). Using OSF to share data: A step-by-step guide. *Advances in Methods and Practices in Psychological Science, 1*, 115–120.

Spector, P. E. (2006). Method variance in organizational research: Truth or urban legend? *Organizational Research Methods, 9*, 221–232.

Spellman, B. A. (2015). A short (personal) future history of revolution 2.0. *Perspectives on Psychological Science, 10*, 886–899.

Stanley, T. D., Carter, E. C., & Doucouliagos, H. (2018). What meta-analyses reveal about the replicability of psychological research. *Psychological Bulletin, 144*, 1325–1346.

Stewart, N., Ungemach, C., Harris, A. J. L., Bartels, D. M., Newell, B. R., Paolacci, G., & Chandler, J. J. (2015). The average laboratory samples a population of 7,300 amazon mechanical Turk workers. *Judgment and Decision Making, 10*(5), 479–491.

Tihanyi, L. (2020). From "That's interesting" to "That's important". *Academy of Management Journal, 63*, 329–331.

Tiokhin, L., Hackman, J., Munira, S., Jesmin, K., & Hruschka, D. (2019). Generalizability is not optional: Insights from a cross-cultural study of social discounting. *Royal Society Open Science, 6*, 181386.

Tourish, D. (2019). *Management studies in crisis: Fraud, deception and meaningless research.* Cambridge University Press.

Vazire, S. (2018). Implications of the credibility revolution for productivity, creativity, and progress. *Perspectives on Psychological Science, 13*, 411–417.

Vermeulen, F. (2005). On rigor and relevance: Fostering dialectic progress in management research. *Academy of Management Journal, 48*, 978–982.

Vicente-Saez, R., & Martinez-Fuentes, C. (2018). Open science now: A systematic literature review for an integrated definition. *Journal of Business Research, 88*, 428–436.

Viswesvaran, C., Ones, D. S., & Schmidt, F. L. (1996). Comparative analysis of the reliability of job performance ratings. *Journal of Applied Psychology, 81*, 557–574.

Washburn, A. N., Hanson, B. E., Motyl, M., Skitka, L. J., Yantis, C., Wong, K. M. Sun, J., Prims, J.P., Mueller, A.B., Melton, C.J. & Carcel, T.S. (2018). Why do some psychology researchers resist adopting proposed reforms to research practices? A description of researchers' rationales. *Advances in Methods and Practices in Psychological Science, 1*, 166–173.

Wicherts, J. M., Veldkamp, C. L. S., Augusteijn, H. E. M., Bakker, M., van Aert, R. C. M., & van Assen, M. A. L. M. (2016). Degrees of freedom in planning, running, analyzing, and reporting psychological studies: A checklist to avoid *p*-hacking. *Frontiers in Psychology, 7*.

Wiebels, K., & Moreau, D. (2021). Leveraging containers for reproducible psychological research. *Advances in Methods and Practices in Psychological Science, 4*. https://doi.org/10.1177/25152459211017853

Wilkinson, M. D., Dumontier, M., Aalbersberg, I. J., Appleton, G., Axton, M., Baak, A. Bloomberg, N., Boiten, J., onino da Silva Santos, L, Bourne, P.E., Bouwman, J., Brookes, A.J., Clark, T., Crosas, M., Dillo, I., Dumon, O., Edmunds, S., Evelo, C.T. Finkers. R. ... Mons, B. (2016). The FAIR guiding principles for scientific data management and stewardship. *Scientific Data, 3*, 160018.

Woznyj, H. M., Grenier, K., Ross, R., Banks, G. C., & Rogelberg, S. G. (2018). Results-blind review: A masked crusader for science. *European Journal of Work and Organizational Psychology, 27*, 561–576.

4

USING DATA IN ORGANIZATIONS

Alexis A. Fink and Keith McNulty

The early part of the twenty-first century has been shaped in part by the tsunami of data, processing power, and rapidly evolving methods for ingesting, transforming, connecting, storing, analyzing, and sharing those data. Perhaps no organizational function has been so affected by this as Human Resources. Although the history of quantitative approaches to solving organizational problems dates back over a century (Kozlowski, Chen & Salas, 2017), recent years have seen an increase in the popularity, volume, complexity, and influence of data-based Human Resources work.

This larger volume considers important questions regarding this such as the overall role of theory (Chapters 9–11) and the research environment created by the issues addressed (Chapter 12). In this chapter, we will complement those considerations with practical issues relevant to data work in organizations. Here, the important stakeholders are less concerned with the theory and more interested in the practical impact of data in informing organizational strategies and practices, dispelling long-held myths, and measuring and evaluating the fairness, effectiveness, and efficiency of strategies and programs (Fink & Sturman, 2017).

In this chapter, we will address the fundamentals of using data in organizations, including the types of data, quality of data, systems used to gather, store, and access data, issues with data security, privacy, and confidentiality, and why all of this is harder than one might initially believe. From there, we will discuss using data in organizations, describing maturity models, the role of metrics, and the spectrum of analytical work conducted by most practitioners, from reporting through to forecasting and optimization.

DOI: 10.4324/9781003015000-5

For the analytical work to have a genuine impact, it must address relevant problems or opportunities that are valued by important stakeholders. We will highlight important elements of influencing with data in organizations, including business acumen, analytic translation, consulting, and collaboration as ways of working, visualization, and storytelling as a way of helping convey meaning, and the interplay between analytics and strategy in a human resource context. Finally, we will close the chapter with a discussion of important considerations for creating impact: embedding findings into business processes and working inside complex systems.

Fundamentals of Using Data in Organizations

Types of Data

Advances in technology have yielded a plethora of new data sources. Chapter 1 in the volume dives deeply into the "changing face of data." Many new forms of data are indeed available and create new opportunities for insight. However, to be useful in a practical setting, data must not only be available but also accurate (reliable and valid) and relevant. The collection, storage, use, and sharing of the data must conform to the appropriate policy requirements. Further, the use of the data must be acceptable to the organization members. Violations of the psychological contract (Argyris, 1960) may yield short-term insight, but ultimately harm trust in a way that makes future work more difficult to conduct and act upon.

Our increasingly digitized working (and personal) lives mean that many of us create a raft of "digital exhaust" as we go about our workdays. The increasing efficiency of computerized systems and decreasing cost of digital storage means that the time we spend doing activities, our locations, and our interaction patterns are increasingly being measured and stored. Ambient data and "digital exhaust," the trail of data left behind by one's interactions with digitized systems, are gaining traction in organizational research as more and more of our lives are digitally mediated (Chakrabarti & McCune, 2020). Researchers can now conduct organization network analyses based on a digital record of interactions via email, chat, or workplace collaboration software, rather than relying on self-ratings. For example, digital capture of meeting interactions between an organizational newcomer and her manager and colleagues permits examination of patterns that can help tease apart how successful onboarding support is different from unsuccessful onboarding support. New patterns of interactions can be identified between in-group versus out-group members in a team by examining email use (e.g., Turnage & Goodboy, 2016).

Advances in Natural Language Processing have created tremendous opportunity to efficiently process large quantities of unstructured, text-based data (e.g., Dutta & O'Rourke, 2020). Existing open-source libraries and commercially available tools can estimate meaning, sentiment, and emotion and in many cases can do it in near real time. In a rapidly developing technological field, capabilities have developed quickly from basic sentiment dictionaries and word frequency counts to the modeling of entire topics in unstructured text and the ability to determine relationships between words through an analysis of their relative positioning in multidimensional space. Leading organizations are now able to clearly and sharply identify the most common topics being referred to in corpuses of text such as survey comments. Each individual comment can be attributed a mapping to the topics and an associated sentiment or emotion. Even the subtle contextual meaning of words is becoming more and more understood through automated analytics – most recently, Google's Bidirectional Encoder Representations from Transformers has shown a significantly improved ability to identify different meanings from the same word used in different sentences. However, as is common with Machine Learning approaches, these new methodologies are often released with proof of improved performance, but without a full understanding of *why* the performance is better (e.g., Devlin et al., 2019).

Digital exhaust can be external to an organization as well as internal. The rise of professional social networks and collaboration platforms can offer the possibility of "market indicator" data on many factors of interest to Human Resources, such as skills, jobs, and turnover, or movement among and attractiveness of various organizations, business sectors, and geographies, as well as provide opportunities to source and evaluate talent at scale using automation and artificial intelligence tools. The commercialization of such information has been a feature of the development of many of these platforms in recent years.

Some employees may bristle at the idea that the contents of their email or chat messages are cataloged and analyzed (e.g., Wells, Moorman & Werner, 2007). However, it is not necessary to include details such as those in analysis to gain useful insights. Many organizations not only include comments in their employee surveys but also have some forms of collaboration software where analyzing the frequency, content, and sentiment is less likely to evoke concerns about privacy or employee monitoring. Similarly, competency modeling, once laboriously investigated with interviews, diaries, surveys, and workshops (e.g., Campion et al., 2011), can now be supported at least to some degree through automated analysis of content related to the jobs in question (e.g., Garman, Standish & Kim, 2018).

Data Quality

Unfortunately, not all data within an organization can be trusted. The ways in which errors can creep into an organization's data are too numerous to inventory and may be unique to each organization's particular configuration and history. For example, it may seem that "start date" would be a simple enough variable.

However, in the case of employees who were part of an acquisition, it may be important to capture both the start date with the acquiring company for some purposes, and still retain the original start date with the acquired company for other purposes, such as vesting of a 401(k). Some organizations will give credit for an employee's prior work history if they are rehired. In those cases, they may have an original start date, a start date that aligns to the date of their rehire, and a 3rd calculated date which adds their original service to the new start date and manufactures a date that essentially gives them "credit" for the total days worked for purposes of seniority, paid time off allotment, or other years-of-service-related benefits. Manager indicators, demographic information, and whether attrition was regrettable or not regrettable can also be defined differently across organizations or even within the same organization. Mixed definitions can yield a dataset that essentially does not mean what you think it means, adding error into calculations and making it more difficult to make appropriate conclusions.

Further, stakeholders may notice discrepancies across reports, creating questions about the credibility and accuracy of analyses. One of the great frustrations of practitioners in many organizations is the frequency with which small discrepancies can derail a conversation into a dissection of why the number of, say, exits on one slide or section of a report differs from the ostensibly same number later in the same or a related document. Even very, very small differences, as small as a single case, and where the overall trend is confirmed in both instances, can be highly disruptive.

These differences can be caused by definitional differences as noted above, or by procedural differences, such as when data was accessed. In some cases, even data nominally representing the same data with the same definitions can vary. For example, the complexity of most HRIS ecosystems means that data must flow among several interrelated systems, often with refreshes happening overnight. Thus, data with an effective date of the last day of the month may change for a few days after that. As an example, data accessed on the 31st of the month may show six non-regrettable exits (i.e., a turnover that does not have a net negative effect on the team or organization). One exit might be effective on the 31st and recoded from the default of regrettable to non-regrettable on that day. However, that record might not be updated in third-party analytic platforms used to query attrition rates until the following day, meaning that data with an effective date of the 31st that is accessed on the 1st of the following month might show seven non-regrettable exits instead.

Data Systems (HRIS and Beyond)

Organizations capture a great deal of information about their employees as a natural part of the course of doing business. Much of this data is contained in Human Resource Information Systems (HRIS), such as Workday or PeopleSoft.

At first blush, this seems like a gold mine; enormous quantities of data, standardized and indexed. This is certainly true for answering questions about what happened. For example, it is generally straightforward to examine who got promoted. The larger challenge comes in understanding. Essentially, HRISs are designed to manage transactions, rather than provide nuanced insight. As a result, HRISs tend to be quite weak on contextual data; why was Juan promoted, while his peer Sarah, with the same team size, tenure as a manager and performance history, was not? While in some fields, it is sufficient to understand what is happening, frequently in HR, it is important to understand why something is happening so that action can be taken to nudge a pattern this way or that.

This presents a nontrivial risk to high-quality research. Quite simply, the data is available and relatively easy to use, requiring much less investment of researcher time and much less imposition on employees, whose time is typically among organizations' most precious and scarce resources. The temptation to use them is great. However, those data typically capture transactions rather than context or meaning. Unfortunately, searching in the readily available, but largely dessicated HRIS data is unlikely to yield useful insights.

Beyond this risk, HRIS data quality and reliability depend entirely on the data entry practices of humans. The less reliable these practices, the less reliable the data and the insights that can be drawn from it. While business-critical event data, such as hiring and termination, can generally be expected to be more reliable, other data such as changes in employee status (promotion, leave of absence, and changes in work schedule) may not be so religiously captured. Data entry processes which are thoughtfully designed and rules-based in order to capture as much data as possible are less likely to suffer from these problems, but these issues remain substantially prevalent among many organizations.

Despite the limitations, examining HRIS data is very popular; it creates no extra demand on employees' time, it avoids the time delay inherent in even short surveys, and the de facto participation rate approaches 100%. These nominal advantages in convenience are enough to overcome the fact that sometimes the data is poor proxies for the actual concepts of interest. Thoughtful researchers are urged to treat this sort of data with appropriate caution and to design studies that will yield relevant and actionable insights rather than simply convenient ones.

Data Security, Confidentiality, and Privacy

To the layperson, data security, data confidentiality, and data privacy likely seem synonymous; after all, each is concerned with making sure that data is only accessed based on a valid need, purpose, and permission. However, while related, each has distinct attributes that are important. Data security is usually understood in a systems context and is concerned with protection against electronic events that could compromise the data of an organization. The growth in hacking as a skill and discipline, and the number of high-profile hacking events that have occurred in recent years have resulted in a high level of concern in organizations about the data they hold, be it HR data or otherwise. The emergence, and economic attractiveness, of cloud-based systems which mean that data is no longer stored on hardware owned and managed by the organization itself has further complicated the landscape of data security recently, with differing levels of anxiety among organizations about ceding this control outside of their infrastructure. Hacks on highly prevalent third-party software – for example, the *SolarWinds* hack in late 2020 – are of particular concern, potentially resulting in data breaches across multiple major organizations at the same time.

Data confidentiality has always been an important preserve in Human Resources, dating back to the time of filing cabinets rather than electronic systems. Confidential data generally have identifying information attached to them but are gathered with the promise that names will not be revealed (anonymous data in turn is fully separated from identifying information). However, in the era of readily available digital data, the expectations and interest across the broader organization of exploring and analyzing data have raised the bar on protecting confidentiality. Many HR analysts find themselves put under pressure to send line-level data – often with identifying information, such as names, unique employee identifiers, or sensitive demographic information, to interested colleagues for the purpose of their own analysis, and without appropriate investment in data confidentiality training and approval systems organizations risk breaching confidentiality obligations in ways that are less obvious than the handing over of paper files. While these colleagues – or researchers – are typically acting with honorable intentions, it is usually inappropriate, and in many cases illegal, to share row-level data beyond the explicit purpose for which the data was collected. Just because you have it doesn't mean you can use it any way you want.

Data privacy as a term and concept is relatively new and is a child of the era of ambient data. Governments and regulators, driven by high-profile incidents and political events, have increasingly concerned themselves with how and why individual data is stored, used, and analyzed, as well as questions surrounding the ownership of data. The most developed regulatory environment at the time of writing is the European Union, where the advent of the extensive General Data Protection Regulation (GDPR) in 2018 enshrined into law the standards of appropriate use and ownership of personal data and the permissions required in using it, and instituted large penalties for any breach. For organizations with operations in the European Union, GDPR has introduced new definitions and operational considerations which will have a substantial impact on how information on their members is collected, stored, and analyzed. For the purposes of GDPR regulation, "personal data" has an expansive definition that includes most data where an individual is potentially identifiable (whether anonymized/coded or not). Where personal data is to be collected, requirements have been placed on the organization to obtain the consent of individuals for the use of their personal data for a specific and limiting purpose. Importantly, individuals have the right to request transparency on how their personal data is being used, and organizations must respond in detail to such a request from an employee or organization member within a specified time period.

Due to the proliferation of data and the increasing levels of regulation, managing data security, confidentiality, and privacy is substantially more challenging for organizations today compared to the past. It is also likely to continue in this trajectory as data will continue to proliferate and more countries will likely follow the example of the European Union in regulating data privacy. What might previously have been considered sufficient workarounds for the protection of individual data, such as anonymization of certain data fields, are becoming increasingly inadequate in both their effectiveness and in the eyes of regulators. For example, distributing a dataset containing the demographics of a set of individuals and removing their names does not prevent an individual being identified via a unique combination of demographics.

Data Coherence

Many organizations have multiple systems containing data relevant to the people within them, and there are often many people and groups accessing those data. As noted earlier in this chapter, incoherence in its simplest form might simply be a matter of when data is pulled or refreshed for a pair of companion purposes, where one is pulled on the last day of the month, but the other is pulled 3 days later, with an effective date of the end of the month, to allow for corrections and post-dated transactions to update. Nominally the same data for the same month might disagree due to a procedural quirk. Similarly, recruiting data might reflect a certain percentage of new hires as diverse based on self-report during the recruiting process, and that might not match the self-report offered by candidates in their official employee record, leading to a disconnection between figures regarding the success of diverse hiring initiatives. From time to time, organizations may update their job codes and move some people between titles, with or without the knowledge of the person or their manager. In some organizations, HR functions have permissions to update demographic data on an employee's record on the basis of their "visual ID." In some systems, individuals have permissions to update portions of their own employee records, such as educational level. Organizations that have invested in gamification may have many people with permissions to award "badges" for various skills or performance levels. Some organizations that use formal goal setting systems permit them to be updated while others do not. When all these sorts of possible data system changes above are taken together, it becomes clear that HR data systems, while theoretically a clear, rules-based single source of truth, can often be inconsistent and inaccurate. Beyond inconvenience to researchers, these inconsistencies can have material real-world consequences, affecting critical outcomes like pay.

Employee attrition (or retention) is a common topic of interest among organizational stakeholders and one where analytics is often expected to offer insight. While it may seem simple, attrition is defined in many different ways, adding confusion within and across organizations. For example, attrition can be characterized as voluntary or involuntary, as regrettable or non-regrettable, and can be calculated as an annualized percentage or a rolling 12-month percentage, or only attrition for certain cohorts or within certain time periods, plus many other permutations. If the organization is changing size, what denominator do you use? As you dig deeper, additional questions arise – should retirements count as attrition at all? If so, how should they be counted? For recruiting purposes, every exit may be backfilled (or captured as a headcount reduction), so all exits should count. For purposes of evaluating the impact of, say, a new training initiative, it might make sense to omit retirements if "attrition" is a success criterion. For researchers evaluating new selection procedures, specific time periods may be important, and the corrective action associated with regrettable attrition may be different from that for non-regrettable attrition. For researchers looking across organizations, simply receiving a file with a column labeled "attrition" might not be useful without additional information about how that organization calculates attrition. If the attrition is focused on a particular job type, should internal transfers out of that job type count as attrition? Even getting the raw figures may not be helpful without additional information – different businesses and industries may have different seasonality trends, perhaps attached to their fiscal year or bonus schedule that might influence attrition 6 months after an intervention in ways that are inconsistent from organization to organization.

Many organizational questions are more complicated than they sound at first blush, exacerbating these definitional challenges. For example, organizations may be concerned about burnout, but prefer not to ask employees directly and instead look to their existing data for clues. Organizational stakeholders might decide that the important thing is that people take their vacation time so that they can restore themselves. Well-meaning analysts in different parts of a business might then operationally define "taking vacation" as the percent of people who have taken any vacation, the percentage of people who have taken no vacation, the average number of days of vacation taken, the percent of people who have accumulated the maximum hours of vacation time, the average balance of available vacation hours or the average percentage of vacation hours available, or any number of other permutations. Those analysts might also use different time periods for their calculations.

Organizational researchers, in turn, may be busy trying to connect those vacation patterns to attrition rates, manager ratings, or other outcomes, generating correlations or predictions to help inform organizational actions. While each individual component of that system may be sensible in its own right, this often leads to different stakeholders having different understandings of a core problem, yielding frustrating sessions where figures from one analysis are incorrectly compared to another analysis, derailing the opportunity for action and progress while frustrated stakeholders swirl and try to deconstruct how the seemingly contradictory figures emerged. Unfortunately, not only does this waste time and resources but it also lays waste to researcher credibility. Thus, creating and agreeing clear definitions and "single sources of truth" become a critical foundation to any credible analytics operation.

For scholars dependent on internal partners to gather and share information, and especially for those working across organizations, clarity and consistency in definitions is critically important. For those conducting quantitative research in a discipline where underlying true effects are likely no greater than moderate in scale, poor metric definitions and coherency can completely obscure these effects, leading to false-negative conclusions on the relevance and importance of the constructs being studied.

Using Data in Organizations

Several maturity models have been suggested to describe how organizations use data. All of these originate from various elements of underlying truth, but the important thing to note is that analytics work in organizations is not singular and its development and maturity is not linear. That is, organizations that have advanced to prescriptive work are also continuously delivering and improving on their foundational metrics and reporting work as well. Leek and Peng (2015) describe six core types of data analytics – descriptive, exploratory, inferential, predictive, causal, and mechanistic – of which all except the last are relevant in a Human Resources context.

Descriptive analytics usually involves the calculation of previously defined metrics, ranging from the intuitively obvious to the highly bespoke. Exploratory analytics involves the processing of raw data in order to understand dimension and effect in a way that helps support the optimal definition of new metrics or the investigation of new topics. Both descriptive and exploratory analytics are primarily focused on past and present states.

Inferential analytics focuses on the quantitative modeling of past and present states in order to infer relationships that could apply to future states. Usually, the purpose of inferential analytics is to suggest possible causality in order to effect action to influence this causality where needed. Predictive analytics involves quantitative modeling with the primary goal of accurate prediction of future events.

While similar mathematical models can often underlie both inferential and predictive analytics, they are primarily differentiated by the processes involved. For example, with a primary focus on accurate prediction, datasets for predictive analytics need to be split into training and testing sets before any modeling is conducted, while such a split is not necessary if the inference is the primary objective. The precise statistical tools used can also differ between inferential and predictive analytics.

Causal analytics involves the extension of analytic techniques beyond inferred causation and into reasonable proof of causation. Causal analytics is underdeveloped and is rarely used in practice. Substantial effort and deliberate experimentation are usually required to satisfy a burden of proof on causality and organizations rarely have the appetite for the time, effort, and cost of such work. However, clever researchers with solid partnerships across the organization can sometimes embed true experimental designs within a complex rollout, creating useful intervention and control groups. This generally requires partnership in advance to design an approach that meets both business and research needs effectively, but when done well is very useful. For example, researchers wishing to demonstrate the impact of a new competency system on internal movement within a firm might take advantage of the necessity of a phased rollout to gauge differences in internal movement within the same firm at the same point in time where some employees have been treated to a new competency modeling system and others have not (as the project has not yet addressed their jobs). If the employees in the treatment group experienced a statistically significant increase in internal mobility compared to those still awaiting a new competency model, it can be reasonably assumed that something about the new competency system contributed to the increased internal movement.

In a typical Human Resources analytics context, these five types of analytics are generated through several key activities: measurement, reporting, exploratory data analysis (EDA), modeling, experimenting, and prescribing.

Measurement

As organizations grow larger and more complex, it becomes increasingly important to monitor things systematically. Given the previously noted challenges in doing this without measurement coherency, defining and generating metrics is a popular and effective foundational step to any analytics maturity model. Configuring these metrics into scalable solutions, such as queryable dashboards or auto-generated reports requires nontrivial time up front but can free up considerable analyst time to focus on action.

Metrics are important for driving accountability around outcomes the organization has decided are important. However, as noted in the HRIS section, there is a material risk that those things which are most easily measured will be incorporated into dashboards, even when they may be poor indicators of the true strategic or operational priority. Context is typically important; knowing a patient's weight gives you some information, it is much more useful to balance that information with height and body composition information. Similarly, in organizations, combining variables into ratios and standardized indices, such as Z-scores can be helpful.

Further, though it is currently fashionable to focus primarily on performance or event outcomes, such as ratings or attrition, it should be remembered that a substantial proportion of these outcomes are the direct effect of employee behavior (e.g., Campbell & Wiernik, 2015). Many organizations make a distinction between performance – what is accomplished – and behavior – how it is accomplished, with attention to both. Practitioners can help organizations by compiling metrics that address the effectiveness, efficiency, and impact of HR activities and by devising systems that appropriately capture and prioritize both the "what" and the "how" aspects of employee performance.

Constructing effective portfolios that address leading and lagging indicators and span the domains of interest is much more difficult than it sounds. Program owners might need a raft of metrics to manage their book of work where organizational decision makers would benefit from a much smaller, more focused set that may diverge considerably from the operational concerns prioritized in program dashboards. Thus, different stakeholder groups might need different views of the same domain space to support their own decisions or information needs. Configuring the ecosystem as a whole is harder than simply rolling up every available figure.

Reporting

Reporting data and metrics is in many ways the foundation of analytical work in organizations. For most organizations, this is a mix of self-service dashboards containing descriptive metrics and custom reports or data pulls. Often internal practitioners must serve a wide range of intended audiences with these products, from sharing the results of employee engagement surveys with all employees to helping managers monitor the health of their teams to helping program owners gauge the effectiveness of their interventions to helping executives set strategy to responding to legal suits to participating in cross-company academic research.

For many of the reasons discussed in previous sections, reporting is rarely as straightforward as it appears. In most cases, some level of data management will be required, even if that is invisible to the end user of a system. Decisions must be made about relevant audience and time period, for example, and frequently multiple variables must be combined, such as identifying managers of managers, or managers with less than 1 year of tenure. System upgrades or acquisitions mean that archived systems may need to be accessed, particularly for longitudinal studies. The data must be presented effectively. Decisions must be made about who can have access to which figures; this is especially relevant for performance management, diversity, or assessment data.

Exploratory Data Analysis

EDA involves the manipulation and summarization of data for the purposes of better understanding and exploring its patterns and structures, and usually involves calculating and visualizing common univariate and bivariate statistical descriptors, such as means and correlations (e.g., Hoaglin, Mosteller & Tukey, 1983; Tukey, 1977). This can be done for a number of purposes. Often, the data is considered to be of interest in the measurement of a certain construct of interest, and analysis is conducted to determine if the data has sufficient statistical properties to be a reasonable representation of such a construct. For example, the aggregated sentiment of anonymous survey comments might be considered a proxy for general organizational sentiment, but exploratory data analysis may determine that the comment fields were used mostly for the expression of negative sentiment and therefore is not a good measure of the full range of sentiment in the organization.

EDA can also be purely for the purpose of better understanding new sources of data that have become available. Techniques can be used to understand the level of completeness, the reliability, the separability, and many other factors which can result in an overall judgment about how useful the data source is overall.

EDA is a common precursor to modeling. It can establish prima facie relationships between variables and measures that can inform modeling efforts, contributing to safe dimensionality reduction and simplification of modeling efforts. For example, missing data can be identified for potential imputation methods in predictive models or collinear variables can be identified that can inform the approach or conclusions of inferential models.

Modeling

Modeling is a fundamental quantitative method for understanding organizational outcomes, their possible causes, and their likely future states. It involves the application of parametric or nonparametric mathematical relationships to data in order to determine if any of these relationships can be considered an acceptable representation of reality. In most cases, the purpose is to describe or infer how certain constructs influence or do not influence an outcome of interest (inferential or explanatory modeling). In a smaller but increasing number of cases, the purpose is to apply the mathematical relationship to future data in order to make direct predictions of an outcome for the purposes of action or planning (predictive modeling).

Inferential modeling involves the use of statistical techniques such as multiple regression and hypothesis testing to estimate the nature of how constructs influence an outcome. This can involve proving or disproving that certain constructs have a meaningful relationship with an outcome, estimating the size of the effect of each construct on the outcome, and determining how much of the outcome is explained by the constructs being studied. These insights are generated in order to inform strategy or action in the future. For example, the relationship between engagement survey responses and future attrition, if well understood, can be used to inform stakeholders about the aspects of employee experience that are most important in retaining them. Datasets do not need to be very large in order to be used for inferential modeling. It is entirely possible that inferential insights are visible in datasets as small as a few hundred observations (McNulty, 2021)

Predictive modeling uses a wide range of techniques or algorithms to try to use currently available data to generate as accurate as possible a prediction of future outcome metrics. In organizational settings, for example, it can be valuable to try to predict attrition rates in a specific future period based on internal factors, such as current employee sentiment and performance, and external factors, such as projected economic growth and competition. If an accurate enough model can be generated, it can provide estimated predictions which can feed into various operational planning processes with the aim of improved effectiveness. The most accurate techniques used in predictive modeling – often involving nested trees of probabilities, multidimensional linear algebra, or multilevel neural networks – are often highly complex in nature and not designed to *explain* what influences an outcome in an easily understandable or intuitive way. This can be problematic in generating trust in these models among stakeholders – especially where acting on their output can have a real effect on people's work and lives. Furthermore, accurate prediction usually requires a large number of observations as well as reliable data that is not too sparse, rendering it unattainable for many small to medium-sized organizations. For this reason, predictive modeling is not as commonly used in a Human Resources context compared to inferential modeling but its use is growing particularly among larger institutions.

Experimenting

The "gold standard" for causal analysis is a true experiment. In some cases, for example, looking for bias in resume reviews or interviews, prospective experiments can be designed, launched, and analyzed relatively quickly. In other cases, clever experiments can look backward in time for retrospective quasi-experiments (e.g., Shadish, Cook & Campbell, 2002; Cook & Campbell, 1979), for example, multiple cohorts through different versions of a leadership development program, or employees whose managers did or did not complete a particular management training course. In some organizations, separate locations, such as individual stores within a franchise operation or separate manufacturing sites building the same products, can form nicely controlled units where interventions can be compared both across sites and within the same sites over time.

In most organizations, prospective experimenting is still a practice and discipline that is considered the preserve of the academic. Although a small but increasing number of teams with academically minded principles are now being set up within business enterprises, it remains unusual for those enterprises to approve any experiments that would substantially disrupt the day-to-day work of employees or require time out from their normal duties. Further, organizations typically wish to gain the advantages from a new strategy as quickly as possible; it is inefficient and perhaps even unethical to withhold a beneficial intervention from some groups in the name of experimentation. The most common forms of prospective experiments currently seen in organizations tend to be lower-risk activities, such as participation in voluntary testing of new survey items or user research.

Prescribing

Prescribing involves the use of analytic outputs to drive a recommendation and action. In many cases, prescribing is not an analytic task but a strategic one, where actions are decided by stakeholders on the basis of both the analytic results and broader contextual considerations. However, instances of the application of artificial intelligence to HR through automated recommendations and actions are growing. The motivation of this automation is primarily to save the time of decision makers and administrators on activities that are considered subcritical and to speed up the time to action on important operational decisions.

Automation in this context usually takes one of two forms. Firstly, it can be the result of a set of rules or a recommendation system that has been generated based on prior inferential analytics. For example, a recommendation can be automatically generated for an action to be taken by a Human Resource professional based on the occurrence of certain words in an email from an employee, or the employee can receive an automated response from a system with a suggested answer to their question based on the words it contained.

Secondly, the automation can be the result of a direct calculation or prediction by a model or algorithm. For example, the data on a job application could be sent to an algorithmic model which could generate a recommendation on how the application could be routed based on its similarity to prior applications received. The trick here of course is ensuring that the treatment of prior applications was free from bias.

The appropriate use of automation and algorithmic methods in a Human Resource context is the subject of fierce debate. Concerns about algorithmic bias and fair treatment render the blind and inconsiderate use of these technologies a risky move for organizations and employers. The risk of adverse impact from these technologies depends on many factors including the context in which they are used, the process through which the recommendation is generated and the nature of the decision-making process in which the output is considered.

Influencing with Data

Business Acumen

While many organizational scholars and people analytics practitioners are deep experts in human processes at work, they may be less facile with the details of how businesses in general, and the business they are currently supporting, works. Understanding core operations, such as finance, operations, product, and sales, as well as the specific organization's key strategies and challenges, helps practitioners design inquiries and research projects that will advance the organization's objectives. Being aware of the organizational culture, its values and constraints can empower practitioners with better judgment about the types of research and the modes of influence that have the greatest likelihood of success.

All of these elements of knowledge and experience represent what is commonly termed as "business acumen" and much of this equation is unique to each organization. Therefore, practitioners are only likely to gain it through immersion in their environment and curiosity about the broader context of their work. Equally, organizations should have reasonable expectations on how quickly a people analytics practitioner can generate impact in a new position and provide the relevant support in enabling them to have an impact. Not only is this business acumen essential to formulating compelling and relevant questions but it is also necessary for designing and effectively implementing strategies that are feasible and effective within that specific organization at that point in time.

Understanding how a specific organization competes in the market is important to identify the people strategies and interventions that will matter most to the organization's success. For example, diagnosing what specifically is meant by the nearly universal claim that "We have the best team in the world!" is important to effectively prioritizing useful research projects, as well as to appropriately accounting for context in designing and analyzing studies. The theoretical "best team" might mean hiring exclusively from the top 1% of talent and providing enormous freedom as a means of nurturing innovation. It might refer to extraordinary levels of efficiency and very low defects, through highly consistent processes, where the individual actor is less important than the processes that actor is executing. It might refer to a nurturing environment where those who may be unemployable in conventional organizations due to legal or other troubles have the opportunity to gain skills and self-confidence and where success is measured less in revenue or shrinkage and more in recidivism rate or the ability to independently secure housing and transition to other employment. Each of those definitions of "success" might lead a researcher to explore different approaches to selection, performance appraisal, and management development, each being fitted to the circumstances of their mission and charter. Attempting to compare research on those programs across such different organizations would require at the minimum a carefully controlled design and potentially may introduce sufficient error to entirely obscure interesting results.

Business acumen is critical for helping practitioners and researchers identify problems that will make a difference to the businesses they serve, in judging the appropriate research and actions that will have the greatest chance of success, and in determining the organizational support needed to ensure successful resourcing and implementation. Practitioners can flounder if their approach is too intellectually or academically driven and not focused enough on the practical objectives and constraints of the organization in which they are working. Regular consultation with stakeholders as well as strong user research principles is critical in designing projects and solutions. Timelines need to be rapid enough to maintain momentum, and project delivery may need to align to other internal processes that are either complementary or need to be retired as the new work is launched. Agility in adjusting objectives or approach is increasingly critical given the rapidly changing nature of today's workplace.

Consulting and Translation

Too often, excellent research and important insight do not result in thoughtful action within an organization. Similarly, large bodies of research may amass without clear synthesis into a coherent theme. Tying data insights to organizational action is a critical, but often neglected, part of data work. This consulting and translation function is less about innovative research methods and more about understanding and influencing organizational leaders and relevant business processes.

Often, the first step is to synthesize a business problem, research findings, and solution proposal into a single coherent statement or document. This requires a different skillset, more grounded in influence and application than academic research writing and is often an area where stakeholders become frustrated with researchers.

Translating results into action is sometimes complicated by practical and ethical considerations. For example, a common early project among internal analytics teams is identifying attrition risk. After all, loss aversion (Kahneman & Tversky, 1979) makes attrition inherently painful, and replacing the staff lost through attrition is expensive (Cascio, Boudreau & Fink, 2019). However, while many vendors and internal practitioners tout their ability to accurately predict who might leave, making use of that information creates multiple challenges.

Where using the information in aggregate to inform recruiting needs may be useful without creating harm to the individuals identified, the more targeted interventions often suggested entailing more risk. For example, proactively approaching select individuals with strategies designed to retain them, such as promotions or bonuses (e.g., Sullivan, 2014), may not only backfire through increasing attrition risk later they may also create bad patterns by rewarding counterproductive behaviors like disengaging, or they may create or exacerbate equity problems if some demographic groups are more frequently identified as attrition risks than others. Thus, an interesting and repeatable finding might not have much practical utility, if its use creates more harm than good.

Findings developed under controlled scientific conditions often do not translate effectively to organizational implementation (Kuncel et al., 2013). Across a variety of organizational processes, findings were consistent that validity was much lower once an intervention was fully implemented than was demonstrated when features were examined individually. For example, a new selection test may be implemented as part of candidate screening to identify proficiency with an emerging area necessary for the organization to compete effectively. However, the gains in identifying that candidate pool with novel skills can be undone at the interview stage if that stage has not also been updated with new questions, new interviewer training and possibly a different bench of interviewers familiar with the new skills, thus eroding the impact of the improved test.

Another practical consideration is whether employees are willing and able to effectively participate, or whether an organization is willing to ask. For example, academics may recommend extensive pilot testing and lengthy, robust measures as a means to ensure healthy reliability and validity (e.g., Ingels, Keeton & Spitzmueller, 2020). Organizations may deem such cumbersome tools unacceptable, or employees may decline to participate. Similarly, managers and HR professionals are frequently stretched and may lack the time or skills to effectively implement or manage yet another process. While each individual item may be quite manageable, in aggregate the load on people managers and on HR professionals can become quite high if new demands on them are not replacing existing processes in a way that reduces the overall burden rather than increasing it. Considering and managing the demand on users of the various interventions and processes is an important part of effective implementation.

Finally, independently identified processes, tools, and models often proliferate across organizations in ways that sew confusion and dampen the effectiveness of each component part. Organizations may have multiple explicit or implicit models of employee engagement, manager effectiveness, team cohesion rubrics, required competencies, leadership models, cultural priorities, performance management standards, behavioral principles, and organizational values. Each one may seem clear and compelling in the training class that introduces it but may run into confusion with other models in the system when an employee tries to figure out which one applies when. This is exacerbated when the various models and frameworks don't align or even contradict. For example, manager may be told to be empathetic and listen to the experiences of their employees so they can help everyone live up to their full potential in one training class, then receive messaging about the importance of integrity as a manager capability, and then a few weeks later be required to apply a forced distribution to their team as part of an annual calibration process, labeling some employees with unsatisfactory performance, even when they do not believe that's a true and fair reflection of performance. While researchers and program owners often only have to think about the impacts of a single process, employees, managers, and HR professionals typically exist in the intersection of several at once. Taking the time to inventory the models and frameworks in use within an organization and adapting processes to resolve conflicts can help organizations spend less time wrestling with these sorts of disconnects and more time fulfilling their core organizational missions.

Language, Purpose, and Intent

One of the most foundational challenges in ensuring the impact of analytic work is the technical language barrier, which can result in misaligned ideas around the purpose and intent of the work between different parties. Stakeholders can often describe their intent in ways that do not accurately reflect their true need, and equally, technical analytics professionals can understand their requirements too literally. A typical example is when stakeholders express interest in finding out about factors that "predict" an outcome, when in fact they are not interested in making predictions but only in knowing explanatory or causal factors. This language can result in technical professionals attacking the problem using suboptimal tools given the true interests of the stakeholders. A level of translation and interpretation is often required in ensuring that the true objectives of the stakeholders are well understood. Similarly, and reciprocally, without appropriate translation, the language used by technical analytics professionals can easily overwhelm laypeople and result in disengagement from the work due to perceived complexity.

Managing Fact Versus Intuition

Sometimes data and analysis will not be welcomed, even by those who claim to be data driven. The insights may disrupt power structures, or contradict beliefs, statements, or intuitions to which stakeholders are wedded. The go-to move in many of these cases is to ask for more or different data. Sometimes this is genuine and helpful feedback, as the original analysis may have missed an important nuance. Frequently, however, it's the organizational equivalent of a youngster asking for one more story at bedtime.

Peter Block's classic text (2011) on consulting delves deeply into resistance, and how to identify and address it. Without the ability to identify and manage this dynamic, analytics professionals and their research partners can end up in a lengthy and demotivating iterations with ever-diminishing returns. Research on organizational processes such as selection may be especially prone to resistance, in part due to stakeholders' belief in the unique value of their own expertise (e.g., Highhouse, 2008). Where status and power are accorded due to perceptions of a unique savvy in, say, identifying scarce skills, it is very difficult to convince people to yield that status and power. One way to avoid this problem is active engagement with key stakeholders early in the process. Active, frequent stakeholder engagement generally improves the overall quality of the final product as well as enrolling would-be resisters as active members of the project team, thus putting them in the role of an advocate rather than objector. While it is often tempting to work toward a big reveal, active, ongoing partnership generally yields better outcomes.

Change and Stakeholder Management with Data

For those steeped in data, it may seem self-evident that findings should be acted upon. The reality of organizational life is that stakeholders must be brought along through the research project. The most successful projects tend to consider change management and stakeholder management from the outset, asking not only "what is happening" but "how can we incorporate these findings into the way we do business?" It is still the case in many organizations that people analytics groups are set up in an "ivory tower" way that discourages collaborative problem solving in favor of solutions driven primarily by centralized expertise.

Many regard change management as little more than the communications plan announcing some new thing. This is an error. Effective change management is a systematic approach to ensuring effective change within a group. Kotter (2012) describes an 8-step process that includes steps often overlooked by organizational researchers and practitioners, such as building a guiding coalition and enabling action by removing barriers.

Working Across Organizations

A great many of the fundamental questions of human behavior and success in the context of organizational life require looking across organizations to thoroughly test hypotheses and ensure that results are not esoteric to a particular context. Several trends conspire against this, however. A trend to jealously guarding employees' time can make it more difficult to launch research without a clear and immediate value proposition back to each participating organization. A tremendous flowering in the HR industry, and in particular the HR Technology industry, means a balkanized ecosystem where the component parts may not align across organizations. An evolving approach to employee privacy means that simply removing names from a data file is no longer considered sufficient anonymization.

Researchers, then, are faced with some novel challenges and opportunities. Researchers may need to invest more in consulting skills to identify mutually beneficial opportunities or to take a Trojan Horse approach to research, where the research is sort of "snuck in" as part of an intervention, rather than as a standalone bit of research.

Storytelling and Visualization

To garner the organizational support needed to prioritize and successfully implement analytic initiatives, stakeholders must clearly see the thread from concept through to impact. The logic of the work needs to be clearly laid out, the evidence needs to be understandable and compelling and the relevance to broader organizational goals needs to be clear and undeniable.

Building a compelling narrative or a "story" around an analytics initiative is critical but requires deft touch in striking the right balance to ensure it is a true and honest reflection of the reality that is not overly influenced by "groupthink" or misdirected enthusiasm. There is a role here for good old-fashioned research skills in conducting literature reviews, statistical testing, and other principles that are strongly relied upon in an academic context.

In fast-moving nonacademic environments, it is also critical to convey narratives succinctly and memorably, acknowledging constraints in time and in the share of mind among decision makers and stakeholders. Simply hewing to the default presentation software format of bulleted hierarchy is a poor method of conveying meaning and relationships among a set of ideas and outcomes (Tufte, 2006). Effective use of attributes like the use of white space and color, avoiding "walls of text," and incorporating as well as well-chosen visuals, are important in effectively conveying messages to organizational audiences.

Data visualization is one of the most powerful tools we have for effectively and efficiently conveying meaning. Visualization has moved far beyond simple line charts and histograms and can effectively convey patterns that are difficult to detect in numerical tables (e.g., Sinar, 2020). Further, particularly in cases where large volumes of data render statistical significance less important, visualization can help stakeholders quickly and easily comprehend larger patterns and relative significance of different features of a problem.

Data visualization is much more than simply making results visually appealing. Well-constructed visualizations will use features like position, hue, shape, texture, and volume, among others to convey complex relationships or attributes efficiently and accurately (Tufte, 2020). Recent advancements allow the animation to demonstrate change in a way that was previously very challenging to do. As data work in organizations has to conform to the norms of the organization rather than the norms of academic journals, effective visualization is important in engaging with organizational stakeholders.

Summary

The recent explosion of data and data-related technology presents a unique opportunity for data-driven advancements in Human Resources. The possibilities of having a genuinely data-driven approach to people management are much more real today than they were even a few years ago, and we are no longer constrained to structured numeric formats when we try to interpret meaning from the data around us. Improved systems and data storage has massively reduced the time taken to conduct quantitative research. The availability of a plethora of open source and commercial analytics tools allows access to models and algorithms which were once the preserve of the specialized academic, and which can often be run in a matter of seconds. Data visualization and reporting options now allow us to engage and inform stakeholders in new, effective, and efficient ways and, with automation technologies offering us the possibility to reproduce regular reporting analytics at scale with minimal human effort.

To take full advantage of this opportunity, practitioners need to be aware of the challenges of working in a data-driven environment. They will need a patient and careful approach to overcoming these challenges and will need to carefully balance considerations of expediency against the risk of ineffective or inaccurate analytics, or breaches of important policy or regulation around security, privacy, or confidentiality. Successful HR analytics leaders of the future will need to be able to simultaneously build the skills of their teams to address the most critical organizational questions, communicate effectively with their stakeholders, improve foundational data quality and metric definitions, and oversee an operation that complies with all the relevant organizational and regulatory requirements.

References

Argyris, C. (1960). *Understanding organizational behavior*. Homewood, IL: Dorsey.

Block, P. (2011). *Flawless Consulting: A Guide to Getting Your Expertise Used* (3rd ed). Jossey-Bass.

Campbell, J. P., & Wiernik, B. (2015). The modeling and assessment of performance at work. *Annual Review of Organizational Psychology and Organizational Behavior, 2*, 47–74.

Campion, M. A., Fink, A. A., Ruggeberg, B. J., Carr, L. Phillips, G. M., & Odman, R. B. (2011). Doing competencies well: Best practices in competency modeling. *Personnel Psychology, 64* (1), 225–262.

Cascio, W. F., Boudreau, J. B., & Fink, A. A. (2019). *Investing in People: Financial Impact of Human Resource Initiatives* (3rd ed). Alexandria, Virginia: Society for Human Resources Management.

Chakrabarti, M., & McCune E. (2020). Is the engagement survey the only way? Alternative sources for employee sensing. In Macey, W. H., & Fink, A. A. (Eds), *Employee Surveys and Sensing: Driving Organizational Culture and Performance* (pp. 219–235). New York, NY: Oxford University Press.

Cook, T. D., & Campbell, D. T. (1979). *Quasi-Experimentation: Design and Analysis Issues for Field Settings*. Chicago: Rand McNally.

Devlin, J., Chang, M.-W., Lee, K., & Toutanova, K. (2019). *BERT: Pre-training of Deep Bidirectional Transformers for Language Understanding*. Accessed April 18, 2021. https://arxiv.org/pdf/1810.04805v2.pdf

Dutta, S., & O'Rourke, E. M. (2020). Open-ended questions: The role of natural language processing and text analytics. In Macey, W. H. & Fink, A. A. (Eds), *Employee Surveys and Sensing: Driving Organizational Culture and Performance* (pp. 202–218). New York, NY: Oxford University Press.

Fink, A. A., & Sturman, M. C. (2017). HR metrics and talent analytics. In Collings, D., Mellahi, K., & Cascio, W. (Eds), *The Oxford Handbook of Talent Management* (pp. 375–396). New York: Oxford University Press. https://doi.org/10.1093/oxfordhb/9780198758273.013.25

Garman, A. N., Standish, M. P., & Kim, D. H. (2018). Enhancing efficiency, reliability, and rigor in competency model analysis using natural language processing. *The Journal of Competency-Based Education, 3*(3), e01164. https://doi.org/10.1002/cbe2.1164

Highhouse, S. (2008). Stubborn reliance on intuition and subjectivity in employee selection. *Industrial and Organizational Psychology, 1*(3), 333–342.

Hoaglin, D. C., Mosteller, F., & Tukey, J. W. (1983). *Understanding Robust and Exploratory Data Analysis*. New York: Wiley.

Ingels, C., Keeton, K. & Spitzmueller, C. (2020). Writing Organizational Survey Items that Predict What Matters in Organizations. In Macey, W. H., & Fink, A. A. (Eds), *Employee Surveys and Sensing: Driving Organizational Culture and Performance* (pp. 186–201). New York, NY: Oxford University Press.

Kotter, J. P. (2012). *Leading Change*. Cambridge, MA: Harvard Business School Press.

Kuncel, N., Klieger, D., Connelly, B., & Ones, D. (2013). Mechanical versus clinical data combination in selection and admissions decisions: A meta-analysis. *Journal of Applied Psychology, 98*. https://doi.org/10.1037/a0034156

Leek, J. T., & Peng, R. D. (2015). What is the question? *Science, 20*(6228), 1314–1315. https://doi.org/10.1126/science.aaa6146

Kahneman, D., & Tversky, A. (1979). Prospect theory: An analysis of decision under risk. *Econometrica, 47*(2), 263–291. https://doi.org/10.2307/1914185

Kozlowski, S. W. J., Chen, G., & Salas, E. (2017). One hundred years of the *Journal of Applied Psychology*: Background, evolution, and scientific trends. *Journal of Applied Psychology, 102*(3), 237–253. https://doi.org/10.1037/2017-06966-001

McNulty, K. (2021). *Handbook of Regression Modeling in People Analytics*. Chapman & Hall/CRC.

Sinar, E. (2020). Data visualization. In Macey, W. H., & Fink, A. A. (Eds), *Employee Surveys and Sensing: Driving organizational Culture and Performance* (pp. 306–323). New York, NY: Oxford University Press.

Shadish, W. R., Cook, T. D., & Campbell, D. T. (2002). *Experimental and Quasi-Experimental Designs for Generalized Causal Inference*. Boston: Houghton Mifflin.

Stanton, J. M. (2000). Reactions to employee performance monitoring: Framework, review, and research directions. *Human Performance, 13*, 85–113.

Sullivan, J. (2014). *What's Wrong With Retention Bonuses? Pretty Much Everything*. Accessed April 18, 2021. https://www.ere.net/whats-wrong-with-retention-bonuses-pretty-much-everything/

Tufte, E. R. (2006). *The Cognitive Style of PowerPoint: Pitching Out Corrupts Within* (2nd ed). Cheshire, CT: Graphics Press LLC.

Tufte, E. (2020). *Seeing with Fresh Eyes: Meaning, Space, Data, Truth*. Cheshire, CT: Graphics Press.

Tukey, J. W. (1977). *Exploratory Data Analysis*. Reading, MA: Addison-Wesley.

Turnage, A. K., & Goodboy, A. K. (2016). E-mail and face-to-face organizational dissent as a function of leader-member exchange status. *International Journal of Business Communication, 53*(3), 271–285. https://doi.org/10.1177/2329488414525456

Wells, D. L., Moorman, R. H., & Werner, J. M. (2007). The impact of the perceived purpose of electronic performance monitoring on an array of attitudinal variables. *Human Resource Development Quarterly, 18*(1), 121–138. https://doi.org/10.1002/hrdq.1194

PART 2
Methods

5

EVALUATING DATA

*Louis Hickman, Q. Chelsea Song,
and Sang Eun Woo*

How should one evaluate the validity and meaning of new types of data? Are the currently available methods and models for evaluating reliability and construct validity adequate? What questions need to be answered in order to develop methods for evaluating new types of data? How does one handle the potential conflict between the volume and novelty of available data versus the quality and relevance of such data? These are the key questions we will attempt to answer in this chapter.

Evaluating data is closely connected to data *usage*: The ultimate focus is on the former, but the latter must be taken into account to address the former. Data themselves are neither good nor bad, as it can only be evaluated against a clearly defined purpose – *what* is the data good for? Only when you have a clear purpose for the data (e.g., "the organization-wide employee attitude survey data shall inform us about how satisfied and motivated our employees are") can it be evaluated (SIOP, 2018). In the current chapter, we discuss methods of data evaluation in the context of how data is used for *psychological measurement*. In other words, one must identify (either *a priori* or *post hoc*) the psychological constructs that are being captured in new types of data to be able to assess the psychometric quality of such data. In a traditional case of psychological measurement, such construct identification normally occurs in the beginning of the process. However, we will also discuss some applications in which data is used primarily for prediction of particular outcomes rather than measurement of specific constructs (and thus construct identification does not happen until after the fact, if ever). With this in mind, consider the following phrases that signify three distinctive ways in which one may approach data evaluation.

"Garbage In, Garbage Out"

DOI: 10.4324/9781003015000-7

This phrase means that incorrect or poor quality input will always produce faulty output. It represents a traditional perspective on psychological measurement, where one takes a theory-driven, hypothetico-deductive approach in clearly defining constructs of interest *a priori*, and then creates and refines elements of the measurement tool accordingly. Throughout the process of developing a measure, each indicator (or item) is designed, evaluated, and selected for a specific construct. In addition to this, we describe below two additional (and alternative) concepts of psychological measurement relevant to new forms of data.

"Sewage In, Drinkable Water Out"

To get from sewage to drinkable water, one must inject a certain chemical formula and conduct a rigorous cleaning process before the water is usable for drinking. In a similar fashion, one can start with messy and unstructured data that is not intentionally designed to capture a psychological construct and contain a lot of construct-irrelevant information. The data will then go through a computational (e.g., supervised machine learning[1]) process of cleaning and refinement so that the resulting data and associated algorithms become suitable for approximating an existing measure of the target construct. This approach can still be characterized as theory-bound, or "construct-driven," where the goal is to arrive at a clear destination (i.e., we must come up with a solid measure of "Construct A" from these inputs).

"Leftover In, Casserole Out"

This expression could be used to describe a largely or completely data-driven approach (e.g., dustbowl empiricism), where the goal is to either "see what hangs together in the data" or "see if a combination of X_1 through X_{100} predicts Y," and then to make sense out of the patterns observed from the data. The initial choice of ingredients (X_k variables) is dictated by what is available to the cook (analyst), who may decide to leave out certain ingredients that they know to be irrelevant or has poor quality in light of the analyst's purpose. In this scenario, the analyst is not trying to measure a specific psychological construct; instead, the goal is to maximize one's ability to predict a practically important outcome from the data. Nonetheless, once you have a casserole (model) that people like to eat (or use; "practical utility"), you can name the dish based on what is in it ("stress and burnout") and/or for what occasion(s) it is good for (e.g., "turnover propensity index").

We will come back to these metaphorical concepts at the end of this chapter to suggest different ways in which data's psychometric value may be evaluated. For now, we stress that, regardless of which specific approach one may choose to adopt, the process of "data evaluation" requires evaluating the content and structure of data themselves as well as the way data is utilized (e.g., analyzed and interpreted) in light of a specific target psychological construct. In the following sections, we will first discuss various sources of (new and emerging) data and their relevance to constructs or phenomena of interest (Part 1); review the general psychometric principles used to evaluate data, such as reliability and validity (Part 2); and discuss various forms of data evaluation that vary in the degree in which data and theory are involved (Part 3). In doing so, we will revisit the aforementioned three concepts and call for more diversified ways in which new types of data are evaluated and harnessed for both scientific and practical utility.

Part 1: Linking New Data Sources to Psychological Constructs

Data can be used to describe individual and collective behaviors, affects, and cognitions, as well as work environment characteristics. Depending on the volume, breadth, and complexity of data available, the observation (or description) can be done in a much more fine-tuned and dynamic way than what was possible just a decade ago. In this section, we identify seven major sources of newer, technology-driven data that are particularly relevant to organizational and psychological science (i.e., social media, internet activities, wearable sensors, smartphones, network cameras, targeted audiovisual records, electronic personnel records), and discuss how they can inform our ability to observe and describe psychological constructs and/or workplace phenomena. These data sources are relevant to organizational psychologists because they can potentially generate useful information to describe psychological and/or organizational phenomena of interest. To this end, we review the existing literature on the linkage between the data sources and key psychological constructs that are already established in organizational psychology research. Table 5.1 summarizes key characteristics of each of the seven data sources, and Table 5.2 presents an overview of relevant constructs, potential opportunities, and challenges associated with each data source.

Social Media

Social media can be defined as web-based platforms that allow individuals to "(1) construct a public or semi-public profile within a bounded system, (2) articulate a list of other users with whom they share a connection, and (3) view and traverse their list of connections and those made by others within the system" (Boyd & Ellison, 2007, p. 211). Some of the most popular social media platforms as of year 2021 include Facebook, Twitter, YouTube, and Instagram. These social media platforms generate and collect a variety of data types, such as text posts, endorsement patterns (e.g., Facebook likes), and social connection (e.g., Twitter follows vs. followed by's). Previous research has utilized social media data to measure a variety of psychological constructs, including personality (Gosling et al., 2011; Kosinski et al., 2013), attitudinal and affective constructs (e.g., stress,

TABLE 5.1 Key characteristics of the seven major data sources

Data source	Data characteristics							
	Allow targeted measures	Individual-level	Location	Time	Active user engagement	Interactive	Connection with others	Momentary assessment
Social media		X	X	X	X	X	X	X
Internet activities			X	X				X
Wearable sensors		X	X	X			X	X
Smartphone	X	X	X	X	X	X		X
Network camera			X	X	X	X		X
Targeted audiovisual records	X	X					X	
Electronic personnel records		X		X			X	X

Note: "Allow targeted measures": allows actively soliciting content-specific responses (e.g., self-reported personality items), contributing to content validity. "Individual-level": data could be linked to individuals, allowing for individual-level analysis (in addition to group-level analysis). "Location": capture physical location and proximity, allow analysis of geography (e.g., country) and context (e.g., work vs. home). "Time": allow momentary ecological analysis. "User engagement": active user engagement requires users actively generating data (e.g., user posts a tweet); on the contrary, passive user engagement does not require user input (e.g., unobtrusive collection of motion data by network cameras). Data sources that require active user engagement is susceptive to impression management. "Interactive": user receives real-time feedback, potentially intervening and influencing user behavior. "Connection with others": captures association with other users (e.g., through profile linkage, proximity with others), allowing for examination of interpersonal relations and group structures. "Momentary assessment": allow data collection of daily events as they unfold over time, contributing to the generalizability of findings.

TABLE 5.2 A summary of relevant constructs, potential opportunities, and challenges associated with the major seven data sources

Data source	Construct	Example	Potential opportunity	Challenge
Social media	• Personality • Attitudes and affects • Interpersonal relationships	Kosinski et al. (2013) Li et al. (2020) Manago et al. (2012)	• Behavioral intentions	• Social desirability bias • Sample only represent active social media users
Internet activities	Group-level • Emotions • Mental/physical health • Behavioral intentions	Ford et al. (2018) Ayers et al. (2013) Kalichman and Kegler (2015)	• Organizational culture	• Construct contamination • Sample only represent web users
Wearable sensors	• Interpersonal relationships • Team dynamics • Stress	Kozlowski et al. (2015) Chaffin et al. (2017) Can et al. (2019) Kyriakou et al. (2019)	• Skills and abilities • Attitudes • Personality	• Construct contamination
Smartphone	• Stress • Depression	Kido et al. (2016) Hung (2016)	• Organizational culture • Interpersonal relationships	• Social desirability bias?
Network camera	• Emotion • Personality traits • Consumer behavior	Urizar et al. (2017) Tay et al. (2017)	• Team dynamic	• Construct contamination
Targeted audiovisual records	• Personality • Cognitive ability	Hickman et al. (2021)	• Emotional intelligence	• External validity • Social desirability bias
Electronic personnel records	• Social network • Job performance	Nurek and Michalski (2020) Speer (2020)	• Productivity • Personality	• Construct contamination

affect, mood, sentiment; e.g., Li et al., 2020), job satisfaction (Saha et al., 2021), interpersonal relationships (e.g., tie strength, communications patterns, network structures; e.g., Gilbert & Karahalios, 2009; Manago et al., 2012), and prosocial behavior (e.g., Nai et al., 2018).

One of the major advantages of social media as a data source for organizational psychology is that they can provide useful information to understand the structure and characteristics of one's social network. Connection among users is the founding block of social media platforms. These include Facebook friends and LinkedIn connections, follows and followed by's in Twitter, as well as interest groups, such as Facebook groups and Reddit communities. These connections provide valuable insights into the centrality and ties of a social network, information flow, and attitudes, preferences, and value orientations of individuals. Social media can also provide momentary behavioral traces of psychological constructs as it manifests in everyday life. For example, Facebook likes, Twitter posts, and YouTube livestreams capture individual's real-time reactions, expressions, and actions toward events taking place in different times of the day. In addition, social media data often involves self-expression through text posts, image sharing, video publication, providing insights into individual's attitude, behavior, and personality traits.

Despite its potentials, social media data also comes with a number of methodological challenges. For example, social media activities are often influenced by users' impression management, introducing social desirability bias. This is especially a concern when the data was used to measure attitudes, beliefs, and traits (e.g., extraversion) in situations where the desired response is clear to users. In addition, samples collected on social media only represent a subpopulation with stable internet accessibility and active social media users. Caution is needed when interpreting the results derived from social media data (e.g., public sentiments, political tendency).

Internet Activities

Internet activities are digital footprints that reflect user's online behavior, commonly captured in webpage search history, page views, clicks, time spent online, and location of online access (Ford, 2020). Internet activity data collected from online websites and search engines (e.g., Google Trends) provide important insights to wide-spread collective phenomena. These include group-level sentiment, subjective well-being (e.g., depression, anxiety; Ayers et al., 2013), and behavioral intentions (e.g., intention toward vaccination; Kalichman & Kegler, 2015). It could be further broken down by location (based on Internet Protocol address, IP), allowing closer examination of trends across different regions. Internet activities that are collected in the individual-level highlight behavioral patterns that could reflect or predict the user's mental states or behavioral intentions. For example, search history for information about job burnout or stress may suggest that the individual is suffering from mental issues and may be predictive of low performance at work in the near future.

Internet activity reflects group-level phenomenon: it captures wide-spread group-level trends that could be used to predict public attitudes and behavior in the near future. However, internet activity data is limited to capturing complex, high-level attitudes, thoughts, and traits of individuals (Woo et al., 2020). This is because the majority of internet activity data passively traces the online behavior of individuals but do not actively solicit individuals' responses (e.g., self-reports, reaction to certain text or images) that reflect attitudes, cognition, and behavioral tendencies. In addition, similar to social media, internet activity is limited to individuals with stable access to the World Wide Web and thus might not be a full representation of the population.

Wearable Sensors

Wearable sensors, such as fitness trackers, smart watches, and sociometric badges, are portable devices (often with Internet connectivity) that could measure and record a continuous stream of data on the user and their environmental context (Chaffin et al., 2017; Swan, 2012; Woo et al., 2020). They share similar advantages as smartphones (as discussed below); yet compared to smartphones, wearable sensors are especially capable of measuring physiological signals, which include blood pressures, heart-rate variability, and temperature. Because of this, wearable sensors are commonly adopted to measure stress and emotional states. For example, researchers utilized the skin conductance, heart-rate variability, and accelerometer signals captured from wearable sensors to assess stress (e.g., Can et al., 2019; Kyriakou et al., 2019). Compared to the traditional methods for stress detection (e.g., electroencephalography [EEG], electrocardiography [ECG]), wearable sensors are easily accessible devices that contribute to stress detection. They also provide real-time feedback to the users, allowing stress management and intervention.

Wearable sensors are also capable of recording behavioral and location data, such as proximity and time spent in a conversation, and are able to synchronize the information among multiple devices (Gravina et al., 2017). This information could be used to study interpersonal relationships and group-level social phenomena. As an example, how closely (proximity) two coworkers sit or stand from each for how long (duration) could inform relationships and interaction patterns among coworkers (Matusik et al., 2019). Wearable sensors have been used to study leadership emergence within groups, group problem-solving performance, and team process dynamics (Chaffin et al., 2017; Dong & Pentland, 2010; Kozlowski, 2015).

Wearable sensors provide a myriad of data, yet to guarantee measurement accuracy, it is important to establish a link between the data source and the construct of interest. For example, if two individuals spend a certain amount of time working in close proximity, does infrequent proximity with long duration or frequent proximity with short duration imply collaboration? If we were to measure team cohesion, what data need to be taken into account for comprehensive measurement? As wearable sensors provide rich data sources, it is even more important to establish accurate operationalization of a construct.

In addition, similar to internet activity data, wearable sensors are passive recordings of physiological and behavioral traces, and thus they are limited in exploring complex, high-level psychological constructs. To allow a more comprehensive analysis of an individual's traits and states, wearable sensors are often used in conjunction with smartphones and other data collection methods to obtain a comprehensive picture of one's high-level attributes as well as momentary states and behaviors.

Smartphones

Smartphones are ubiquitous, sensor-rich, and computationally-powered devices that can automatically collect multimedia data (e.g., text, audio, and video) capturing users' in-the-moment thoughts and behaviors. It could also host mobile assessments and surveys actively soliciting user responses (e.g., Harari et al., 2016). With smartphone data, researchers can triangulate behavioral data (e.g., social interactions, movement) with survey data (e.g., self-reported emotion) to capture a holistic account of one's psychological states. Smartphones are also widely used and increasingly integrated into people's everyday life, allowing them to continuously collect data in a seamless way. Due to these advantages, smartphones are often used for experience sampling studies, for instance, to measure daily variations in emotional states (Sandstrom et al., 2017) and interpersonal activities (Schmid Mast et al., 2015).

The communication capability of smartphones (e.g., text messages and phone calls) provides insights into social networks (Kobayashi et al., 2015), and some sensor capability allows for the measurement of physiological data. For example, smartphones could be used to measure stress through pulse frequency from fingers pressed against the camera lens (Kido et al., 2016). That being said, compared to wearable sensors, smartphones tend to offer less sensor capability and measurement accuracy and thus are often combined with wearable sensors for higher-quality physiological measurement. Wearable sensors provide continuous measurement of various physiological, behavioral, and location data, whereas smartphones, with their powerful computational capacity, software capabilities, and internet connectivity, analyze the data in real-time and allow active user inputs. Smartphone data is rich and versatile, capturing both behavioral traces and complex, high-level attitudes and cognition.

Network Cameras

Network camera data is gathered from stationary surveillance cameras placed in certain physical spaces and are connected to networks. They capture various surface-level appearances and behaviors of people in the space (e.g., facial expressions, body languages, gestures, movements, and locations), that can be used to measure emotion (e.g., collective emotions of crowds) through smiles (Hernandez et al., 2012), social interactions (Cocca et al., 2016), and behavioral contexts in which the behaviors are "enacted, facilitated, or constrained" (Tay et al., 2017, p. 17).

Network cameras capture patterns in individual, interpersonal, and group behaviors (Woo et al., 2020). The recent COVID-19 pandemic accelerated the use of public network cameras to assist in identifying and managing infections. For example, the governments of China and South Korea utilized facial recognition and thermal imaging to identify individuals with high temperatures and potential virus carriers (Chen et al., 2020; Sonn et al., 2020). In addition to pandemic control, public network cameras are also widely used to monitor behavioral patterns and predict future behaviors, such as identifying restlessness and other potentially suspicious body language to prevent theft and crime (e.g., Yamato et al., 2017).

That said, compared to other data sources (e.g., wearable sensors, smartphones), network camera is constrained to certain physical locations, and thus the behaviors captured are limited by context and environment. Analysis of network camera data requires careful examination of content validity and *a priori* decisions on the unit of analysis. In addition, to ensure measurement accuracy, considerations should be given to the choice of the time frame and the images to include or exclude (Woo et al., 2020).

Targeted Audiovisual Records

Targeted audiovisual records contain verbal, paraverbal, and nonverbal behaviors in a particular context, where behaviors are often elicited by certain stimuli related to constructs of interest (or target constructs). Common examples include job interview questions are often used in personnel selection to measure knowledge, skills, abilities, and personality. Targeted audio visual records (or video-recorded interviews) provide a rich collection of self-expressions focused on one or two target constructs and thus provide unique advantages in studying complex affect, cognition, and traits, including cognitive ability and personality traits (Hickman et al., 2021).

One concern with audiovisual data is that it could be contaminated by impression management/faking and anxiety. Individuals are often aware that their behaviors are being recorded, especially in high-stakes contexts such as personnel selection interview and performance appraisal, which could compromise the construct validity of the data.

Electronic Personnel Records

Electronic personnel records are workplace data routinely collected by organizations for human resource purposes. These records include job performance appraisals, absentee/attendance records, task log files, and communication trails within organizations (e.g., email, intranet direct messaging). It involves records of all employees within the organization or a team, allowing for a focused analysis of interpersonal dynamics as well as individual behaviors. For instance, email communications and task completion records could be used to study social network and collaboration within a workplace (Nurek & Michalski, 2020); performance appraisal narratives from supervisors could be used to study individual performance (Speer, 2020), as well as to compare across multiple employees in the organization, identifying factors influencing job performance.

Because electronic personnel records are often collected routinely, it captures workplace activities with less risk in social desirability bias. However, because electronic personnel records are often collected for administrative and management purposes and not for the purpose of measuring or studying a certain psychological construct (such as the case with targeted audiovisual records), similar to data from wearable sensors, internet activities, and network cameras, analysis of electronic personnel records requires extra care toward content and construct validity.

Part 2: General Principles of Psychometric Data Evaluation

This section discusses the applicability of traditional and emerging techniques for evaluating the psychometric properties of new data sources. These properties can describe the indicators themselves (e.g., the granular variables generated from organic data) or some combination of indicators that represents a construct (e.g., Big Five traits).

Reliability

Data used for psychological measurement must be reliable to be considered high quality. Reliability is concerned with the extent to which measurement scores contain random error (as opposed to systematic error, known as bias; SIOP, 2018). Reliability estimates, then, can be considered approximations of the amount of true score variance versus the amount of error variance. When considered this way, reliability sets an upper limit on validity because error cannot contribute to validity (per classical test theory; Lord et al., 1968). Traditionally, researchers have been concerned with the reliability of aggregate scores (e.g., the sum or average of multiple items) that represent latent constructs.

Traditional scale scores are generated by unit weighting (i.e., summing/ averaging) their items. Assuming that the k scale items have uncorrelated errors, the scale will contain $1/k$ of the average item's error variance (Cronbach, 1990). This suggests the importance of also attending to item-level psychometric properties because they are the *data* being *used* to measure some meaningful construct. Indeed, scale items sometimes exhibit reliability superior to their scales because the less reliable items in a scale may negatively affect the scale's reliability (McCrae, 2015). The properties of items are particularly relevant with new forms of data because fallible, single indicators are sometimes used to measure constructs. For example, when Bluetooth sensors are used to measure physical proximity, the estimates follow a Gaussian normal distribution around the true distance (Matusik et al., 2019). A single measurement, then, can contain large amount of error, yet taking repeated measurements during an interaction should generate estimates with uncorrelated errors that cancel out and provide an estimate close of the true value.

Generalizability theory (G-theory; Cronbach et al., 1972) is the predominant alternative to classical test theory and provides theoretical explanations of measurement reliability. G-theory is concerned with the contexts under which measurement scores generalize – such as across time, raters, items, conditions of measurement, and so on – in other words, G-theory recognizes that measures contain multiple, differentiable sources of error. An implication is that the classical test theory claim that reliability sets an upper limit on validity may not always be accurate because different estimates of reliability (e.g., internal consistency; test-retest; parallel forms) have distinct values and capture different elements of error.

Generally, reliability is estimated as scale-level internal consistency and, in particular, Cronbach's alpha (Cortina, 1993). Due to an overreliance on Cronbach's alpha (Cortina et al., 2020), alpha is sometimes used synonymously with reliability. Internal consistency concerns whether a measure generalizes across a universe of interchangeable items but ignores other sources of error. Scale development generally relies on factor analytic methods for item selection and elimination (Hinkin, 1998), and factor analytic methods are concerned only with scale internal consistency. Indeed, item selection and elimination during scale development often relies exclusively on internal consistency. However, Cronbach's alpha is one flawed estimate of one aspect of reliability. Alpha is flawed in that it is conflated with scale length (although similarly, intraclass correlations conflate reliability with the number of raters), and a scale with a large number of items will often produce a large alpha value, even if the items are not highly homogeneous[2]. Further, neither alpha nor any other estimate of internal consistency can be used for single item measures. Nor are estimates of internal consistency appropriate for empirically keyed scales (e.g., such as developed via supervised machine learning; Hickman et al., 2021) because empirically keyed scales are not designed to be internally consistent (Simms et al., 2005).

Cronbach's alpha assumes scale homogeneity or *unidimensionality*. When scales are not unidimensional, Cronbach's alpha underestimates internal consistency (Schmitt, 1996). Although unidimensionality and internal consistency is important, scale items that are too highly intercorrelated (i.e., too internally consistent) may be redundant and fail to capture all aspects of the focal construct (i.e., the measure is construct deficient). In other words, internal consistency reliability and construct validity can be in opposition, as increasing levels of internal consistency can actually attenuate correlations with other measures – a problem referred to as the attenuation paradox (Loevinger, 1954). This is a paradox because classical test theory assumes that unreliability attenuates correlations, yet high internal consistency reliability can also attenuate them. The attenuation paradox can be particularly problematic when developing short forms of scales because fewer items are available to capture all aspects of a construct (Clark & Watson, 2019), and short forms are increasingly common in modern organizational research (Cortina et al., 2020). Factor analytic techniques are used both to generate scales and their short forms – this will tend to narrow scale content, increase item redundancy/homogeneity, and reduce the amount of construct-relevant variance captured by the test, thereby changing the nature of the measured construct (Clark & Watson, 2019). Item heterogeneity, on the other hand, will tend to reduce internal consistency reliability but may increase other aspects of reliability (McCrae, 2015) as well as the breadth and validity of the measure (Clark & Watson, 2019). This perhaps helps to explain why low values of Cronbach's alpha may not seriously attenuate correlations (Schmitt, 1996) and why, when test-retest reliability is controlled for, internal consistency reliability estimates do not predict the validity of personality scales (McCrae et al., 2011).

We believe that, moving forward, test-retest reliability of both scales and individual items/indicators will be especially informative (e.g., McCrae, 2015). As long as the constructs we aim to measure are relatively stable over short time periods, their indicators (which are generally considered interchangeable) should also be relatively stable. Returning to the example of physical proximity captured via Bluetooth sensors, multiple measurements generated in a short period of time should converge to the true value because the random error in each individual measurement will tend to cancel out. The correlation among these many estimates can be considered a measure of test-retest reliability, because each estimate is from the same measure. Additionally, test-retest reliability appears to be more predictive of validity than internal consistency reliability (McCrae et al., 2011), at least partially because a scale's test-retest reliability also carries information about internal consistency *if* internal inconsistency indeed attenuates correlations between measures. Test-retest reliability measures are not only sensitive to internal consistency, but also to temporal stability in measures.

Our general recommendation for estimating reliability is to take a holistic approach and examine multiple aspects simultaneously, rather than being limited by one or two indices of reliability (a point echoed by Cortina et al., 2020). For example, inter-algorithm reliability recently emerged in the literature (Sajjadiani et al., 2019; Tay et al., 2020) and involves comparing the results gleaned from multiple algorithms during supervised machine learning (e.g., elastic net regression and random forest). Sajjadiani et al. (2019) compared the accuracy of models developed from multiple algorithms and found that they were similarly accurate, which increased their confidence that true score variance was being captured. More in line with traditional notions of reliability, one could correlate the scores from multiple supervised machine learning models to estimate the amount of construct-irrelevant variance (i.e., error) that is specific to the algorithm used during model training (Tay et al., 2020). This could be likened to differences in using dominance or ideal point modeling to generate scale scores – these two forms of scoring tend to be highly correlated, but in some instances they may not be. In particular, specific regions of the score distributions generated by these two methods may not be highly correlated – for example, Stark et al. (2006) found that the top 5% of distributions between dominance and ideal point model scores on selection tests were *negatively* correlated, which could cause different selection decisions to be made during top-down selection.

Overall, we implore researchers to *make G-theory great again*. G-theory advocates for accounting for multiple sources of error instead of using a single estimate of reliability to estimate error. Internal consistency reliability may not be appropriate (e.g., in the case of empirically keyed scales) or possible (e.g., in the case of single item scales or when evaluating the reliability of indicators), and it does not necessarily relate to validity (McCrae et al., 2011; Schmitt, 1996). Further, we suggest that reliability be investigated for both indicators and scale scores, because both can be informative.

Validity

In addition to being reliable, data should capture something theoretically substantive to be considered high quality. As made clear above, reliability does not guarantee this, since high internal consistency can be obtained by using multiple, redundant scale items that capture only a narrow aspect of a construct. Validity regards whether or not something theoretically substantive is captured and is a characteristic of the interpretation of test scores. Test scores can be interpreted either as indicating one's standing on some construct (e.g., Extraversion) or to predict something – for example, job performance. Adapting the definition of validity in the SIOP *Principles*, the validity of *data* regards the degree to which accumulated evidence and theory supports specific interpretations of scores from a measurement procedure – whether the goal is for the data to be indicative of a psychological construct and/or predictive of important workplace outcomes. Therefore, the validity of data (or a test) cannot be examined until a clear purpose behind the data collection and use is defined.

Validity today is considered a unitary concept to be ascertained by investigating the relevance of a measure's content, the measure's internal structure, external relations with other measures, and response processes (American Educational Research Association [AERA] et al., 2014; Cronbach & Meehl, 1955; Loevinger, 1957; Messick, 1995). For example, two measures should converge at least $r = .70$ to be confident that external relationships between the two measures and other variables will be relatively consistent (Carlson & Herdman, 2012). However, what makes for adequate convergence varies depending on the characteristics of the measures under investigation (Clark & Watson, 2019). For example, two self-reports of the same construct converging $r = .45$ is unlikely to be adequate, yet it may be adequate to evidence convergence between self- and other-ratings of a construct, in part because this latter comparison involves two different measurement methods, and each method may involve unique sources of variance. Additionally, convergent correlations should be larger than (and potentially significantly larger than) discriminant correlations (Clark & Watson, 2019).

In industrial-organizational psychology, predicting job performance is often considered the *sine qua non* of validation efforts. However, we believe that the increasing use of big data and supervised machine learning will increase the importance of other pieces of evidence to avoid capitalization on chance and being criticized for engaging in dustbowl empiricism (but for other perspectives on this issue, see Hansen, 1998). Using supervised machine learning to predict workplace outcomes runs the risk of capturing spurious relationships that exist without any causal relationship between the predictor and the outcome. Additionally, such predictive models can reinforce existing inequalities in the data because they will tend to inherit biases in the training data (Hickman et al., 2021). Even when these models are not given explicit demographic information, they will often use predictors that act as proxies for demographic information, allowing them to perpetuate and/or exacerbate outcome disparities (Barocas & Selbst, 2016). Such considerations are important with new data sources because it can be very easy to contaminate one's measure with construct-irrelevant variance.

Therefore, we call for research going beyond correlations with other variables (i.e., convergent-, discriminant-, and criterion-related validity evidence) when working with new forms of data. Special emphasis should be placed on three aspects of validity that are commonly overlooked in contemporary research: (1) response processes, (2) content relevance, and (3) the consequences of data use (e.g., bias and fairness). Response processes help shed light onto data validity by advancing our theoretical understanding of why various behaviors are engaged in and that understanding can enrich our interpretation of the resulting scale.

Further, understanding the causal relationships between the focal construct and behaviors used to assess it is a necessary part of the formulation of a measure (Tay et al., 2020). The psychological processes that explain how construct A causes behavior B should be explained. Borsboom et al. (2004) notion of validity is relevant here, as it emphasizes causality and focuses on the ontology (i.e., the truth regardless of observability) of concepts instead of the epistemological (i.e., the truth as observability) perspectives on validity and validation implicitly endorsed by the unitarian conception.

Content relevance is often assumed in traditional scales because it is a foundational part of the scale development process (Hinkin, 1998). However, with the increasing adoption of data-driven methods, content relevance is often subordinated to an ad hoc, postmortem analysis (e.g., Park et al., 2015). We echo Bleidorn and Hopwood's (2019) recommendation to inspect model content during supervised machine learning in order to differentiate between *theory-expected* and *theory-unexpected* content. This requires, first, a clear specification of the theory undergirding the construct-behavior response process. Further, these construct-behavior relationships should be examined across different populations and over time. Such content investigations help to ensure the consistency and replicability of the scale. Another option is to utilize the Brunswik (1956) lens model to explore cue validity. This involves checking whether cues related to the machine learning model scores are also empirically related to the focal construct, as well as investigating cues that were related to the focal construct but not the machine learning model scores (Tay et al., 2020).

The consequences of using new types of data are often only investigated after negative effects have been observed (e.g., Dastin, 2018). Incorporating bias and fairness considerations into the scale development and validation process should be beneficial for two reasons. First, the likelihood that unfair and/or biased measures will become widely adopted for assessment should be reduced. Second, methods for mitigating unfairness and/or measurement bias can be investigated and applied prior to the adoption of the measure. Applying methods that industrial-organizational psychologists are already familiar with (e.g., checking mean-level differences and for differential prediction and validity) will likely be informative in this regard.

Finally, the generalizability of validity evidence is important as well (and, in some regards, is related to G-theory). Echoing our point regarding content relevance, validity evidence should be investigated across multiple time points and populations (Bleidorn & Hopwood, 2019; Tay et al., 2020). Doing so increases confidence that the construct-behavior relationships are etic (i.e., universal) and not emic. Further, at least one group of participants in a validity study should be representative of the intended population for test use (Clark & Watson, 2019).

Organic data also has some concerns specific to it that differ from traditional data. For example, changing technological conditions may cause changes in the patterns of behavior observed, affecting the veracity of the data (Xu et al., 2020). For example, several years ago, Twitter doubled the allowable length of tweets, and any machine learning models trained on the shorter tweets may not be as accurate on the longer tweets. Therefore, validation must be an ongoing process, as suggested by both the *Principles* and *Standards*. This process involves continually evaluating the validity of data and scales via multiple methods of investigation that consider multiple aspects of validity. Much like we advocate for exploring multiple aspects of reliability, we advocate for construct validation being a process of exploring multiple sources of evidence and doing so as long as the measure continues to be used.

Part 3: Multiple Approaches to Evaluating New Forms of Data

As illustrated in the first two parts of this chapter, there are multiple points of consideration when new forms of data are evaluated for their psychometric value. In this concluding section, we return to our earlier "big picture" discussion of various approaches to data evaluation such as: (1) theory-driven, hypothetico deductive approach ("Garbage In, Garbage Out"); (2) construct-driven, data-flexible approach ("Sewage In, Drinkable Water Out"); and (3) data-driven, construct-informing approach ("Leftover In, Casserole Out"). These approaches vary in the degrees and manners in which theory and data are incorporated into the process.

On the one end of the theory-data spectrum, one might exclusively focus on explanation (i.e., theoretical interpretability) in evaluating data. When this view is taken to the extreme, the fact that data can be used to predict something of practical importance does not necessarily bear on the scientific merit of the data. However, we contend that this is an overly restrictive mindset for data evaluation because it dismisses the value of inductive and abductive reasoning in the progress of our scientific field (Woo et al., 2017). On the other end of the spectrum, one might consider following a completely atheoretical and data-driven ("dustbowl empiricism") process, where the sole focus is on detecting replicable patterns in the data in a purely descriptive and/or predictive manner without an attempt to unpack the "black box" from a theoretical standpoint. In this case, data is considered good as long as they can reliably describe and/or predict something of practical importance. This perspective appears to be endorsed by many researchers and practitioners in data science and industry (McAbee et al., 2017). However, from the scientific perspective of industrial-organizational psychology, restricting our goals to only description and prediction is neither wise nor productive. Being able to explain causal links among variables is the ultimate goal of science, and careful interpretation of empirical insights or observations obtained from data (i.e., phenomenon detection; Jebb et al., 2017) can lead to greater theoretical understanding of such causality – e.g., development of a new theory and/or refining existing theories. In between these two extremes, we suggest that there exist at least three viable frameworks for utilizing, evaluating, and validating new forms of data.

Theory-Driven Approach

Traditionally, the psychological testing and assessment community has (almost exclusively) endorsed a theory-driven, hypothetico-deductive approach to scale development and validation (AERA et al., 2014). In this approach, one starts with a clearly-defined construct that has been well researched in the literature and intentionally generates content-relevant items and scoring algorithms for measuring the target construct. As such, data (e.g., responses to survey items, behavioral observations in a controlled environment) are gathered and analyzed through a mechanism that is carefully designed *a priori*. Specifically, one is recommended to follow the steps as outlined below (e.g., Hinkin, 1998):

1. Decide on a well-defined construct
2. Item generation: Come up with content-relevant items
3. Scale (measure) administration
4. Initial item reduction: Exploratory factor analysis, internal consistency reliability (and potential others)
5. Confirmatory factor analysis
6. Convergent/discriminant/predictive relations with external variables
7. Replication (using new data source and/or analytic method, evaluate reliability, internal structure, and relations with external variables)
8. If changes are made to the measure, repeat Steps 2–6.

Although this framework is most suited for traditional survey/questionnaire development, it can also be applied to some of the new data sources quite well. For example, using smartphone applications, a researcher can send out notifications to the participants' mobile phones and ask them fill out multiple short surveys throughout the day (i.e., event sampling method and/or momentary ecological assessment; Sandstrom et al., 2017) while also collecting time and location data that can be added to a multilevel structure of the survey data. In another example, electronic personnel records can be used to collect a predefined set of information that is deemed theoretically relevant to the constructs of work and/or job withdrawal, such as absence, tardiness, and frequent breaks. In both cases, the researcher clearly lays out *a priori* scoring strategies based on theory, rather than influenced by data in the analytic process.

Construct-Driven, Data-Flexible Approach

In the second approach, a few modifications to the aforementioned theory-driven approach are implemented to allow flexibility in the scoring (modeling) stage, where supervised machine learning techniques can be used to develop psychological measurement through an iterative computational process. When the goal is to measure a specific target construct with existing theory and (conventional) measurement tool readily available while utilizing data that were not specifically designed for such purposes, it may be useful to take a more flexible approach to developing scoring algorithms. This is because, in many cases of using new forms of data, the linkage between variables in the input data and output (i.e., scores of target construct) cannot be clearly spelled out *a priori* due to lack of prior research and/or the nature of computational approaches used for scoring (e.g., neural networks and deep learning). In some cases, it may not even be feasible to identify "indicators" from the input data. When there is a need for accommodating such flexibility, we suggest the following steps:

1. Decide on a well-defined construct (e.g., extraversion) and an existing measure of the construct to be used as "ground truth" (e.g., self-reported extraversion using well-validated survey items).
2. Data Preparation
   2a. Select data sources potentially suitable for measuring the construct (e.g., social media behaviors).
   2b. Extract indicators or features from each source in light of the target construct. Allow possible construct contamination by "casting a wide net" in order to maximize the algorithm's ability to predict ground truth scores.
3. Use machine learning algorithm to create a scoring model (or a composite of indicators with differential weights) that maximizes the prediction of target construct. Use cross-validation to establish model specifications (e.g., indicator weights).
4. In a new sample, assess the congruence between algorithmically-derived and ground-truth scores (which is often referred to as algorithm's predictive accuracy; Tay et al., 2020). In addition, assess other psychometric properties of the algorithmically-derived scores following the recommendations offered in Part 2 (e.g., inter-algorithm reliability, criterion predictions).
5. If findings from Step 3 suggest that certain indicators or data features need to be removed or scoring algorithms altered, repeat Steps 2–3 to re-generate and re-evaluate the prediction and content relevance.
6. Replicate the entire process in additional studies.

It is important to note that these steps are described at a broad, and somewhat abstract, level in order to accommodate various analytic approaches and data characteristics. Providing more context-specific elaborations of this process would be well beyond the scope of this chapter. That said, readers may be interested in a recent study on automated video interviews for personality assessment (Hickman et al., 2021), which describes a fairly comprehensive process that is in line with the "construct-driven, data-flexible" approach discussed in this section. Also, an article by Sajjadiani et al. (2019) describes a rigorous, multistep process of developing measures of "work experience relevance, tenure history, and history of involuntary turnover, history of avoiding bad jobs, and history of approaching better jobs" (p. 1207), which were then used to predict various work outcomes, such as job performance and turnover.

Data-Driven and Construct-Informing Approach

When one's primary goal is to predict an important outcome of interest (e.g., job performance) rather than to measure a specific construct, the psychometric process of utilizing and evaluating data requires one additional step: *post-hoc* content analysis and construct development. Consider the following steps:

1. Define a clear purpose for the data collection (e.g., predicting future job performance from behaviors recorded in one-way asynchronous video interviews).
2. Data Preparation
   2a. Select data sources that could potentially be useful for the prediction (e.g., verbal, para-verbal, non-verbal behaviors).
   2b. Extract indicators or features from each source.
3. Use machine learning algorithm to create a scoring model (or a composite of indicators with differential weights) that maximizes the prediction. Use cross-validation to establish model specifications (e.g., indicator weights).
4. Content analyze the model. Interpret the content through indicators with nonzero weights.
5. Link the main indicators in the composite to theoretical constructs that are well established in the literature. If there were some indicators that were not able to link to existing theory, revise existing theories, generate a new theory (abduction), or drop them from the scoring model (measure) if deemed construct-irrelevant (e.g., related to protected group status).
6. If indicators are removed, repeat Steps 2–4 to re-generate and re-evaluate the prediction and content relevance.
7. Replicate the entire process in a new sample.

Approaching psychological measurement this way deviates from the traditional, theory-driven approach, in that data collection, processing, and analysis are all done without a predetermined target construct in mind (if there is a construct of interest, it is only loosely defined and used as an initial guideline for selecting input data sources). As Speer et al. (2019) have pointed out, a traditional construct-centric psychometric approach has limited practical value in utilizing new data sources for workplace applications (e.g., attrition modeling), as it restricts the organization's ability to garner empirical insights from multiple sources of data that are often unstructured and less-understood, yet potentially useful for predicting and managing key organizational phenomenon (e.g., turnover). However, even data-driven modeling approaches focusing on predicting organizational outcomes can incorporate an element of host-hoc psychometric analysis in the process (e.g., Steps 3 and 4 above), which will significantly contribute to scientific progress by enhancing the field's theoretical understanding of the workplace phenomena. Although we attempted to provide some initial recommendations for the process of evaluating and establishing psychometric data quality, there are many areas in which more nuanced methodological/practical considerations will be needed.

Closing Remarks

As the technologies evolve, workplace applications to measure individual and group-level constructs will continue to increase in popularity. While the traditional psychometric principles offer a solid foundation for evaluating data for reliability and validity, the field needs to evolve in providing practical guidelines for data evaluation that effectively accommodate new forms of data as well as how they are analyzed. Such guidelines should account for multiple sources of error in evaluating reliability and validity and adopt a holistic approach to data evaluation that incorporates both theory and data.

Authors' Note

All three authors contributed equally to writing the chapter. We thank Dan Putka for reading an early outline of the chapter content and providing helpful comments.

Notes

1 Machine learning can be unsupervised (i.e., no human intervention is used as algorithms search for patterns in data) or supervised (i.e., where datasets are carefully chosen and shaped to train algorithms to perform specific tasks such as predicting a ground truth).
2 This conflation does not occur if (and only if) the k scale items' errors are completely independent/uncorrelated.

References

American Educational Research Association, American Psychological Association, & National Council on Measurement in Education. (2014). *Standards for educational and psychological testing.* American Educational Research Association.

Ayers, J. W., Althouse, B. M., Allem, J.-P., Rosenquist, J. N., & Ford, D. E. (2013). Seasonality in seeking mental health information on Google. *American Journal of Preventive Medicine, 44*(5), 520–525. https://doi.org/10.1016/j.amepre.2013.01.012

Barocas, S., & Selbst, A. D. (2016). Big data's disparate impact. *California Law Review, 104*(3), 671–732.

Bleidorn, W., & Hopwood, C. J. (2019). Using machine learning to advance personality assessment and theory. *Personality and Social Psychology Review, 23*(2), 1088868318772990. https://doi.org/10.1177/1088868318772990

Borsboom, D., Mellenbergh, G. J., & van Heerden, J. (2004). The concept of validity. *Psychological Review, 111*(4), 1061–1071. https://doi.org/10.1037/0033-295X.111.4.1061

Boyd, D. M., & Ellison, N. B. (2007). Social network sites: Definition, history, and scholarship. *Journal of Computer-Mediated Communication, 13*(1), 210–230. https://doi.org/10.1111/j.1083-6101.2007.00393.x

Brunswik, E. (1956). *Perception and the representative design of psychological experiments* (2nd ed.). University of California Press.

Can, Y. S., Chalabianloo, N., Ekiz, D., & Ersoy, C. (2019). Continuous stress detection using wearable sensors in real life: Algorithmic programming contest case study. *Sensors, 19*(8), 1849. https://doi.org/10.3390/s19081849

Carlson, K. D., & Herdman, A. O. (2012). Understanding the impact of convergent validity on research results. *Organizational Research Methods, 15*(1), 17–32. https://doi.org/10.1177/1094428110392383

Chaffin, D., Heidl, R., Hollenbeck, J. R., Howe, M., Yu, A., Voorhees, C., & Calantone, R. (2017). The promise and perils of wearable sensors in organizational research. *Organizational Research Methods, 20*(1), 3–31. https://doi.org/10.1177/1094428115617004

Chen, B., Marvin, S., & While, A. (2020). Containing COVID-19 in China: AI and the robotic restructuring of future cities. *Dialogues in Human Geography, 10*(2), 238–241. https://doi.org/10.1177/2043820620934267

Clark, L. A., & Watson, D. (2019). Constructing validity: New developments in creating objective measuring instruments. *Psychological Assessment, 31*(12), 1412–1427. https://doi.org/10.1037/pas0000626

Cocca, P., Marciano, F., & Alberti, M. (2016). Video surveillance systems to enhance occupational safety: A case study. *Safety Science, 84*, 140–148. https://doi.org/10.1016/j.ssci.2015.12.005

Cortina, J. M. (1993). What is coefficient alpha? An examination of theory and applications. *Journal of Applied Psychology, 78*(1), 98–104. https://doi.org/10.1037/0021-9010.78.1.98

Cortina, J. M., Sheng, Z., Keener, S. K., Keeler, K. R., Grubb, L. K., Schmitt, N., Tonidandel, S., Summerville, K. M., Heggestad, E. D., & Banks, G. C. (2020). From alpha to omega and beyond! A look at the past, present, and (possible) future of psychometric soundness. *Journal of Applied Psychology, 105*(12), 1351–1381. https://doi.org/10.1037/apl0000815

Cronbach, L. J. (1990). *Essentials of psychological testing.* Harper & Row.

Cronbach, L. J., Gleser, G. C., Nanda, H., & Rajaratnam, N. (1972). *The dependability of behavioral measurements: Theory of generalizability for scores and profiles.* John Wiley & Sons.

Cronbach, L. J., & Meehl, P. E. (1955). Construct validity in psychological tests. *Psychological Bulletin, 52*(4), 281–302. https://doi.org/10.1037/h0040957

Dastin, J. (2018, October 10). Amazon scraps secret AI recruiting tool that showed bias against women. *Reuters.* https://www.reuters.com/article/us-amazon-com-jobs-automation-insight-idUSKCN1MK08G

Dong, W., & Pentland, A. "Sandy." (2010). Quantifying group problem solving with stochastic analysis. *International Conference on Multimodal Interfaces and the Workshop on Machine Learning for Multimodal Interaction,* 1–4. https://doi.org/10.1145/1891903.1891954

Ford, M. T. (2020). Internet search and page view behavior scores: Validity and usefulness as indicators of psychological states. In *Big data in psychological research* (pp. 89–107). American Psychological Association. https://doi.org/10.1037/0000193-005

Ford, M. T., Jebb, A. T., Tay, L., & Diener, E. (2018). Internet searches for affect-related terms: An indicator of subjective well-being and predictor of health outcomes across US states and metro areas. *Applied Psychology: Health and Well-Being, 10*(1), 3–29.

Gilbert, E., & Karahalios, K. (2009). Predicting tie strength with social media. *Proceedings of the 27th International Conference on Human Factors in Computing Systems – CHI 09,* 211. https://doi.org/10.1145/1518701.1518736

Gosling, S. D., Augustine, A. A., Vazire, S., Holtzman, N., & Gaddis, S. (2011). Manifestations of personality in online social networks: Self-reported Facebook-related behaviors and observable profile information. *CyberPsychology, Behavior & Social Networking, 14*(9), 483–488. https://doi.org/10.1089/cyber.2010.0087

Gravina, R., Alinia, P., Ghasemzadeh, H., & Fortino, G. (2017). Multi-sensor fusion in body sensor networks: State-of-the-art and research challenges. *Information Fusion, 35,* 68–80. https://doi.org/10.1016/j.inffus.2016.09.005

Hansen, J.-I. C. (1998). Cognitions of a dustbowl empiricist. *The Counseling Psychologist, 26*(3), 499–513. https://doi.org/10.1177/0011000098263013

Harari, G. M., Lane, N. D., Wang, R., Crosier, B. S., Campbell, A. T., & Gosling, S. D. (2016). Using smartphones to collect behavioral data in psychological science: Opportunities, practical considerations, and challenges. *Perspectives on Psychological Science, 11*(6), 838–854. https://doi.org/10.1177/1745691616650285

Hernandez, J., Hoque, M. (Ehsan), Drevo, W., & Picard, R. W. (2012). Mood meter: Counting smiles in the wild. *Proceedings of the 2012 ACM Conference on Ubiquitous Computing,* 301–310. https://doi.org/10.1145/2370216.2370264

Hickman, L., Bosch, N., Ng, V., Saef, R., Tay, L., & Woo, S. E. (2021). Automated video interview personality assessments: Reliability, validity, and generalizability investigations. *Journal of Applied Psychology.* https://doi.org/10.1037/apl0000695

Hinkin, T. R. (1998). A brief tutorial on the development of measures for use in survey questionnaires. *Organizational Research Methods, 1*(1), 104–121. https://doi.org/10.1177/109442819800100106

Hung, S., Li, M. S., Chen, Y. L., Chiang, J. H., Chen, Y. Y., & Hung, G. C. L. (2016). Smartphone-based ecological momentary assessment for Chinese patients with depression: An exploratory study in Taiwan. *Asian Journal of Psychiatry, 23,* 131–136.

Jebb, A. T., Parrigon, S., & Woo, S. E. (2017). Exploratory data analysis as a foundation of inductive research. *Human Resource Management Review, 27*(2), 265–276. https://doi.org/10.1016/j.hrmr.2016.08.003

Kalichman, S. C., & Kegler, C. (2015). Vaccine-related Internet search activity predicts H1N1 and HPV vaccine coverage: Implications for vaccine acceptance. *Journal of Health Communication*, *20*(3), 259–265. https://doi.org/10.1080/10810730.2013.852274

Kido, S., Hashizume, A., Baba, T., & Matsui, T. (2016). Development and evaluation of a smartphone application for self-estimation of daily mental stress level. *International Journal of Affective Engineering*, *15*(2), 183–187.

Kobayashi, T., Boase, J., Suzuki, T., & Suzuki, T. (2015). Emerging from the cocoon? Revisiting the tele-cocooning hypothesis in the smartphone era. *Journal of Computer-Mediated Communication*, *20*(3), 330–345. https://doi.org/10.1111/jcc4.12116

Kosinski, M., Stillwell, D., & Graepel, T. (2013). Private traits and attributes are predictable from digital records of human behavior. *Proceedings of the National Academy of Sciences*, *110*(15), 5802–5805. https://doi.org/10.1073/pnas.1218772110

Kozlowski, S. W. J. (2015). Advancing research on team process dynamics: Theoretical, methodological, and measurement considerations. *Organizational Psychology Review*, *5*(4), 270–299. https://doi.org/10.1177/2041386614533586

Kyriakou, K., Resch, B., Sagl, G., Petutschnig, A., Werner, C., Niederseer, D., Liedlgruber, M., Wilhelm, F. H., Osborne, T., & Pykett, J. (2019). Detecting moments of stress from measurements of wearable physiological sensors. *Sensors*, *19*(17), 3805. https://doi.org/10.3390/s19173805

Li, S., Wang, Y., Xue, J., Zhao, N., & Zhu, T. (2020). The impact of COVID-19 epidemic declaration on psychological consequences: A study on active Weibo users. *International Journal of Environmental Research and Public Health*, *17*(6), 2032. https://doi.org/10.3390/ijerph17062032

Loevinger, J. (1954). The attenuation paradox in test theory. *Psychological Bulletin*, *51*(5), 493–504. https://doi.org/10.1037/h0058543

Loevinger, J. (1957). Objective tests as instruments of psychological theory. *Psychological Reports*, *3*, 635–694. https://doi.org/10.2466/PR0.3.7.635-694

Lord, F. M., Novick, M. R., & Birnbaum, A. (1968). *Statistical theories of mental test scores*. Addison-Wesley.

Manago, A. M., Taylor, T., & Greenfield, P. M. (2012). Me and my 400 friends: The anatomy of college students' Facebook networks, their communication patterns, and well-being. *Developmental Psychology*, *48*(2), 369–380. https://doi.org/10.1037/a0026338

Matusik, J. G., Heidl, R., Hollenbeck, J. R., Yu, A., Lee, H. W., & Howe, M. (2019). Wearable Bluetooth sensors for capturing relational variables and temporal variability in relationships: A construct validation study. *Journal of Applied Psychology*, *104*(3), 357–387. https://doi.org/10.1037/apl0000334

McAbee, S. T., Landis, R. S., & Burke, M. I. (2017). Inductive reasoning: The promise of big data. *Human Resource Management Review*, *27*(2), 277–290. https://doi.org/10.1016/j.hrmr.2016.08.005

McCrae, R. R. (2015). A more nuanced view of reliability: Specificity in the trait hierarchy. *Personality and Social Psychology Review*, *19*(2), 97–112. https://doi.org/10.1177/1088868314541857

McCrae, R. R., Kurtz, J. E., Yamagata, S., & Terracciano, A. (2011). Internal consistency, retest reliability, and their implications for personality scale validity. *Personality and Social Psychology Review: An Official Journal of the Society for Personality and Social Psychology, Inc*, *15*(1), 28–50. https://doi.org/10.1177/1088868310366253

Messick, S. (1995). Validity of psychological assessment: Validation of inferences from persons' responses and performances as scientific inquiry into score meaning. *American Psychologist, 50*(9), 741–749. https://doi.org/10.1037/0003-066X.50.9.741

Nai, J., Narayanan, J., Hernandez, I., & Savani, K. (2018). People in more racially diverse neighborhoods are more prosocial. *Journal of Personality and Social Psychology, 114*(4), 497–515. https://doi.org/10.1037/pspa0000103

Nurek, M., & Michalski, R. (2020). Combining machine learning and social network analysis to reveal the organizational structures. *Applied Sciences, 10*(5), 1699. https://doi.org/10.3390/app10051699

Park, G., Schwartz, H. A., Eichstaedt, J. C., Kern, M. L., Kosinski, M., Stillwell, D. J., Ungar, L. H., & Seligman, M. E. P. (2015). Automatic personality assessment through social media language. *Journal of Personality and Social Psychology, 108*(6), 934–952. https://doi.org/10.1037/pspp0000020

Saha, K., Yousuf, A., Hickman, L., Gupta, P., Tay, L., & De Choudhury, M. (2021). A social media study on demographic differences in perceived job satisfaction. *Proceedings of the ACM on Human-Computer Interaction, 5*(CSCW1), 167:1–167:29. https://doi.org/10.1145/3449241

Sajjadiani, S., Sojourner, A. J., Kammeyer-Mueller, J. D., & Mykerezi, E. (2019). Using machine learning to translate applicant work history into predictors of performance and turnover. *Journal of Applied Psychology, 104*(10), 1207–1225. https://doi.org/10.1037/apl0000405

Sandstrom, G. M., Lathia, N., Mascolo, C., & Rentfrow, P. J. (2017). Putting mood in context: Using smartphones to examine how people feel in different locations. *Journal of Research in Personality, 69*, 96–101. https://doi.org/10.1016/j.jrp.2016.06.004

Schmid Mast, M., Gatica-Perez, D., Frauendorfer, D., Nguyen, L., & Choudhury, T. (2015). Social sensing for psychology: Automated interpersonal behavior assessment. *Current Directions in Psychological Science, 24*(2), 154–160. https://doi.org/10.1177/0963721414560811.

Schmitt, N. (1996). Uses and abuses of coefficient alpha. *Psychological Assessment, 8*(4), 350–353. https://doi.org/10.1037/1040-3590.8.4.350

Simms, L. J., Casillas, A., Clark, L. A., Watson, D., & Doebbeling, B. N. (2005). Psychometric evaluation of the restructured clinical scales of the MMPI-2. *Psychological Assessment, 17*(3), 345–358. https://doi.org/10.1037/1040-3590.17.3.345

SIOP. (2018). Principles for the validation and use of personnel selection procedures. *Industrial and Organizational Psychology: Perspectives on Science and Practice, 11*(Supl 1), 2–97. https://doi.org/10.1017/iop.2018.195

Sonn, J. W., Kang, M., & Choi, Y. (2020). Smart city technologies for pandemic control without lockdown. *International Journal of Urban Sciences, 24*(2), 149–151. https://doi.org/10.1080/12265934.2020.1764207

Speer, A. B. (2020). Scoring dimension-level job performance from narrative comments: Validity and generalizability when using natural language processing. *Organizational Research Methods.* https://doi.org/10.1177/1094428120930815

Speer, A. B., Dutta, S., Chen, M., & Trussell, G. (2019). Here to stay or go? Connecting turnover research to applied attrition modeling. *Industrial and Organizational Psychology, 12*(3), 277–301. https://doi.org/10.1017/iop.2019.22

Stark, S., Chernyshenko, O. S., Drasgow, F., & Williams, B. A. (2006). Examining assumptions about item responding in personality assessment: Should ideal point methods be considered for scale development and scoring? *Journal of Applied Psychology, 91*(1), 25–39. https://doi.org/10.1037/0021-9010.91.1.25

Swan, M. (2012). Sensor mania! The Internet of Things, wearable computing, objective metrics, and the quantified self 2.0. *Journal of Sensor and Actuator Networks, 1*(3), 217–253. https://doi.org/10.3390/jsan1030217

Tay, L., Jebb, A. T., & Woo, S. E. (2017). Video capture of human behaviors: Toward a big data approach. *Current Opinion in Behavioral Sciences, 18*, 17–22.

Tay, L., Woo, S. E., Hickman, L., & Saef, R. (2020). Psychometric and validity issues in machine learning approaches to personality assessment: A focus on social media text mining. *European Journal of Personality, 34*, 826–844. https://doi.org/10.1002/per.2290

Urizar, O. J., Barakova, E. I., Marcenaro, L., Regazzoni, C. S., & Rauterberg, M. (2017). Emotion estimation in crowds: A survey. In *8th International Conference of Pattern Recognition Systems (ICPRS 2017), Madrid, Spain* (pp. 1–6). IET.

Woo, S. E., O'Boyle, E. H., & Spector, P. E. (2017). Best Practices in developing, conducting, and evaluating inductive research. *Human Resource Management Review, 27*(2), 255–264. https://doi.org/10.1016/j.hrmr.2016.08.004

Woo, S. E., Tay, L., Jebb, A. T., Ford, M. T., & Kern, M. L. (2020). Big data for enhancing measurement quality. In *Big data in psychological research* (pp. 59–85). American Psychological Association. https://doi.org/10.1037/0000193-004

Xu, H., Zhang, N., & Zhou, L. (2020). Validity concerns in research using organic data. *Journal of Management, 46*(7), 1257–1274. https://doi.org/10.1177/0149206319862027

Yamato, Y., Fukumoto, Y., & Kumazaki, H. (2017, January). Security camera movie and ERP data matching system to prevent theft. In *2017 14th IEEE Annual Consumer Communications & Networking Conference (CCNC)* (pp. 1014–1015). IEEE.

6

ORGANIC DATA AND THE DESIGN OF STUDIES

Nan Zhang, Heng Xu, and Le Zhou

Introduction

Information technology and the Internet are transforming social sciences. With emerging digital platforms enabling the collection and analysis of massive datasets capturing human behavior and their interactions, social scientists now have the opportunity to study more phenomena in greater detail than ever before. The trend of Big Data has brought a fundamental shift in data collection from experiments and surveys toward digital records (Paxton & Griffiths, 2017). Groves (2011) introduced the notion of "organic data" to capture the new sources of data that are organically generated with no explicit research design, e.g., data generated by ubiquitous sensors, social interaction data from Twitter feeds, social media websites, click streams, etc. Meanwhile, Groves (2011) used the label of "designed data" to refer to those data that originated from traditional research using rigorously designed surveys or experiments.

There is a rapid rise in volume with organic data, given the more and more prevalent use of automated systems that track, collect, and make available datasets of all sorts 24/7. Examples of such systems include Twitter and other social media platforms, web e-commerce websites that track the price and popularity of products, and traffic cameras that have continuous video feeds posted online. With such massive sources of organic data, we see efforts of academic interests built on them. For example, we observe a growing trend of using Twitter as a source of research data to test or develop theories in social sciences, from the influential construal-level theory of psychological distance (Snefjella & Kuperman, 2015) to the cognitive theory of emotions (Doré et al., 2015), from

DOI: 10.4324/9781003015000-8

social movement theories (Vasi et al., 2015) to theory on media influences on social outcomes (Kearney & Levine, 2015).

Meanwhile, the rapidly growing prevalence of organic data also provides a unique opportunity for social scientists to supplement traditional designed data with organic data and to address ongoing challenges in studies using traditional design, such as increasing nonresponse rates, small sample sizes, and cross-sectional design. Such a promising prospect of integrating designed and organic data has been well recognized in social sciences (Groves, 2011; Ruggles, 2014). A few recent studies have already attempted the manual integration of administrative and social media data. For example, Barberá et al. (2015) matched users in a Twitter corpus with voter registration rolls to analyze the political sentiments of individuals in different socioeconomic groups. With the promising results shown in these studies, the full potential of organic data is just starting to get unlocked.

Research using organic data, however, has its own limitations – e.g., the sampling biases stemming from the overrepresentation of certain subpopulations (Mislove et al., 2011; Smith, 2011), the technological barriers enforced by the platform design (Morstatter et al., 2013, 2014; Morstatter & Liu, 2017), the errors produced by automated data processing techniques (Imran et al., 2015), or even misleading information intentionally posted by platform users (Cook et al., 2014). Further, the great volume, variety, and complexity of such data, including complex individual, spatial, and network dependencies, challenge the standard capabilities of algorithms, tools, and analytical methods and paradigms of social science (Salganik, 2018). Moreover, Big Data may come with "Big Error" (Lazer et al., 2014; McFarland & McFarland, 2015) that leads to inaccurate inferences built on hidden biases in the data or in the measurement.

As the use of organic data is increasingly popular in social science research (e.g., Doré et al., 2015; Vasi et al., 2015; Snefjella & Kuperman, 2015), it is of essence for social scientists to carefully study the potential issues concerning the usage of organic data that could affect the robustness of research findings. These issues are often distinct from the robustness issues facing traditional "designed"-data-based research in social sciences. As we will elaborate later in the chapter, a key reason for this distinction is that, while research design usually precedes data collection in traditional research, organic-data-based research often requires researchers to work with data already generated *before* a detailed research design emerges as researchers start to interact with the data. To illustrate the distinct challenges for the use of organic data, this chapter first provides an overview of the unique characteristics of organic data, followed by illustrating how the unique characteristics manifest as operational challenges in the design of research studies involving organic data. After identifying the validity threats posed by these challenges, we discuss potential solutions to address the validity threats and improve the robustness of research using organic data. We conclude the chapter by a call for interdisciplinary research on developing methodologies that make organic data a robust part of future research in organizational science.

Characteristics of Organic Data

In most instances, the "organic data" later identified for research purposes are not captured by an explicit research instrument nor originally generated for the purpose of research, but by a technology or device naturally capturing the "digital footprints" of human activity and interaction (McFarland et al., 2016). In other words, these organic data are *not* generated to test a theory-driven hypothesis (McFarland et al., 2016). Owing to the lack of a research-focused design in the data-generation process, organic data exhibits distinct characteristics from the canonical, "designed," research data produced by randomized experiments, surveys, interviews, etc. In this section, we discuss three unique characteristics of organic data: (1) the opaqueness of the process through which the data were generated, (2) the large data volume that requires a high computational cost to process, and (3) the low signal-to-noise ratio.

Overview

Before discussing these three characteristics in detail, we would like to note that the differences between organic and designed data should be viewed as a multidimensional continuum rather than a dichotomy. In other words, different datasets could exhibit a characteristic to varying extents. Further, a dataset could exhibit some of the characteristics but not others. Consider the US Census data as an example. The data-generation process, e.g., the sampling mechanism, was meticulously designed and explicitly specified. From this perspective, such data is more closely aligned with the conventional designed data. Yet the dataset is certainly voluminous, triggering computational challenges similar to those encountered in processing organic data.

Thus, when examining an organic dataset, it is important to analyze each of the three characteristics respectively, rather than assuming that all of them apply to every organic dataset. The reason why doing so is important for research is that the design of research practices in general, and the data-analysis workflow in particular, is often influenced by different characteristics in different ways. For example, the algorithmic filtering of input data is often driven by the prohibitive computational cost of processing an extremely large dataset (in its entirety). On the other hand, a low signal-to-noise ratio often leads to the use of information extraction algorithms that can automatically discern signals from noise. Only when researchers have a clear understanding of the unique characteristics of an organic dataset can they properly decide whether a research practice is warranted and, if so, whether appropriate precautions have been taken to avoid the common pitfalls discussed later in the chapter. In other words, when analyzing the validity issues facing a research design, one should avoid chalking an issue up to the dataset being "organic." Instead, an analysis at finer granularity is warranted to identify the specific characteristics of the dataset that give rise to the validity threats.

Opaque Data-Generation Process

The data-generation process refers to the process through which the data were generated in the real world. That is, it is the "ground-truth model" that explains all patterns and regularities in the data. Unless the data was synthetically generated (e.g., through numeric simulations), the data-generation process is rarely, if ever, known to researchers *a priori*. Nonetheless, research studies can unveil certain aspects of the data-generation process. For example, consider a dataset consisting of job satisfaction of workers in a given organization with multiple units. While we cannot claim complete knowledge of the data-generation process, i.e., how an individual's job satisfaction is what it is, we do know certain aspects of the data-generation process. For example, differences in unit leaders can produce a probability distribution of job satisfaction that is the mixture of two Gaussian distributions, one corresponding to those with an abusive unit manager and the other to those without. Note that such knowledge of the data-generation process is extremely important for the design of a research study involving the data. For example, if we were to design a study on people's job satisfaction, we know we would have to stratify the subjects according to unit membership instead of mixing them together in one group, because otherwise statistical artifacts like Simpson's paradox (i.e., the trend in the overall population is the reverse of that in every individual group; Wagner, 1982) may arise and threaten the validity of the research findings. Thus, the less knowledge we have about the data-generation process, the more likely it is for validity threats to arise in our research design and data analysis.

It is exactly this (amount of) knowledge about the data-generation process that often distinguishes organic data from designed data. Compared with data collected in a laboratory setting, the data-generation process that underlies an organic dataset "out in the world" could involve numerous extraneous factors beyond the behavior of the individual participants. For example, when the data was collected from an online platform (e.g., a social media platform), the data-generation process is often influenced by the platform design, such as how it computes and personalizes recommendations (e.g., Facebook posts displayed on a user's news feeds) for each user. Further, technical issues impeding the normal operation of an online platform could result in abnormal patterns in the organic data. For example, when the content delivery network (CDN) used by a website malfunctions in one geographic region but not another, the composition of user activities on the website may change sharply without any underlying shift of user behavior. Finally, cyberattacks and malicious activities on an online platform could also alter the data-generation process. When a large percentage of users on a website are bots posing as human users (Ott, Cardie & Hancock, 2012), the data-generation process could be largely shaped by the acts of bot operators rather than the behavior of *bona fide* users.

Large Data Volume

One feature of organic datasets that has long held intuitive appeal to researchers is their large sizes. Without the resource constraints of a laboratory experiment (e.g., physical space) or a survey (e.g., financial cost), organic datasets can be orders of magnitude larger than datasets produced by most traditional studies in social sciences. The advantage from a larger dataset size is well recognized: since a larger sample size reduces the standard error of the mean and, in turn, increases the statistical power of common hypothesis tests, it is more likely to shed clarity on the phenomena of interest to researchers. A larger dataset also has the potential to offer a broader representation of the general population than laboratory experiments or surveys using convenience samples, which are known to have sampling bias toward the Western, educated, industrialized, rich, and democratic (WEIRD) populations (Henrich, Heine & Norenzayan, 2010). Further, a larger dataset may have a higher chance of covering rare events that are difficult to capture in a study collecting a smaller number of observations. All these advantages speak to the value of a large data volume to research involving organic data.

Organic datasets are often larger in terms of not only the number of records but also the number of variables. This is especially pronounced for organic data collected through technological platforms and sensory devices, which are usually designed to assemble as wide a variety of information as possible. This stands in contrast with designed data, which tend to limit the collected variables to those theoretically linked to a research question. As a result of the large number of variables collected in an organic dataset, many of the collected variables may be highly correlated with each other. For example, Twitter provides a wide variety of variables related to how a tweet attracts interests and engagement from Twitter users, including the number of times the tweet has been viewed, made "favorite," retweeted, quoted in other tweets, or replied to; the number of times a video embedded in the tweet has been viewed; the number of followers of the user who posted the tweet, etc. These variables have been found to be strongly correlated with each other (Morchid et al., 2014). On the one hand, the correlated variables provide researchers with the opportunity to compare and contrast different aspects of the phenomenon to identify their subtle distinctions. On the other hand, it also brings about questions on how to properly choose which variables to use in research.

Note that the large volume of an organic dataset could exacerbate the opaqueness of the data-generation process. When there are a large number of records in the raw data, the extraction from such data to construct a dataset for further analysis is often constrained by technical limitations that could form part of the (opaque) data-generation process. For example, consider the collection of user profiles from LinkedIn.com through online search. LinkedIn limits the number of profiles returned per search query to at most 1,000, no matter how many profiles actually match the search. If one were to construct a research dataset using the search results of LinkedIn, then the proprietary ranking algorithm used by LinkedIn to order the returned profiles becomes part of the data-generation process, exacerbating its opaqueness. Similarly, many variables provided by (and thus collectible from) technological platforms are often generated with proprietary algorithms that are not fully known to the external researchers. Consider the aforementioned Twitter example. While Twitter provides through its API the number of times a video embedded in a tweet has been watched, it is unclear (based on the publicly available description from Twitter) whether repeated viewing of a video by the same user on the same device is counted only once or multiple times; whether there is a minimum threshold on the amount of time the video is played (e.g., 5 seconds) before it is counted as a view; etc. Again, the inclusion of these steps in the process of gathering the research dataset introduces additional opaqueness to the data-generation process.

Low Signal-to-Noise Ratio

For a given research dataset, if we consider the part of data relevant to the focal research study as "signal" and the part irrelevant as "noise," then organic datasets likely feature lower signal-to-noise ratios than designed data. An important reason is that, by definition, an organic dataset is generated from a process beyond a researcher's control. As such, large parts of the data are bound to be irrelevant to the phenomena of interest to the researcher. For example, consider a study that examines people's emotional reactions to an event, with the research dataset being the set of tweets that include the hashtag corresponding to the event. Many of these tweets may be irrelevant to the research interest: some tweets may not be about the event at all, instead just using the "trendy" hashtag for promotional purposes. Some tweets may simply be reports about the event, with no emotional reactions attached to them. Other tweets may appear to be emotional responses but were indeed posted by bots rather than bona fide Twitter users. The presence of all these "noise" tweets reduces the signal-to-noise ratio of the organic dataset and requires researchers to carefully filter the data before conducting further data analysis.

Besides the independence between the data-generation process and the research interests, there are a multitude of other reasons that could lower the signal-to-noise ratio for organic datasets. First, the precision of sensory devices used to generate the organic dataset may not have been scrutinized as closely as measures used in scientific research. For example, step counts collected by Fitbit devices are known to be underestimates in controlled settings but overestimates in practice (Feehan et al., 2018). Second, in the case of online technological platforms, the accurate curation of certain data may be computationally expensive, in which case the platform providers may elect to replace the data with "quick-and-dirty" estimates without explicitly disclosing the potential error of such estimates. It is well known, for example, that the count of matching documents provided by all major search engines are highly inaccurate estimates that could deviate from the real value by orders of magnitude (Uyar, 2009). In this case, the search engines' practices not only lower the signal-to-noise ratio but also introduce further opaqueness to the data-generation process, as the design of the quick-and-dirty estimates is rarely disclosed to researchers.

Challenges in Study Design Involving Organic Data

Challenges that are commonly faced by researchers when designing studies involving organic datasets, due, in large part, to the unique characteristics discussed in the last section. Note that, by "research studies," we specifically focus on those that are designed to explain certain mechanisms that give rise to some behavior, outcomes, or phenomena captured in the organic data (i.e., explanation-focus studies; Yarkoni & Westfall, 2017). Organic data could also be used to support many other types of research studies, such as those that develop machine learning algorithms (cf. algorithmic modeling culture; Breiman, 2001) for use on an organic dataset. These research studies, while important, are beyond the scope of this chapter.

In this section, we identify two types of challenges. The first type is associated with the need of using computational algorithms to process organic data with a large volume and a low signal-to-noise ratio, while the second type of challenges stem from the opaqueness of the data-generation process underpinning many organic datasets.

Use of Computational Algorithms

A low signal-to-noise ratio, coupled with a large data volume, gives rise to the need of extracting "signals" from the large amounts of input data in an efficient and cost-effective manner. The most common way for researchers to address the need is to adopt computational algorithms that automate the extraction process according to certain filtering conditions specified by the researchers. Consider the aforementioned example of studying people's emotions based on their tweets. Compared with a designed survey in which researchers can directly quantify an emotion variable from participants (e.g., through self-report measures), here the variable has to be coded from the tweets filled with "noise." Since manual coding is often prohibitively expensive for a voluminous dataset, the only remaining choice is to deploy (automated) computational algorithms that make use of various types of machine learning techniques, such as computer vision, Natural Language Processing (NLP), etc.

The use of computational algorithms can occur in different stages of the research design and data-analysis process involving organic data: researchers may incorporate the filter for the observations of interest into the design of web scraping algorithms, so as to selectively curate data from web pages (Landers et al., 2016). Alternatively, they can leverage the filtering algorithms (e.g., the "search" feature) already provided by an online platform. For example, it is not uncommon to see research studies that compile a list of keywords relevant to the research interest, before using the keywords to search an online platform and extract relevant data. Yet another alternative is to scrap the full dataset before filtering the collected data with algorithms that predict the relevance of each data point to the phenomena of interest (e.g., Wang, Hernandez, Newman, He, & Bian, 2016). Once the organic dataset is collected, algorithms may be used to code structured variables from unstructured input data, like text, image, and video (Jiang, Yin & Liu, 2019), or directly used to identify relationships between structured variables (Shrestha et al., 2020).

Two specific complications arise from the use of computational algorithms: (1) almost all such algorithms incur errors in their outputs, and (2) many such algorithms require a subtle parameter-tuning process before they can function properly on a specific dataset. With regard to the first complication, it is important to note that an information-extraction algorithm could miss relevant information, extract information that is not relevant, or completely misrepresent the input data in the coded variables. For example, to code responses to open-ended questions in job-performance reviews, researchers may need to leverage NLP algorithms that are known to be prone to errors when the text contains irony or sarcasm (Davidov, Tsur & Rappoport, 2010) or is written by nonnative speakers (Zhiltsova, Caton & Mulway, 2019). Note that the presence of such errors is not in and of itself a problem. After all, human coders also incur errors, and computational algorithms could be even more accurate than human coders for tasks like recognizing faces from images (Taigman et al., 2014) or identifying events from text (King & Lowe, 2003). The fundamental challenge here lies in a *lack of understanding* of the origin of such errors. With the rapid, practice-driven advancement of machine-learning techniques in recent years, it is often the case that even the designers of an algorithm (or, more broadly, the computer science research community at large) cannot fully explain how the algorithmic errors were generated over a specific dataset. A notable reason for this is akin to the famous quote by Heraclitus, "No man ever steps in the same river twice." Collecting an organic dataset, like social media posts, with the same design again does not mean that the newly collected data would follow the same data-generation process as the old data, as both the social media users and the topics they discuss shift over time. With this lack of ability to resample the input data comes the challenge of determining whether errors produced by an algorithm reflect a lack of sample representation, the inherent uncertainties in the data-generation process or algorithmic design issues that can be rectified in the future (Gal & Ghahramani, 2016). As a result, the distribution of the algorithmic errors could be biased in certain ways that have nontrivial implications. For example, some NLP algorithms have been found to work better on text written by some race/gender combinations than others (Blodgett & O'Connor, 2017) or exhibit unintended biases against nonnative English speakers (Zhiltsova et al., 2019). Similarly, computer-vision techniques such as gender-recognition algorithms were also found to be more accurate for certain racial/ethnic groups than others (Buolamwini & Gebru, 2018). All these issues could potentially lead to unfair treatments when NLP or computer-vision algorithms are used to screen job applicants or aid decisions on compensation and promotion.

With regard to the second complication, it is important to understand why parameter tuning is often necessary for the proper functioning of algorithms yet could trigger concerns on the robustness of research findings. There are two main reasons: (1) the large number of parameters involved in information-extraction algorithms, and (2) the lack of theoretical guidance on how to set these parameters without first accessing the data. Both issues were exacerbated by the rapid advance of machine-learning techniques in recent years, specifically the advent of deep-learning algorithms (LeCun, Bengio & Hinton, 2015) such as Convolutional Neural Network (CNN), Recurrent Neural Network (RNN), etc. On the one hand, the space of parameters for deep-learning algorithms is notoriously large, so much so that some were found to have the expressive power to "memorize" an entire input dataset (Zhang, Bengio et. al., 2017). The scientific community's understanding of the theoretical link between these parameters and the algorithmic outputs, on the other hand, is nascent at best, requiring researchers to engage in manual parameter tuning with no clear theoretical guidance (Bergstra, Yamins & Cox, 2013). Therefore, the parameter-tuning challenge can exacerbate the "many analysts" problem (Silberzahn et al., 2018) in social science research. Bau et. al. (2017), for example, examined numerous variations of a CNN on benchmark datasets and found a wide variation in terms of whether the algorithmic outputs can be interpreted based on the input parameters and the input data. Despite recent efforts on improving the interpretability of machine-learning outputs (Zhang, Wu & Zhu, 2018) and on automating the parameter-tuning process (Rhys, 2020), there is not yet an established method that a researcher could directly use to set the parameters for complex machine-learning algorithms.

The two complications also interact with each other to incur additional subtleties in the use of computational algorithms. For example, many NLP algorithms are known to incur excessive errors on short text due to ambiguity and lack of context (Hua et al., 2015). To reduce the amount of algorithmic errors, it is not uncommon to see research studies that start with a preprocessing step such as "excluding tweets with fewer than 5 words." While this step is certainly reasonable for addressing the first complication, it indeed adds to the second complication, as taking this step implies a choice of two parameters: one is the basis of filtering (i.e., the number of words rather than characters or sentences), and the other is the threshold (i.e., "5" words instead of "6"). These parameter settings are clearly dependent upon the specific research study. For example, if the input text was legal documents rather than tweets, the basis of filtering is more likely to be the number of sentences rather than words. Similarly, the more complex the variable-coding task is, the higher the threshold is likely to be. As discussed before, for machine-learning algorithms, the context- and data-dependent nature of these parameters settings makes it difficult to develop general-purpose guidelines that researchers can follow in setting the parameters, suggesting that sensitivity tests are often needed to know robustness of the findings.

Difficulty of Making Causal Inferences

By definition, organic data is not generated in a properly randomized and controlled fashion like in the designed experiments. Stripped of this only known way of unequivocally establishing causality (Pearl, 2009), causal inference is clearly a major challenge for research using organic data. Two complications tend to arise when attempting to infer causality from any observational dataset (Cochran, 1972), and both are exacerbated by the opaqueness of the data-generation process underpinning organic data. One complication is the difficulty of establishing a "comparative structure" (Cochran, 1972) due to the absence of experimental manipulation. For example, in order to establish a causal relationship $X \rightarrow Y$, we need to at least be able to distinguish between study units within the same sample with different levels of X (e.g., different places on the spectrum of the same personality trait). In other words, we need an accurate measure of X based on the variables included in the organic dataset – a nontrivial task when the link between X and the observable variables is not fully known. The other complication is the lack of randomization, which gives rise to "bias due to extraneous variables" (Cochran, 1972), a problem commonly known as confounding.

With regard to the first complication, a key obstacle is that researchers are severely constrained in terms of how to operationalize a construct when studying organic data. In a design experiment, researchers can either design an instrument or choose one that has been carefully scrutinized by the scientific community. With an organic dataset, however, the operationalization is limited to the variables that are already included in the dataset. Since these variables were not designed according to the research question on hand, researchers almost always have to figure out a way to operationalize each construct of interest using the observable variables that are available. Unfortunately, when the data-generation processes behind the observable variables are not well documented or understood, even ostensibly straightforward operationalizations could function poorly in practice. For example, consider a study of Twitter data that attempts to measure the geographic location of a Twitter user (e.g., as disclosed in the user's tweets) and use it to construct an independent variable X (e.g., aggregated emotions or opinions of users in each US state). It may appear straightforward to first query Twitter's API to retrieve the latitude/longitude coordinates for the user's location. Yet doing so could incur a plethora of issues for downstream data analysis. For example, the latitude/longitude pair returned by Twitter's API is generated by applying geocoding over the text specified in the "location" field of the user profile. Many Twitter users provide fake or sarcastic locations in their profiles (Hecht et al., 2011), like "Mars," which unfortunately could be misinterpreted as "Mars, Pennsylvania" in geocoding. Even when a user provides the real location, the latitude/longitude pair returned by Twitter's API is determined by the granularity of the location specified (e.g., whether it is at the city, state, or country level). Thus, if a study assumes the latitude/longitude pair as a user's precise location, the state of Kansas in the US will likely be severely overrepresented because many geocoding services return a latitude/longitude pair in Kansas (i.e., the geographic center of the contiguous 48 states) when the input text is simply "United States" or "USA" (i.e., at the country level).

The second complication is even more pronounced: when the data-generation process is opaque, we cannot exclude the possibility for an unknown common cause to simultaneously affect both sets of variables used to operationalize X and Y. As a result, the unknown variable becomes a confounder that jeopardizes the inference of causal relationship $X \rightarrow Y$. For example, any causal inference over Twitter data is likely vulnerable to a potential confounder of whether a Twitter user is (or whether a tweet is from) a bona fide user or a bot, because human users and bots could behave differently on all characteristics, including the observed variables for both X and Y. While certain causal inference techniques, such as the use of instrumental variables, could function in the presence of unknown confounders, these techniques also require a clear understanding of the data-generation processes behind the observed X and Y. For example, the use of an instrumental variable Z requires that all associations between Z and Y must be through the association between X and Y. It is often difficult for researchers to make such assertions when the data-generation processes behind the observed X and Y remain opaque.

Validity Threats From the Use of Computational Algorithms

In this section, we illustrate the validity threats posed by the two complications arising from the use of computational algorithms in processing organic data: (1) the errors of algorithmic outputs, and (2) the parameter-tuning process required for the proper functioning of the algorithms. As discussed earlier, computational algorithms can be used at various stages of the research process to code different types of variables (e.g., independent, dependent, and moderating variables) and/or to infer their relationships. Consequently, the threats posed by the (improper) use of these algorithms also cut across different types of validity (e.g., construct, internal, and external validity). Thus, instead of attempting to pinpoint the specific types of validity threats emerging from each specific usage scenario, we instead focus our discussions on the characteristics of the computational algorithms that could threaten the overall validity of research findings based on organic data.

Validity Threats from Algorithmic Errors

The validity threat stemming from algorithmic errors might appear to be straightforward: the more errors an algorithm incurs, the more serious the validity threat. If this were true, then researchers should be optimistic because, as computer scientists continue improving the accuracy of information-extraction algorithms, the use of these algorithms may soon pose no threat to the validity of research on organic data. Unfortunately, this oversimplified understanding of how algorithmic error affects validity is a serious misconception. As elaborated in the passages that follow, an algorithm could incur a much larger amount of errors than human coders yet pose no significant threat to validity. Meanwhile, an algorithm that outperforms human coders in terms of accuracy could still manifest serious validity threats. The key factor is *not* the amount of errors but whether researchers have sufficient knowledge of such errors so as to be able to account for them in the research design. To illustrate this point, we discuss two types of algorithmic errors, *benign errors* and *malignant errors*, respectively, as follows.

Benign Errors

A broad class of computational algorithms, called *randomized algorithms* (Motwani & Raghavan, 1995), is known to produce incorrect outputs (or fail to produce any product) with certain probability, yet can be extremely useful in practice. For example, consider an organic dataset consisting of the software products (e.g., GitHub repositories) developed by different teams, and a research study that measures the performance of a team through the quality of its products, e.g., by counting the number of security vulnerabilities in the software code (Arcuri & Briand, 2014). Since security vulnerabilities may emerge in any potential execution path of a software product, which branches out exponentially according to the running environment, it is infeasible for not just human experts, but even computational algorithms, to exhaustively search for all possible execution paths to identify all potential vulnerabilities. Thus, most, if not all, computational algorithms designed for this purpose are randomized ones (Harman & McMinn, 2010) that randomly sample the branch to follow at every turn in running the code. Clearly, the vulnerability count returned by such an algorithm is error-prone. Yet such an error, even when numerically large, is *benign* in terms of research validity because not only the error distribution is clearly known (i.e., a shifted binomial distribution), but the error stems solely from the randomness of the (vulnerability-counting) algorithm and is provably independent of any other study variables of theoretical interest in the study (e.g., characteristics of the team). Thus, other than potentially reducing the statistical power of the study, the error is unlikely to result in Type I error in the research findings.

Malignant Errors

Standing in sharp contrast are malignant errors, which may be numerically small yet pose serious threats to the validity of research findings. An example is the deep-learning-based algorithms for recognizing gender from facial images. Buolamwini and Gebru (2018) examined three commercial algorithms and found that, despite having very low overall error rates (e.g., the Microsoft algorithm achieved an overall accuracy of 93.7%), the errors incurred by the algorithms are highly imbalanced across gender and racial groups. For example, the Microsoft algorithm has a 0.0% error rate for lighter-skinned males yet a 20.8% error rate for darker-skinned females. Such disparate error rates, in essence, manifest an artificial dependency of the algorithm-coded gender on race. As a result, any gender-related research finding, like whether there is a gender difference on a criterion variable like job performance, could reflect either the artifact introduced by the algorithm or the effect of race on the criterion variable (or both). In this case, the algorithmic errors, while small, pose serious threats to the validity of research findings. Note from this example that a key reason why the algorithmic errors become malignant is that the data-generation process behind such errors is unknown to researchers, making it impossible for them to account for the errors in the research design or statistical analysis. Unfortunately, many recent machine-learning-based information extraction methods, like deep-learning algorithms (Krizhevsky, Sutskever & Hinton, 2012), are known to produce outputs (which probably contain errors) that are difficult to interpret by human experts (Bau et al., 2017; Szegedy et al., 2013), likely exacerbating the validity threats posed by malignant errors.

Validity Threats from Parameter Tuning

As explained earlier, parameter tuning is a common presence in the use of computational algorithms to process data. Some algorithms, like k-means clustering (Brusco, Shireman & Steinley, 2017), *require* the specification (and, therefore, tuning) of a parameter k (i.e., the number of clusters) before the algorithm can be used. While parameter tuning may be optional for other algorithms (e.g., the number of trees in the random forest algorithm; Liaw & Wiener, 2002), doing so is often essential for the proper functioning of some algorithms (Hastie, Tibshirani & Friedman, 2009). Before discussing the validity threats that could emerge from the parameter-tuning process in the use of computational algorithms, it is important to note that tuning parameters for an algorithm is not *in and of itself* a problem. Indeed, the process of parameter tuning can be both practically necessary and theoretically sound. Practically, many computational algorithms require users to tune their parameters based on a dataset in order to perform properly (Bergstra et al., 2013). Theoretically, consider the case where researchers have access to an infinite amount of samples, and tune the parameters to achieve the optimal algorithmic performance over the entire population. In this case, the tuned parameter settings become a function of the data-generation process and independent of the sample that happens to be taken in the research study, making the parameter-tuning process free of threatening the validity of research findings.

To understand how parameter tuning could pose serious validity threats, it is helpful to juxtapose the process of parameter tuning with the questionable research practice of *p*-hacking (Nelson, Simmons & Simonsohn, 2018), e.g., the repeated attempts of searching through a large space of variable combinations for a statistically significant relationship. Like discussed before for parameter tuning, if *p*-hacking were conducted over an infinite amount of samples produced by the data-generation process (rather than a dataset with a limited sample size), then the outcome of it would reflect the data-generation process rather than being the spurious relationships that only hold over the limited-sample dataset. In other words, what truly threatens the validity of research findings is the tendency for certain research practices, like *p*-hacking, to generate results that hold over nothing else but the dataset on hand. Following the same logic, parameter tuning becomes a validity threat when the tuned parameters function in a substantially different way between the dataset on hand than and other datasets stemming from the same data-generation process.

This problem is known as the out-of-sample generalization problem in machine learning (Zhang et al., 2017). In essence, when the parameter space (i.e., the set of all possible value combinations for the parameters) is large enough, if a researcher attempts too many parameter settings, then simply by chance some settings will lead to considerably more favorable (i.e., preferred by the researcher) results over the specific samples on hand than over the true data-generation process (Hofman, Sharma & Watts, 2017). If such results, in turn, alter the research findings, then clearly the parameter-tuning process poses a serious validity threat akin to the practice of cherry-picking test results in studies using designed data (Nelson et al., 2018).

Validity Threats from the Opaqueness of the Data-Generation Process

In this section, we discuss the validity threats stemming from the opaqueness of the data-generation process underpinning organic data. Specifically, we focus on two types of validity threats: (1) the threats to construct validity from the design of data filtering and/or the measurement of theoretical constructs and (2) the threats to internal validity from unknown confounders and measurement errors.

Threats to Construct Validity from Filtering and Measurement Design

As discussed earlier, the opaqueness of the data-generation process leads to the complication of mapping constructs of theoretical interests to variables included in an organic dataset. An improper mapping gives rise to construct validity threats. In the passages that follow, we discuss two common steps in the processing of organic data that could introduce intuitively appealing yet practically flawed mappings that threaten the construct validity of a research design: (1) the filtering of organic data to a subset that fits the research interests and (2) the measurement design for theoretical constructs.

Data Filtering

Many organic datasets, especially those derived from technological platforms like Twitter, have to be filtered before research use due to the sheer volume of data. In the case of Twitter, even when computational algorithms are used, it is still infeasible to process each and every tweet to determine whether one is relevant to the research interests. Thus, researchers usually have to rely on the filters provided by the technological platforms, such as Twitter's search API, to preselect a subset of tweets that serve as the input data to subsequent research activities. Doing so requires researchers to map the research interests to a set of *keywords* that are then entered to the search interface. The proper selection of keywords (which is part of the research design), however, can be blunted by two types of opaqueness in the data-generation process.

First, it is unclear what words people (e.g., Twitter users) tend to use in reference to the research interests. For example, it might appear reasonable to use the keyword "Obamacare" to identify tweets relevant to the Affordable Care Act (ACA). Yet, at least when ACA was first enacted, the use of the word "Obamacare" carried a negative connotation that expressed a person's opposition to the law. In contrast, the use of the word "ACA" carried a positive connotation that signaled support. Thus, if a researcher was to use either "ACA" or "Obamacare" as the keyword (but not the other), the filtered data during a certain time would likely be a severely biased sample of the overall sentiment toward ACA. Phenomena like this are indeed the norm, not the exceptions, as Zhang, Hill, and Rothschild (2016) found that the words different individuals use to discuss the same topic may have little overlap, instead reflecting the individual's own experience or opinion about the subject. Clearly, if a researcher is unaware of this association between word choice and attitudes toward the research topic (i.e., opaqueness in the way in which individuals "generate" their data), then bias in the design of data filters could threaten the construct validity and internal validity of the research design. On the other hand, by taking, (at least part of) the data-generation process into consideration, a researcher could include a more comprehensive set of keywords in the data-filtering process and thereby amorliate the corresponding robustness issues.

The second type of opaqueness is the (unknown) ambiguities associated with a filtering condition, especially a filter relying on the data provider. For example, a seemingly straightforward way to filter tweets by its relevance to a city (e.g., Houston, Texas) is to use the city name as a filtering keyword. Yet a name like "Houston" could retrieve many more irrelevant tweets (e.g., those mentioning "Whitney Houston") than a name like "Indianapolis." Such ambiguities can be compounded by the opaqueness of the filtering mechanism provided by a technological platform. For example, if a filtering keyword is specified as "Houston, Texas," a platform equipped with NLP-based entity resolution techniques (Getoor & Machanavajjhala, 2012) would be able to recognize this as a location and only returns results in which Houston also appears as a location (rather than as part of a person's name). A platform without such capability, on the other hand, could return results that match either "Houston" or "Texas." If a researcher is unaware of such subtle differences when processing the filtered data, construct validity threats may emerge in the research design.

Measurement Design

The opaqueness associated with the data-generation process also directly affects how the variables in an organic dataset can be used to measure constructs of theoretical interests. Like in the case of data filtering, ostensibly straightforward measures could be tainted by the opaqueness of individual behavior and technological design. For example, consider the issue of measuring the similarity between two companies' presence on Twitter. A seemingly straightforward idea is to measure the amount of overlap between their followers, with the premise being that two companies attracting the same type of followers must be similar to each other. Unfortunately, such a measure is likely affected by many factors beyond a researcher's reach. For example, Meeder et al. (2011) found that nearly half of all following events occur within one day of a user joining Twitter. In other words, if two companies happen to be trending on Twitter, like appearing on Twitter's "Trends" list, at the same time, they could inadvertently acquire a large number of common followers without having any similarity between them. Similarly, without knowing the design underpinning Twitter's "Who to follow" service (Gupta, Goel, Lin, Sharma, Wang, & Zadeh, 2013), it is difficult for researchers to determine whether two companies are likely to appear on the list at the same time, again acquiring a large number of common followers. As

can be seen in these examples, the opaqueness of both user behavior and platform design could manifest as construct validity threats even when the design of
a measurement is both intuitively appealing and simple.

Threats to Internal Validity from Unknown Confounders and Measurement Errors

As discussed before, the infeasibility of randomization for creating organic
datasets gives rise to the problem of confounding, with which an unknown
confounder could jeopardize the inference of causality from observational data.
Further, the presence of measurement errors in an organic dataset may also affect
causal inference, especially when machine learning is used to delineate nonlinear
relationships. We first discuss three common types of confounders: (1) time or,
more precisely, the rapid evolution of technological design, (2) unknown links
between data sources, and (3) unknown links between variables from the same
data source, before discussing the threats of measurement errors.

Time

Many organic datasets are collected over months or years. On the one hand, the
long period of data collection contributes to the large volume of collected data, the
advantages of which were discussed earlier in the chapter. On the other hand, it also
exposes the collected data to potential changes in the technological design underpinning data collection. For example, consider an organic dataset consisting of
Instagram users' activity logs on mobile devices. According to uptodown.com, the
Instagram app on Android was updated 31 times in December 2020 alone. Some of
these updates were security fixes that do not affect functionalities, but many others could change how the platform functioned (Segarra, 2018) and, consequently,
altered the users' activities on the mobile platform or how such activities are logged.
If some of these logged activities are used for measuring the independent variables
and some for the dependent variable, then the technological changes over time
become a confounder that threatens the internal validity of the research finding.

This issue is even more pronounced if the research involves a longitudinal perspective. For example, in Apple's iOS app store, the way of computing the average review score for an app has changed repeatedly over the years (Dillet, 2017),
from the average score of all reviews for the app to the average score of reviews
for the current version only to allowing app developers to choose whether to
reset the average review score after each app update. If researchers were not
aware of such policy changes, they could easily misinterpret a recent increase of
average review scores as an improvement of app quality, while the increase could
simply be an artifact of the app developers now having the ability to design their
score-reset strategies to boost their displayed average scores. Again, technological
changes over time could manifest as internal validity threats for the inferences.

Links Between Features

As technological platforms become more sophisticated, so are the links between different variables collected from the platform. When seemingly irrelevant variables are indeed linked through the backend technological design, a researcher's lack of awareness of such links and thus failure to account for them could threaten the internal validity of a research. For example, consider an organic dataset consisting of users' activities on an e-commerce website that allows users to connect with each other as friends. Suppose that a user who never shopped for books before started buying books after befriending a savvy book buyer. It might appear straightforward to attribute such changes to the word-of-mouth effect. But a subtler, technological, link might exist that offers an alternative explanation. Specifically, almost all e-commerce websites offer users with recommendations of products to buy. It is plausible that, even though the user never noticed what their new friend was buying, the recommender system took into account the new friendship when generating the recommendation list and thus included books in the recommendations for the first time. In other words, the new book purchases could simply reflect the user following recommendations, rather than being influenced by any word-of-mouth effect. As can be seen in this example, the recommender system becomes a confounder for the causal relationship between different users' purchase patterns. In other words, such confounders threaten the internal validity of the research.

Link Between Data Sources

It is no secret that joining multiple organic datasets together can amplify their values to research. For example, by matching the time-series visitor counts for two websites, a researcher can discern the correlation between the two, e.g., how much traffic on one website is likely driven by referral links on the other (Sismeiro & Mahmood, 2018). It is important to note, however, that if there are links between datasets that are unknown to researchers, then such links could become confounders that threaten the internal validity of research design. This threat is especially pronounced when the organic datasets were collected from technological platforms, which are increasingly and intricately linked today thanks to the proliferation of open source software, cloud computing, etc. Back in 2016, one individual's decision to remove an open-source package called left-pad, which has a total of 11 lines of code, disrupted the development of numerous web services around the world, including Facebook and Netflix (Abdalkareem et al., 2020), because all these services, through the open-source packages they use (and the ones these packages use), had an ultimate dependency on left-pad. This incident demonstrates the scale and complexity of the web of dependencies between different technological platforms. If a researcher were to study the associations between activities on different web services yet were unaware of their common dependencies like left-pad then incidents like this become confounders that threaten the validity of causal inference.

Threats from Measurement Errors

Measurement errors in observed independent variables have been long known to bias (specifically, attenuate) the linear relationships inferred from regression analysis (Gustafson, 2003). When measurement errors are induced by classic instruments such as tests or survey questionnaires, researchers can correct for the resulting bias by examining the reliability of the instruments used. Yet such reliability information is rarely available for measures constructed from organic datasets. This challenge is compounded by the fact that measurement errors could introduce an even more pronounced bias into estimates of *nonlinear* relationships than linear ones, especially when data-driven inference tools like machine learning are used to infer such nonlinear relationships (Jacobucci & Grimm, 2020). The vast majority of machine learning algorithms are designed to unveil the relationships among the *observed* measurements rather than the ground-truth relationships among latent constructs. In other words, when researchers attempt to infer complex, nonlinear, relationships among theoretical constructs with complex measurement models from organic datasets prone to measurement errors, such errors could have an outsized influence on the robustness of the research findings.

Potential Solutions to Improve the Design of Organizational Science Studies

In this section, we discuss potential solutions to three critical problems facing the design of research studies involving organic data: (1) how to examine the validity threats from algorithmic errors, (2) how to prevent the parameter-tuning process from overfitting the data, and (3) what should researchers try to learn about the data-generation process underlying organic data?

How to Examine the Errors of a Computational Algorithm?

As discussed earlier in the chapter, the validity threat posed by algorithmic errors is less about the magnitude of the errors and more about researchers' knowledge of the error distribution. This indicates that the canonical ways of ensuring the reliability of human-coded data, like inter-coder reliability, are unlikely to be effective in dealing with algorithmic errors. Instead, researchers need to closely examine the design of an algorithm to determine whether the errors it generates are likely benign or malignant. In the former case (i.e., when the errors can be purely attributed to chance), errors could be mitigated with a larger dataset or, for certain randomized algorithms, by running the algorithm multiple times.

In the latter case (i.e., malignant errors), the burden is on the researcher to examine whether there are likely associations between the algorithmic errors and the other variables involved in the research study. This examination could start with seeking guidance from the related technical literature but, in the absence of such guidance, may require an empirical test of algorithmic performance. Such tests could include comparisons vis-à-vis other competing algorithms. For example, if the final research findings changed when replacing one algorithm with a competitor, then the researcher would have to convincingly demonstrate that the change can be explained by the algorithm having superior accuracy to the competitor rather than the research design just capitalizing on chance. The tests could also involve manual crosscheck of algorithmic errors (for a small sample) or evaluating the algorithm over other, similar, datasets. Recall from earlier discussions that the amount of algorithmic errors could differ drastically between different subpopulations (e.g., in the case of gender recognition from facial images). Thus, researchers may need to study the algorithmic errors in a stratified manner to fully understand the range of variables that could interact with the outputs of the algorithms.

How to Ensure Out-of-Sample Generalizability in Using Computational Algorithms

Given the earlier-discussed analogy between p-hacking and the over-tuning of parameters for computational algorithms, it would appear natural to assume that the existing remedies for p-hacking, like preregistration (e.g., Nelson et al., 2018), could also be used to prevent parameter tuning from overfitting the research dataset. Unfortunately, the use of preregistration in this context is blunted by the question of whether it is at all possible to predetermine the parameter settings. In preventing p-hacking, preregistration generally happens before a researcher collects the data. Adopting the same rule is difficult here because, without first seeing the organic dataset, researchers may not even be able to determine which algorithms are needed for processing the data. For example, without knowing how many values are missing in a dataset, it is unclear whether a researcher should simply discard samples with missing values (Daniel et al., 2012) or adopt complex prediction algorithms, like multiple imputation (Sterne et al., 2009) or semi-supervised learning (Zhu, Ghahramani & Lafferty, 2003), to fill in the missing values. It might be theoretically possible for researchers to consider all possible cases and preregister all potential solutions. Yet in practice, given the many different aspects of data quality that could affect the selection of algorithms for data preprocessing (Rahm & Do, 2000), it is usually infeasible for a researcher to anticipate all contingencies before even seeing the data.

If decisions on the parameter settings must come after observing the data, an obvious step to prevent the overfitting of parameters is to split the research datasets into two parts, one used to determine the parameter settings and the other to ensure the generalizability of such settings. The split can happen in different ways. For example, if the number of parameters is relatively small, one could use a small fraction of the dataset as a *pilot sample* to tune the parameters, before using the tuned parameters to carry out the research design over the remaining data. Alternatively, if the algorithms being used require a large number of parameters, one has to retain a large part of the dataset for tuning the parameters, meaning that a small fraction of the dataset will be left as a *hold-out sample* to test the generalizability of the parameter settings (cf. Campion et al., 2016). For example, if applying the same research design and parameter settings over the hold-out sample returns the same research findings, researchers can safely conclude that there is unlikely to be validity threats stemming from the overfitting of parameters to data.

It is important to note that, no matter how the dataset is split, the tuning of parameters *cannot* happen again after seeing the other part of the data. For example, consider the use of an algorithm that recognizes gender from facial images, and suppose that a researcher observed a systematic pattern for the chosen parameters to misclassify men as women in the hold-out sample. An intuitively appealing solution is for the researcher to use such an observation to retune the parameters to rectify the systematic bias. Yet doing so is *inappropriate* because it would disqualify the hold-out sample from serving as a validation tool (as specific properties of the hold-out sample, such as the facial feature of individuals within, have already been incorporated into the parameter design; Dwork et al., 2015). There are considerable subtleties in determining how hold-out samples should be used, as recent research in machine learning found widespread abuse of hold-out samples that led to significant overfitting problems (Cawley & Talbot, 2010; Reunanen, 2003). Fortunately, recent research in computer science developed randomization techniques that can enable the reuse of hold-out samples without incurring the overfitting problem (see further explanations in Dwork et al., 2015). The use of these techniques could significantly ease the precautions needed to guard against validity threats in the parameter-tuning process.

Besides the technical solution, there are also editorial policies that can help address the validity threats stemming from the parameter-tuning process. For example, researchers may be required or recommended to justify the parameter settings used in the research design, e.g., by disclosing the parameter settings or algorithms attempted but not adopted, and explaining the reason behind the decisions. For parameter settings that cannot be theoretically justified (e.g., the aforementioned example of whether to set the threshold of "short text" as 5 or 6 words), researchers may be encouraged to perform robustness checks to ensure that the research findings will not change drastically under a different, yet equally reasonable, parameter setting.

What Can Be Done About the Opaqueness of the Data-Generation Process?

The ideal solution to address the validity threats from an opaque data-generation process is to thoroughly "unpack" the process (e.g., the design of the technological platform from which the data were collected). Unfortunately, this is also an impractical solution given that the design of technological platforms is not only complex but often proprietary. The aforementioned recommender system design, for example, is usually considered as "highly guarded industrial secrets" (Milano, Taddeo & Floridi, 2020). Without the ability to fully unpack the data-generation process, there are still practices that researchers can follow to prevent the most common validity threats. We discuss some of these practices in the passages that follow.

First, it is important for researchers to *not* presuppose what drives people's behavior on a technological platform, but to carefully document the information users are exposed to on these platforms. In the previous e-commerce website example, instead of simply assuming that the sudden change of a user's purchase pattern must be a result of the word-of-mouth effect, a researcher should carefully examine the ways users interact with the e-commerce website by identifying the types of information displayed to users on the web interface, the potential data sources (e.g., the user's historic browsing records, other users' browsing patterns) that were used to generate the displayed information, the frequency in which such displayed information is updated, whether different users may see different interface designs, etc. These examinations will likely illuminate the importance of product recommendations in users' purchase decisions and, in turn, reveal to the researcher the possible role of recommender-system design on the change of a user's purchase pattern.

Similarly, even though it is unlikely for a researcher to learn *all* the technological design details that could possibly affect the organic dataset, it is still possible for the researcher to carefully research the characteristics of the technological design that are publicly known. Many examples discussed earlier in the chapter, e.g., the prevalent use of open-source packages and the frequent update of web services and apps, illustrate the importance of such research on identifying the potential confounders that could jeopardize the efforts of discerning causal relationships from the organic data.

Finally, performing robustness checks, e.g., by attempting different ways of filtering the input data or measuring theoretical constructs, can also help alleviate the validity threats. For example, instead of relying on researchers' manual efforts to identify the relevant keywords for data filtering, one could attempt automated solutions, like the bootstrapping technique commonly used in information retrieval (e.g., Zhang, Zhang & Das, 2013), which starts with a small set of keywords and then iteratively extracts additional keywords from the data retrieved by the earlier-identified keywords. Many alternative strategies also exist for measurement design. For the earlier example of measuring the similarity between two companies' Twitter profiles, researchers could count the number of common followers who joined Twitter before the creation of the companies' Twitter accounts (hence eliminating the confounder discussed earlier) or the number of common followers who frequently engage with both companies' Twitter accounts (e.g., through retweets). Researchers could also measure the similarity by analyzing the common language patterns between the tweets posted by the two companies. If the research findings remain similar across multiple measures, this convergence of evidence would alleviate concerns about the validity threats posed by the opaque data-generation process.

Increasing Need of Interdisciplinary Methodological Research

While much of the earlier discussions focused on the issues of using organic data, we caution against a "defeatist" view of abandoning research that involves organic data altogether due to the validity concerns. Given the critical roles served by organic data in organizations today, it is important for the research community to invest more in facilitating the proper use of organic data and the development of research methodologies to support such use, rather than deserting this valuable source of knowledge (Paxton & Griffiths, 2017). To this end, we conclude the chapter with a call for interdisciplinary research on the methodological issues related to the research use of organic data.

Organic data is extensively used for research in both computer science and social sciences. On the surface, the focus of research using organic data in the two camps are markedly different: the focus in computer science is often to develop algorithms that are more accurate and/or faster than the existing ones for performing certain tasks over organic datasets. Correspondingly, the empirical examinations in computer science focus on comparing the performance of different algorithms. Usually, researchers assert the superiority of their algorithm by demonstrating that it outperforms competitors over multiple *benchmark* datasets (e.g., Rajpurkar et al., 2016), which are often organic datasets recognized by the research community as representative of real-world data. In contrast, the focus of organic-data research in organizational science in particular, and social sciences in general, tends to be on using one organic dataset to test certain hypotheses derived from theory (e.g., see Min et al., 2021). Indicatively, empirical examinations frequently apply statistical tools for hypothesis testing over variables derived from the organic dataset, with the outcomes of statistical testing serving as the basis for the inferences from a research study.

The distinct purposes and research designs of the two camps would ostensibly suggest that they will likely follow divergent pathways for methodological development, with the only intersection being the need for social science researchers to make use of the computational algorithms developed by computer scientists. We argue that this view underestimates the degree of commonality between the two camps. At a high level, if we conceptualize the statistical models (e.g., regression models or confirmatory factor analysis models) tested in social sciences also as algorithms, then both camps, in essence, share a common goal of testing the (in-)distinguishability of the outputs of two algorithms over one dataset. In computer science, the two algorithms can be competitors for data filtering, from which the one with a better performance needs to be identified. For social sciences, the two algorithms represent the null and the alternative hypotheses, so a markedly better accuracy (i.e., model-data fit) of the latter would allow the rejection of the null hypothesis.

Viewed through this lens, there is considerable synergy in the future development of research methodologies across both camps. For social scientists, a proper understanding of algorithmic/technological design is instrumental to addressing the validity threats discussed earlier in the chapter. Further, there are also lessons to be learned from the design of empirical studies in computer science. For example, while social scientists value the curation of new datasets for answering novel research questions, it could also be extremely helpful to assemble a set of domain-specific "benchmark" datasets that can be used to identify validity threats in a research design. For example, if a research design frequently returns statistically significant findings over datasets that are known to be consistent with the null effect (e.g., Keogh & Lin, 2005), then researchers may be prompted to examine the potential sources of false positives in their research design. Similarly, these benchmark datasets could either directly serve as the basis for parameter tuning or augment a research dataset for such purpose, alleviating the earlier discussed validity threat from the overfitting of the tuned parameters to the research dataset. Finally, the availability of these benchmark datasets could also motivate computer scientists to optimize their algorithms for the specific domain, thereby contributing to the methodological development in both fields.

While there are many potential ways for generating such benchmark datasets, one method that is already familiar to many organizational science researchers is stochastic simulations based on the existing empirical evidence (e.g., covariance between variables reported in existing meta-analyses or primary studies). This method has been extensively used in areas such as personnel selection (Finch, Edwards & Wallace, 2009). Since researchers have full control on the data-generation process for the simulated data, biases and errors in the outputs of an algorithm could be easily identified and diagnosed (Keogh & Lin, 2015). The drawback of this method is that there are bound to be considerable differences between the distribution of the simulated data and that of the real-world data, especially when there are many variables, due to the so-called "curse of dimensionality" (Zhang et al., 2017). If left unattended, such differences could distort the parameters learned from the simulated data. To address this problem, researchers may need to deploy technical solutions designed to reduce such differences, such as augmenting the data-generation process with distribution information learned from the organic dataset (Zhang et al., 2017).

The need of social scientists could also inspire future research in computer science. For example, with the increasing adoption of machine learning algorithms in social science research, it is not uncommon to see studies that compare the accuracy of different machine learning algorithms/models using standard hypothesis testing tools like the paired t-test to determine which algorithm/model has a better predictive power for a criterion of interest. The problem here, however, is that the design of statistical tests for comparing the performance of different machine learning algorithms is not yet a settled area in computer science. Dieterich (1998), for example, found that the paired t-test is fundamentally incompatible with a common method of assessing the accuracy of machine learning algorithms, i.e., the k-fold cross validation, because cross validation breaks the independence between different runs of a machine learning algorithm. While later research suggested the use of nonparametric testing for this purpose (Demšar, 2006), future research is needed to identify the appropriate methods for comparing different measures of algorithmic performance, such as the F_1 score, AUC, etc.

In sum, organic data is likely to present ongoing challenges to researchers, but the potential value of data of this sort is clear, and the use of organic data is likely to grow in the organizational sciences. We hope that the warnings and advice offered here will assist researchers in making the best use of organic data.

References

Abdalkareem, R., Oda, V., Mujahid, S., & Shihab, E. (2020). On the impact of using trivial packages: An empirical case study on npm and pypi. *Empirical Software Engineering, 25*(2), 1168–1204.

Arcuri, A., & Briand, L. (2014). A hitchhiker's guide to statistical tests for assessing randomized algorithms in software engineering. *Software Testing, Verification and Reliability, 24*(3), 219–250.

Barberá, P., Jost, J. T., Nagler, J., Tucker, J. A., & Bonneau, R. (2015). Tweeting from left to right: Is online political communication more than an echo chamber? *Psychological Science, 26*(10), 1531–1542.

Bau, D., Zhou, B., Khosla, A., Oliva, A., & Torralba, A. (2017). Network dissection: Quantifying interpretability of deep visual representations. In *Proceedings of the IEEE conference on computer vision and pattern recognition* (pp. 6541–6549).

Bergstra, J., Yamins, D., & Cox, D. (2013, February). Making a science of model search: Hyperparameter optimization in hundreds of dimensions for vision architectures. *International conference on machine learning* (pp. 115–123). PMLR.

Blodgett, S. L., & O'Connor, B. (2017). Racial disparity in natural language processing: A case study of social media African-American English. *arXiv* preprint arXiv:1707.00061.

Breiman, L. (2001). Statistical modeling: The two cultures (with comments and a rejoinder by the author). *Statistical Science, 16*(3), 199–231.

Brusco, M. J., Shireman, E., & Steinley, D. (2017). A comparison of latent class, K-means, and K-median methods for clustering dichotomous data. *Psychological Methods, 22*(3), 563.

Buolamwini, J., & Gebru, T. (2018, January). Gender shades: Intersectional accuracy disparities in commercial gender classification. In *Conference on fairness, accountability and transparency* (pp. 77–91). PMLR.

Campion, M. C., Campion, M. A., Campion, E. D., & Reider, M. H. (2016). Initial investigation into computer scoring of candidate essays for personnel selection. *Journal of Applied Psychology*, *101*(7), 958–975.

Cawley, G. C., & Talbot, N. L. (2010). On over-fitting in model selection and subsequent selection bias in performance evaluation. *The Journal of Machine Learning Research*, *11*, 2079–2107.

Cochran, W. G. (1972). Observational Studies, In *Statistical Papers in Honor of George W. Snedeor*, 77–90. Ames, Iowa: Iowa State University Press.

Cook, D., Waugh, B., Abdipanah, M., Hashemi, O., & Rahman, S. A. (2014). Twitter deception and influence: Issues of identity, slacktivism, and puppetry. *Journal of Information Warfare*, *13*(1), 58–71.

Daniel, R. M., Kenward, M. G., Cousens, S. N., & De Stavola, B. L. (2012). Using causal diagrams to guide analysis in missing data problems. *Statistical Methods in Medical Research*, *21*, 243–256.

Davidov, D., Tsur, O., & Rappoport, A. (2010, July). Semi-supervised recognition of sarcasm in Twitter and Amazon. In *Proceedings of the fourteenth conference on computational natural language learning* (pp. 107–116).

Demšar, J. (2006). Statistical comparisons of classifiers over multiple data sets. *The Journal of Machine Learning Research*, *7*, 1–30.

Dietterich, T. G. (1998). Approximate statistical tests for comparing supervised classification learning algorithms. *Neural Computation*, *10*(7), 1895–1923.

Dillet, R. (2017). The new iOS App Store lets devs choose whether or not to reset ratings when updating. TechCrunch. Retrieved on July 15, 2018, from https://techcrunch.com/2017/06/07/ios-app-developers.

Doré, B., Ort, L., Braverman, O., & Ochsner, K. N. (2015). Sadness shifts to anxiety over time and distance from the national tragedy in Newtown, Connecticut. *Psychological Science*, *26*(4), 363–373.

Dwork, C., Feldman, V., Hardt, M., Pitassi, T., Reingold, O., & Roth, A. (2015). The reusable holdout: Preserving validity in adaptive data analysis. *Science*, *349*, 636–638.

Feehan, L. M., Geldman, J., Sayre, E. C., Park, C., Ezzat, A. M., Yoo, J. Y., … Li, L. C. (2018). Accuracy of Fitbit devices: Systematic review and narrative syntheses of quantitative data. *JMIR mHealth and uHealth*, *6*(8), e10527.

Finch, D. M., Edwards, B. D., & Wallace, J. C. (2009). Multistage selection strategies: Simulating the effects on adverse impact and expected performance for various predictor combinations. *Journal of Applied Psychology*, *94*(2), 318–340.

Gal, Y., & Ghahramani, Z. (2016, June). Dropout as a bayesian approximation: Representing model uncertainty in deep learning. In *International conference on machine learning* (pp. 1050–1059). PMLR.

Getoor, L., & Machanavajjhala, A. (2012). Entity resolution: Theory, practice & open challenges. *Proceedings of the VLDB Endowment*, *5*(12), 2018–2019.

Groves, M. R. (2011). Three eras of survey research. *Public Opinions Quarterly*, *75*(5), 861–871.

Gupta, P., Goel, A., Lin, J., Sharma, A., Wang, D., & Zadeh, R. (2013, May). Wtf: The who to follow service at twitter. In *Proceedings of the 22nd international conference on World Wide Web*, 505–514.

Gustafson, P. (2003). *Measurement error and misclassification in statistics and epidemiology: Impacts and Bayesian adjustments*. CRC Press.

Harman, M., & McMinn, P. 2010. A theoretical and empirical study of search-based testing: Local, global, and hybrid search. *IEEE Transactions on Software Engineering, 36*, 226–247.

Hastie, T., Tibshirani, R., & Friedman, J. (2009). Random forests. In *The elements of statistical learning* (pp. 587–604). Springer, New York, NY.

Hecht, B., Hong, L., Suh, B., & Chi, E. H. (2011, May). Tweets from Justin Bieber's heart: The dynamics of the location field in user profiles. In *Proceedings of the SIGCHI conference on human factors in computing systems* (pp. 237–246).

Henrich, J., Heine, S. J., & Norenzayan, A. (2010). Most people are not WEIRD. *Nature, 466*(7302), 29–29.

Hofman, J. M., Sharma, A., & Watts, D. J. (2017). Prediction and explanation in social systems. *Science, 355*(6324), 486–488.

Hua, W., Wang, Z., Wang, H., Zheng, K., & Zhou, X. (2015, April). Short text understanding through lexical-semantic analysis. In *2015 IEEE 31st International Conference on Data Engineering* (pp. 495–506).

Imran, M., Castillo, C., Diaz, F., & Vieweg, S. (2015). Processing social media messages in mass emergency: A survey. *ACM Computing Surveys (CSUR), 47*(4), 67.

Jacobucci, R., & Grimm, K. J. (2020). Machine learning and psychological research: The unexplored effect of measurement. *Perspectives on Psychological Science, 15*(3), 809–816.

Jiang, L., Yin, D., & Liu, D. (2019). Can joy buy you money? The impact of the strength, duration, and phases of an entrepreneur's peak displayed joy on funding performance. *Academy of Management Journal, 62*(6), 1848–1871.

Kearney, M. S., & Levine, P. B. (2015). Media influences on social outcomes: The impact of MTV's 16 and pregnant on teen childbearing. *The American Economic Review, 105*(12), 3597–3632.

Keogh, E., & Lin, J. (2005). Clustering of time-series subsequences is meaningless: Implications for previous and future research. *Knowledge and Information Systems, 8*(2), 154–177.

King, G., & Lowe, W. (2003). An automated information extraction tool for international conflict data with performance as good as human coders: A rare events evaluation design. *International Organization*, 617–642.

Krizhevsky, A., Sutskever, I., & Hinton, G. E. (2012). Imagenet classification with deep convolutional neural networks. *Advances in Neural Information Processing Systems, 25*, 1097–1105.

Landers, R. N., Brusso, R. C., Cavanaugh, K. J., & Collmus, A. B. (2016). A primer on theory-driven web scraping: Automatic extraction of big data from the Internet for use in psychological research. *Psychological Methods, 21*(4), 475.

Lazer, D., Kennedy, R., King, G., & Vespignani, A. (2014). The parable of Google Flu: Traps in big data analysis. *Science, 343*(6176), 1203–1205.

LeCun, Y., Bengio, Y., & Hinton, G. (2015). Deep learning. *Nature, 521*(7553), 436–444.

Liaw, A., & Wiener, M. (2002). Classification and regression by random forest. *R News, 2*(3), 18–22.

McFarland, D. A., & McFarland, H. R. (2015). Big data and the danger of being precisely inaccurate. *Big Data and Society*, July–December, 1–4.

McFarland, D. A., Lewis, K., & Goldberg, A. (2016). Sociology in the era of big data: The ascent of forensic social science. *American Sociologist, 47*, 12–35.

Meeder, B., Karrer, B., Sayedi, A., Ravi, R., Borgs, C., & Chayes, J. (2011, March). We know who you followed last summer: Inferring social link creation times in Twitter. In *Proceedings of the 20th international conference on World Wide Web* (pp. 517–526).

Milano, S., Taddeo, M., & Floridi, L. (2020). Recommender systems and their ethical challenges. *Artificial Intelligence and Society, 35*(4), 957–967.

Min, H., Peng, Y., Shoss, M., & Yang, B. (2021). Using machine learning to investigate the public's emotional responses to work from home during the COVID-19 pandemic. *Journal of Applied Psychology, 106*(2), 214–229.

Mislove, A., Lehmann, S., Ahn, Y. Y., Onnela, J. P., & Rosenquist, J. (2011). Understanding the demographics of Twitter users. In *Proceedings of the international AAAI conference on web and social media, 5*(1), 554–557.

Morchid, M., Dufour, R., Bousquet, P. M., Linares, G., & Torres-Moreno, J. M. (2014). Feature selection using principal component analysis for massive retweet detection. *Pattern Recognition Letters, 49*, 33–39.

Morstatter, F., & Liu, H. (2017). Discovering, assessing, and mitigating data bias in social media. *Online Social Networks and Media, 1*, 1–13.

Morstatter, F., Pfeffer, J., & Liu, H. (2014, April). When is it biased?: Assessing the representativeness of twitter's streaming API. In *Proceedings of the 23rd international conference on World Wide Web* (pp. 555–556). ACM.

Morstatter, F., Pfeffer, J., Liu, H., & Carley, K. (2013, June). Is the sample good enough? Comparing data from twitter's streaming api with twitter's firehose. In *Proceedings of the international AAAI conference on web and social media, 7*(1), 400–408.

Motwani, R., & Raghavan, P. (1995). *Randomized algorithms.* Cambridge University Press.

Nelson, L. D., Simmons, J., & Simonsohn, U. (2018). Psychology's renaissance. *Annual Review of Psychology, 69*, 511–534.

Ott, M., Cardie, C., & Hancock, J. (2012, April). Estimating the prevalence of deception in online review communities. In *Proceedings of the 21st international conference on World Wide Web* (pp. 201–210).

Paxton, A., & Griffiths, T. L. (2017). Finding the traces of behavioral and cognitive processes in big data and naturally occurring datasets. *Behavior Research Methods, 49*(5), 1630–1638.

Pearl, J. (2009). *Causality: Models, reasoning and inference.* Cambridge University Press.

Rahm, E., & Do, H. H. (2000). Data cleaning: Problems and current approaches. *IEEE Data Engineering Bulletin, 23*, 3–13.

Rajpurkar, P., Zhang, J., Lopyrev, K., & Liang, P. (2016, January). SQuAD: 100,000+ Questions for Machine Comprehension of Text. Proceedings of the 2016 Conference on Empirical Methods in Natural Language Processing (EMNLP), Austin, TX.

Reunanen, J. (2003). Overfitting in making comparisons between variable selection methods. *Journal of Machine Learning Research, 3*, 1371–1382.

Rhys, H. I. (2020). *Machine learning with R, the tidyverse, and mlr.* Manning Publications.

Ruggles, S. (2014). Big microdata for population research. *Demography, 51*, 287–297.

Salganik, M. J. (2018). *Bit by bit: Social research in the digital age.* Princeton, NJ: Princeton University Press.

Segarra, L. M. (2018). Instagram is making a big change and now new posts will show up first again. *Time.* Retrieved on July 15, 2018, from http://time.com/5210976/instagram

Shrestha, Y. R., He, V. F., Puranam, P., & von Krogh, G. (2020). Algorithm supported induction for building theory: How can we use prediction models to theorize? *Organization Science*, 856–880.

Silberzahn, R., Uhlmann, E. L., Martin, D. P., Anselmi, P., Aust, F., Awtrey, E., … Nosek, B. A. (2018). Many analysts, one data set: Making transparent how variations in analytic choices affect results. *Advances in Methods and Practices in Psychological Science, 1*(3), 337–356.

Sismeiro, C., & Mahmood, A. (2018). Competitive vs. complementary effects in online social networks and news consumption: A natural experiment. *Management Science, 64*(11), 5014–5037.

Smith, A. (2011). Who's on what: Social media trends among communities of color. *Pew Internet and American Life Project*.

Snefjella, B., & Kuperman, V. (2015). Concreteness and psychological distance in natural language use. *Psychological Science, 26*(9), 1449–1460.

Sterne, J. A., White, I. R., Carlin, J. B., Spratt, M., Royston, P., Kenward, M. G., … Carpenter, J. R. (2009). Multiple imputation for missing data in epidemiological and clinical research: Potential and pitfalls. *BMJ*, 338.

Szegedy, C., Zaremba, W., Sutskever, I., Bruna, J., Erhan, D., Goodfellow, I., & Fergus, R. (2013). Intriguing properties of neural networks. *arXiv* preprint:1312.6199.

Taigman, Y., Yang, M., Ranzato, M. A., & Wolf, L. (2014). Deepface: Closing the gap to human-level performance in face verification. In *Proceedings of the IEEE conference on computer vision and pattern recognition* (pp. 1701–1708).

Uyar, A. (2009). Investigation of the accuracy of search engine hit counts. *Journal of Information Science, 35*(4), 469–480.

Vasi, I. B., Walker, E. T., Johnson, J. S., & Tan, H. F. (2015). "No fracking way!" Documentary film, discursive opportunity, and local opposition against hydraulic fracturing in the United States, 2010 to 2013. *American Sociological Review, 80*(5), 934–959.

Wagner, C. H. (1982). Simpson's paradox in real life. *American Statistician, 36*(1), 46–48.

Wang, W., Hernandez, I., Newman, D. A., He, J., & Bian, J. (2016). Twitter analysis: Studying US weekly trends in work stress and emotion. *Applied Psychology: An International Review, 65*(2), 355–378.

Yarkoni, T., & Westfall, J. (2017). Choosing prediction over explanation in psychology: Lessons from machine learning. *Perspectives on Psychological Science, 12*(6), 1100–1122.

Zhang, C., Bengio, S., Hardt, M., Recht, B., & Vinyals, O. (2017). Understanding deep learning requires rethinking generalization. *International Conference on Learning Representations*.

Zhang, J., Cormode, G., Procopiuc, C. M., Srivastava, D., & Xiao, X. (2017). Privbayes: Private data release via bayesian networks. *ACM Transactions on Database Systems (TODS), 42*(4), 1–41.

Zhang, H., Hill, S., & Rothschild, D. (2016, March). Geolocated Twitter panels to study the impact of events. In 2016 *AAAI Spring Symposium Series*.

Zhang, Q., Wu, Y. N., & Zhu, S. C. (2018, June). Interpretable convolutional neural networks. In *The IEEE conference on computer vision and pattern recognition (CVPR)* (pp. 8827–8836).

Zhang, M., Zhang, N., & Das, G. (2013). Mining a search engine's corpus without a query pool. *Proceedings of the ACM conference on information and knowledge management*, 29–38. ACM.

Zhiltsova, A., Caton, S., & Mulway, C. (2019). Mitigation of unintended biases against non-native English texts in sentiment analysis. In *AICS* (pp. 317–328).

Zhu, X., Ghahramani, Z., & Lafferty, J. D. (2003). Semi-supervised learning using Gaussian fields and harmonic functions. *Proceedings of the 20th international conference on machine learning*, 912–919. AAAI Press.

7

SURVIVING THE STATISTICAL ARMS RACE

Kevin R. Murphy

In this chapter, I will argue four main points. First, data analysis in the behavioral and social sciences has become increasingly complex. There are good reasons to believe that these methods of analysis promise a great deal more than they typically deliver, and they have contributed significantly to the decreasing interpretability and importance of our research. Second, changes in the types and volume of data available to organizational researchers are likely to make these methods even more difficult to appropriately use and interpret. Third, complex analysis is having an increasingly negative effect on the types of theories we develop and the types of studies we perform. Fourth, this "statistical arms race" – i.e., a continuing pursuit of increasingly complex and opaque methods of analysis, is a losing game, and our best chance for using statistical analyses as a tool for making sense of data is to make them simpler and more direct and to avoid unnecessary complexity.

The Lure of Complex Analytic Methods

The methods used to collect and analyze data in research on behavior in organizations have become increasingly complex. In part, the complexity and variety of data analytic methods in our field are a reflection of the diversity of the questions organizational researchers pursue, as well as the diversity in levels of analysis for this research. Twenty-five years ago, organizational researchers with a solid understanding of ordinary least squares (OLS) regression and its applications to a range of analytic questions and methods (e.g., analysis of experimental data, field research) would be well-positioned to understand the analyses included in most of the research published in leading journals. This is no longer the case.

DOI: 10.4324/9781003015000-9

There is a continuing embrace of new analytic methods, in part because they sometimes appear to open new and useful lines of inquiry. For example, there has been a great deal of attention to level of analysis questions in the last 25 years (Chen, Mathieu & Bliese, 2004; Klein, Dansereau & Hall, 1994; Klein & Kozlowski, 2000), driven in part by the widespread availability of multilevel modeling methods. Without adequate analytic methods, it is unlikely that our understanding of the complex issues or inference or the theoretical implications of aggregation would have advanced so far. On the other hand, papers in which multilevel analytic models are used, even though there are no meaningful cross-level questions or credible aggregation effects present seem increasingly common. There sometimes can be statistical advantages to using these methods even in the absence of substantial aggregation effects (Bliese, Maltarich & Hendricks, 2018), but as I will explain in the sections that follow, there are also substantial disadvantages to wandering from the familiar territory of OLS regression.

As new types of data and new research designs become available, it is possible that the statistical toolkit of organizational researchers will become increasingly diverse and complex. For example, data mining (automated processes for detecting unsuspected patterns in large databases) uses a very different set of tools than those used by organizational scientists to analyze data, and it is not always clear what role most of our most common analytic tools might play in the analysis of "big data" (Friedman, 1997; Kuonen, 2004). Data mining often involves tasks, such as anomaly detection, clustering to discover groups, and building models to capture relationships among variables in the dataset (Hand, 1998; Nisbett, Elder & Miner, 2009), and it is likely that organizational researchers will be increasingly drawn to these methods, regardless of whether they have a sufficient understanding of how they work. In a later section, I will examine the implications of data mining and, more generally, big data for data analysts trained in the methods most frequently encountered in organizational journals.

Statistical Methods in Organizational Research Are Complex and Diverse

There is clear evidence that the methods used to analyze data in organizational research are becoming increasingly varied and complex. To quantify the range and complexity of these statistical methods, I reviewed research from two journals, *Journal of Management* (JOM) and *Journal of Applied Psychology* (JAP). These journals were chosen because of their combined breadth of coverage and quality; both are top-tier journals that cover a wide remit.

I reviewed all of the papers published in these two journals in 2018 and 2019 (Volumes 44, 45 of *JOM* and 103,104 of *JAP*, respectively). Several papers were editorials, recommendations regarding research methods, meta-analyses or theory-development papers, but there were 248 papers that used quantitative

TABLE 7.1 Principal analytic methods – *JAP* and
JOM 2018–2019

Method	Percentage
OLS regression and variants[1]	16.9
Regression with qualitative DVs[2]	9.6
Moderated multiple regression	16.5
Advanced regression variants[3]	13.7
Latent variable analysis[4]	14.9
Multilevel modeling	20.6
Other[5]	7.2

Note:

[1] Includes ANOVA, ANCOVA.
[2] Includes logistic probit, tobit analyses.
[3] Includes polynomial regression, 2-stage regression, random
coefficient models, panel regression.
[4] Includes latent path analysis, SEM, CFA.
[5] Includes event history/hazard models, visualization
methods.

methods to test the principal hypotheses advanced by the authors. Table 7.1 sum-marizes the results of this analysis. Forty-two of these papers (16.9%) relied on OLS regression or some variant (e.g., ANOVA) to test their main hypotheses.[1]

Twenty-four papers, (9.6%) used some form of regression with qualitative dependent variables (e.g., logistic regression). Moderated or mediated regression methods were quite popular (41 papers, or 16.5%); advanced variants of regression (e.g., polynomial regression, random coefficient models) were almost equally popular (34 papers, or 13.7%). Latent variable analyses and multilevel analyses were common (37 and 52 papers, or 14.9% and 20.6%, respectively); multilevel modeling represented the most common analytic method in this set of papers. A grab-bag of other methods (e.g., event history/hazard models, visualization methods) was used in a handful of papers (18 papers, or 7.2%). On the whole, this quick review reinforces the idea that complex and sophisticated methods of data analysis have become the norm in organizational research.

Increasing complexity in analysis brings some real benefits; the range of questions that can be attacked using SEM, multilevel modeling (MLM), random coefficient models, and the like is arguably wider than questions that can be adequately addressed using OLS regression. However, there are many potential costs. First, complex analyses are often done incorrectly. For example, Cortina et al. (2017) reviewed over 700 SEM models reported in leading organizational models. A quarter of the analyses did not report degrees of freedom or the information needed to compute them, and in cases where it was possible to obtain or compute them, degrees of freedom were wrong in over 1/3 of the models examined, throwing doubt on these analyses and their interpretation. Second, complex analyses are often difficult to interpret in a meaningful way. If an article presents a multilevel model with measurements of unknown or dubious quality, the odds that the average reader will correctly interpret the coefficients that result from this analysis are often small. Third, as Saylors and Trafimow (2021) point out, as models become increasingly complex, the likelihood that they are true diminishes steadily. The same principle can be applied to data analyses; as they become complex, the likelihood that they are useful and understandable probably decreases.

It is important to note that errors in testing models and interpreting results are not limited to complex multilevel or latent variable models. Evan a statistic as simple, familiar and widely used as coefficient alpha is routinely misunderstood (Cho & Kim, 2015). The difficulties researchers are having making clear sense of factor models or reliability indices are symptomatic of a broader problem — i.e., that the statistical methods used in evaluating the results of organizational research are quickly overrunning researchers' ability to truly understand and make sense of research in our field.

These Methods Depend on a Dubious Foundation – Tests of Statistical Significance

One noteworthy and worrisome finding is that many of the methods of analysis presented in these 248 articles rely entirely on the results of some form of null hypothesis statistical significance testing (e.g., significance tests of key parameters, the significance of changes in model fit) to evaluate and make sense of results. In most analyses, no meaningful attention is paid to how well the proposed model predicts or explains the dependent variable, and even where there is some attention to how well the model explains the dependent variable, or to the size of the effects being tested, effect size virtually never trumps statistical significance in evaluating study results.

Table 7.2 shows the proportion of 248 JAP and JOM papers analyzed earlier that include effect size information, such as the proportion of variance explained

TABLE 7.2 Are effect size measures provided?

	Proportion
Regression[a]	.728
Multilevel modeling	.381
Regression with qualitative DV[b]	.430
SEM[c]	.110
Other	.000

Note: a – OLS regression, random coefficient models, moderated and mediated regression; b – logistic regression, probit and tobit regression; c – SEM, latent growth models, latent variable analyses.

or the proportion of correct vs. incorrect predictions. Nearly three-quarters of the papers using OLS regression reported effect size information (usually R^2 or eta^2). This is not to say that of these papers paid serious attention to the size of the effects; in many papers effect sizes were presented in tables with virtually no comment or reference in the text. However, in the majority of OLS analyses, effect size information was at least available. The same cannot be said for any of the other data analytic methods used in these papers.

The Perils of Reliance on Significance Testing

Current analytic methods (particularly the increasingly popular alternatives to OLS regression and its variants) depend heavily, if not entirely on the outcomes of null hypothesis tests to evaluate models and coefficients. Unfortunately, at the very time that scientists across a wide range of disciplines are rising up against the uncritical use of significance tests as tools for evaluating research results (Amrhein, Greenland & McShane, 2019; Wasserstein & Lazar, 2016; Wasserstein, Schirm & Lazar, 2019), organizational scientists are increasing their reliance on these dubious tools. This is a serious mistake.

There is an extensive literature dealing with conceptual and statistical arguments against overreliance on tests of statistical significance (see, e.g., Cohen, 1994; Cortina & Dunlap, 1997; Cortina & Landis, 2011; Meehl, 1978; Schmidt, 1996). The value of tests of the null hypothesis is always dubious in large part because the null hypothesis is virtually never true (Murphy, Myors & Wolach, 2014). The value of these tests shrinks to near zero when large samples are used, something that is increasingly likely with the increasing use of archival datasets and big data. Given that methodologists routinely advise using larger samples in order to attain at least respectable levels of statistical power (Cohen, 1988; Murphy et al., 2014; Wilcox, 1992), you might wonder why having a large N is a problem.

Power curves are asymptotic, and regardless of how small a population effect might be, the probability of rejecting the null hypothesis inevitably approaches 1.0 as N increases. Thus, in large N samples, null hypothesis tests are essentially trivial, in the sense that the null will always be rejected (see Cohen, 1988; Kraemer & Thiemann, 1987; Maxwell, Kelley & Rausch, 2008; Murphy et al, 2014, for discussions of the role of sample size in significance tests).

The perils of reliance on null hypothesis tests when samples are large is vividly illustrated by Amenson, Sackett, and Beatty (2011), who examined the relationship between measures of cognitive ability and measures of performance in jobs, in school, etc. In one part of their study, they examined the relationship between SAT scores and Freshman GPA in a sample over 150,000 students. They found a moderately strong linear relationship ($R^2 = .181$), and their visual presentation of this relationship shows only trivial deviations from linearity. Adding a quadratic term to the prediction model led to virtually no increase in R^2 (.001), but this increase in R^2 was statistically significant ($p < .001$), and if you take significance tests seriously, you would conclude, incorrectly, that the relationship between SAT and GPA was nonlinear.

In an earlier paper, Coward and Sackett (1990) examined data from 174 studies with a mean sample size of 210 to test the hypothesis that the relationship between several ability measures and measure of performance was linear. They found significant deviations from linearity in only a small proportion of their tests, no more than would have been expected by chance, and concluded that the relationship between ability and performance is linear. However, suppose this study was repeated with sample sizes of 2,100, 21,000, or 210,000. There is little doubt that as the power of the studies to detect nonlinearity went up, the conclusions one would reach on the basis of significance tests for deviations from linearity would change, and that there would be a real risk of concluding that this relationship is nonlinear, when it manifestly is not.[2]

Alternatives to NHST

One strategy for overcoming the limitations placed on the value of NHST when samples are large is to choose some alternative to the traditional NHST.[3] Stanton (2021) describes a number of equivalence tests that can be used to determine whether differences between the population value predicted by some theory (either a prediction of no effect or the prediction of any specific effect) are sufficiently small as to be trivial. Suppose, for example, that some theory predicted that the correlation between X and Y should be .40. You find a value of .401. If your sample is very large (e.g., $N = 40,000$), you will reject the null hypothesis and conclude that the theory is wrong when, in fact, the fit between your theory and the data is very good.

In a similar vein, Murphy et al. (2014) described a method of using the noncentral F statistic to evaluate the hypothesis that the difference between groups or the association between variables is so small that it can be regarded as trivial; this method can be easily applied to any of the variations on the general linear model (e.g., t tests, ANOVA, regression). Murphy et al. (2014) suggest that in many settings, differences that account for less than 1% of the variance in the dependent variable might be regarded as so small as to be meaningless, but their methods can be applied no matter what threshold is used to define trivial vs. meaningful effects.

The downside of the various alternatives that have been proposed in decades of criticism of NHST (e.g., more intelligent use of confidence intervals) is their limited uptake. Despite all of the criticism of traditional NHST, there is no sign that tests of the traditional null hypothesis will go away, and no evidence that any of the alternatives are likely to replace it.

Analytic Complexity Undermines the Interpretability and Utility of Research

The growing diversity and complexity of the methods used to analyze research in organizations create two problems that threaten to undermine the interpretability and value of research in organizations. First, as was noted earlier, analytic methods that stray from the familiar range of applications of the general linear model via OLS regression often rely heavily, if not exclusively on significance tests to evaluate results. This reliance on significance testing was deeply problematic even before the advent of big data and is likely to become even more problematic as large, unstructured datasets become more common (Ratner, 2017).

Second, there is a difficult trade-off between complexity and interpretability in the analyses that are frequently published in leading journals. The likelihood that both the authors and the readers of articles will fully understand the meaning and implications of statistical analysis is inversely related to the complexity of those analyses, and as analyses become more complex, the cadre of researchers and readers who truly understand them is likely to shrink. Consider an analysis that involves multiple control variables, all of which are correlated. A regression coefficient for the first predictor represents the average change in Y per unit change in that predictor, holding control variables as well as other predictors constant. It is challenging for experts to fully understand what holding several other variables, all of which are likely to be imperfectly reliable and valid indicators of the constructs they represent, really means (see Becker, 2005; Berneth et al., 2018, for discussions of the challenges of interpreting control variable effects).

Complexity-Interpretability Trade-Offs

The reliance on most of the methods of analysis that appears in our journals on significance testing is not only a problem because of the implausibility of the traditional null hypothesis. The reliance on significance testing also has disturbing implications for the interpretability of those analyses. If pressed to explain *why* a particular coefficient is or is not significantly different from zero, or what it really means when that parameter it is significantly different from zero, you might find it increasingly difficult to answer this question as analyses become increasingly complex.

Suppose you are testing the hypothesis that the value of some parameter in a statistical model (e.g., the population difference between two means) is different from zero. This hypothesis is tested by comparing a sample estimate of that parameter with its standard error, and your ability to make sense of this test and its results depends to a large extent on your ability to understand precisely what this standard error indicates and what factors determine the value of this standard error.

The standard errors that are used to test hypotheses about correlation coefficients (after conversion to Fisher's z prime) are determined entirely by N. The standard errors used to test hypotheses about simple regression coefficients include three components, the variability of errors in prediction (which is a function of r_{xy} and the variability of Y), N, and the variability of X. The standard errors of tests of coefficients in multiple regression includes all of these components plus: (1) R_y – the multiple correlation between all of the X variables and Y, and (2) R_i^2 – the squared correlation between X_i and all other X variables In a multilevel model, the standard error of coefficients for level-2 variables (i.e., group-level variables) is a function of the intraclass correlation, an indicator of the degree of clustering and N, while the standard errors of coefficients representing level-1 variables are similar to standard errors in multiple regression, but the values of these coefficients are also affected by the number of clusters and the strength of the clustering of values within groups (Longford, 2000). The statistical power of model comparisons in MLM is a complex function of N, cluster sizes and the distributions of both level 1 and level 2 variables (Olvera Astivia, Gadermann & Guhn, 2019), and this function is sufficiently complex that the most common method for evaluating power in these models is to use simulations.

The point of this comparison is that it becomes increasingly difficult to understand *why* particular coefficients or parameters are or are not significantly different from zero as analyses become more complex. In a complex structural equation model or a moderated moderation model, making sense of the standard errors, and therefore the meaning (if any) of significance tests may elude all but a few methodologists.

Significance tests for coefficients are not the only tools used to interpret complex statistical models; many studies also use comparisons of model fit, for example, testing whether the addition of more variables, more factors, more links between factors or interactions among variables to a model leads to an increment in fit. The power of these tests is determined by a complex mix of factors (e.g., number of parameters, number of cases, intercorrelations among variables for both latent variable models (Hermida et al., 2015; MacCallum, Browne & Sugawara, 1996; MacCallum, Lee & Browne, 2010; Satorra & Saris, 1985) and regression-based models (e.g., moderated multiple regression; Murphy & Russell, 2017), making it difficult for authors or readers to understand precisely why a more complex model fits or fails to fit better than a simpler one. In most cases, N is an important determinant of the power of model comparisons, and in studies, where N is unusually large, researchers may be likely to accept complicated models even if the increment in fit over more parsimonious models is trivially small.

The "Flavor of the Month" Leads us to Choose Complex Over Simpler Methods

Researchers in the organizational sciences have tend to gravitate to data analytic methods that appear to be popular with their colleagues. Organizational researchers are susceptible to peer pressure, and the pressure to use methods of analysis that achieve the status of "flavor of the month" is often hard to resist. Throughout the 1990s and early 2000s, structural equation modeling was widely used in organizational research[4], and in the current era, favorites include multilevel modeling and moderation/mediation analyses. It is important, however, to understand that complex methods of analysis are not always the authors' first choice. For example, Green, Tonidandel, and Cortina, (2016) noted that a frequent criticism of studies that hypothesized that some third variable (Z) mediated the relationship between X and Y was that "authors used *outdated* (my italics) tests for mediation – i.e., Baron and Kenny. One implication of this criticism is that authors would be better off choosing more current (and more complex) methods of evaluating claims of mediation. It is far from clear that they really would be better off.

The Baron and Kenny (1986) method for evaluating mediation hypotheses is indeed dated, but it is admirably direct, asking researchers to: (1) verify that X is related to Y, (2) verify that X is related to Z, and (3) verify that Z is related to Y, before asking the question of whether controlling for Z pushed the relationship between X and Y near zero. There are more statistically sophisticated alternatives available, notably Hayes' (2017) PROCESS macro, which provide detailed information about the strength of direct and indirect effects, but it is unclear that they provide information that is both valuable and interpretable.

As I will noted in a later section, the hypothesis that Z fully mediates the relationship between X and Y is rarely true; full mediation can only be supported if the average of r_{xz} and r_{yz} is considerably larger than r_{xz} (Murphy, 2021). Current methods of testing mediation hypotheses often leave researchers in the limbo known as "partial mediation," which is rarely meaningful, because for any set of three intercorrelated variables (e.g., X, Y, and Z), any of those variables will act as a partial mediator of the relationship between the other two. More modern methods evaluating claims of mediation are more sophisticated, but if all they tell you in the end is the X, Y, and Z were all intercorrelated, it is far from clear that they lead to a clearer understanding than the old standby articulated by Baron and Kenny (1986).

Researchers are sometimes encouraged, if not coerced, to use methods that are more mathematically sophisticated but arguably less informative by reviewers and editors. I believe it is time for reviewers and editors to argue for *simpler* rather than more complex methods of analysis.

Big Data Is Likely to Make Analyses More Complex and Less Interpretable

Big data is increasingly being used to study topics that range from turnover and retention (Hausknect & Li, 2016) to the study of teams (Kozlowski et al., 2016). For example, Sajjadiani et al. (2019) combined selection research and theory with applied machine learning to examine over 16,000 job applications to develop measures of work experience relevance, tenure history, and history of involuntary turnover, history of avoiding bad jobs, and history of approaching better jobs. They showed that these measures showed some value (albeit with small validity coefficients) as predictors of several organizational-relevant criteria. Because N was so large in this study, it was no surprise that most of the coefficients in the prediction model they developed were significantly different from zero.

Big data creates a unique set of challenges for researchers, especially when relatively unrestricted methods are used to search for patterns or interesting combinations in large datasets. In his engaging volume *How not to be Wrong: The Power of Mathematical Thinking,* Ellenburg (2015) presents two startling examples of the problems that arise when applying familiar statistical procedures and null hypothesis tests to big data.

The Perils of Analyzing Big Data

As noted in several chapters in the volume (e.g., Chapter 1), big data presents many unique opportunities to develop rigorous research on important problems in organization. However, the very size and diversity of the databases that are becoming increasingly available also present opportunities to draw absurd conclusions from research, especially when automated tools of arbitrary criteria (e.g., significance tests) take the place of informed judgment in trying to make sense of data.

For example, claims are often made about the ability of functional Magnetic Resonance Imaging (fMRI) studies to detect specific types of mental activity, but there are reasons to believe that at least some of these claims are artifacts of the huge amount of data these scans produce. The fMRI uses differences in detected brain activity in different parts of the brain, comparing activity in over 130,000 spatial regions (voxels), which gives the potential for huge numbers of statistical contrasts. The potential for statistical analyses of these huge datasets to provide misleading pictures of the value of these scans was illustrated by Bennett et al. (2009) demonstration of the remarkable ability of dead salmon to detect expressions of emotion in photographs of humans.

Their methods section is primer on deadpan humor, describing the subject in this study as "One mature Atlantic Salmon (Salmo salar) participated in the fMRI study. The salmon measured approximately 18 inches long, weighed 3.8 lbs, and *was not alive at the time of scanning* (my italics)." Without adequate correction for the number of contrasts, and with only weak criteria for determining which comparisons indicate specific emotions, it is no surprise that even dead salmon perform significantly better than chance in detecting emotion in fMRI scans of hundreds of thousands of voxels. Bennett et al. (2009) suggest that corrections for the number of comparisons are necessary, and perhaps even sufficient to control for this. However, as Lyon (2017) notes, the extreme flexibility of the technique (i.e., the availability of an extensive range of settings, contrasts, methods) also contributes to the difficulty of specifying adequate statistical models for these huge and unstructured datasets, because different criteria, settings, comparisons, and the like make it almost impossible to know how many choices and comparisons might actually be involved in this type of study.

Bennett et al. (2009) used a purposefully ridiculous experimental procedure to illustrate the perils of relying on thousands of relatively unstructured comparisons when judging whether or not dead salmon can accurately detect human emotion. Other applications of standard statistical methods to analyze big data are less transparently silly and potentially more worrisome. In particular, if an algorithm is let loose on a large dataset with the implicit instruction to find something interesting, it will probably do exactly that, even if there is nothing real to find.

The peril of relying on unstructured automated searches in large datasets to draw conclusions about what those data mean is vividly illustrated in a series of numerical studies of the Torah and Christian and Islamic scriptures. In a careful and rigorous statistical analysis of letter patterns in the Torah, Witztum, Rips, and Rosenberg (1994) claimed to find statistical evidence of specific and accurate predictions of particular events in that occurred hundreds to thousands of years after the Torah was written.[5] Witztum et al. (1994) applied the method of equidistant letter sequence (ELS) analysis to the Torah, which attempts to uncover subtexts in the Torah on the basis of sets of letters that are equally spaced in the main text. In a simple example, the text stream "New York Standard" includes the subtext "not a" if we focus on every fifth letter. In a series of best-sellers, Drosnin (1997) applied similar methods to mine the Torah to foretell assassinations, attacks, and many other events. Drosin gained attention by making predictions about the assassination of Yitzhak Rabin, and there have been reports that he and other similar researchers were consulted by governments to foretell future events.[6]

The use of statistical analysis of large and unstructured datasets to predict the future is worrisome mainly because some readers take this analysis seriously. In a devastating rebuke to this method, McKay et al. (1999) showed that applying the same methods to *War and Peace* yielded similarly impressive predictions; other analysts have done just about as well with *Moby Dick* as a source document. The predictive power of hidden meanings in text is clearly not limited to sacred documents.

Three Methodological Challenges Presented by Big Datasets

There are ways of using traditional methods of analysis with big datasets (Ratner, 2017), but different types of big datasets can create specific and important problems when coupled with standard methods of statistical analysis. First, some datasets are consistently structured, in the sense that each subject or unit is typically measured on the same variables. This type of dataset can be configured into an $N \times k$ data frame that is fairly well populated (i.e., without inordinate amounts of missing data). Here, the dataset might be considered "big" if N and/or k (the number of variables) is unusually large. Datasets with very large N make tests of the null hypothesis essentially trivial because virtually any statistical relationship will be significant (Cohen, 1988). If these tests are the primary tool used to tell researchers what the data mean, the usefulness of methods that depend on null hypothesis tests in datasets with very large N tests is questionable.

Big data presents especially difficult challenges when the data collected do not fall neatly into a well-defined $N \times k$ array. In a poorly structured big dataset, the indicators and variables might change over time, and the number of observations at any one point in time might be unpredictable. There is likely to be a substantial amount of missing data, and there will often be systematic patterns of missing data as indicators change, populations change, etc. Nonrandom missing data can create numerous problems for analysis (Little & Rubin, 2002). Our standard analytic methods might prove useless if there is no well-defined population or no clear definition of what does and does not constitute an observation. Poorly structured datasets are difficult to analyze; the interpretation of inferential statistics in a context where the population cannot be clearly defined is completely up in the air.

The third methodological challenge presented by big data is that it is likely to lead to an increased reliance on data mining methods that are poorly understood by organizational researchers. As the examples of using dead salmon to detect emotion or mining the Torah to predict the future presented earlier suggest, it is easy to go badly off the rails when using very large datasets, especially when they are coupled with automated processes for detecting patterns or anomalies. If the results presented by these analyses are on their face ridiculous, this might not be a problem, but many automated analyses of big data present results that might seem entirely plausible, and organizational researchers are usually ill-equipped to critically evaluate the results these methods produce.

Tails Wagging Dogs: How Analysis Drives Theory and Design

Methods of data analysis wax and wane in their popularity, sometimes because they have been replaced by better methods (e.g., exploratory factor analysis has largely been replaced by confirmatory factor analysis), and sometimes because they simply go out of fashion (e.g., during the 1960s and 70s, path analysis was very much in vogue). During their heyday, popular methods of analysis have the potential to shape theories, not always in ways that are positive. The history of the relationship between factor analysis and theories of cognitive ability provides a vivid example.

Virtually every important theories of cognitive ability developed during the period 1930–1970 (e.g., Two-Factor theory, Primary Mental Ability Theory, Cattell's explication of fluid vs. crystallized intelligence, Vernon's hierarchical theory) was based primarily on factor analyses of ability data. Carroll's (1993) hierarchical model the structure of cognitive ability is sits firmly within this tradition. Factor analysis forms the basis of the Carroll-Horn-Cattell (CHC) model, the most widely accepted model of the structure of cognitive ability (McGrew, 2009).

Early factor analysts believed that their analytic methods revealed meaningful latent structures; Thurstone (1934) referred to factor analysis as a method for uncovering the "vectors of the mind." Later researchers have been more circumspect, but theories driven by factor analysis have long attempted to sort human cognitive ability into orthogonal bundles, not because orthogonality makes good theoretical sense, but because this is a bedrock feature of exploratory factor analysis, which has its roots in principal components analysis (PCA). There are reasons to believe that a similar pattern of methods dictating theory is underway today in research in which multilevel analysis is a common tool.

The availability of user-friendly software for performing MLM for datasets where people are grouped into potentially meaningful units (e.g., classrooms, companies, nations) has coincided with an explosion in multilevel research. Much of this work pursues important questions, but it is hard to escape the impression that multilevel analyses are in vogue because these analyses are now relatively easy to carry out and because everyone is doing them.

Would we really be worse off if multilevel modeling methods had never been developed? There are extensions of traditional methods of OLS regression that can be used for examining and taking into account both group-level and individual-level effects, but these are rarely applied. Bickel (2007), for example, argues that MLM is "just regression." Bliese et al. (2018) show how OLS regression methods might be used to analyze multilevel data.

There is clear evidence that MLM provides better estimates of standard errors and therefore more accurate significance tests than OLS when it is used to analyzed clustered data (Bliese et al., 2018; Huang, 2018a, 2018b). In Table 7.2, I noted that nearly 2/3 of the MLM analyses reported in recent issues of top journals failed to even mention, much less pay serious attention to statistics such as R^2 or other indications of how well the models developed by researchers explain key dependent variables. OLS analyses of the same data would produce worse significance tests, but if these tests are of limited value in the first place

(Amrhein et al., 2019; Murphy et al., 2014), MLM might have few meaningful advantages over OLS, and the proliferation of cross-level theories and studies in context where cross-level effects are small or meaningless would arguably be reduced if the field accepted Bikel's (2007) advice that "it's just regression."

Can We Afford to Abandon the Statistical Arms Race?

How should organizational researchers respond to the increasing complexity of the methods used to analyze and make sense of the data they collect or obtain? Our usual response has been to pile on more analytic training and more methods, but perhaps we would be better off abandoning the statistical arms race for newer and more complex methods in favor of tools and techniques that will help us understand what our data really mean. I believe this entails going back to basics and sticking with simple and easily understandable methods whenever possible.

First, they must get better at and more practiced in using the sort of simple statistics usually presented in Table 7.1 of a research paper to understand their data and to communicate that understanding. Second, the training of organizational scientists needs to focus on building and understanding a compact analytic toolkit that centers around a handful of familiar techniques (e.g., multiple regression, PCA) that researchers thoroughly understand. Third, in those rare cases where complex statistical methods are both necessary and useful, organizational researchers need to develop partnerships with researchers in other disciplines who have true expertise in those methods. There is clear evidence that organizational researchers are routinely over their heads in performing and interpreting many common methods of analysis (Cho & Kim, 2015; Cortina et al., 2017; Green et al., 2016). Rather than continuing to spread ourselves more thinly over the an increasingly large methodological ground, researchers, editors and reviewers need to carefully assess the conditions under which complex analytic methods are truly useful and to develop partnerships with researchers who have genuine expertise rather than continuing to perform analyses they do not thoroughly understand.

Restoring the Primacy of Descriptive Statistics

Earlier in this chapter, I described an analysis of 248 papers from *JAP* and *JOM* (2018–2019) that documented the growing complexity and variety of the data analytic methods used in the organizational sciences. One of the depressing features of these papers, and of research in the social sciences more generally, is that journal articles typically give scant attention to descriptive statistics. Virtually every one of these 248 papers reported some descriptive statistics, but 64.5% of these papers said nothing about descriptive statistics other that "Descriptive statistics are presented in Table 7.1" or its equivalent. Approximately 2/3 of the papers that *did* comment on descriptive statistics restricted their comments to assessments of potential multicollinearity, typically measured in terms of a variance inflation factor.[7]

For too long, descriptive data has been consigned to Table 7.1, which is likely to be briefly mentioned and subsequently ignored, and attention has been focused on inferential tests. The growing recognition of the limits of null hypothesis significance testing (Amrhein et al., 2019; Benjamin et al., 2018; Cortina & Landis, 2011; Murphy et al., 2014) suggests that this imbalance is likely to change. Bedeian (2014) gives thoughtful advice for interpreting and using descriptive statistics (e.g., correlations based on *N* less than 500 lack stability beyond the first digit, if the mean is less than twice the SD, this may indicate a skewed distribution) and he advocates starting one's paper and one's analysis with a thorough understanding of the descriptive statistics and their meaning. As our field moves toward an increasing use of with very large datasets, we will no longer be able to lean on the familiar tool of null hypothesis significance testing; no matter what hypothesis or parameter we test, we are likely to achieve "significant" results, and these tests will have little value in helping us understand our data.

First and foremost, organizational researchers need to develop skills in presenting and interpreting their descriptive statistics. For example, researchers should be routinely asking questions about whether the distribution of values of key measures is consistent with the hypotheses or theories they wish to test. Thus, if there are severe distributional anomalies in key variables (e.g., range restriction, extreme skew, few values representing theoretically important regions in the distributions of independent or dependent variables) that can plausibly influence the interpretation of analyses, researchers and readers need to know this and understand the implications of these anomalies. At a minimum, authors should know whether the range and distribution of values of key measures will allow them to meaningfully test their hypotheses before launching and complex data analyses.

Two tools are likely to be particularly useful in helping researchers and the consumers of organizational research make sense and make better use of descriptive statistics: (1) visualization and (2) plausibility testing.

Visualization and Descriptive Statistics

Tukey has long advocated Exploratory Data Analysis (EDA) as an alternative to the typical statistical approaches that depend on significance tests and related techniques (Hoaglin, Mosteller & Tukey, 1983; Mosteller & Tukey, 1977; Tukey, 1977). EDA represents an approach to making sense of data that puts emphasis on visualization and understanding the data you have collected, with relatively less emphasis on statistical inference. Other statisticians have noted the limited relevance of inferential statistics, observing that these methods are often ill-suited to the types of data scientists in many disciplines collect (Hubbard, Haig & Parsa, 2019). Our most familiar statistical methods were designed for something we rarely do – i.e., estimating fixed population parameters from random samples, and there are good arguments for placing more emphasis of descriptive than on inferential statistics.

EDA places strong emphasis on visualization tools, such as boxplots and stem and leaf plots. The increasing use of **R** in the social sciences has opened the door for better visualizations, with numerous built-in visualization functions and packages, and the increasing availability of supplemental materials linked to journal articles is helping to remove one of the barriers to the widespread use of visualization in publications – i.e., the fact that graphs and plots take considerable space and resources (e.g., printing in color is expensive when done in hard copy) to publish. Simple visualizations such as boxplots give researchers considerable insight into the distributions of important variables in a study, and there are a range of tools for obtaining good two and three-dimensional visualizations of one's data.

R is a good starting point for visualization, but we should think of the set of methods for visualization data that **R** provides as a starting point rather than the only option for visualization. In a series of extraordinary books, Tufte (1983, 1990, 2020) has shown the range of methods for presenting complex data visually; organizational research would be substantially enriched by the better use of graphics.

Visualization is a useful tool, but it is not the only way of making better use of descriptive statistics. At a minimum, journals should require that researchers at least comment on the implications of their descriptive statistics for the hypotheses they intend to test. For example, if the main theory is being used to explain data in a study deals with the way organizations react to a particular class of events (e.g., disagreements between home and host norms in a multinational corporation), it should be incumbent on authors to show that there are, in fact, a reasonable number of cases this actually occurs. More generally, before they move on to complex statistical tests, authors should be required to demonstrate, on the basis of the simplest descriptive statistics possible, that their key hypotheses are at least plausible (Murphy, 2021).

Plausibility Tests

Suppose an author proposes that outcomes are better for subjects who receive a treatment than for those who do not. Our research would be easier to understand and less likely to be misinterpreted if, before launching a complex statistical analysis, authors at least demonstrated that the mean score on an important dependent variable is indeed higher than the mean for the controls, and that the difference in means is large enough to be plausibly important [e.g., is the standardized mean difference (*d*) .20 or larger?]. There may be cases where the observed means do not meet this simple test but where statistical controls and complex models lead to the conclusion that there are group differences that are statistically significant and meaningful. In this case, the onus should be on the author to clearly and convincingly explain why the complex model rather than the simple descriptive statistics should be believed.

Two of the most common hypotheses in the behavioral and social sciences are that the nature of the relationship between two variables is *moderated* (i.e., influenced) by a third variable or that the relationship between two variables is *mediated* (i.e., explained) by a third variable (Aguinis, Edwards & Bradley, 2017; Gardner et al., 2017; Wood, Goodman & Beckman, 2008). Murphy (2021) explains simple plausibility tests that could easily precede any complex analyses of moderator or mediator hypotheses. These tests are especially important because the likelihood that significant and meaningful moderation effects will be found (and replicated) or that some variable or set of variables will fully mediate the relationship between X and Y is often low (Murphy, 2021; Murphy & Russell, 2017). The improbability of meaningful moderator or mediator effects can be obscured by complex statistical models; thinking through what these hypotheses require helps to establish ways of using simple descriptive statistics to test their plausibility.

The usual method for testing moderation hypothesis involves using moderated regression to test the hypothesis that cross-product terms between the predictors (X) and moderators (Z) account for variance in Y not accounted for by the predictors and moderators alone (Aguinis & Gottfredson, 2010; Aguinis, Gottfredson & Wright, 2011). The statistical power of these tests is shockingly low, especially when there is a nontrivial correlation between the X and Z or Y and Z variables (Murphy & Russell, 2017). This suggests that a simple examination the correlations between X, Y, and Z, considered in the light of N can often establish that moderator hypotheses are implausible, in which case any complex analysis that suggests that there *is* a moderator effect should be considered with caution. If r_{xz} and/or r_{yz} are even moderately large, moderator effects will be very small and difficult to detect; even if they can be detected, they are unlikely to be important or meaningful.

The conditions under which the hypothesis that Z mediates the relationship between X and Y are surprisingly restrictive. As Murphy (2021) shows, unless the values of if r_{xz} and r_{xz} are both substantially larger than the value of r_{xy}, Z cannot fully account for the correlation between X and Y.[8] If a simple examination of r_{xz}, r_{xz}, and r_{xy} shows that Z will, at best, act as a partial mediator, there may be no sense in proceeding to a more complex test. If you know on the basis of an examination of r_{xz}, r_{xz}, and r_{xy} that this is where you will end up, there may be little point in going any further.

Murphy (2021, p. 467) proposed that: *Any result that is established on the basis of a complex data analysis that cannot be shown to be at least plausible on the basis of the types of simple statistics shows in Table 7.1 (e.g., means, standard deviations, correlations) should be treated as suspect and interpreted with the utmost caution*. I believe that rigorously following this proposition would reduce the frequency of complex (and often uninterpretable) analyses *and* would bolster the interpretability of complex tests that did show moderator or mediator effects, intervention effects, and the like.

The Analytic Tools Organizational Scientist Need

What analytic tools are necessary for a well-trained organizational scientist? I believe that the basic toolkit every organizational scientist should master is relatively small, and that when a genuine occasion for a complex analysis that falls outside of this toolkit arises, that it is better to collaborate with experts than to attempt to learn and truly master new analytic methods on the fly. There are a handful of basic tools/skills that all organizational scientists should master in order to make sense of the data collect. First, as noted above they must become skilled at examining, presenting, and making sense of descriptive data. Second, organizational researchers must develop a clear understanding of what happens when linear combinations of variables are formed. Weighted linear combinations of variables are at the heart of the general linear model, and while there has been some movement away from the most traditional forms of OLS regression in our field, there are few analytic methods that do not depend on combining multiple variables into weighted linear composites, using weights that satisfy some statistical criterion. Whether you are using analysis of variance, multiple regression, logistic regression, random coefficient models, or multilevel models to analyze your data, you are operating within the same general linear model framework. If you are using PCA, factor analysis (exploratory or confirmatory), or structural equation models to make sense of your data, you are in the business of forming weighted linear combinations of variables to estimate latent factors and their relationships.

Regardless of the analytic context, there are a few principles of the algebra of linear combinations that apply regardless of whether the analysis is part of the general linear model family of methods, multilevel models, factor or latent variable models, and regardless of whether OLS, or some other statistical criterion (e.g., restricted maximum likelihood) is employed. First, following Wilks' theorem, as the correlations among variables increase, the choice of values for regression weights becomes increasingly unimportant and uninformative (Bobko, Roth & Buster, 2007; Dawes & Corrigan, 1974; Einhorn & Hogarth, 1975; Ree, Carretta & Earles, 1998; Wainer, 1976; Wilks, 1938). When the matrix of correlations among predictors and criteria is uniformly positive (positive manifold), with many large values, it hardly matters what weights are used when combining predictors, and the value of statistically optimal combinations (e.g., multiple regression) is no longer high in comparison to other systems for combining variables. In addition, as correlations among predictors increase, hypotheses about whether particular variables will receive more or less weight in any type of prediction model become progressively less tenable.

Second, the number of variables in a model is critically important. For example, the standard errors coefficients in a regression model tend to increase as the number of variables increases (in large part because the multiple correlation between each variable in the model and other variables will increase). It is not unusual to see multiple control variables and many predictors in regression models in the organizational sciences, and this will create increasing instability and uncertainty in the interpretation of these analyses. The case for models built on the basis of weights that make theoretical or practical sense vs. statistical optimal models becomes increasingly ambiguous as intercorrelations increase. A researcher who understands the instability and virtually irrelevance of regression weights in a complex linear model will be less likely to base important decisions on their significance or the lack thereof.

Third, organizational researchers need to understand how to evaluate and compare models without relying on the crutch of null hypothesis tests. The interpretation of alternate models is likely to depend on informed judgments about the predictive power of the models in question. Earlier I noted that in nearly 2/3 of the multilevel studies published in *JAP* and *ORM* in 2018 and 2019 paid little or no attention to how well their models explained the dependent variables, relying instead on the outcomes of significance tests. It is imperative that researchers look carefully at how well particular models explain dependent variables, and if they key hypothesis in a study that a particular facet of a predictive model is important (e.g., cross products in moderated multiple regression), the most useful test of this hypothesis is to demonstrate that a model with this variable or set of variables predicts important dependent variables better than a model without them. Significance tests can be used to evaluate increases in predictive power, but we would be better served by relying on informed judgment, based on the relevant literature, of whether the increase in predictive accuracy is sufficient to support the hypothesis in question.

As a practical matter, it is more important for organizational researchers to truly and thoroughly understand a handful of analytic methods; researchers who have an in-depth understanding of descriptive statistics, multiple regression and PCA is well-situated to understand virtually any type of data they collect. If your research deals extensively with qualitative dependent variables, a good understanding of logistic regression is called for. Unfortunately, for the foreseeable future, organizational researchers will need to know how to *perform* analyses the types of analysis summarized earlier in this chapter (Tables 7.1 and 7.2), in large part because reviewers and editors will continue to demand them, but they should resist whenever possible performing analyses that they do not fully understand.

We can make the process of simplifying your approach to data analysis easier by emphasizing the links among methods that appear to be different. For example, Bikel (2007) makes a compelling case that multilevel analysis is "just regression", and organizational researchers who thoroughly understand multiple regression will be well situated to perform its many variants (e.g., moderator and mediator analysis, logistic regression, multilevel modeling). For example, moderated mediation analyses (Preacher, Rucker & Hayes, 2007) are becoming increasingly popular; researchers who understand regression will recognize that these methods test the proposition that X, Y, and Z are intercorrelated (partial mediation), and that their correlations change depending on the values of Z (moderation). Whether there is much value in testing this hypothesis depends on the context, but the analysis itself only *looks* complex. Similarly, suppose N subjects are grouped into k units and both individual and unit-level predictors are present. This would seem to call for multilevel modeling, but simpler methods are often applicable, including OLS (Bliese et al., 2018) and even regression that combines coded variables representing groups (i.e., ANOVA) with continuous measures. If we were statisticians or devotees of null hypothesis significance testing, we would be drawn to MLM because it gives smaller standard errors and does a better job handling the degrees of freedom for specific statistical tests, but we are not statisticians and (hopefully) not slaves to significance testing. Simple analyses that help us understand the data serve us better than analyses that get the standard errors right but mystify and misdirect researchers and readers.

In the long term, our analytic toolbox is likely to become more compact, with a greater emphasis on understanding how to ask simple and direct questions about our data. There is a proverb attributed to the ancient Greek poet Archilochus, "a fox knows many things, but a hedgehog knows one big thing." We need to become more hedgehog-like, focusing on a small number of big things rather than trying to learn many different methods of analysis. In our field, analytic complexity is not our friend, and as we move to embrace larger datasets, our ability to understand what the data mean is more and more likely to depend on sensible handling of descriptive statistics, forming combinations of variables on the basis of theory or policy rather than statistical optimization, and careful attention to and judgments about the predictive power of our models.

The simplest principle for data analysis should be that if you cannot explain an analysis (e.g., why is the standard error of the parameter you are interested in large or small), don't use it. In those rare occasions where a complex method of data analysis is needed, collaborate with a real expert, but above all strive for simplicity. Complex analyses are likely to be done incorrectly, reported incorrectly and misunderstood by your readers, and our increasing use of complex methods of analysis should be recognized as a threat to the viability of our research, not a sign of sophistication.

What If We Need Complex Analyses?

What if descriptive statistics, simple regression and related techniques that combine variables into linear combinations to predict your dependent variable are not enough? There are likely to be some studies in which there is a genuine payoff for doing a more complex analysis, and there will be instances where a well-intentioned but perhaps poorly trained reviewers or editors insist on analyses that neither you nor they are likely to fully understand. The best approach is likely to be similar to the one you would take if something went seriously wrong with your house – i.e., *hire an expert*. If a storm destroyed your wiring panel, you would just rewire your house yourself; you would get a qualified electrician. You should take the same stance when approaching the task of performing a complex data analysis. The fact that you *can* do a multilevel moderated mediation analysis does not mean that you *should* or that you will be able to make genuine sense of the results of such an analysis, and in those rare cases where this sort of work is needed, leave it to the experts.

This will require a substantial culture change, especially on the part of reviewers and editors, but imagine the benefits if our analyses were simple and transparent. We would no longer risk thinking that dead salmon could read human emotions. More to the point, our ability to clearly and convincingly communicate our result to others would improve dramatically. Organizational researchers have many goals, but one of them is often to improve organizations, and we will be better prepared to accomplish this if we can speak in a language that makes sense to us and to a wider audience. We can and should avoid the statistical arms race in the organizational sciences, and the sooner the better!

Notes

1 In multistudy papers, I used to last study that tested a substantive hypothesis to classify the analytic methods used.
2 This is a conjecture, but I believe it is reasonable to expect that *any* relationship between any pair of variables that are neither orthogonal or perfectly correlated (e.g., X and the predicted value of Y in a simple regression equation) would be described as nonlinear if the sample is sufficiently large and a significance test is used to determine nonlinearity.
3 Another strategy is to employ a more stringent criterion for statistical significance. A group of 72 prominent statisticians has recently advocating replacing the $p < .05$ standard with $p < .005$ (Benjamin et al., 2018).
4 When I was Associate Editor of *Journal of Applied Psychology*, I received a cover letter with an article that had been submitted that said "I know that structural equation models are required for publication in *JAP*, but…". There was no such requirement, but it was not an unreasonable inference given the popularity of this analytic method.

5 McKay et al. (1999) show how a number of seemingly innocuous choices made by these researchers (e.g., spellings of particular names) could dramatically affect their results.

6 https://www.stltoday.com/suburban-journals/illinois/opinion/garcia-bible-codes-and-prime-minister-netanyahu/article_d2fae4f0-8aff-5d02-a0c3-4eba81af58be.html

7 VIF for the variable $xi = \dfrac{1}{1 - R_i^2}$, where R^2_i is the squared multiple correlation between xi and the other x variables.

8 For example, Z will fully mediate the relationship between X and Y is both r_{xz} and r_{zy} are equal to $\sqrt{r_{xy}}$.

References

Aguinis, H., Edwards, J. R., & Bradley, K. J. (2017). Improving our understanding of moderation and mediation in strategic management research. *Organizational Research Methods, 20,* 665–685.

Aguinis, H. & Gottfredson, R. K. (2010). Best-practice recommendations for estimating interaction effects using moderated multiple regression. *Journal of Organizational Behavior, 31,* 776–786.

Aguinis, H., Gottfredson, R. K., & Wright (2011). Best-practice recommendations for estimating interaction effects using meta-analysis. *Journal of Organizational Behavior, 32,* 1033–1043.

Amrhein, V., Greenland, S., & McShane, B. (2019). Scientists rise up against statistical significance. *Nature, 567,* 305–307.

Amenson, J. J., Sackett, P. R., & Beatty, A. S. (2011). Ability-performance relationships in education and employment settings: Critical tests of the more-is-better and the good-enough hypothesis. *Psychological Science, 22,* 1336–1342.

Baron, R. M., & Kenny, D. A. (1986). The moderator-mediator variable distinction in social psychological research: Conceptual, strategic, and statistical considerations. *Journal of Personality and Social Psychology, 51,* 1173–82.

Becker, T. E. (2005). Potential problems in statistical control variables in organizational research: A qualitative analysis with recommendations. *Organizational Research Methods, 8,* 274–289.

Bedeian, A. G. (2014). "More than meets the eye": A guide to interpreting the descriptive statistics and correlation matrices reported in management research. *Academy of Management Learning & Education, 13,* 121–135.

Benjamin, D. J. et al. (2018). Redefine statistical significance. *Nature Human Behavior, 2,* 6–10.

Bennett, C. M., Baird, A. A., Miller, M. B., & Wolford, G. L. (2009). Neural correlates of interspecies perspective taking in the post-mortem Atlantic salmon: An argument for proper multiple comparisons correction. *Journal of Serendipitous Unexpected Results, 1,* 1–5.

Berneth, J., Cole, M. S., Taylor, E. C., & Walker, H. J. (2018). Control variables in leadership research: A qualitative and quantitative review. *Journal of Management, 44,* 141–160.

Bickel, R. (2007). *Multilevel analysis for applied research: It's just regression.* New York: Guilford.

Bliese, P. D., Maltarich, M. A., & Hendricks, J. L. (2018). Back to basics with mixed-effects models: Nine take-away points. *Journal of Business and Psychology, 33,* 1–23.

Bobko, P., Roth, P. L., & Buster, M. A. (2007). The usefulness of unit weights in creating composite scores: A literature review, application to content validity, and meta-analysis. *Organizational Research Methods, 10,* 689–709.

Carroll, J. B. (1993). *Human cognitive abilities: A survey of factor-analytic studies.* Cambridge, UK: Cambridge University Press.

Chen, G., Mathieu, J. E., & Bliese, P. D. (2004). A framework for conducting multilevel construct validation. In F. J. Yammarino & F. Dansereau (Eds.), *Research in multilevel issues: Multilevel issues in organizational behavior and processes* (Vol. 3, pp. 273–303). Elsevier: Oxford, UK.

Cho, E., & Kim, S. (2015). Cronbach's alpha: Well-known but poorly understood. *Organizational Research Methods, 18,* 207–230.

Cohen, J. (1988). *Statistical power analysis for the behavioral sciences* (2nd ed.). Hillsdale, NJ: Erlbaum.

Cohen, J. (1994). The earth is round (p < .05). *American Psychologist. 49,* 997–1003.

Cortina, J. M., & Dunlap, W.P. (1997). On the logic and purpose of significance testing. *Psychological Methods, 2,* 161–173.

Cortina, J. M., Green, J. P., Keeler, K. R., & Vandenberg, R. J. (2017). Degrees of freedom in SEM: Are we testing the models that we claim to test? *Organizational Research Methods, 20,* 350–378.

Cortina, J. M., & Landis, R. S. (2011). The earth is *not* round (*p.*=.00). *Organizational Research Methods, 14,* 332–349.

Coward, W. M., & Sackett, P. R. (1990). Linearity of ability-performance relationships: A reconfirmation. *Journal of Applied Psychology, 75,* 297–300.

Dawes, R. M., & Corrigan, B. (1974). Linear models in decision making. *Psychological Bulletin, 81,* 95–106.

Drosnin, M. (1997). *The Bible Code.* New York: Touchstone.

Einhorn, H., & Hogarth, R. (1975). Unit weighting schemes for decision making. *Organizational Behavior and Human Performance, 13,* 171–192.

Ellenbeg, J. (2015). *How not to be wrong: The power of mathematical thinking* (Illustrated ed.). New York: Penguin Books.

Friedman, J. H. (1997, May). Data mining and statistics: What is the connection? *Proceedings of the 29th symposium on the interface between computer science and statistics.* Houston.

Gardner, R. G., Harris, T. B., Li, N., Kirkman, B. L., & Mathieu, J. E. (2017). Understanding "it depends" in organizational research: A theory-based taxonomy, review, and future research agenda concerning interactive and quadratic relationships. *Organizational Research Methods, 20,* 610–638.

Green, J. P., Tonidandel, S., & Cortina, J. M. (2016). Getting through the gate: Statistical and Methodological issues raised in the reviewing process. *Organizational Research Methods, 19,* 402–432.

Hand, D. J. (1998). Data mining: Statistics and more? *The American Statistician, 52,* 112–118.

Hausknect, J. P., & Li, H. (2016). Big data in turnover and retention. In S. Tonidandel, E. King, and J. Cortina (Eds.). *Big data at work: The data science revolution and organizational psychology* (pp. 250–271). New York: Routledge.

Hayes, A. F. (2017). *Introduction to mediation, moderation and conditional process analysis* (2nd ed.). New York: Guilford.

Hermida, R., Luchman, J. N., Nicolaides, V., & Wilcox, C. (2015). The issue of statistical power for overall model fit in evaluating structural equation models. *Computational Models in Social Sciences, 3,* 25–42.

Hoaglin, D. C., Mosteller, F., & Tukey, J. W. (1983). *Understanding robust and exploratory data analysis.* New York: Wiley.

Huang, F. L. (2018a). Multilevel modeling and ordinary least squares regression: How comparable are they? *The Journal of Experimental Education, 86*, 265–281.

Huang, F. L. (2018b). Multilevel modeling myths. *School Psychology Quarterly, 33*, 492–499.

Hubbard, R., Haig, B. D., & Parsa, R. A. (2019). The limited role of formal statistical inference in scientific inference, *The American Statistician, 73* (sup1), 91–98.

Klein, K. J., Dansereau, F., & Hall, R. J. (1994). Levels issues in theory development, data collection, and analysis. *Academy of Management Review, 19*, 195–229.

Klein, K. J., & Kozlowski, S. W. J. (2000). *Multilevel theory, research and methods in organizations: Foundations, extensions and new directions.* San Francisco, CA: Jossey-Bass.

Kozlowski, S. W. J., Chao, G. T., Chang, C., & Fernandez, R. (2016). Using big data to advance the science of team effectiveness. In S. Tonidandel, E. King, and J. Cortina (Eds.). *Big data at work: The data science revolution and organizational psychology* (pp. 272–309). New York: Routledge.

Kraemer, H. C., & Thiemann, S. (1987). *How many subjects?* Newbury Park, CA: Sage.

Kuonen, D. (2004). Data mining and statistics: What is the connection? *The Data Administration Newsletter.*

Little, R. J. A., & Rubin, D. B. (2002). *Statistical analysis with missing data* (2nd ed.). New York: Wiley.

Longford, N. T. (2000). On estimating standard errors in multilevel analysis. *The Statistician, 49*, 389–398.

Lyon, L. (2017). Dead salmon and voodoo correlations: Should we be skeptical about functional MRI? *Brain, 140*, E53–68.

Maxwell, S. E., Kelley, K., & Rausch, J. R. (2008). Sample size planning for statistical power and accuracy in parameter estimation. *Annual Review of Psychology, 59*, 537–563.

MacCallum, R. C., Browne, M. W., & Sugawara, H. M. (1996). Power analysis and determination of sample size for covariance structure modeling. *Psychological Methods, 1*, 130–149.

MacCallum, R. C., Lee, T., & Browne, M. W. (2010). The issue of isopower in power analysis for tests of structural equation models. *Structural Equation Modeling, 17*, 23–41.

McGrew, K. S. (2009). CHC theory and the human cognitive abilities project: Standing on the shoulders of the giants of psychometric intelligence research. *Intelligence, 37*, 1–10.

McKay, B., Bar-Natan, B., Bar-Hillel, M., & Kalai, G. (1999). Solving the Bible Code puzzle. *Statistical Science, 14*, 150–173.

Meehl, P. (1978). Theoretical risks and tabular asterisks: Sir Karl, Sir Ronald, and the slow progress of psychology. *Journal of Consulting and Clinical Psychology, 46*, 806–834.

Mosteller, F. & Tukey, J. W. (1977). *Data analysis and regression: A second course in statistics.* Reading, MA: Addison-Wesley.

Murphy, K. R. (2021). In praise of Table 1: The importance of making better use of descriptive statistics. *Industrial and Organizational Psychology, 14*, 461–477.

Murphy, K. R., Myors, B., & Wolach, A. (2014). *Statistical power analysis: A simple and general model for traditional and modern hypothesis tests* (4th ed.). New York: Taylor & Francis.

Murphy, K. R., & Russell, C. J. (2017). Mend it or end it: Redirecting the search for interactions in the organizational sciences. *Organizational Research Methods, 20*, 549–573.

Nisbett, R., Elder, J., & Miner, G. (2009). *Handbook of statistical analysis and data mining applications.* Oxford, UK: Elsevier.

Olvera Astivia, O. L., Gadermann, A., & Guhn, M. (2019). The relationship between statistical power and predictor distribution in multilevel logistic regression: A simulation-based approach. *BMC Medical Research Methodology, 19*, 97–107.

Preacher, K. J., Rucker, D. D., & Hayes, A. F. (2007). Addressing moderated mediation hypothesis: Theory, methods and prescriptions. *Multivariate Behavioral Research, 42*, 185–227.

Ratner, B. (2017). *Statistical and machine-learning data mining* (3rd ed.). Boca Raton, FL: CRC Press.

Ree, M., Carretta, T., & Earles, J. (1998). In top-down decisions, weighting variables does not matter: A consequence of Wilk's theorem. *Organizational Research Methods, 1*, 407–420.

Sajjadiani, S., Sojourner, A. J., Kammeyer-Mueller, J. D., & Mykerezi, E. (2019). Using machine learning to translate applicant work history into predictors of performance and turnover. *Journal of Applied Psychology, 104*, 1207–1225.

Satorra, A., & Saris, W. E. (1985). Power of the likelihood ratio test in covariance structure analysis. *Psychometrika, 50*, 83–90.

Saylors, R., & Trafimow, D. (2021). Why the increasing use of complex causal models is a problem: On the danger sophisticated theoretical narratives pose to truth. *Organizational Research Methods, 24*, 616–629.

Schmidt, F. L. (1996). Statistical significance testing and cumulative knowledge in psychology: Implications for training of researchers. *Psychological Methods, 1*, 115–129.

Stanton, J. M. (2021). Evaluating equivalence and confirming the null in the organizational sciences. *Organizational Research Methods, 24*, 491–521.

Thurstone, L. L. (1934). The vectors of mind. *Psychological Review, 41*, 1–32.

Tufte, E. (1983). *The visual display of quantitative information*. Cheshire, CT: Graphics Press.

Tufte, E. (1990). *Envisioning information*. Cheshire, CT: Graphics Press.

Tufte, E. (2020). *Seeing with fresh Eyes: Meaning, space, data, truth*. Cheshire, CT: Graphics Press.

Tukey, J. W. (1977). *Exploratory data analysis*. Reading, MA: Addison-Wesley.

Wasserstein, R. L., & Lazar, N. A. (2016). The ASA's statement on p-values: Context, process, and purpose. *The American Statistician, 70* (2), 129–133.

Wasserstein, R. L., Schirm, A. L., & Lazar, N. A. (2019). Moving to a World Beyond "$p < 0.05$". *The American Statistician, 73* (sup1), 1–19.

Wilcox. R. R. (1992). Why can methods for comparing means have relatively low power, and what can you do to correct the problem? *Current Directions in Psychological Science, 1*, 101–105.

Wilks, S. (1938). Weighting systems for linear functions of correlated variables when there is no dependent variable. *Psychometrika, 3*, 23–40.

Witztum, D., Rips, E., & Rosenberg, Y. (1994). Equidistant letter sequences in the Book of Genesis. *Statistical Science, 9*, 429–438.

Wood, R. E., Goodman, J. S., & Beckman, N. (2008). Mediation testing in management research: A review and proposals. *Organizational Research Methods, 11*, 270–295.

PART 3

Theory

8

HOW DO THEORIES IN THE BEHAVIORAL AND SOCIAL SCIENCES EMERGE, DEVELOP, AND DECLINE?

The Evolution of Politics Perceptions Theory

Wayne Hochwarter, Christopher C. Rosen, Samantha L. Jordan, and Maira E. Ezerins

Led by superstar Michael Jordan, the Chicago Bulls racked up six NBA championships, establishing themselves as one of the league's great dynasties. During the 1992–1993 season, the NBA chose Charles Barkley of the Phoenix Suns as the league's most valuable player, an award dominated by Jordan in the previous years. This decision did not sit well with many, including one person in particular. On episode five of ESPN's documentary, The Last Dance, Jordan admitted, "I was a little bit upset that I didn't get the MVP that year and they gave it to Charles [Barkley]. But I thought, OK, you can have that, I'm going to have this." In this case, "this" was the NBA championship contested between the Chicago Bulls and the Phoenix Suns – a series won by the Bulls in six games. Jordan's "this" wish resulted in his third (of six) Final's MVP award.

Michael Jordan's competitive nature was legendary. He would look for any advantage to destroy anyone or anything in his way of winning championships. One approach would be to teach lessons, often in person, to those who questioned his abilities or whom he considered obstacles. As another example, journalists compared Portland Trail Blazers superstar Clyde Drexler as a potential rival to Jordan's standing as the league's best player. Jordan took this personally, viewing the 1991–1992 NBA Finals as an opportunity to dispel any similarity between himself and Drexler. In Jordan's biography, David Halbersham (2000) noted, "He set out to do nothing less than destroy, not just Portland, but Drexler

DOI: 10.4324/9781003015000-11

as well." During a card game before Game 1, Jordan confided to Magic Johnson, "You know what's going to happen tomorrow; I'm going to give it to the dude" – the gift, 39 points in a 122-89 blowout win.

The mere presence of others, especially those considered a threat, served as a source of drive for Jordan. In many ways, this perspective is consistent with the tenets of social facilitation theory (SFT; Guerin, 1986). The principle, which emphasizes changes in task performance in others' presence versus when alone (Aiello & Douthitt, 2001), represents one of the oldest social psychology theories (Allport, 1968). Initially, Triplett (1898) noticed that cyclists raced fastest when competing with others. Performance declined when racing against the clock in tandem with others and reached its lowest point when riders practiced with no pacesetter. Triplett then reported that children would turn a fishing reel faster when side-by-side than alone. Fast forward a hundred years to Michael Jordan, whose competitive ruthlessness led to bets with the winner determined by who could drink water the fastest.

Social facilitation remains a topic of considerable scholarly attention across disciplines (Gonzalez & Aiello, 2019). For example, recent studies explored how social facilitation and neural networks combine to impact pay-based performance (Chib, Adachi & O'Doherty, 2018) and a theoretical drive of employee accountability (Han & Perry, 2020). In a practical sense, SFT's foundations help explain a myriad of real-world phenomena, ranging from Fitbit step count to Olympic competitions. The question is, "Why has SFT endured when other performance-focused theories have fallen out of favor or discounted entirely?" We see this as an essential question. Given the importance of theory for science and practice, understanding how and why theories emerge and grow, and providing explanations for possible decay, is necessary.

There are several reasons to assess a particular theory's state, from emergence to (possible) extinction. First, theories do not emerge in a vacuum. Sometimes the vacuum changes – a situation that can make practical and scientific interest in a theory sturdier. On the other hand, the vacuum can suck the life out of a theory rendering it obsolete if viewed wincingly by researchers. Accordingly, assessing a particular theory's status must be done within its operational realm to achieve a nuanced interpretation. Second, society, journal editors, and reviewers clamor for novelty (Pfeffer, 1993), often at the expense of familiarity (Ferris et al., 2006). Coining novel and previously implicit theories can establish careers (Bell, Den Ouden & Ziggers, 2006). We agree with Popper (1969), who advocated for developing theory that offers greater explicatory power and precision. However, are there times when the rush to establish unique thinking patterns is harmful to science? McKinley (2010) argued, "displacement of ends toward the goal of new theory development has brought excitement, novelty, and less attention to organized empirical verification work" (p. 56). Rather than move ahead to new theories, we advocate for reflection as a means for growth and a way to avoid decline or condemnation (Ferris, Hochwarter & Buckley, 2012).

To this end, this chapter evaluates political theory in organizations, specifically in employee perceptions of organizational politics (POPs), by charting its emergence and identifying current and future opportunities and threats. We view this as an appropriate time for doing so. First, despite the impressive growth of research, the topic has been in existence for just over 30 years (Ferris, Russ & Fandt, 1989; Hochwarter, Rosen et al., 2020). As one of the "newer" social science theories, POPs has not received the scrutiny afforded more mature organizational science theories. Second, and related, reviews of POPs have summarized the accumulated evidence of Ferris, Russ, and Fandt (1989) model (Chang, Rosen & Levy, 2009), mainly noting support for its initial tenets (Bedi & Schat, 2013). Fewer discussions have reviewed the contextual effects and philosophical directions that future generations of POPs research will take. Third, because research on POPs has increased exponentially (especially in recent years) (Hochwarter, Rosen et al., 2020), the emphasis has been on expanding the theory (Hochwarter, Kapoutsis et al., 2020). Few have mentioned decline or replacement despite widespread acceptance that "social and economic theories are ever-changing as social and economic life and conditions change…" (Richter, 1913, p. 285).

Ostensibly, theories are "perpetually changing" (Popper, 2002, p. 50), positioned in cycles (Turner, Baker & Kellner, 2018) similar to those used in economics and the natural sciences (Mueller, 1972). Although several reviews document the emergence of the POPs construct (Ferris & Judge, 1991; Hochwarter, Rosen et al., 2020), few discussions consider the decline or replacement of the theory presented to account for this phenomenon. As such, the current chapter provides an opportunity to discuss the emergence and evolution of contemporary POPs theory since first introduced by Ferris, Russ, and Fandt (1989) almost 35 thirty years ago.

This chapter unfolds as follows. First, we discuss reasons why theories decline, are replaced, or are rejected outright. Second, we review POPs theory and research to offer the reader a basic understanding of its previous work's conceptualization, highlighting the growth and maturation of POPs theory over time. Our treatment is intentionally brief as: (a) wide-ranging reviews (Ferris et al., 2019; Hochwarter, Rosen et al., 2020) and edited volumes (Vigoda-Gadot & Drory, 2016) are available elsewhere and (b) our focus is to understand where POPs theory is in its developmental trajectory, not on developing a new theory, per se.

Third, drawing from our discussion of why theories decline and our review of POPs theory, we look forward and discuss avenues capable of extending POPs research, thus avoiding the decline and death experienced by many once well-regarded theories (Cady et al., 2019). These recommendations cover social and contextual factors (i.e., what is going on in the world) shaping the practice of politics in organizations and the tools and cognitive approaches (i.e., how we conceptualize and analyze human behavior) available to scholars.

Emergence and Decline of Theory

For centuries, scholars have acknowledged that theories assume a life of their own (Van Maanen, Sørensen & Mitchell, 2007). Boltzman (1901) argued that theory's evolution "has been by no means so continuous as we might be inclined to believe, but rather that it is full of gaps and has not taken place, to appearances at least, along the simplest and most logical paths" (p. 229). Much like human existence, theories emerge, grow, and attract enough attention to determine what is next following maturation (Kuhn, 1970). Similarly, life cycle (and product cycle) proponents (Cady et al., 2019) argue that much goes on between emergence and decline/death (Clegg, Cunha & Berti, 2020), and the pace of evolution is unique, dependent mainly upon the people and realities in which it resides. Although assumed largely unpredictable, scholars recognize that unchanged theories have little practical or scientific value (Weick, 1995).

Scholars have discussed the emergence of theory across disciplines, including political science (King, Keohane & Verba, 1995), applied health (Vågerö, 2006), child development (Meltzoff, 1999), and exchange relationships (Muldoon, Liguori & Bendickson, 2013). Fewer discussions focus on decline and death, despite their importance in theory's ecological advancement. Darwinist views of natural selection argue that some theories are apt to die-off while others would survive, perhaps only transitorily (Narskii, 1980). The evolutionary perspective also implies that a controlled burn of the existing theoretical landscape spurs development by eliminating clutter and allowing resilient views to be increasingly prominent (Popper, 1961).

Why might a theory decline? Theories receive less attention or perish for several reasons. First, *a theory can experience its final death when abandoned by its originator* (or morbidly, when its originator or staunchest advocate dies) (Goldsmith, 1995). Whether it be passion, identity, unmatched knowledge of its underpinnings, or sheer stubbornness, originations are more apt to resuscitate "their theory" than let it evolve into something that takes on a different appearance or pull the plug. As evidence, research reports that collaborators of star scientists who die (albeit prematurely in this case) submitted fewer papers on the topic postmortem. Conversely, outsiders offered more research on the topic, perhaps due to a hesitancy to challenge the scholar or the theory's existing tenets while the original creator was alive (Azoulay, Fons-Rosen & Graff Zivin, 2019).

Second, *time also affects a theory's popularity* (Nehrbass, 1979; Popper, 1969). Older theories often assume an inverted-U form (Mingers & Burrell, 2006). Attractiveness wanes as new knowledge (extensions, modification) makes earlier knowledge antiquated and less exploited (Bell, Kennebrew & Blyden, 2015).

As an example, Martin (1917; *Journal of Applied Psychology's* first edition) advocated for studying mental hygiene, describing it as work dedicated to "creating, maintaining, and restoring normal mental activity in a given individual" (p. 67). In the next edition, Fish's (1917) work in human engineering recognized that advancement opportunities and personal growth were critical in minimizing turnover and that the "shop shall be comfortable in both a physical and mental way" (p. 162). Seemingly, both works evolved from blue-collar discussions of wellness in industrial contexts into the increasingly flourishing job stress domain, focusing in recent years on white-collar service workers (Bliese, Edwards & Sonnentag, 2017). Interestingly, these essential early discussions of employee welfare have been cited a total of 13 times (Martin – seven times; Fish – six times) over the past 108 years.

Third, *theories also decline when the context is unsupportive* (i.e., the world has changed) or has moved in directions warranting changes or egress. In JAP's first year, Baird (1917) examined the legibility of the New York Telephone Company's directory, while Rasely's (1917) "Golden Text" principle advised business letters to have, among others, a "friendly touch." Good luck explaining a phonebook and letter writing to a Millennial or conjuring up interest in a fledgling behavioral scientist. As noted, occupations previously staffed by blue-collar employees "doing things with their hands" have been supplanted by professional workers who "do things with their heads." Accordingly, theories related to production in piece work settings (e.g., Parkinson's Law; Latham & Locke, 1975) and industrial accident predisposition (e.g., Theory of Increased Accident Proneness; Mintz, 1954) do not exist in contemporary research. Organizational science research is particularly amenable to change-induced development due to its emphasis on specific, temporary, and ephemeral social behaviors within dynamic environments (Geisler, 2001).

Fourth, *theories die because scholars find them untestable or,* in a more discouraging sense, uninterpretable. Historically, the *Academy of Management Review* represented the primary outlet to "publish theoretical insights that advance our understanding of management and organizations" (AMR's mission statement). In recent years, outlets for theoretical research have increased considerably (i.e., journals and special editions). As a result, there are "more theories out there to test." Because these journals (and chapters) place a premium on novelty and a unique contribution to the field, practical approaches to test the theory's basic tenets are often afterthoughts. Sadly, it seems that some scholars find joy in developing theoretical contributions that are indecipherable, too vast to partition in any meaningful way, or require data that is impossible to gather (Leblanc & Schwartz, 2007). Therefore, many accepted theories are not theories (or science) (Popper, 1969) because they offer no falsification opportunities (Bacharach, 1989). It is encouraging to note that the Southern Management Association (publisher of *Journal of Management*) has announced the launch of a new journal,

Journal of Management Scientific Reports, designed to empirically test and refine theories.

Fifth, *theories fall out of favor as a result of their own success*. Novel and thought-provoking theories garner attention as scholars seek evidence to confirm, refute, or suggest modified forms (Wisdom, 1972). As a noteworthy example, Locke (1689) proposed that children are a "blank slate (i.e., Tabula rasa)," born without mental content and systems for processing information. Instead, the mind relies exclusively on sensory experiences to establish rules for operation. If accepted, this argument assumes all humans have the same capacities (and possibilities) at birth (Dobzhansky, 1976). Labeled as a myth (Pinker, 2002), a fallacy and dismissed out of hand by Darwin (Munz, 2006), the approach was denounced in favor of those that consider inherited factors and prenatal/perinatal conditions (Cavanagh, 2006). In terms of personality development, Locke's view is ensconced in the "nature" side of nature versus nurture debates, where "experiences write all the contents" (Holmes, 1930, p. 248).

Sixth, although theory evaluation is not as combative as efforts examining Locke's work, *natural evolution (e.g., narrowing/expanding) justifies redirection*. Before the turn of the last century, Simmel's (1895) Theory of Socialization recognized that "Society, in its broadest sense, is found wherever several individuals enter into reciprocal relations" (p. 414). Subsequent discussions focused on reciprocal relationships in social groups ("… cohesion of parts, and hence unity of the whole" Simmel, 1898, p. 664), superior-subordinate associations (e.g., the sum of interests uniting interacting individuals; Simmel, 1896), and secret societies (i.e., "friends reciprocally refrain from obtruding themselves into the range of interests and feelings not included in the special relationship…" Simmel, 1906, p. 458). Reciprocity, according to Simmel (1990), is a process of exchange, a compromised exchange of something valued (Simmel, 1904) based on equivalence (Simmel, 1908).

Contemporary scholars often reference Homans (1958), Gouldner (1960), Blau (1964), and Thibaut and Kelley (1959) when acknowledging foundational theories of social exchange (SET). Elaborations of SET, including organizational support (Eisenberger et al., 1986), equity (Adams, 1965), and justice/fairness (Cropanzano & Greenberg, 1997) theories, pay similar homage to these important works. Accordingly, scholars (Muldoon, Liguori & Bendickson, 2013) have anointed Homans as the "father of social exchange" and Gouldner as "the founding father of the norm of reciprocity" (Thijssen, 2016). This acknowledgment begs the question, "what about Grandpa"? Grandpa was important since "George Homans, Alvin Gouldner, and Peter Blau used Simmel to help justify their new focus on exchange as the governing metaphor for sociological" (Levine, 1989, p. 163). Though perhaps not immediately visible, we argue that Simmel's DNA continues to influence science across disciplines.

The focus of the current chapter is on understanding the current state of theory in POPs research, and, in so doing, we hope to shed light on the processes through which theories evolve and mature. In the following section, we review and take stock of POPs theory and research to identify where POPs currently falls in the trajectory of theory development, growth, and decline (Kapoutsis et al., 2011). We begin by providing a brief overview of POPs theory and research. We then provide additional insight into the process through which theory grows and declines by considering: (a) the extent to which external factors influenced the growth and development of POPs theory and (b) how contemporary issues (e.g., changes to the nature of work) will impact this area of study going forward. We conclude by identifying where POPs theory currently is in its evolution and identify steps that scholars must take to ensure that POPs remain relevant in current (and future) work contexts.

Critical Issues in POPs Theory and Research

Although discussion of organizational politics dates back to the early 1900s (see Farrell & Petersen, 1982), consideration of organizational politics as a scientific construct began in earnest when Burns (1961) discussed politics in the process of organizational change. In the 1970s, research focused on understanding politics in the context of power, influence tactics, and decision-making (e.g., Schein, 1977). This research led to increasing interest in politics as a work-situated phenomenon during the late 1970s and early 1980s.

At this point, scholars began to view politics as a process involving specific tactics (i.e., political behaviors, such as ingratiation, impression management, and self-promotion) that employees use to influence the thoughts, decisions, and actions (e.g., Kipnis et al., 1980). Notably, there was adequate theory from different disciplines (e.g., persuasion, social influence, self-serving behavior) to support the legitimacy of studying politics in organizations during this time (e.g., Cavanagh, Moberg & Velasquez, 1981; Pfeffer & Salancik, 1974).

Scholarship from the early 1980s (e.g., Gandz & Murray, 1980) influenced later researchers to reconsider previous conceptualizations of politics. Notably, the focus shifted from political influence tactics to viewing politics as a part of the social fabric of organizations that can influence employee attitudes and behaviors. More explicitly, work was needed to "address both conceptual and empirical limitations of prior work on organizational politics, while also providing mechanisms for integrating several streams of research that seem to be addressing essentially the same phenomenon" (Ferris, Russ & Fandt, 1989, p. 145). Accordingly, Ferris, Russ, and Fandt (1989) conceptual model emphasized the role of employee POPs. Definitionally, POPs reflect the extent to which workers engage in behavior that "is strategically designed to maximize short-term or long-term self-interest, which is either consistent with or at the expense of others' interests" (Ferris, Russ & Fandt, 1989, p. 145). Grounded in appraisal-based theories of work stress (McGrath, 1976), Ferris, Russ, and Fandt (1989) argued that employees typically view organizational politics as a work threat both caused by and a creator of uncertainty. Such appraisals and reactions are a function of one's understanding of the nature of politics in their organization, as well as the degree of control that employees feel they have over the "political game" (Ferris, Russ & Fandt, 1989, p. 162).

Ferris, Russ, and Fandt (1989) conceptualization of organizational politics as a subjective state aligned with previous scholarship (e.g., Gandz & Murray, 1980) which asserted that politics is more of a state of mind, existing in the eye of the beholder, rather than an objective state of reality. Moreover, the assertion that employee *perceptions* affect attitudes and behaviors rather than a "something quantifiable" aligns with Lewin's (1936) idiographic view of reality. Kacmar and Ferris (1991) subsequently developed the perceptions of organizational politics scale (POPS). The POPS was the first generally accepted measure of organizational politics, and it allowed for the systematic evaluation of Ferris, Russ, and Fandt (1989) model. We provide POPs scale items and other established politics perceptions measures in the Appendix.

Over the past three decades, research has generally supported Ferris, Russ, and Fandt (1989) model, providing evidence that: (a) individual differences (e.g., Machiavellianism, affectivity, and locus of control), features of the work context (e.g., job autonomy, feedback, leader-member exchange, and trust), and organizational influences (e.g., centralization, formalization, and justice) serve as antecedents to POPs; (b) POPs are associated with psychological (e.g., stress, anxiety, burnout), perceptual (e.g., diminished perceptions of trust, justice, and relationship quality), attitudinal (e.g., reduced job satisfaction and commitment, increased turnover intentions), and behavioral (e.g., reduced organizational citizenship behavior and task performance) consequences; and (c) personal (e.g., political skill), perceptual (e.g., perceived control and understanding), and organizational (e.g., whether the organization is in the public or private sector) factors serve as moderators of the effects of POPs on attitudinal and behavioral outcomes (Ferris et al., 2002; Hochwarter, Rosen et al., 2020). This research provides strong support for Ferris, Russ, and Fandt (1989) model, indicating that POPs elicit a stress response with considerable potential to influence employee and organizational outcomes (Chang, Rosen & Levy, 2009).

In the years immediately following the publication of Ferris, Russ, and Fandt (1989) seminal chapter, many notable and well-referenced works came from a limited number of scholars. However, interest in POPs began to increase substantially in the mid-1990s, following the publication of Kacmar and Ferris's (1991) POPs measure. This work was reviewed and summarized in several comprehensive reviews (e.g., Ferris et al., 2002; Kacmar & Baron, 1999) published in the 1990s and early 2000s. These reviews generally upheld Ferris et al.'s conceptualization of POPs as a stressor. Subsequently, primary (e.g., Rosen, Levy & Hall, 2006) and meta-analytic studies (e.g., Chang, Rosen & Levy, 2009) provide additional support (and momentum) for viewing POPs as a workplace stressor.

As scholars continued to document the stress-based effects of POPs, several challenges to this conceptualization emerged. In particular, an implicit assumption of this research is that employees generally appraise POPs as a threat (Chang, Rosen & Levy, 2009), which has led some scholars to identify POPs as a hindrance stressor (e.g., LePine, Podsakoff & LePine, 2005). However, stress theories have guided research (e.g., the transactional model of stress; Lazarus & Folkman, 1984) suggesting that POPs can potentially represent threats *or* opportunities. Individual differences, such as cognitive styles (Rosen & Hochwarter, 2014), contextual and personal resources (De Clercq & Belausteguigoitia, 2017), and personality traits (e.g., political skill and Machiavellianism; Perrewé, Rosen & Maslach, 2012) also affect perceptions and subsequent reactions. Accordingly, this research questions whether POPs elicit a stress response in all employees. Scholars have gone so far as to suggest that POPs may signal the presence of an opportunity for growth and achievement for some employees, further countering arguments that POPs represent a hindrance (rather than a challenge) stressor (Byrne et al., 2017).

In addition to these decades-long challenges, scholars have focused on alternative mechanisms accounting for POPs' harmful effects on employee outcomes. To this end, exchange-related means (e.g., psychological contract breach and employee-organization social exchange relationship quality) and motivational constructs (e.g., the satisfaction of basic psychological needs) also emerged as alternative explanations (Rosen et al., 2014), challenging earlier conceptualizations and models of POPs. The growth of POPs research has triggered additional challenges to the theory, with some scholars arguing that POPs might not be a universally harmful experience (Hochwarter, 2012). Despite these challenges, or perhaps because of them, research on POPs is robust and has continued to increase in recent years (i.e., annually, studies examining POPs have more than doubled over past ten years: 2010 = 157 articles; 2020 = 422 articles; Google Scholar Search). Presumably, opposition to theory and indoctrinating alternative views can benefit (rather than harm) theory development. Importantly, and as documented above, challenges can result from the "normal" scientific process (Kuhn, 1970), such that theory is revised, updated, and modified as part of the cumulative research process. However, as discussed below, external factors (e.g., technological advancements, statistical innovations, changes to the context and nature of work, societal influences) can also motivate theory changes.

External Factors that Motivate Theory Change

Technological advancements and statistical innovations, and related trends in the organizational sciences (e.g., the recent focus on within-person phenomena and temporal influences on organizational phenomena), led to adopting a new theory that challenges consensus in the POPs literature. For example, scholars have recently begun to view constructs, such as organizational justice (Koopman et al., 2020), workplace incivility (Rosen et al., 2016), and leadership (Rosen et al., 2019) as dynamic, within- (rather than between-) person phenomena. Similarly, countering decades of research identifying POPs as a relatively static, between-person phenomenon (Chang, Rosen & Levy, 2009), Hochwarter, Rosen et al. (2020) argued for POPs as a within-person phenomenon influenced by events (i.e., discrete political behaviors) occurring in the work environment. More explicitly, Hochwarter, Rosen et al. (2020, p. 879) theorized POPs as "a discrete phenomenon capable of being evaluated in terms of its novelty, disruption, and criticality." This conceptualization provides insight into employees' everyday experiences with organizational politics. Doing so identifies additional factors beyond understanding and control (e.g., Ferris, Russ & Fandt, 1989) likely to influence how employees perceive and respond to organizational politics daily (or perhaps even hourly).

Viewing POPs as a discrete workplace phenomenon represents a radical departure from previous conceptualizations, which have typically identified organizational politics as an enduring feature of the work context in which employees exist (e.g., Chang, Rosen & Levy, 2009). This perspective adds critical nuance to understanding how employees perceive and respond to daily discrete political behaviors. We were unable to identify any published empirical studies that have tested Hochwarter, Rosen et al.'s (2020) model or evaluated event-based antecedents and outcomes of POPs. Since Ferris, Russ, and Fandt (1989) seminal model, however, technological advancements (e.g., smartphone ownership and widespread access to the internet throughout the workday) and statistical innovations (e.g., user-friendly software that allows for the rapid assessment of multilevel models) have facilitated the development and testing of dynamic theory (Gabriel et al., 2019). Thus, testing a dynamic multilevel model such as the one presented by Hochwarter, Rosen et al. (2020) is now possible. We anticipate that further revision to POPs theory will occur as scholars begin to adopt the event-based outlook prescribed by Hochwarter, Rosen et al. (2020).

In addition to external factors directing attention toward POPs as a dynamic, within-person phenomenon, the ever-evolving context of work also played a role in the evolution of POPs as a theory. Only within the past generation has context become a focal consideration in organizational psychology research (Johns, 2006; McLaren & Durepos, 2021). This lack of emphasis is both practically and scientifically bewildering when one considers that work must take place "somewhere." In support, "one might think that organizational context receives more explicit consideration with the growth of the OB [organizational behavior] field, but scholars have with regular intervals questioned the extent to which context plays any serious, prominent role in OB theory or empirical research" (Felin, Foss & Ployhart, 2015, p. 603). Reasons for this disregard are many (Johns, 2018). However, treatments remain speculative and undetermined (Johns, 2006), primarily driven by scholars' "on-again, off-again" relationship with contextual influences (Schneider, Ehrhart & Macey, 2012).

In addition to technical and statistical innovations, other external factors (e.g., the changing nature and context of work) also drive theory changes. Johns (2001) noted that context plays an essential role in theory growth, development, and decline. In this regard, politics perceptions research has grown exponentially down a path with few major contextual disruptions, especially in its early years (e.g., 1985–2000). To a great extent, changes in work environments had only minimal lasting effects on POPs research. Accordingly, few reasons existed to reexamine the constructs underlining theoretical tenets despite widespread agreement that context matters. Nonetheless, scholars claim that context shapes assessments and reactions (McFarland, Van Iddekinge & Ployhart, 2012). In this regard, Kapoutsis et al. (2011, p. 124) argued that context "is preeminently important to scholars and practitioners for a myriad of reasons" when examining work politics. To this point, research examining POPs' role in downsizing (Rosen et al., 2009), economic tumult (Lawong et al., 2021), abusive leadership (Liu & Liu, 2018), and in non-Western contexts (Haider, Fatima & de Pablos-Heredero, 2020) exists. Nevertheless, discussions of contextual influences on POPs are often relegated to discussion sections as an "interesting avenue of future research."

More recently, the COVID-19 pandemic has drawn politics researchers to the proverbial fork in the road. The pandemic effects have been felt worldwide and caused considerable disruption to work environments previously replete with instability. As representative examples, recent studies assessed COVID-19's impact on work stability and financial insecurity (Probst, Lee & Bazzoli, 2020), work-family responsibilities (Restubog, Ocampo & Wang, 2020), the safety of essential workers (Dennerlein et al., 2020), and the potential to respond to future natural disasters (Cardiol & de-Miguel, 2020). COVID-19 abruptly transformed all aspects of work-life, including where job responsibilities are performed (Chong, Huang & Chang, 2020).

Pervading pandemic-related "jolts" create unprecedented levels of global uncertainty (Kniffin et al., 2021), affecting employees in industries, including air travel (Sobieralski, 2020), hospitality (Teng, Wu & Lin, 2020), and higher education (Charoensukmongkol & Phungsoonthorn, 2020). Employees are uncertain whether they will have jobs (Kniffin et al., 2021), if mental health will return to pre-pandemic levels (Rettie & Daniels, 2020), if bosses still expect pre-pandemic work output (Restubog, Ocampo & Wang, 2020), if they are returning home with a contagious disease (Zhou et al., 2020), or if work is "even worth it" (Ferns, Gautam & Hudak, 2021). So, what do these disruption-based uncertainties have to do with POPs as a component of an organization's social fabric? In particular, to what extent do these changes affect how we theorize about the phenomenon? The answer – a great deal.

Scholars agree that politics and uncertainty are inexplicable linked (Cropanzano et al., 1997), forming an impactful and constant flux relationship. Because of this dynamism, the "chicken or egg" analogy does not apply (see Hochwarter, Rosen et al., 2020 for a discussion). Extricating the POPs – uncertainty relationship is futile. For example, "…politics are a source of uncertainty that in turn affects the way that employees act in that social context" (Li, Liang & Farh, 2020, p. 462). Also, "uncertainty leads to increases in both political behavior and perceptions of politics" (Brouer et al., 2006, p. 189).

Are our current theories/conceptualizations capable of supporting the upward trajectory of POPs research considering the disruptions occurring at work and globally? It is conceivable that the theory is generally sound will require only modest development to remain supportive, as we have seen with other recent challenges to the theory that have resulted in consideration of additional explanatory mechanisms and boundary conditions. Alternatively, widespread societal and technological changes may indicate a point of bifurcation. Accordingly, it may become necessary to put previous theorizations in the rearview mirror and create scientifically and practically sound foundations that account for how the rapidly changing world of work may impact the relevance and value of POPs theory in its current form. Time will tell. In the following section, we discuss considerations required to ensure that POPs research flourishes. We also discuss methodological issues that must work part and parcel with theory for an accurate picture to emerge at this critical juncture.

The Next Two Decades of POPs Theory

Is Ferris, Russ, and Fandt (1989) a Theory, a Meta-Theory, or an Excellent Start?

Building off of Mintzberg (1985), Ferris, Russ, and Fandt (1989) defined POPs as perceptions of "…behavior not formally sanctioned by the organization, which produces conflict and disharmony in the work environment by pitting individuals and/or groups against one another, or against the organization" (Ferris et al., 1996, p. 234). Despite widespread acceptance and use across disciplines, occupations, and countries, the theory may not be expansive enough to capture the width of political activity at work. This discussion assumes that political action is harmful, causing competition for finite resources (e.g., a "zero-sum game";

Kane-Frieder et al., 2014). However, Ferris and Hochwarter (2011) maintained, "scholars advertise their studies as inspections of organizational politics when, in fact, the research is limited to confirming the existence and impact of negative politics" (p. 443).

Lately, research assumes that politics is not always destructive (Maslyn, Farmer & Bettenhausen, 2017), and discounting a positive role is inconsistent with practical or academic realities. For example, Eldor (2017) found that observing politics was beneficial for highly engaged workers, increasing their initiative, ingenuity, and willingness to share. Moreover, Hochwarter (2012) argues that politics can uncover resources that would otherwise remain obscured or unused. In instructional terms, universities offer standalone undergraduate courses in organizational politics, often coupled (dare we say) with ethics. Finally, maximizing one's return on political engagement is an often-covered module in many contemporary leadership development programs (Hochwarter, Kapoutsis et al., 2020).

This discussion begs the question, "how can theory best serve POPs' development" moving forward? We argue that *A* theory (should it be one theory) is unlikely given the intricacies of the phenomenon recognized in science and practice. Instead, we see prior theory as the trunk of a tree with many sturdy branches extending in unique and often-unpredicted directions. Both the trunk and branches are essential to moving science forward. The trunk offers scholars a communal space to build a foundation. As wrought to do, branches accommodatingly operate within the natural environment to tell a more complete (and accurate) story. To quote *The Gospel in All Lands* (Simpson & Smith, 1881), "we planted our tree, but a tree without branches would be very unsightly" (p. 279). Noted plant pathologist Alex Shigo more recently argued, "a tree without branches is not a tree" (1986, p. 208). In short, it is time to replace *A Theory of POPs* with *Theories of POPs*.

Stabbing Me in the Back in Person or Posting Things Online?

When initially conceptualized, scholars envisioned politics as gossiping or rumormongering at the water cooler, corporate lunchroom, or behind closed office doors (Byrne et al., 2017). Accordingly, discussions centered on perceptions of others in their "work environment" (Parker, Dipboye & Jackson, 1995), the "workplace" (Ferris et al., 1996), and in the "office" (Fedor et al., 1998). During COVID-19, however, many workers became comfortable working away from the office (Wang et al., 2021). Concurrently, organizations recognized the cost savings (e.g., rent, facilities operations, and maintenance) associated with a remote workforce adding significantly to their bottom line (Prasad et al., 2020). Predictions regarding returning to the traditional office vary (Parker, 2020), including *within a year, never,* and *"who knows"* (Parker, 2020). On the one hand, the lack of in-person exchange may minimize politics, and subsequent perceptions of others' behavior, simply because they are less visible.

Conversely, technology offers various previously untapped mechanisms for seeking influence (Ferris et al., 2019), providing anonymity to those unable to act politically in traditional office settings (D'Cruz & Noronha, 2018). For example, videoconferencing technology can make it challenging to interpret contextual cues and nonverbal behavior (i.e., reduced media richness; Daft, Lengel & Trevino, 1987) in meetings, making it more challenging to discern political behavior from sincerity. Additionally, consider how big data use and analysis have grown exponentially over the last decade. Although many believe that mathematical algorithms are objective, even slight manipulations to visual displays, like the truncation of axis markers, can significantly impact decision-making (Parikh, 2014). Finally, projections of automation estimate that by 2030 anywhere from 75 to 375 million employees will need to change occupations or tasks (Manyika et al., 2017). The need to maneuver into different jobs or levels within an organization may incentivize at-risk employees' political behavior.

Consequently, technology may facilitate more accessible methods of engaging in political behavior while simultaneously creating a perceived need for such behavior. We thus argue that little evidence for a decline in political activity exists. The shroud of uncertainty permeating society alone reinforces political actions' sensemaking function to reduce insecurities (Hochwarter et al., 2010). Accordingly, the theory of POPs needs to consider these dramatic changes in the context of influence. Without doing so, the long-term prognosis of an acceptable theory of POPs is, at best, dubious.

Methodological Considerations in POPs Theory

Early conceptualizations (Zhou & Ferris, 1995) identified POPs as a multidimensional phenomenon. Nevertheless, scholars generally have treated POPs as unidimensional, combining the dimensions into a single measure (e.g., Rosen, Levy & Hall, 2006) or focusing on a specific subdimension (e.g., going along to get ahead) POPs. As noted above, technological and statistical advancements have opened the door for considering new conceptualizations of POPs, such as viewing it as a within-person phenomenon or at the event level. In addition to these advances, scholars argue that adopting person-centered approaches, such as latent profile analysis (LPA), is necessary to enhance understanding of how variables operate conjointly and within-persons (Gabriel et al., 2018). In addition to addressing specific research questions, LPA also serves to "develop and expand theoretical thinking regarding the existence of different configurations of profiles in variables of interest in organizational behavior...including their predictors and outcomes" (Spurk et al., 2020, p. 2). It may, therefore, behoove scholars to adopt a person-centered approach to examining POPs, as this may provide additional insight into the complex nature and impact of POPs in contemporary work settings.

Discussion

Despite advocating for research viewing POPs from a time-series perspective (Hochwarter et al., 2003; Hochwarter, Rosen et al., 2020), often a snapshot is preferred to gauge the status of a particular phenomenon or stream of research (Ferris & Hochwarter, 2011). In terms of its place along a continuum of growth (e.g., conception, introduction, progression, maturity [plateau leading to acceleration or decline], and death; Cady et al., 2019; Hirsch & Levin, 1999), most would agree that POPs occupies *mature* status, capable of explaining complicated political dynamics but still with room for development or replacement.

Simplistically put, POPs theory to date can be viewed as a child's dot-to-dot picture, where each dot represents a meaningful element of our political domain (i.e., constructs, phenomena, contingencies, contexts, methodologies, etc.), and our current theoretical understanding reflects the lines or predetermined route from one dot to the next. Currently, prior POPs theories (e.g., persuasion, social influence, self-serving behavior) present a meaningful picture of a horse; however, a few dots remain unconnected or unexplained. Although the image makes sense now, emerging theorization may link the remaining dots to show a more accurate picture of a unicorn instead. Alternatively, new advancements (e.g., neutral and positive political behaviors, virtual contexts, within-person methodologies) may replace our entire existing picture, providing researchers with an unlined dot-to-dot canvass ready for future theoretical connection. Given the exponential rate of technological change and the ever-changing complexity of our world, the replacement approach is arguably more likely.

Regardless, the landscape suggests that POPs theory is mature, positioned to explain contemporary workplace phenomena, or eventually fade into obscurity if adaptations to emerging challenges are not made. Fortunately, however, mechanisms are in place for continued growth for many years to come, including: (a) an increasing number of practitioners interested in the topic, (b) a heightened interest in the construct as a legitimate area of inquiry, (c) an accelerated interest in POPs in nontraditional and non-western contacts, (d) a recognition that politics is as much a component of an entity's social fabric as other confirmed realities, (e) its connection to "social politics," and (f) its visibility in popular media, including film (e.g., *Horrible Bosses*) and broadcast (e.g., *The Office*) outlets. Nevertheless, it is faulty to assume that our existing dot-to-dot picture of POPs is a perfect reflection of the future state of the construct. To many, POPs theory has lagged precipitously behind the reality of the situation. This situation is hardly uncommon (Doldor, Silvester & Atewologun, 2017). Because work evolves faster than theory, we do not expect the next generation of research to catch up completely. However, closing the gap is achievable if proactive approaches to explaining the phenomenon replace the reactive tactics seeped into most POPs research. Now, who will take on this challenge?

Conclusion

Twenty-five years ago, few were interested in organizational politics. During this time, everything has grown – the number of articles, citations, summary chapters, edited reading books, practical discussions of the phenomenon, and widespread acceptance of its critical role in shaping careers and organizations. We argue that the phenomenal growth is likely attributed to the number of insightful and dedicated scholars actively engaged in this research. Perhaps there is something to this *social facilitation thing* after all.

Appendix

Scale	Items
Perceptions of Organizational Politics Scale (POPS; Kacmar & Ferris, 1991)	*General political behavior* 1. One group always gets their way 2. Influential group no one crosses 3. Policy changes help only a few 4. Build themselves up by tearing others down 5. Favoritism, not merit, gets people ahead 6. Don't speak up for fear of retaliation *Go along to get ahead* 7. Promotions go to top performers (R) 8. Rewards come to hard workers (R) 9. Encouraged to speak out (R) 10. No place for yes men (R) *Pay and promotion* 11. Pay and promotion policies are not politically applied (R) 12. Pay and promotion decisions are consistent with policies (R)
Perceptions of Organizational Politics Scale (POPS; Kacmar & Carlson, 1997)	*General political behavior* 1. People in this organization attempt to build themselves up by tearing others down 2. There has always been an influential group in this department that no one ever crosses *Go along to get ahead* 3. Employees are encouraged to speak out frankly even when they are critical of well-established ideas (R) 4. There is no place for yes-men around here; good ideas are desired even if it means disagreeing with superiors (R) 5. Agreeing with powerful others is the best alternative in this organization 6. It is best not to rock the boat in this organization

(Continued)

Scale	Items
	7. Sometimes it is easier to remain quiet than to fight the system
	8. Telling others what they want to hear is sometimes better than telling the truth
	9. It is safer to think what you are told than to make up your own mind
	Pay and promotion policies
	10. Since I have worked in this department, I have never seen the pay and promotion policies applied politically (R)
	11. I can't remember when a person received a pay increase or promotion that was inconsistent with the published policies (R)
	12. None of the raises I have received are consistent with the policies on how raises should be determined
	13. The stated pay and promotion policies have nothing to do with how pay raises and promotions are determined
	14. When it comes to pay raise and promotion decisions, policies are irrelevant
	15. Promotions around here are not valued much because how they are determined is so political
Perceived Politics (Parker, Dipboye & Jackson, 1995)	1. Getting rewarded is political- It's who you know
	2. Having a manager at a higher level take a personal interest in you is important for advancement
	3. The real-world within (the organization) is one of under-cutting and behind the scenes politics
	4. (The organization) can be described as a system of empires, and there is very little sharing among them
	5. We talk about teamwork and sharing, but people quietly hold onto their power and authority
	6. (The organization) values organization politics
Politics Perceptions (Hochwarter, Kacmar, Perrewé, et al., 2003)	1. There is a lot of self-serving behavior going on
	2. People do what's best for them, not what's best for the organization
	3. People spend too much time sucking up to those who can help them
	4. People are working behind the scenes to ensure that they get their piece of the pie
	5. Many employees are trying to maneuver their way into the in group
	6. Individuals are stabbing each other in the back to look good in front of others
Political Work Environment (Hochwarter, Kacmar, Treadway, et al., 2003)	1. On a scale of 0 [none] to 100 [extremely], please indicate the level of politics in your organization

References

Academy of Management Review mission statement. Available at: https://journals.aom. org/journal/amr

Adams, J. (1965). Inequity in social exchange. In L. Berkowitz (Ed.), *Advances in experimental social psychology* (pp. 267–299). New York, NY: Academic Press.

Aiello, J., & Douthitt, E. (2001). Social facilitation from Triplett to electronic performance monitoring. *Group Dynamics: Theory, Research, and Practice, 5*, 163–183.

Allport, D. (1968). Phenomenal simultaneity and the perceptual moment hypothesis. *British Journal of Psychology, 59*, 395–406.

Azoulay, P., Fons-Rosen, C., & Graff Zivin, J. S. (2019). Does science advance one funeral at a time? *American Economic Review, 109*, 2889–2920.

Bacharach, S. (1989). Organizational theories: Some criteria for evaluation. *Academy of Management Review, 14*, 496–515.

Baird, J. (1917). The legibility of a telephone directory. *Journal of Applied Psychology, 1*, 30–37.

Bedi, A., & Schat, A. (2013). Perceptions of organizational politics: A meta-analysis of its attitudinal, health, and behavioural consequences. *Canadian Psychology / Psychologie Canadienne, 54*, 246–259.

Bell, J., Den Ouden, B., & Ziggers, G. (2006). Dynamics of cooperation: At the brink of irrelevance. *Journal of Management Studies, 43*, 1607–1619.

Bell, R., Kennebrew, D., & Blyden, L. (2015). An increasing utility for the early management theories: An exploratory study. *International Journal of Management and Human Resources, 3*, 1–22.

Blau, P. (1964). *Exchange and power in social life*. New York, NY: Wiley.

Bliese, P., Edwards, J., & Sonnentag, S. (2017). Stress and well-being at work: A century of empirical trends reflecting theoretical and societal influences. *Journal of Applied Psychology, 102*, 389–402.

Boltzmann, L. (1901). The recent development of method in theoretical physics. *The Monist, 11*, 226–257.

Brouer, R., Ferris, G., Hochwarter, W., Laird, M., & Gilmore, D. (2006). The strain-related reactions to perceptions of organizational politics as workplace stressor: Political skill as a neutralizer. In E. Vigoda-Gadot, & A. Drory (Eds.), *Handbook of organizational politics* (pp. 187–206). Cheltenham, UK: Elgar.

Burns, T. (1961). Micropolitics: Mechanisms of institutional change. *Administrative Science Quarterly, 6*, 257–281.

Byrne, Z., Manning, S., Weston, J., & Hochwarter, W. (2017). All roads lead to well-being: Unexpected relationships between organizational politics perceptions, employee engagement, and worker well-being. In P. Perrewé, C. Rosen, & J. Halbesleben (Eds.), *Research in occupational stress and well being* (pp. 1–32). Bingley, UK: Emerald.

Cady S., Wheeler, J., Schlechter, A., & Goodman, S. (2019). A proposed theory life cycle model: Standing on the shoulders of giants. *The Journal of Applied Behavioral Science, 55*, 428–452.

Cardiol, A., & de-Miguel, S. (2020). COVID-19 jeopardizes the response to coming natural disasters. *Safety Science, 130*, 104861.

Cavanagh, G., Moberg, D., & Velasquez, M. (1981). The ethics of organizational politics. *Academy of Management Review, 6*, 363–374.

Cavanagh, M. (2006). Moral imperviousness and the Tabula Rasa Fallacy: A contribution from the neurosciences. *Journal of College and Character, 7*, 1–12.

Chang, C., Rosen, C., & Levy, P. (2009). The relationship between perceptions of organizational politics and employee attitudes, strain, and behavior: A meta-analytic examination. *Academy of Management Journal, 52,* 779–801.

Charoensukmongkol, P., & Phungsoonthorn, T. (2020). The effectiveness of supervisor support in lessening perceived uncertainties and emotional exhaustion of university employees during the COVID-19 crisis: The constraining role of organizational intransigence. *The Journal of General Psychology.* https://doi.org/10.1080/00221309.2020.1795613

Chib, V., Adachi, R., & O'Doherty, J. (2018). Neural substrates of social facilitation effects on incentive-based performance. *Social Cognitive and Affective Neuroscience, 13,* 391–403.

Chong, S., Huang, Y., & Chang, C. (2020). Supporting interdependent telework employees: A moderated-mediation model linking daily COVID-19 task setbacks to next-day work withdrawal. *Journal of Applied Psychology, 105,* 1408–1422.

Clegg, S., Cunha, M., & Berti, M. (2020). Research movements and theorizing dynamics in management and organization studies. *Academy of Management Review.* https://doi.org/10.5465/amr.2018.0466

Cropanzano, R., & Greenberg, J. (1997). Progress in organizational justice: Tunneling through the maze. In C. Cooper, & I. Robertson (Eds.), *International review of industrial and organizational psychology* (pp. 317–372). New York, NY: Wiley.

Cropanzano, R., Howes, J., Grandey, A., & Toth, P. (1997). The relationship of organizational politics and support to work behaviors, attitudes, and stress. *Journal of Organizational Behavior, 18,* 159–180.

Daft, R., Lengel, R., & Trevino, L. (1987). Message equivocality, media selection, and manager performance: Implications for information systems. *MIS Quarterly: Management Information Systems, 11,* 355–366.

De Clercq, D., & Belausteguigoitia, I. (2017). Mitigating the negative effect of perceived organizational politics on organizational citizenship behavior: Moderating roles of contextual and personal resources. *Journal of Management & Organization, 23,* 689–708.

D'Cruz, P., & Noronha, E. (2018). Target experiences of workplace bullying on online labour markets. *Employee Relations, 40,* 140–154.

Dennerlein, J., Burke, L., Sabbath, E., Williams, J., Peters, S., Wallace, L., Karapanosm M., & Sorensen, G. (2020). An integrative total worker health framework for keeping workers safe and healthy during the COVID-19 pandemic. *Human Factors, 62,* 689–696.

Dobzhansky, T. (1976). The myths of genetic predestination and of Tabula Rasa. *Perspectives in Biology and Medicine, 19,* 156–170.

Doldor, E., Silvester, J., & Atewologun, D. (2017). Qualitative methods in organizational psychology. In W. Rogers, & C. Willig (Eds.), *The SAGE handbook of qualitative research in psychology* (pp. 520–540). London, UK: Sage.

Eisenberger, R., Huntington, R., Hutchison, S., & Sowa, D. (1986). Perceived organizational support. *Journal of Applied Psychology, 71,* 500–507.

Eldor, L. (2017). Looking on the bright side: The positive role of organisational politics in the relationship between employee engagement and performance at work. *Applied Psychology, 66,* 233–259.

Farrell, D., & Petersen, J. C. (1982). Patterns of political behavior in the organization. *Academy of Management Review, 7,* 403–412.

Fedor, D., Ferris, G., Harrell-Cook, G., & Russ, G. (1998). The dimensions of politics perceptions and their organizational and individual predictors. *Journal of Applied Social Psychology, 28,* 1760–1797.

Felin, T., Foss, N., & Ployhart, R. (2015). The microfoundations movement in strategy and organization theory. *Academy of Management Annals, 9*, 575–632.

Ferns, S., Gautam, S., & Hudak, M. (2021). COVID-19 and gender disparities in pediatric cardiologists with dependent care responsibilities. *The American Journal of Cardiology.* https://doi.or/10.1016/j.amjcard.2021.02.017

Ferris, G., Adams, G., Kolodinsky, R., Hochwarter, W., & Ammeter, A. (2002). Perceptions of organizational politics: Theory and research directions. In F. Yammarino, & F. Dansereau (Eds.), *Research in multi-level issues, Vol. 1. The many faces of multi-level issues* (p. 179–254). Oxford, UK: Elsevier.

Ferris, G., Bowen, M., Treadway, D., Hochwarter, W., Hall, A., & Perrewé, P. (2006). The assumed linearity of organizational phenomena: Implications for occupational stress and well-being. In P. Perrewé, & D. Ganster (Eds.), *Research in occupational stress and well being* (pp. 205–232). Oxford, UK: JAI Press/Elsevier Science.

Ferris, G., Ellen III, B., McAllister, C., & Maher, L. (2019). Reorganizing organizational politics research: A review of the literature and identification of future research directions. *Annual Review of Organizational Psychology and Organizational Behavior, 6*, 299–323.

Ferris, G., Frink, D., Bhawuk, D., Zhou, J., & Gilmore, D. (1996). Reactions of diverse groups to politics in the workplace. *Journal of Management, 22*, 23–44.

Ferris, G., Frink, D., Galang, M., Zhou, J., Kacmar, K., & Howard, J. (1996). Perceptions of organizational politics: Prediction, stress-related implications, and outcomes. *Human Relations, 49*, 233–266.

Ferris, G., & Hochwarter, W. (2011) Organizational politics. In S. Zedeck (Ed.), *APA handbook of industrial and organizational psychology* (pp. 433–459). Washington, DC: APA Press.

Ferris, G., Hochwarter, W., & Buckley, M. (2012). Theory in the organizational sciences: How will we know it when we see it? *Organizational Psychology Review, 2*, 94–106.

Ferris, G., & Judge, T. (1991). Personnel/human resources management: A political influence perspective. *Journal of Management, 17*, 447–488.

Ferris, G., Russ, G., & Fandt, P. (1989). Politics in organizations. In R. Giacalone, & P. Rosenfeld (Eds.), *Impression management in the organization* (pp. 143–170). Hillsdale, NJ: Lawrence Erlbaum.

Fish, E. (1917). Human engineering. *Journal of Applied Psychology, 1*, 161–174.

Gabriel, A., Campbell, J., Djurdjevic, E., Johnson, R., & Rosen, C. (2018). Fuzzy profiles: Comparing and contrasting latent profile analysis and fuzzy set qualitative comparative analysis for person-centered research. *Organizational Research Methods, 21*, 877–904.

Gabriel, A., Podsakoff, N., Beal, D., Scott, B., Sonnentag, S., Trougakos, J., & Butts, M. (2019). Experience sampling methods: A discussion of critical trends and considerations for scholarly advancement. *Organizational Research Methods, 22*, 969–1006.

Gandz, J., & Murray, V. (1980). The experience of workplace politics. *Academy of Management Journal, 23*, 237–251.

Geisler, E. (2001). Good-bye dodo bird (*Raphus cucullatus*): Why social knowledge is cumulative, expansive, and evolutionary. *Journal of Management Inquiry, 10*, 5–15.

Goldsmith, D. (1995). *Einstein's greatest blunder? The cosmological constant and other fudge factors in the physics of the universe.* Cambridge, MA: Harvard University Press.

Gonzalez, M., & Aiello, J. (2019). More than meets the ear: Investigating how music affects cognitive task performance. *Journal of Experimental Psychology: Applied, 25*, 431–444.

Gouldner, A. (1960). The norm of reciprocity: A preliminary statement. *American Sociological Review, 25*, 161–178.

Guerin, B. (1986). Mere presence effects in humans: A review. *Journal of Experimental Social Psychology, 22,* 38–77.

Haider, S., Fatima, N., & de Pablos-Heredero, C. (2020). A three-wave longitudinal study of moderated mediation between perceptions of politics and employee turnover intentions: The role of job anxiety and political skills. *Journal of Work and Organizational Psychology, 36,* 1–14.

Halbersham, D. (2000). *Playing for keeps: Michael Jordan and the world he made.* New York, NY: Broadway Books.

Han, Y., & Perry, J. (2020). Employee accountability: Development of a multidimensional scale. *International Public Management Journal, 23,* 224–251.

Hirsch, P., & Levin, D. (1999). Umbrella advocates versus validity police: A life-cycle model. *Organization Science, 10,* 199–212.

Hochwarter, W. (2012). Positive politics. In G. Ferris and D. Treadway (Eds.), *Politics in organizations: Theory and research considerations* (pp. 20–45). New York, NY: APA Press.

Hochwarter, W., Ferris, G., Laird, M., Treadway, D., & Coleman Gallagher, V. (2010). Nonlinear politics perceptions-work outcomes relationships: A three-study, five-sample investigation. *Journal of Management, 36,* 740–763.

Hochwarter, W., Kacmar, K., Treadway, D., & Watson, T. (2003). It's all relative: The distinction and prediction of political perceptions across levels. *Journal of Applied Social Psychology, 33,* 1995–2016.

Hochwarter, W., Kapoutsis, I., Jordan, S., Khan, A., & Babalola, M. (2020). Dyads of politics and the politics of dyads: Implications for leader development. In M. Buckley, J. Halbesleben, & A. Wheeler (Eds.), *Research in personnel and human resources management* (pp. 103–144). Bingley, UK: Emerald.

Hochwarter, W., Rosen, C., Jordan, S., Ferris, G., Ejaz, A., & Maher, L. (2020). Thirty years and growing: Review and identification of research challenges in perceptions of politics research. *Journal of Management, 46,* 879–907.

Holmes, S. (1930). Nature versus nurture in the development of the mind. *The Scientific Monthly, 31,* 245–252.

Homans, G. (1958). Social behavior as exchange. *American Journal of Sociology, 63,* 597–606.

Johns, G. (2001). In praise of context. *Journal of Organizational Behavior, 22,* 31–42.

Johns, G. (2006). The essential impact of context on organizational behavior. *Academy of Management Review, 31,* 386–408.

Johns, G. (2018). Advances in the treatment of context in organizational research. *Annual Review of Organizational Psychology and Organizational Behavior, 5,* 21–46.

Kacmar, K., & Baron, R. (1999). Organizational politics: The state of the field, links to related processes, and an agenda for future research. In K. Rowland, & G. Ferris (Eds.), *Research in personnel and human resources management* (pp. 1–39). Greenwich, CT: JAI.

Kacmar, K., & Ferris, G. (1991). Perceptions of organizational politics scale (POPS): Development and construct validation. *Educational and Psychological Measurement, 51,* 193–205.

Kane-Frieder, R., Hochwarter, W., Hampton, H., & Ferris, G. (2014). Supervisor political support as a buffer to subordinates' reactions to politics perceptions. *Career Development International, 19,* 27–48.

Kapoutsis, I., Papalexandris, A., Nikolopoulos, A., Hochwarter, W., & Ferris, G. (2011). Politics perceptions as moderator of the political skill-job performance relationship: A two-study, cross-national, constructive replication. *Journal of Vocational Behavior, 78,* 123–135.

King, G., Keohane, R., & Verba, S. (1995). The importance of research design in political science. *American Political Science Review, 89*, 475–481.

Kipnis, D., Schmidt, S., & Wilkinson, I. (1980). Intraorganizational influence tactics: Explorations in getting one's way. *Journal of Applied Psychology, 65*, 440–452.

Koopman, J., Lin, S., Lennard, A., Matta, F., & Johnson, R. (2020). My coworkers are treated more fairly than me! A self-regulatory perspective on justice social comparisons. *Academy of Management Journal, 63*, 857–880.

Kniffin, K., Narayanan, J., Ansell, F., Antonakis, J., Ashford, S., & Vugt, M. (2021). COVID-19 and the workplace: Implications, issues, and insights for future research and action. *American Psychologist, 76*, 63–77.

Kuhn, T. (1970). *The structure of scientific revolutions.* Chicago, IL: University of Chicago Press.

Latham, G., & Locke, E. (1975). Increasing productivity and decreasing time limits: A field replication of Parkinson's law. *Journal of Applied Psychology, 60*, 524–526.

Lawong, D., Ferris, G., Hochwarter, W., & Fitzgerald, M. (2021). Going to heck in a handbasket? Organizational politics in economically challenged environments. In M. Buckley, J. Halbesleben, & A. Wheeler (Eds.), *Research in personnel and human resources management, 37.* Bingley, UK: Emerald Group Publishing Ltd.

Lazarus, R., & Folkman, S. (1984). *Stress, appraisal, and coping.* New York, NY: Springer.

Leblanc, R., & Schwartz, M. (2007). The black box of board process: Gaining access to a difficult subject. *Corporate Governance: An International Review, 15*, 843–851.

LePine, J., Podsakoff, N., & LePine, M. (2005). A meta-analytic test of the challenge Stressor-hindrance stressor framework: An explanation for inconsistent relationships among stressors and performance. *Academy of Management Journal, 48*, 764–775.

Levine, D. (1989). Simmel as a resource for sociological metatheory. *Sociological Theory, 7*, 161–174.

Lewin, K. (1936). *Principles of topological psychology.* New York, NY: McGraw-Hill.

Li, C., Liang, J., & Farh, J. (2020). Speaking up when water is murky: An uncertainty-based model linking perceived organizational politics to employee voice. *Journal of Management, 46*, 443–469.

Liu, Y., & Liu, X. (2018). Politics under abusive supervision: The role of Machiavellianism and guanxi. *European Management Journal, 36*, 649–659.

Locke, J. (1689). An essay concerning human understanding, Part 1, Volume 1. Available [online] also at http://oll.libertyfund.org/title/761 on 2012-12-15

Manyika, J., Lund, S., Chui, M., Bughin, J., Woetzel, J., Batra, P., Ko, R., & Sanghvi, S. (2017). Jobs lost, jobs gained: What the future of work will mean for jobs, skills, and wages. *McKinsey.* https://www.mckinsey.com/featured-insights/future-of-work/jobs-lost-jobs-gained-what-the-future-of-work-will-mean-for-jobs-skills-and-wages#

Martin, L. (1917). Mental hygiene and the importance of investigating it. *Journal of Applied Psychology, 1*, 67–70.

Maslyn, J., Farmer, S., & Bettenhausen, K. (2017). When organizational politics matters: The effects of the perceived frequency and distance of experienced politics. *Human Relations, 70*, 1486–1513.

McFarland, L., Van Iddekinge, C., & Ployhart, R. (2012). Measurement and methodology in organizational politics research. In G. Ferris, & D. Treadway (Eds.), *Politics in organizations: Theory and research considerations* (pp. 99–129). New York, NY: Routledge.

McGrath, J. (1976). Stress and behavior in organizations. In M. Dunnette (Ed.), *Handbook of industrial and organizational psychology* (pp. 1351–1395). Chicago, IL: Rand-McNally.

McKinley, W. (2010). Organizational theory development: Displacement of ends? *Organization Studies, 31*, 47–68.

McLaren, P., & Durepos, G. (2021). A call to practice context in management and organization studies. *Journal of Management Inquiry, 30*, 74–84.

Meltzoff, A. (1999). Origins of theory of mind, cognition and communication. *Journal of Communication Disorders, 32*, 251–269.

Mingers, J., & Burrell, Q. (2006). Modeling citation behavior in management science journals. *Information Processing & Management, 42*, 1451–1464.

Mintz, A. (1954). Time intervals between accidents. *Journal of Applied Psychology, 38*, 401–406.

Mintzberg, H. (1985). The organization a political arena. *Journal of Management Studies, 22*, 133–154.

Mueller, D. (1972). A life cycle theory of the firm. *The Journal of Industrial Economics, 20*, 199–219.

Muldoon, J., Liguori, E., & Bendickson, J. (2013). Sailing away: The influences on and motivations of George Caspar Homans. *Journal of Management History, 19*, 148–166.

Munz, P. (2006). Popper's Darwinism. In I. Jarvie, K. Milford, & D. Miller (Eds.), *Karl Popper: A centenary assessment* (pp. 131–141). Burlington, VT: Ashgate.

Narskii, I. (1980). The philosophy of the late Karl Popper. *Soviet Studies in Philosophy, 18*, 53–77.

Nehrbass, R. (1979). Ideology and the decline of management theory. *Academy of Management Review, 4*, 427–431.

Parikh, R. (2014). How to lie with data visualization. HuffPost. https://www.huffpost.com/entry/lie-with-data-visualization_b_5169715

Parker, L. (2020). The COVID-19 office in transition: Cost, efficiency and the social responsibility business case. *Accounting, Auditing & Accountability Journal, 33*, 1943–1967.

Parker, C., Dipboye, R., & Jackson, S. (1995). Perceptions of organizational politics: An investigation of antecedents and consequences. *Journal of Management, 21*, 891–912.

Perrewé, P., Rosen, C., & Maslach, C. (2012). Organizational politics and stress: The development of a process model. In G. Ferris, & D. Treadway (Eds.), *Politics in organizations: Theory and research considerations* (pp. 213–255). New York, NY: Routledge.

Pfeffer, J. (1993). Barriers to the advance of organizational science: Paradigm development as a dependent variable. *Academy of Management Review, 18*, 599–620.

Pfeffer, J., & Salancik, G. (1974). Organizational decision making as a political process: The case of a university budget. *Administrative Science Quarterly*, 135–151.

Pinker, S. (2002). *The blank slate.* London, UK: Penguin.

Popper, K. (1961). Evolution and the tree of knowledge. In K. Popper (Ed.), *Objective knowledge. An evolutionary approach* (pp. 256–284). Oxford, UK: Clarendon.

Popper, K. (1969). *Conjectures and refutation: The growth of scientific knowledge.* London, UK: Routledge & Kegan Paul.

Popper, K. (2002). *Popper: The logic of scientific discovery.* New York, NY: Routledge.

Prasad, D., Rao, M., Vaidya, D., & Muralidhar, B. (2020). Organizational climate, opportunities, challenges and psychological wellbeing of the remote working employees during COVID-19 pandemic: A general linear model approach with reference to information technology industry in Hyderabad. *International Journal of Advanced Research in Engineering and Technology (IJARET), 11*, 372–389.

Probst, T., Lee, H., & Bazzoli, A. (2020). Economic stressors and the enactment of CDC-recommended COVID-19 prevention behaviors: The impact of state-level context. *Journal of Applied Psychology, 105*, 1397–1407.

Rasely, H. (1917). Improving business correspondence. *Journal of Applied Psychology*, *1*, 220–231.

Restubog, S., Ocampo, A., & Wang, L. (2020). Taking control amidst the chaos: Emotion regulation during the COVID-19 pandemic. *Journal of Vocational Behavior*. https://doi.org/10.1016/j.jvb.2020.103440

Rettie, H., & Daniels, J. (2020). Coping and tolerance of uncertainty: Predictors and mediators of mental health during the COVID-19 pandemic. *American Psychologist*. https://doi.org/10.1037/amp0000710

Richter, A. (1913). A legislative curb on the judiciary. *Journal of Political Economy*, *21*, 281–295.

Rosen, C., Chang, C., Johnson, R., & Levy, P. (2009). Perceptions of the organizational context and psychological contract breach: Assessing competing perspectives. *Organizational Behavior and Human Decision Processes*, *108*, 202–217.

Rosen, C., Ferris, D., Brown, D., Chen, Y., & Yan, M. (2014). Perceptions of organizational politics: A need satisfaction paradigm. *Organization Science*, *25*, 1026–1055.

Rosen, C., & Hochwarter, W. (2014). Looking back and falling further behind: The moderating role of rumination on the relationship between organizational politics and employee attitudes, well-being, and performance. *Organizational Behavior and Human Decision Processes*, *124*, 177–189.

Rosen, C., Koopman, J., Gabriel, A., & Johnson, R. (2016). Who strikes back? A daily investigation of when and why incivility begets incivility. *The Journal of Applied Psychology*, *101*, 1620–1634.

Rosen, C., Levy, P., & Hall, R. (2006). Placing perceptions of politics in the context of the feedback environment, employee attitudes, and job performance. *Journal of Applied Psychology*, *91*, 211–220.

Rosen, C., Simon, L., Gajendran, R., Johnson, R., Lee, H., & Lin, S. (2019). Boxed in by your inbox: Implications of daily e-mail demands for managers' leadership behaviors. *The Journal of Applied Psychology*, *104*, 19–33.

Schein, V. (1977). Individual power and political behaviors in organizations: An inadequately explored reality. *Academy of Management Review*, *2*, 64–72.

Schneider, B., Ehrhart, M., & Macey, W. (2012). A funny thing happened on the way to the future: The focus on organizational competitive advantage lost out. *Industrial-Organizational Psychology*, *5*, 96–101.

Shigo, A. (1986). *A new tree biology*. Durham, NH: Shigo and Tree Associates.

Simmel, G. (1895). The problem of sociology. *The ANNALS of the American Academy of Political and Social Science*, *6*, 52–63.

Simmel, G. (1898). The persistence of social groups. *American Journal of Sociology*, *3*, 662–698.

Simmel, G. (1896). Superiority and subordination as the subject-matter of sociology. *American Journal of Sociology*, *2*, 167–189.

Simmel, G. (1900). A chapter in the philosophy of value. *American Journal of Sociology*, *5*, 577–603.

Simmel, G. (1904). The sociology of conflict. III. *American Journal of Sociology*, *9*, 798–811.

Simmel, G. (1906). The sociology of secrecy and of secret societies. *American Journal of Sociology*, *11*, 441–498.

Simmel, G. (1908) *Soziologie: Untersuchungen über die formen der vergesellschaftung*. Leipzig: Dunker und Humblot.

Simpson, A., & Smith, E. (Eds.). (1881). *The gospel in all lands*. New York, NY: Bible House.

Sobieralski, J. (2020). COVID-19 and airline employment: Insights from historical uncertainty shocks to the industry. *Transportation Research Interdisciplinary Perspectives*, *5*, 100123.

Spurk, D., Hirschi, A., Wang, M., Valero, D., & Kauffeld, S. (2020). Latent profile analysis: A review and "how-to" guide of its application within vocational behavior research. *Journal of Vocational Behavior.* https://doi.org/10.1016/j.jvb.2020.103445.

Teng, Y., Wu, K., & Lin, K. (2020). Life or livelihood? Mental health concerns for quarantine hotel workers during the COVID-19 pandemic. *Frontiers in Psychology*, *11*. https://doi.org/10.3389/fpsyg.2020.02168

Thibaut, J., & Kelley, H. (1959). *The social psychology of groups.* New York, NY: Wiley.

Thijssen, P. (2016). Intergenerational solidarity: The paradox of reciprocity imbalance in ageing welfare states. *The British Journal of Sociology*, *67*, 592–612.

Triplett, N. (1898). The dynamogenic factors in pacemaking and competition. *American Journal of Psychology*, *9*, 507–533.

Turner, J., Baker, R., & Kellner, F. (2018). Theoretical literature review: Tracing the life cycle of a theory and its verified and falsified statements. *Human Resource Development Review*, *17*, 34–61.

Vågerö, D. (2006). Where does new theory come from? *Journal of Epidemiology and Community Health*, *60*, 573–574.

Van Maanen, J., Sørensen, J., & Mitchell, T. (2007). The interplay between theory and method. *Academy of Management Review*, *32*, 1145–1154.

Vigoda-Gadot, E., & Drory, A. (2016). *Handbook of organizational politics: Looking back and to the future.* Cheltenham, UK: Elgar.

Wang, B., Liu, Y., Qian, J., & Parker, S. (2021). Achieving effective remote working during the COVID-19 pandemic: A work design perspective. *Applied Psychology*, *70*, 16–59.

Wisdom, J. (1972). Scientific theory: Empirical content, embedded ontology, and weltanschauung. *Philosophy and Phenomenological Research*, *33*, 62–77.

Weick, K. (1995). What theory is not, theorizing is. *Administrative Science Quarterly*, *40*, 385–390.

Zhou, J., & Ferris, G. (1995). The dimensions and consequences of organizational politics perceptions: A confirmatory analysis. *Journal of Applied Social Psychology*, *25*, 1747–1764.

Zhou, Y., Wang, W., Sun, Y., Qian, W., Liu, Z., Wang, R., & Zhang, X. (2020). The prevalence and risk factors of psychological disturbances of frontline medical staff in China under the COVID-19 epidemic: Workload should be concerned. *Journal of Affective Disorders*, *277*, 510–514.

9

THE DATA REVOLUTION AND THE INTERPLAY BETWEEN THEORY AND DATA

Steve W. J. Kozlowski

Introduction and Premise

The organizational sciences are on the cusp of a theory-data revolution. Several decades ago, there was a shift from the primacy of data to one of theoretical primacy. The data revolution – big data and lots of it – promises to shift primacy back to data, or at least some observers think so. I think the issue is much more complicated and important than one of mere primacy. Rather, the issue is about how to achieve a more balanced perspective – an enhanced integration – between theory and data. Whether the result is continued theoretical primacy, data primacy, or better integration, it will have a lasting influence – for better or worse – on the organizational sciences for decades to come. It merits scrutiny.

In 2017, the *Journal of Applied Psychology* celebrated its centennial, marking a major historical milestone in the evolution of organizational psychology. My colleagues and I organized a Special Issue of the journal to recognize and celebrate this achievement and, to open that Special Issue, we conducted an analysis of the evolution of the work published in it across the century (Kozlowski et al., 2017). The *Journal of Applied Psychology* is of course only one of several core journals across the organizational sciences but, as the oldest journal in this space by a wide margin, it is a microcosm for the evolution of organizational psychology and behavior (OPB) theory and research across the twentieth and early twenty-first centuries.

Among the many interesting takeaways from our deep dive into the evolution of the published content was the revelation of just how much of the early research was atheoretical, driven almost entirely by exploratory data. To provide a broad characterization, it was largely driven by the availability of a test or

DOI: 10.4324/9781003015000-12

measure which sparked descriptive comparisons across two or more groups (e.g., *Sex differences shown by 2,544 schoolchildren on a group scale of intelligence, with special reference to variability*), intercorrelations among assessments (*Twenty three serial tests of intelligence and their intercorrelations*) or by purely pragmatic concerns (e.g., *The legibility of a telephone directory*). This shifted rather abruptly in the mid-1950s when John Darley became editor. Since then, the *Journal of Applied Psychology* has had a reputation for publishing theory-driven, rigorous, and impactful empirical research.

Although much of the early research in OPB was driven by curiosity, pure pragmatics, or the availability of a measure, by the time I started graduate school in the organizational sciences, the door had firmly closed on atheoretical exploratory research – so-called "dust bowl empiricism" – and theory was primary. I was trained that well-developed theory was the foundation for impactful empirical research and a cumulative science of organizations. "Theory is about connections among phenomena, a story about why acts, events, structure, and thoughts occur .... Strong theory, in our view, delves into underlying processes so as to understand the systematic reasons for a particular occurrence or nonoccurrence" (Sutton & Staw, 1995, p. 378). Theory describes the nature of the phenomenon or phenomena of interest, identifies relevant constructs and the basis for their relationships, and provides a rationale for the hypotheses to be evaluated. Research methods and measurement, which are essentially *data generation* protocols, follow from the theory and hypotheses. Appropriate analyses then reveal whether the data support the hypotheses and theory or disconfirm it. Theory leads, research methods and data follow, and findings feedback to theory to refine, extend, or prune it for cumulative scientific progress. This is an idealized view of the scientific method.

In this chapter, I will argue that theory and data – the methods that generate data and the analyses that evaluate data – are inherently intertwined. They need to be appropriately balanced and aligned, with neither one nor the other taking an undisputed lead. Indeed, if either theory or data take a completely dominant lead, it will destabilize the necessary balance and interplay between theory and data which will have deleterious implications for progress in the organizational sciences. There are prevailing trends for theory versus data dominance that merit mention.

One trend is that preaching the primacy of theory can become so distorted as to decouple theory development from cumulative empirical science. Many scholars have argued that the adulation of theory for its own sake, particularly novel and/or counterintuitive theory (Davis, 1971), has already exerted a distorting influence on organizational science (Ferris et al., 2012; Hambrick, 2007; McKinley, 2010). Indeed, Pillutla and Thau (2013) highlight that of 260 citations to Davis (1971) – exhorting novel, counterintuitive theory as a desirable goal – 71% appear in organizational science publications. Moreover,

Halbesleben et al. (2004) reported that the vast majority of theory articles published in the *Academy of Management Review* – a top-tier theoretical journal – over a 20-year period (1983–2003) did not generate any citations; that is, the theories were never evaluated. Theory proliferation without critical pruning cannot advance science. The worship of theory for its own sake is a scientific dead end, yielding theory that is rarely evaluated, improved, or pruned. Such theory development does not add to cumulative scientific progress. It only adds noise, making scientific progress more difficult. This is not a desirable direction.

Another trend is the ascendency of big data and advanced analytics under the banner of data science. Good descriptive data can be very informative about the processes underlying a phenomenon, especially in the absence of good theory, and can provide a basis for theory building (Kozlowski, 2009). Big data (i.e., high volume, velocity, and variety; Tonidandel et al., 2018) and advanced analytics (i.e., artificial intelligence [AI], machine learning, smart algorithms) offer the promise of solutions to difficult problems and easy answers to previously difficult to answer questions (Wenzel & Van Quaaquebeke, 2017). The accelerating development of new forms of data generation, most of them with a digital substrate (e.g., email, text, web search, chat, social media, location services, etc.), combined with the ability and motivation to compile that data into truly massive repositories to be mined for knowledge, have led some observers to advance the notion that theory is not needed for scientific advancement; knowledge can advance via big data and AI-driven algorithms (Mayer-Schonberger & Cukier, 2013). Although this may sound futuristic and seductive (Who does not want easy answers?), it is new version of dust bowl empiricism (Silicon Valley empiricism?) with a veneer of technological sophistication. It is another scientific dead end, yielding answers without an understanding of the underlying processes, answers that are often subject to many unknown biases, and answers that do not cumulate science. Worshiping big data in the absence of theory is not a desirable direction either.

Organizational science has advanced considerably over the past century and that success is to be celebrated. However, I assert that it is at a critical juncture with respect to the interplay between theory and data. The theories and the dominant methods/data that populate the literature have some serious limitations that are not often acknowledged directly. With respect to theory, first, there is a proliferation of too many of them, which dissipates limited resources toward too many low-yield research pursuits. Second, many theories are too imprecise, which limits the ability to advance knowledge, replicate, cumulate, and prune. Third, most theories are too static, which limits knowledge gain about the *processes* that are the core drivers of phenomena. With respect to data, first, the findings that constitute the foundation of the vast majority of OBP research are largely based on convenience samples, which are not random, not representative, and subject to bias. Second, most of the data are generated using cross-sectional designs, which limits causal inference and knowledge about the underlying processes that are central to the phenomenon. Third, most of the measures are based on retrospective, self-reports to questions (i.e., items) that are decoupled from the context and the phenomenon of interest, which is a really limited way to assess human behavior. With these many limitations, a continuation of "business as usual" may be the death knell for organizational science as we know it. The promise of data science to answer difficult questions with big data and smart algorithms has much appeal. If organizational science does not advance, it will be overtaken by engineering, computer, and data science.

Fortunately, there is a path forward. It involves an examination of the interplay between theory and data, appreciating the opportunity to adapt and evolve the idealized scientific method, and forging forward with a more balanced alignment between theory and data. We are at a cusp in which new forms of data generation can help to advance improved ways to build theory and in which improved theory can better guide knowledge extraction using big data, digital traces, and advanced analytic techniques. In subsequent sections, I discuss the nature and evolution of theory and how advances in data generation options can support a desirable interplay intended to better balance and improve the yield of the theory-data linkage.

The Nature and Evolution of Theory

What Is Theory?

With theory firmly in the dominant position for current-day organizational science, one would expect that what it is, what makes for good theory, and how good theory is built would be well-established and consensual. But that is not really the case. I am not asserting that there is no consensus whatsoever (e.g., Bacharach, 1989; Dubin, 1978; Whetten, 1989), but there is a remarkable diversity of opinion as to what theory is, how it is built, and what makes it good (Colquitt & Zapata-Phelan, 2007). Ferris and colleagues note that "… there are few issues in the field that have generated more confusion and disagreement among scholars than what constitutes theory …. it is difficult to develop a shared appreciation for theory when scholars are unable to agree upon its definition" (Ferris et al., 2012, p. 95). Since the lack of a "theoretical contribution" is the number one reason for most rejections of submissions to top-tier journals, this is a legitimate concern. Specifics are difficult to pin down and such a judgement is often in the eye of the beholder. Indeed, the many efforts to describe and explicate good theory are a testament to the need to improve the degree of scholarly consensus on this issue (e.g., Colquitt & Zapata-Phelan, 2007; Corley & Gioia, 2011; Ferris et al., 2012; Pillutla & Thau, 2013). In any case, this ambiguity and subjectivity merit closer scrutiny.

I suspect that there are many reasons that contribute to this sense of ambiguity regarding theory, but one of the major contributors goes to the nature of the science of organizations. Organizational science is not a discipline per se, but rather an amalgamation of several basic disciplines that each contribute to its intellectual diversity. Multidisciplinarity is a good thing for scientific progress, and I support it (Kozlowski, 2012). However, there is a downside to multidisciplinarity and it may well be a contributor to the sense that there is limited consensus on theory. Each of the contributing disciplines to organizational science brings different theoretical and data generation traditions, which can lead to contradictions or, at the very least, tensions. Rather than attempting to catalog all the many such differences in perspective across component disciplines, a contrast of quantitative and qualitative research, which are the big tectonic plates that distinguish approaches, is useful for illustrating this issue.

As a point of departure, quantitative research assumes that there is a reality, an essential ground-truth, that undergirds phenomena that we observe and experience. Research is designed to reveal this ground-truth and to add it to the store of human knowledge (Russell, 1931). Qualitive research assumes that the world is socially constructed and interpretive and the goal of the research effort is to reveal the many interpretations "at a particular point in time and in a particular context" (Merriam, 2002, p. 4). These are very distinctive approaches to theory building, research, and evaluation.

Quantitative research is a (largely) deductive approach, starting from a theoretical foundation to explicate specific findings. In the operation of the idealized scientific method noted previously, quantitative research builds or draws from theory, formulates *a priori* hypotheses, employs a research design strategy to generate data relevant to the hypotheses, and uses statistical analyses to evaluate those hypotheses. At this point, the data either support the hypotheses (and by implication the theoretical rationale that led to them) or it fails to support the hypotheses and, thus, should disconfirm the theory. Theories that are supported should be refined and extended. Theories that are not supported should be trimmed from the pool of viable options. Over time, this process should yield fewer, more precise theories that form the core of a cumulative organizational science (remember, this is an idealized process).

In contrast, qualitative research is (largely) inductive, starting from observations and interpretations to explicate the nature of a phenomenon and how it is experienced. In that sense it is exploratory, but it may form the basis for theory building. Qualitative research is inherently interpretive in orientation, focused on attempting to understand the meaning that people and groups ascribe to their interactions within a particular context and time frame. Using a research design (e.g., narrative, phenomenology, ethnography, case study, grounded theory), the researcher is the instrument for data generation, analysis, and interpretation, which are ongoing and intertwined. A key outcome of the research is a rich and deep description of what the researcher has gleaned about the phenomenon using notes, interview excerpts, or other illustrations to add to descriptive richness (Merriam, 2002).

Quantitative and qualitative research are viewed as distinctly different research approaches – and they are so – but, despite their deep philosophical and operational differences, they provide complementary roles in knowledge discovery. Indeed, it is difficult to imagine how any useful theory can be constructed without a foundation of good descriptive research, whether it be from exploratory quantitative or qualitative research methods.

Theory Evolution: A Typology of Theory Building Concepts

Given that there is a range of concepts in the organizational literature pertaining to theory, it is useful to develop a typology to identify and distinguish key theory building concepts as a means to discuss how it has evolved and where it should evolve next.[1] I make no claim that this typology is comprehensive of all theory or theory building concepts across organizational science; the field is simply too broad. Indeed, to make this effort tractable, I am limiting the scope of the typology to theory concepts relevant to micro, meso, and (some) macro OBP research. I believe the typology has broader relevance, but I am mindful that any position taken on theory can be controversial in a broad field with so many different perspectives. Hence, I am bounding its scope to turf on which I am firmly grounded.[2]

The Typology of Theory Building Concepts is shown in Table 9.1. The concepts are organized as a hierarchy (lowest to highest) relevant to theoretical knowledge building. It is foundational in that the categories build on each other. Moreover, this ordering is more or less descriptive of the evolution of theory in the field in the sense that each level (at one time) represented where much of the theoretical activity was clustered. Of course, one must recognize that new areas of inquiry can spring up at any time and make progress across the levels of the hierarchy. The hierarchy is a quasi-continuum because, although the end points are firm, the ordering of one or another of the concepts could be debated and there is no assumption that progress proceeds in a strict hierarchical order. In any case, strict ordering of the typology is not germane to my main point. What I really want to discuss is: (a) how we evolved to where we are (business as usual), (b) where the evolution needs to proceed, and (c) how big data or new forms of data generation can help us move in that desirable direction. Here, I discuss points (a) and (b); point (c) is discussed in a subsequent section.

Pre-Theory

The lowest level of the taxonomy is *pre-theory*, which is a domain of ideas and data that, although not theory driven, provide an essential basis for theory

TABLE 9.1 A typology of theory building concepts

Concept	Comments
• Process theory	• Focused on the underlying *process mechanisms* or rules driving system phenomena; how system phenomena form, evolve, and change over time; often cuts across multiple levels (i.e., emergent phenomena)
• Causal theory/model	• Focused on a dependent variable; specifies antecedent constructs and the network of associations intended to explain or predict the endogenous variable of interest; causal or implied causality; based on one or more substantive theories and research findings; contextualized
• Phenomenon theory	• Describes the nature of a broadly generalizable phenomenon in sufficient detail to explain what it is and how it operates; can underpin many more specific, focused models
• Typology/taxonomy; framework/heuristic	• Differentiate phenomena to distinguish differences and similarities; Organizing broad concepts or constructs, often (but not always) with attention to relations or linkages
• Construct theory	• Defines and explicates the content for phenomena of interest; often not directly observable, theoretical explanation is needed to link the latent construct to manifest indicators and to distinguish the construct of interest from other constructs
• Pre-theory	• Exploratory, descriptive research provides data and insights that can be used as raw material for theory building • Thought experiments as a basis for theory building • Metaphor may aid theory building • Hunches, intuition may initiate theory building

development. From where does theory spring? It springs from hunches, curiosity, and intuition, but it needs descriptive data to give it shape. I started this chapter by recounting the early years of the *Journal of Applied Psychology*, which were characterized by mostly exploratory, descriptive research. Murphy (2021) recently emphasized the importance of paying much closer attention to descriptive information reporting and interpretation in all empirical research. I am a multilevel theorist interested in phenomena, such as team development, adaptation, and effectiveness. I can relate from experience how difficult it is to build such theories, given that most research in our field is cross-sectional and static. Good descriptive research on such phenomena is essential for theory building. Gersick (1988, 1989) constructed the punctuated equilibrium model of team development based on two qualitative observations of eight groups each (i.e., three student and five work groups in the first effort and eight student groups in the second). My efforts to build process theory of team development (Kozlowski et al., 1996, 1999, 2009) was influenced by informal observations of action teams engaged in large-scale training simulations and other such opportunities. Those descriptive observations provided insights that enabled a theoretical synthesis based on the existing literature, but with the processes of interest informed by the observations. More recently, my colleagues and I have been conducting descriptive research on teams in isolated, confined, and extreme (ICE) settings to understand the challenges that astronauts will face on future missions beyond near-Earth orbit. I do not know of an existing theory that will enable predictions regarding how the crew will manage their interpersonal relations under the challenges of confinement (i.e., very small habitat, virtually no privacy), social isolation (i.e., four to six team members define one's entire social world), persistent danger (i.e., equipment failure or habitat rupture a constant concern), high autonomy (i.e., 40 minute communication lags with Earth make the crew very much on their own), and long duration (i.e., approximately 33 months for a mission to Mars). To build theory, we have collected data in a variety of ICE settings, including Antarctica (i.e., eight to twelve months of isolation) and NASA mission simulations (i.e., weeks to a year of isolation) studying one team at a time (Kozlowski et al., 2018, 2015). Good descriptive research data are priceless for theory building and should be more highly valued than they are in our science.

Construct Theory

Perhaps the most fundamental theoretical concept in OPB is that of construct development. Many of the phenomena of interest are psychological in nature that are not directly observable. One's ability to remember facts, organize them, and reason about them is attributed to one's cognitive ability. One's preference to socialize or to keep to oneself is attributed to a personality trait (i.e., extraversion). Constructs are hypothetical psychological explanations that originate within the person and are presumed to account for behavior or some observable manifest variable of interest (Cronbach & Meehl, 1955). Constructs capture the raw person-based content of the field (i.e., knowledge, skills, abilities, and other characteristics) that are used as explanations for a wide range of behavior and outcomes that are studied in OPB. Constructs necessitate a conceptual rationale – a focused theory – that explicates the nature of the hypothetical latent construct (e.g., conscientious personality trait) and connects it to manifest indicators that signify the influence of the trait on behavior (e.g., conscientious persons are detail-oriented and planful) (Binning & Barrett, 1989). Construct development is inextricably linked to operationalization and measurement. That is, the theoretical explanation for the construct is used to justify indicators (i.e., behaviors, self-report items) that are used to assess it. To help ensure that the theoretical explanation for the construct is viable, a variety of data generation efforts are used to support a judgement of construct validity (Landy, 1993). Following the early emphasis on exploratory, descriptive research in OBP, construct development formed a substantial amount of research energy in OPB. Constructs provide the field with much of the fundamental content that is used to develop broader, substantive theories, or models.

Typology/Taxonomy/Framework/Heuristic

The next category, *typology-taxonomy-heuristic-framework*, seeks to classify, order, or organize disparate concepts, constructs, or entities of some sort. I acknowledge that each of these concepts is distinctive, but for purposes of this theory building typology they are sufficiently similar that I have clustered them into a single category. In essence, these concepts help to create a conceptual structure that distinguishes and organizes concepts, constructs, or entities – content – and, in that sense, are often a foundation for theory development, although they are not theories *per se*.

Typologies and taxonomies are a very basic form of conceptual organization that endeavor to classify items into mutually distinct categories and, thus, are useful for distinguishing similarities and differences across the set of categories of interest. In organizational science, the terms are typically used interchangeably, although taxonomies are more correctly used to classify empirical cases, whereas typologies are conceptual categories (Bailey, 1994). Thus, typology is generally the more appropriate term. For example, Cohen and Bailey (1997) created a typology for distinguishing different types of teams (i.e., work, project, parallel, and management) to organize a literature review. Typologies *may* include order or other structural information relevant to linkages among the entities. For example, Hollenbeck et al. (2012) used multidimensional scaling to classify different types of teams along the dimensions of skill differentiation, authority differentiation, and temporal stability. Thompson (1967) developed a typology for organizational conversion technologies (i.e., the process for converting inputs to outputs) that ordered the categories (i.e., long-linked, mediating, and intensive) from least to most complex with respect to their coordination demands. Steiner (1972) developed a typology of interdependent team tasks (i.e., additive, compensatory, disjunctive, conjunctive, and discretionary). Subsequent scholars drew upon these concepts to create a typology of coordination types (i.e., pooled, sequential, reciprocal, and intensive; Van de Ven et al., 1976).

Frameworks and heuristics organize concepts or constructs in ways that begin to shape theoretical progress. For example, the widely used Input-Process-Output (IPO) heuristic of team effectiveness was developed by McGrath (1964) to organize the literature for a review. Hackman and Morris (1975) popularized the heuristic, which has served as the basic conceptual framework for many subsequent literature reviews (e.g., Ilgen et al., 2005; Mathieu et al., 2008), research studies (e.g., Gladstein, 1984), and theories (e.g., Kozlowski et al., 1996). Thus, *typology-taxonomy-heuristic-framework* often provide a basic classification and organization that facilitates theory building and evaluation.

Phenomenon-Oriented Theory

Phenomenon-oriented theory is a category that I believe most scholars in the field would agree is "theory." Such a theory is a description and explanation of a phenomenon of interest. Social identity theory or social cognitive theory are examples of phenomenon-oriented theories, which are usually broad in scope and context free. The explanation of the theory is most typically verbal or narrative in nature (i.e., based on natural language). It *may* have a formal (i.e., logical or mathematical) specification, although that is rare in OPB. There are many phenomenon-oriented theories. They vary in their emphasis on structure versus process, scope, and formality.

Structure Versus Process

Virtually every theory in OPB has some degree of process explanation[3] or it could not be a theory; there would be no "why" or "how it works" in the explanation. Nevertheless, theories vary in the extent to which they emphasize the content or structure – the core constructs – that energize the theory versus the processes by which the phenomenon originates, interacts, evolves, and operates. Consider, for example, theories of leadership. Transformational Leadership (TFL) Theory emphasizes the structure of leadership behavior with respect to its ability to motivate individuals to go beyond their self-interest to contribute to organizational objectives (Bass & Avolio, 1994). Although there is a process explanation, albeit one that has been criticized for not being sufficiently detailed (van Knippenberg & Sitkin, 2013), the emphasis is on the structure and content of the behavioral dimensions – idealized influence, inspirational motivation, individualized consideration, and intellectual stimulation – that capture the transformative aspect of leadership. In contrast, Leader-Member Exchange (LMX) theory emphasizes the unfolding process by which leader-member dyads develop and negotiate their relationship, how that LMX relationship prompts the formation of in-groups and out-groups, and how it influences individual perceptions and behavior (Graen & Scandura, 1987). There is a measure of this relationship that is used to index LMX quality, its core construct, but the theoretical explanation has more process emphasis in comparison with TFL.

Scope

Many phenomenon-oriented theories are quite broad. That is, they are not contextualized or constrained and, in that sense, are intended to apply across the board.

For example, TFL is not constrained and, therefore, is presumed to apply to all leaders in all organizations at any hierarchical level at any time. Although such broad scope is often viewed as a strength because it makes the theory generalizable across many settings and samples, it can also be considered a limitation because it reduces the precision and predictive value of the theory. For example, with respect to TFL, meta-analytic evidence shows that the relationship between the TFL dimensions and leadership effectiveness perceptions varies across samples and settings, which suggests the need for boundary conditions or contextual moderators to improve the precision of the theory (Judge & Piccolo, 2004; Judge et al., 2004). Researchers like broad, generic theories because they can be fit to a variety of research questions and settings. However, for such theories to be evaluated so they can contribute to cumulative knowledge (or pruned), they need to be constrained by boundary conditions or moderators to a more targeted range of settings and samples (Pinder & Moore, 1980). With cumulation, this yields more precise theory with better predictive potential.

Formality

Finally, as noted previously, most theory in OPB is verbal in nature, based on a narrative description using natural language. Unfortunately, natural language is an imprecise form of scientific communication. Readers vary in their comprehension and interpretation, which means that theoretical explanations are often misinterpreted in ways that are not what the theorist intended. This makes it very difficult to evaluate theoretical propositions, operationalize theoretical concepts, replicate theory, and falsify it. Formal theories have a logical or mathematical specification which makes the underlying propositions much more precise, transparent, and less subject to misinterpretation or misspecification. There were some early efforts in OBP to formulate formal theory, but they fell by the wayside. For example, Vroom's (1964) valence, instrumentality, and expectancy theory specified mathematically the form of each construct and the relationships among them that generated motivational force. It is not complicated, but it is formalized. Similarly, the Hackman and Oldham (1975) job characteristics theory also specified mathematically the combination of job characteristics that would yield a motivating potential score. Although these early efforts are notable, perhaps because there was little support for the mathematical combination (for a variety of reasons), there has been very little follow through on the use of formal theoretical specifications in theory building in OPB.

Causal Theory/Model

A causal theory or model is likely the dominant form of theorizing in OPB. This approach to theorizing and analyzing causal relations was developed in the early twentieth century in the form of path analysis (Wright, 1921), but its emergence in OPB as a way of more precisely representing theory did not manifest until decades later. Fueled by the growing popularity of multiple regression for theory testing, it was promoted as a way of evaluating causal structures using correlational techniques (e.g., Feldman, 1975; see Williams et al., 2020). This also coincided with the development and use of structural equations modeling (Jöreskog, 1970) to analyze statistically the measurement model and the covariance relations among latent constructs (James et al., 1982). However, this discussion is not about analyses *per se*, but on the underlying theoretical representation.

A causal model typically draws on one or more phenomenon-oriented theories and research findings to synthesize a network of construct relationships that are intended to explicate an endogenous variable of interest. Such theories are generally represented as "boxes and arrows" models in which the boxes identify the focal constructs and the arrows signify the direction of relationships linking the constructs. Such models strongly imply causality, given the directionality and sequential ordering of the constructs. However, whether such a model can support an inference of causality is entirely dependent on methodology – data generation – to support the temporal ordering of the relationships. Even then, causal inference is complicated (Bollen & Pearl, 2013; Hanges & Wang, 2012; James et al., 1982; Rohrer, 2018). Nonetheless, whether the data generation supports causal inference or not, such models clearly aspire to explain the network of causal relationships that account for the dependent variable of interest.

Relative to purely narrative theory, this form of theorizing represented an advance in the precision of specifying and communicating hypotheses. If there are contradictions or gaps, it is obvious. I still remember vividly when my advisor, Jim Farr, suggested that I represent my dissertation hypotheses using a causal model framework (Kozlowski & Farr, 1988). The effort revealed inconsistencies and gaps that were harder to apprehend in the narrative theoretical rationale. Needless to say, that effort was an instructive one and I became a much better theorist because of it. As part of specifying the theoretical flow of causality, this form of theorizing allows for constructs to mediate relationships between hypothetical causal constructs and the outcome variable. Mediating variables are often treated theoretically as representing processes (or process explanations). For example, the previously mentioned IPO heuristic treats process constructs as mediating the conceptual linkages between the input factors and the output. Indeed, the IPO has frequently been theorized as a causal model in the research literature on team effectiveness. However, as I will explain later, process constructs cannot really capture dynamic processes; they are at best proxies for processes (Marks et al., 2001). In any case, other constructs may also be incorporated that serve as moderating variables – third variables that change the nature of the relationship (i.e., magnitude or sign) between two other constructs – thereby representing boundary conditions or contingencies relevant to the theoretical network of relationships.

From a theory building perspective, a small set of component relationships – one or more predictors, mediating variables, and moderating variables – afford a great deal of flexibility for constructing extended theoretical models of causal relations. With the advent of multilevel theory – a set of meta-theoretical principles for developing theories or models to transcend single levels of analysis (Kozlowski & Klein, 2000) – the causal modeling approach was easily adapted to incorporate cross-level relationships (i.e., higher-level constructs that influence different lower-level constructs) and emergent constructs (i.e., higher-level constructs that originate from a lower level). Decontextualized versions of this form of theorizing are highly prevalent in the *Academy of Management Review*, a premier theory journal, and contextualized versions (i.e., setting, sample, data) are prevalent in the *Academy of Management Journal* and the *Journal of Applied Psychology*, two premier empirical journals. I think it is safe to conclude that this has been the dominant form of theorizing in OPB for the last half century and is generally regarded as the state of the art.

Process Theory

This form of theorizing is nascent in OPB, but I believe it represents the way that theorizing needs to evolve so that it becomes the dominant form in OPB and organizational science more broadly. What is meant by *process theory*? I previously stated that virtually every theory in OPB incorporates some degree of attention to a process explanation; I stand by that statement. The Sutton and Staw (1995) theory quote noted previously is clearly process-centric. However, most theories provide limited process explanations and the way that most theories are examined in research is incapable of capturing processes directly. Process involves interactions among people or entities that unfold over time (Kozlowski & Klein, 2000); processes are, by definition, dynamic (Cronin et al., 2011; Kozlowski & Chao, 2012). Yet, most theoretical representations of processes use static constructs as "process proxies;" a box that mediates input-output relationships or instead focus on the arrow(s) linking constructs. Theory is about actors and acts, not factors *per se*. An examination of mean differences, correlations, or covariance structures cannot support a theory-based *process* explanation. That is, most theoretical explanations of processes are rooted in a narrative that describes a hypothetical process which, imagined over time, is hypothesized to yield linear changes in the level of a variable (i.e., A compared to B as a difference in means) or a relationship. Yet, an observed mean difference or correlation consistent with the hypothesis just means that the process explanation is not disconfirmed. In fact, because the process was not directly measured or examined, the theoretical explanation is merely one of any number of potentially plausible explanations for observed covariation. Support for the theory is at least one step removed from the relevant observations. Virtually the entire research foundation in OPB and organizational science is based on such reasoning; one step removed from the process phenomena of interest. Theory needs to focus on process explanations in a way that can be directly examined with data.

A process approach to theory building in OPB is grounded in the idea that organizations are like open systems. This notion has been a dominant theoretical metaphor in organizational science since at least the 1930s (Roethlisberger & Dickson, 1939), coming into full bloom in the 1950s and 1960s (Katz & Kahn, 1966; Thompson, 1967). This line of thinking was influenced by general systems theory (von Bertalanffy, 1968), with its emphasis on interacting elements and hierarchical structures giving rise to collective, system-level phenomena. However, the focus of general systems theory on the concept of holism – the system can only be understood as an interdependent whole entity – as a counterpoint to reductionism, prevented systems thinking from having any meaningful influence beyond that of a theoretical metaphor (Kozlowski & Klein, 2000). Essentially, there was no feasible way to research organizational behavior holistically using quantitative methods. Such efforts were limited to qualitative researchers (see Kozlowski & Chao, 2012). However, the rise of Complexity theory (e.g., Arthur, 1994; Gell-Mann, 1994; Kauffman, 1994; Nicolis & Prigogine, 1989) as the successor to General Systems Theory in the 1980s and 1990s provided a foundation for incorporating systems thinking in organizational theory. Complexity theory also focuses on the interaction among system elements and simple subsystems, but without being hobbled by holism (Kozlowski & Klein, 2000). Systems can be meaningfully decomposed (i.e., bounded; Simon, 1973) so that the way in which the interactions among system elements or entities give rise to collective phenomena can be made theoretically tractable and subject to empirical investigation (Kozlowski & Klein, 2000). This is what multilevel theory – as a meta-theoretical framework – is all about.

In multilevel organizational theory, the focus of process explanations is on how interactions among individuals, shaped by the context, give rise to team and higher-level collective phenomena. "A phenomenon is emergent when it originates in the cognition, affect, behaviors, or other characteristics of individuals, is amplified by their interactions, and manifests as a higher level, collective phenomenon" (Kozlowski & Klein, 2000, p. 55). I am a multilevel theorist, who studies team effectiveness, interested in understanding how emergent phenomena unfold and manifest at a higher-level. Thus, for example, I am interested the origin and emergence of team cognition and team cohesion (Kozlowski & Chao, 2018). However, process theory is not limited to phenomena that cut across entity levels – micro, meso, and macro. They are also relevant to process phenomena with respect to an entity at a given level (e.g., a person) that emerge as the entity interacts with other entities and the environment over time. The process of human motivation is a good exemplar (Vancouver et al., 2010).

How does one build process theory? What's different? The key difference in process theory is that rather than focusing on explaining covariance relationships, the focus in on explicating the *process mechanisms* or rules that drive entity interactions that yield the unfolding processes and/or emergent phenomenon of interest (Kozlowski et al., 2013). Actors, not factors. Outcomes of the process may ultimately be evaluated as a mean difference or a correlation, but there would be direct specification and observation of the underlying process, thereby closing the inferential loop. Computational modeling or theorizing represents an important means to build process theory.

The *boids* simulation is a good example for illustrating the concept of process mechanism. Boids is an agent-based computer simulation developed by Reynolds (1987) that emulates the emergence of flocking behavior in birds. It is based on three simple process mechanisms or rules that each boid – an agent in the simulation software – endeavors to meet. The *separation mechanism* influences each boid to maintain distance from other boids to limit collisions. The *alignment mechanism* influences each boid to move in the average direction of the other boids. The *cohesion mechanism* influences each boid to move toward the center of the boid cluster. Each boid is programmed to follow these rules *in dynamic interaction with the other boids* endeavoring to maximize the rules. System level behavior – boid flocking – emerges from the complex interactions among the individual entities following the rule set. The process mechanisms – rules – provide a formal theoretical explanation for the emergent process of boid flocking.

For human behavior in organizations, one might opine that the processes are far more complicated than the three simple rules of boid behavior. In general, I agree, but fairly complex phenomena can be represented by parsimonious process mechanisms. For example, Vancouver and colleagues (e.g., Vancouver, 2008; Vancouver et al., 2005, 2010) used modeling to good effect for studying the process of human motivation. Zhou et al. (2019) used systems dynamics modeling to investigate core process mechanisms involved in leadership goal striving in an action team context. My colleagues and I (Grand et al., 2016) investigated a small set of core process mechanisms to theorize about the emergence of team cognition. Gaining insights on the knowledge emergence process from agent-based simulation, we then translated the insights into experimental interventions to improve knowledge emergence in real human teams. March (1991) famously used computational modeling to investigate exploitation and exploration processes during organizational learning (i.e., socialization) and others have used modeling to theorize about firm-level capabilities (Coen & Maritan, 2011). A few simple process mechanisms can model complex, dynamic phenomena. Moreover, this is just a sampling. There is a wide range of phenomena that are suitable for computational modeling investigations relevant to organizational science (Kozlowski et al., 2013; Weinhardt & Vancouver, 2012).

This explanation has focused on the use of computational modeling to facilitate process theory building, but one could also use a variety of other methods that provide intensive longitudinal measurement of the unfolding process to help build and evaluate a process theory (Kozlowski, 2015), albeit without gaining the benefits of more tightly coupling theory and data. However, that brings us to data considerations and how new forms of data generation can support theory building, particularly process theory building, in the organizational sciences.

Toward a Balanced Interplay between Theory and Data

Conventional Data Generation Approaches

Compared to theory, the evolution of data and its generation in organizational science is a much more straightforward story or was, at least, until very recently. The techniques we use are well-developed and have served the field well to fuel a century of research progress. However, the dominant data generation methods in use are largely static (i.e., cross-sectional) or nearly so (i.e., short duration longitudinal studies with a limited number of repeated measurements). Given the goal of promoting the development, evaluation, and refinement of process theory, our data generation techniques need a major evolution. In this section, I first provide a high-level overview of the major data generation techniques in use and consider their limitations with a particular focus on their ability to advance process theory. I then discuss new types of data generation that are largely fueled by the growth and increasing proliferation of big data. Finally, I conclude with a discussion for how big data approaches – properly targeted – can help to advance the development of process theory.

There are two basic types of data that have generally been used in organizational science research: (a) self-reports and (b) measures of behavior. Although the discussion that follows is decidedly focused on quantitative data, qualitative approaches are relevant as well.

Self-Reports

Without question, retrospective self-reports to survey questionnaires have formed the backbone of data generation in the field for most of its history. Self-report measures are generally multi-item scales focused on the respondent's perspective, targeting the assessment of latent constructs, such as ability, personality, attitudes, or perceptions. Because such measures endeavor to capture latent constructs, there are consequent concerns about construct validity and psychometric quality. Self-reports can also capture other types of information, such as demographics (i.e., age, sex), achievements (i.e., educational attainment), or life events (i.e., biodata). These are manifest indicators (i.e., generally directly observable, factual). Although most self-reports are targeted on self-reflection, surveys can ask informants to provide information about a target entity that the informant presumably is in a good position to observe. For example, ratings of the performance of individuals or effectiveness of a team are often provided by supervisors or managers. I would also note that interviews conducted as part of qualitative research are also a form of retrospective self-report, albeit with the meaning interpreted by the researcher rather than being inherent in the development and construct validation of the measure.

The development of construct-oriented theory and procedures for validating construct measures are resource intensive. However, once developed, survey measures, both construct-based and manifest, have many advantages. They are a relatively easy and economical way to collect data, they are (for the most part) comparable across samples and settings,[4] and relationship information gathered via self-reports can be cumulated across studies using meta-analyses to contribute to a cumulative science. Construct-based measures, and the supporting technology of psychometrics, are unquestionably a major success story for organizational science.

However, it is also the case that survey measures – asking questions – are a major limitation when the goal is to unpack processes. Such measures are subject to a host of concerns (i.e., reliability, construct validity, measurement error, reporting accuracy [concept accessibility; (Nisbett & Wilson, 1977) and insufficient effort (Huang et al., 2015)]). The measures are intended to tap constructs. At what rate do they change? The frequency of measurement should at least match the rate of change in the underlying process. As the process becomes more granular, there are upper limits to how frequently one can ask respondents to answer multi-item scales and to get quality data. Some researchers, employing experience sampling methods (ESMs), use very short measures in an effort to get around questionnaire fatigue. Even then, ESM research is obtrusive, interrupting ongoing behavior, and can only assess a few constructs or concepts. Most such research is confined to one or two weeks of data collection. Although ESM opens the window into process insights, the window is merely cracked.

Behavioral Measures

Compared to self-reports, behavioral measurement techniques are used far less frequently in organizational research, although they do provide a point of departure for process measurement. Nevertheless, behavioral measurement techniques are important given the data revolution underway; there are points that merit highlighting. Conventional approaches to behavioral measurement can be clustered into four primary categories: (a) direct, real-time observational coding, (b) video/audio capture and coding, (c) computer-based tasks, and (d) sensor data.

In direct observation, trained raters endeavor to capture target behaviors as they occur. Measurement is typically accomplished using checklists to index the occurrence of the targeted behaviors. This approach may simply cumulate the behaviors of interest, essentially creating a frequency count. In other cases, the observers may use behavioral observation scales. This approached may be used for "live" cases where ratings are obtained in real time (e.g., Salas et al., 2017). This approach may also be used for training simulations in the military or medicine (Rosen et al., 2011; Weaver et al., 2010). In such instances, there is generally a scenario script that dictates a series of events or problems that the trainees, as individuals or teams, must confront. Thus, there is a timeline and, in such cases, the target behaviors may be sequenced or associated with particular phases of the scenario to enable some degree of process assessment (Grand et al., 2013). Although this data generation approach is relatively easy to implement, human judges are fallible, and when there are many behaviors of interest, the technique can encounter problems with data quality (Salas et al., 2017).

As an alternative, researchers may use video and audio recording to capture all manifest behaviors and verbal communications that occur during an event or scripted scenario. A key advantage of this approach is that all behaviors of potential interest can be captured on a permanent record for later coding or labeling by human judges. This approach is often used in research involving medical team effectiveness. The approach allows for behavioral coding that can range in precision from very general to highly granular dimensions (Grand et al., 2013). Coders can be trained and calibrated on a subset of the actual data and coder reliability can be assessed, which is often not possible in real-time observation. Coders can go back to reexamine specific aspects of the scenario, and it is possible to get very precise measures of individual and team behavioral sequences over time (Grand et al., 2013; Lehmann-Willenbrock & Allen, 2018) that can be arrayed against the phases of the scenario (Fernandez et al., 2008). Certainly, coding behavioral data is time consuming, but this approach provides a very useful point of entre to process measurement, albeit limited to the length of the targeted event or problem scenario (e.g., typically around 20–30 minutes). Moreover, there is a wealth of information on behavioral coding and interaction analysis (Brauner et al., 2018).

Several researchers interested in processes have employed computer-based tasks as a means to capture behavioral sequences using computer inputs (i.e., keystrokes, mouse actions). A series of keystrokes and or mouse movement and clicks can be combined to form an assessment of molar behaviors that indicate intention and/or action. Some scholars have modified off-the-shelf games for such purposes (e.g., Mathieu et al., 2004). A well-designed task will timestamp each component behavior, which can be arrayed against the task scenario structure. Such tasks, particularly when they are purpose built, provide very precise assessment of behavioral processes relevant to interaction, coordination, and task performance (e.g., DeShon et al., 2004; Hollenbeck et al., 1995; Moon et al., 2004). Resources and some degree of technical sophistication are required, but this is another good point of entre to process measurement (albeit limited to the length of the scenario and or laboratory session).

Finally, and this begins to make a transition to the data revolution, one can employ sensors to capture behavior. For example, cognitive psychologists have used eye tracking sensors and computer tasks to assess attention and physiological psychologists have used heart rate sensors and galvanic skin resistance sensors to assess arousal for at least a couple of decades. This is by no means a major approach in the organizational literature, but that may be beginning to change with the introduction of team interaction sensors (Pentland, 2007) and other sensing modalities. Using sensor technologies to track interpersonal interactions, movement, and vocalization, researchers have studied interaction networks in organizations (e.g., Olguin et al., 2009; Orbach et al., 2015) and predicted team performance and interaction satisfaction (Olguin & Pentland, 2010). These technologies are by no means a panacea – basic measurement concerns regarding reliability and validity remain key concerns (Chaffin et al., 2017). However, validated sensor platforms can be used to capture patterns of team interactions and to infer affect and cohesion (Zhang et al., 2018a, 2018b).

Many of these investigations have been confined to relatively short-term observations of one to two weeks. However, unobtrusive sensors coupled with really long duration observations (i.e., weeks or months) offer an opportunity to capture detailed and copious amounts of process-oriented behavioral data in a very efficient way. Whereas the other behavioral measurement techniques tend to be confined to "shortitudinal" lab studies, sensor technologies can be deployed in real life or analogs. Research that my colleagues and I have conducted for NASA has studied teams in a space mission simulation for eight to twelve months. Using team interaction sensor data, we were able to predict breakdowns in team cohesion four to seven months into the mission that were also assessed using daily cohesion ratings (Kozlowski et al., 2019). Technological innovations using sensors can increase the accuracy and scope of data collection. Not to mention that many people carry smart phones that are packed with sensors that capture meaningful behavior. Commercial firms have been adept at monetizing such data. Organizational researchers should be harnessing such data in appropriate ways to gain insights too. This is not on the brink of big data, it *is* big data, but it needs to be targeted on specific behaviors of interest (Kozlowski et al., 2015).

The Data Revolution: Big Data and the Future of Organizational Science

A Bit of History

As I noted previously, the idealized scientific method makes an implicit assumption that theory drives data. However, the reality is that data generation (i.e., research methods, measurement, and analyses) place major constraints on theory building. We create theories that conform to the capabilities (and limitations) of our dominant data generation methods so those theories can be evaluated. Even when the goal is to create theory for its own sake, the norms for theorizing are so deeply engrained through graduate training and the publication review process, it is very difficult for scholars to think about theorizing in any other way than what is viewed as normative. *Data generation, and the statistical tools used to analyze data, irrevocably shape theory.*

The beginning of the twentieth century saw the development of most of the data generation and analysis tools that still underpin research – and constrain theory – for organizational science today. Although ability testing has historical roots in Chinese civil service examinations circa 700 AD (Ployhart et al., 2006), the origin of modern psychometrics is attributed to Galton and his work on individual differences with further development by Cattell (Kaplan & Saccuzzo, 2010). The early development of cognitive ability testing, or so-called intelligence tests, occurred in France with the Binet-Simon Scale in 1905 (Becker, 2003). Terman standardized that test on a sample of American participants, which became known as the Stanford-Binet Intelligence Scale (Terman, 1916). With the involvement of the United States of America in World War I, Yerkes developed the written Army Alpha to process recruits (and Beta for illiterate recruits).

Development of the correlation coefficient is attributed to Sir Francis Galton in the late nineteenth century, with further development by Pearson in the early twentieth century (Stanton, 2001). Building on earlier contributions by Gauss and Legendre, by the late 1800s the least squares method of prediction was well known. Regression analysis, which is at the root for many of our statistical tools, is primarily due to the work of Fisher in the early 1920s (Aldrich, 2005). Gosset, publishing under the pseudonym Student, developed the t-distribution (Student, 1908) for his group comparisons using small samples in his work for the Guinness brewery in Dublin, Ireland. Analysis of Variance (ANOVA) was developed by Fisher in 1918 and began to be widely used in social and organizational sciences by the 1930s (Tweney, 2014).

Thus, by the time the *Journal of Applied Psychology* sprang into being in 1917, the technologies for assessing latent constructs with paper and pencil measures, analyzing group differences on them, and examining relationships among different measures were basically in place. Although most of the early research was exploratory, by the mid to late 1950s it became more theory oriented and, as theory matured, more substantive and causally oriented. This is basically the status quo today. Theory is focused on group mean differences or models of relationships because that is what the core data technologies are designed to address. I am not saying that this focus is not useful, it has been extraordinarily productive, but it is the case that the focus impedes our ability to better examine, unpack, and theorize about processes, process dynamics, and emergent phenomena. Although our measurement tools and analytical techniques have become much more sophisticated, they are still strongly influenced by these century old technologies. It is time to widen the net.

The Data Revolution

A little over a decade ago, a group of thought leaders (Lazer et al., 2009) published an insightful essay in *Science* that highlighted the many new forms of digital data generation – email, chat, Internet search, location information, video surveillance, and natural language processing – that capture "… digital breadcrumbs which, when pulled together, offer increasingly comprehensive pictures of both individuals and groups" (p. 2). They opined that this data revolution had positioned organizational science on the threshold of a *computational social science* "… that leverages the capacity to collect and analyze data with an unprecedented breadth and depth and scale" (p. 3). On the other hand, they also noted that there was not a great deal of evidence for the penetration of big data or computational social science in the research published in the leading academic journals at the time. Rather, "… computational social science is occurring, and on a large scale, [but] in places like Google, Yahoo, and the National Security Agency" (p. 3). This was before social media exploded on the scene.

A decade later, this is still largely the status quo. To be sure, there has been a rapid scaling up of the use of big data analytic tools in areas related to hiring – applicant assessment, selection, and talent management (Oswald et al., 2020) – but not widespread adoption in organizational science research at large. There are many, many reasons for this slow rate of adoption, not the least of which is a lack of knowledge and training, but there are two principal ones that I wish to highlight.

First, there is the thorny issue of privacy. Much of the big data touted by proponents is created by technology firms (i.e., Jim Cramer's FAANG stocks: Facebook, Amazon, Apple, Netflix, and Google) that provide services in exchange for user data that can be monetized. The services are often free and are perceived to be useful, but often at the cost of some privacy and anonymity. In theory, the data are deidentified but the shear amount of data and ability to compile it mean that anonymity is thinly veiled. There are many notable examples that illustrate just how easy it is to reidentify data from just a little bit of information (Anthes, 2015). The potential power to surveil entire populations in terms of one's political views, social networks, financial behavior, and location data raise the specter of Big Brother well beyond anything Orwell could have imagined. However, the technology firms collecting the data and most users appear to be sanguine about the potential for privacy abuses. For researchers, however, privacy, anonymity, confidentiality, and informed consent are big concerns. Research ethics guidelines and Institutional Review Boards, which review academic research protocols and informed consent procedures, are not well prepared to address this deluge of data. This has led many researchers to proceed with caution.

Second, there is the critical issue of *what* we – as behavioral scientists – can learn about human behavior in groups and organizations from such big data. Epidemiologists can track Internet search terms by location (Verma et al., 2018) and use other internet tools (Milinovich et al., 2014) to monitor the spread of disease. Big data are a boon to network scholars who, in prior eras, were limited to asking single questions of people in relatively small networks. Now, networks can be huge and encompass many different topic foci. After the fact, it was possible to trace the misinformation, disinformation, and lies spread by state-sponsored troll farms through social media in an effort to influence the American presidential election in 2016 (Leonnig et al., 2017; Shane, 2017). Certainly, these are important capabilities for epidemiologists, political scientists, journalists, policy makers, and the public at large. But big data need to be targeted for it to be useful for organizational science.

Much of the behavioral data generated by web searches or social media are strongly conditioned by the technology itself. For example, social media platforms enable influencers and the merely ignorant to propagate misinformation and disinformation at scale. The viral contagion of political lies in the United States or misinformation about the COVID-19 pandemic is a direct by-product of these technology platforms. Certainly, studying how disinformation propagates across broad social networks should be very useful for generating countermeasures to limit its spread or effects. However, the behavior in question is completely enabled by the existence of the technology platforms; the behavior may even be promoted by the technology firms (e.g., one firm's policies elevated controversial information to promote more sharing; Silverman, 2018). This behavior is quite stylized and a product of the technology design features. It is legitimate to study, but it has little value for advancing organizational science. Such research would not serve a broader mission of understanding normative behavior in groups and organizations, meaningful interpersonal interactions, and process dynamics. I think this is a problem with a lot of the big data that is publicly or privately available. It could appear to be interesting, but it may be nothing more than smoke and mirrors. Big data have much promise for undergirding a computational social organizational science. For that promise to be realized, the data of interest will have to have more substantive relevance for behavior that is of interest to organizational scientists. Rather than harvesting or utilizing data from social media or Internet search firms, organizational science should figure out how to use the new tools created by the data revolution but harness and target them on behavior that is substantively meaningful to us (Tonidandel et al., 2018). To the extent that variants of broader communication and social media tools are contextualized within organizations, then they become more germane to research interest. Alternatively, researchers may scrape the web to purposefully assemble data that can usefully address important questions relevant to OPB while managing the many challenges of data acquisition and assembly (Braun et al., 2018). The goal is to harness and focus the data generated on answering important questions relevant to human, team, and system effectiveness and well-being in organizations.

Process Theory and Targeted Big Data: A Desirable Interplay

A Manifesto

In previous sections of this chapter, I developed a typology of theory concepts used in OPB. I used that typology to anchor process theory at the forefront of theorizing; the direction in which OPB, and organizational science more generally, should be moving. I argued that, although processes are at the core of virtually every theoretical effort, for the most part we do not actually theorize about process dynamics and do not conduct research on processes that capture those dynamics. Rather, the processes in OPB theories are imagined in a general, cumulative fashion so we can predict how they may yield mean differences between groups or relationships between constructs. Mean differences and correlations are not processes; they are outcomes of hypothesized processes.

I then argued that the primary reason for this state of affairs is due to the dominant data generation method used in our science – asking retrospective questions – using static, cross-sectional research designs, and the associated statistical techniques – centered on mean differences and correlations. Because actual processes are not directly observed, the most we can infer when we find support for hypotheses based on mean differences and covariance relations is to conclude that the theory was not disconfirmed. We do not know whether the general, cumulative processes underlying the theorized hypotheses are actually responsible for such findings. The theory and data are one step removed. We have learned a lot using this century old technology, but now it is time to move forward.

For some, notions of big data offer an enticing way to move beyond the perceived limits of current theorizing (Mayer-Schonberger & Cukier, 2013).

However, big data are fundamentally flawed with respect to their ability to provide scientific insights for theory building. It is not representative; it takes resources, knowledge, and status to access the technologies that leave a trail of digital breadcrumbs. It is often biased; that lack of representativeness is not clearly apparent when machine learning techniques are applied to big data and algorithms are developed (i.e., facial recognition software biases; Buolamwini & Gebru, 2018). The behavioral data contained in big data are conditioned by the technology platforms that generate them; this creates stylized data that may have little meaning beyond understanding behavior that is enabled by the platforms themselves. Finally, the behavior measured by big data is subject to influence both seen (e.g., Facebook policies to encourage viral sharing) and unseen (e.g., Russian troll farms harnessing those policies to spread misinformation, disinformation, and lies to influence voting behavior).

My point is that big data, on its own, is not going to be particularly informative about phenomena undergirding organizational behavior. However, the tools and techniques that underlie big data have the potential to be harnessed in ways that better target organizational phenomena. That is a desirable use for big data. The biggest limitation in most theorizing is that it is weak on the underlying processes. The biggest limitation in most conventional organizational research methods – data – is their inability to directly capture processes. This is also mirrored by the data analyses that are typically employed (Putka & Oswald, 2016; Tonidandel et al., 2018). Thus, the way to make progress is to harness big data techniques to help us better theorize about processes in organizations and to better capture processes in our research. To accomplish this, the field will have to move beyond debates of theory driving data or data driving knowledge. Rather, we need to appreciate that theory and data are inherently entwined. We need to take a more balanced approach.

Moving Forward

How do we move forward? I do not have all the answers, but I can see a path forward. First, we need to be willing to partner with colleagues in computer science, engineering, and data science who have tools and techniques that can be used to help provide process insights. Second, we need to rekindle an appreciation for, and learn how to fully embrace, exploratory research that is process oriented. Much like the early days, process-oriented exploratory research will provide a foundation of observations that will help to propel theory building. Third, we need to move toward formalizing theory. This will be a heavier lift for the field, but it is the path toward fully integrating theory and data.

Embrace Multidisciplinary Research. One could argue that organizational science is inherently multidisciplinary; based on the primary component disciplines of economics, psychology, and sociology. However, that would be misleading since the different disciplines have tended to be associated with theory and research conducted at different levels across the organizational system. That is, the different disciplines with their associated theoretical and data preferences have sliced the organizational system into levels – micro, meso, and macro – that fit their assumptions (Roberts et al., 1978). Even within OPB, the field is mostly made up of influences from organizational and social psychology. For the most part, organizational science is siloed from broader influences in science. In an insightful analysis, Allen (2015) showed how OPB imports ideas from other areas of scientific inquiry but has had less influence outside its boundaries; that is, it does not export ideas to other areas of science.

To move forward, we need to partner with colleagues in other disciplines who study similar phenomena and who also have different tools and techniques that can help us to get better measures of behavior or alternative analytical approaches to help study process phenomena. For example, Sandy Pentland, a computer scientist at MIT who popularized the concept of *social physics* – analogous to computational social science – has been prolific in applying techniques from big data and advanced analytics to understand large-scale human problems (Pentland, 2014). On a smaller scale, one of their concepts led to the development of the sensor platform that captures interactions among team members that I described previously. Interpersonal interactions in teams go to the very core of team process dynamics. Interaction dynamics were at the dawn of group research in social psychology (e.g., Bales, 1950), but fell to the wayside no doubt because of the labor-intensive nature of generating and coding interaction data. In any case, several useful studies were conducted using sociometric badges as a means to collect team interaction data. There is a community of computer scientists who are targeting interaction processes, who hold specialized conferences, and publish journal proceedings that provide a window into this multidisciplinary link. I have collaborated with colleagues in computer engineering, computer science, computational modeling, data science, engineering, and medicine in my efforts to unpack team process dynamics. A researcher's choice of collaborators should be driven by their common interests and diverse expertise with respect to the phenomena of interest. The point is to build bridges to enlarge one's data generation and analysis options.

Embrace Exploratory Process Research. The dawn of organizational science saw much research that was purely exploratory. Theoretical sophistication came much later but was better informed by having that exploratory period. Under the pressures of big data and analytics, organizational science needs to advance to address the one key area in which it is most limited – unpacking processes. I have argued that the critical direction for that advance is to directly address processes, process dynamics, and emergent phenomena that are at the core of human behavior in organizational systems. It would be great if there were theory to guide that effort, but I have argued that theory is constrained by data and most current theory and data are a step removed from processes. It is difficult to theorize about processes in the abstract; particularly, micro, meso, and macro processes that are interconnected; that unfold dynamically and often in nonlinear ways in complex organizational systems. Having multiple examples of carefully measured, longitudinally intensive, descriptive data on phenomena that unfold over time would be immensely useful as a point of departure for building process theory. I have related anecdotally that my theoretical efforts to unpack learning, regulation, and developmental processes in teams (Kozlowski et al., 1996, 1999, 2009) were substantially informed by informal opportunities to observe teams in simulated action settings. Those observations provided the insights needed to synthesize relevant theory. I can also note anecdotally that some of my exploratory (unpublished) efforts to assess team development over time were quite revealing. Theoretically, we tend to assume that emergent phenomena in teams are nice, neat, and linearly convergent. However, my experience was that it was not neat, not linear, and not convergent. Those explorations are a primary reason that I began to seek out new methodologies and approaches to advance my theorizing and research. I think it would be highly valuable to have good descriptive data on socialization, team development, and team performance over time, but those are my interests. Whatever class of phenomena one may be interested in, there are important insights to be gained via good, descriptive, exploratory research. Our journals should be accepting of such data, to the extent that it can contribute to process, theoretical insights. *Academy of Management Discoveries* is one such journal. It would be useful for such data to be welcomed in other top-tier empirical journals.

Embrace Formal Process Theory. I have made a case for the field to move toward process theorizing as a core competency. But I want to push this forward one more step. Process theorizing in narrative form is a good point of departure. The theoretical narrative as a communication tool is not going away. We need good, deep, well-articulated narrative theory to continue to be a primary communication medium for organizational science. However, narrative theory is subject to misinterpretation in so many ways. Translating process insights from narrative theory into a set of step-by-step process actions, conditional statements, or equations – specifying process mechanisms – necessitates a level of theoretical precision that goes beyond most theoretical narratives. The theorist invariably must fill in the missing precision (Weinhardt & Vancouver, 2012). Formalizing a theory forces a tighter, deeper, and more precise narrative and yields a formal translation that is transparent and less subject to misinterpretation (Kozlowski et al., 2013).

This is where computation modeling, or what I like to call *computational theorizing*, has an important role to play. A computational model is essentially the instantiation of a set of theoretically based process mechanisms in a computer simulation (Hulin & Ilgen, 2000). I previously used the boids simulation (Reynolds, 1987) to illustrate the process mechanisms that emulate flocking behavior in birds. This illustrates the use of computational modeling in an intellective capacity to support process theory building; it does not evaluate the accuracy of the theoretical mechanisms *per se*. In other words, the data generated by the boids simulation indicate whether the process mechanisms generate the phenomenon in ways predicted by theory. The data generated provide evidence that the theory is plausible. Evaluating whether the theory is correct or not requires additional data collection in which model predictions are coupled with observations of flocking in real birds. Nonetheless, creating a formal theoretical specification and demonstrating it is plausible goes a long way toward advancing theory building.

Grand et al. (2016) lay out a four-step approach for process-oriented computational theory building that is illustrated in Figure 9.1. Step 1 poses a substantive (narrative) theory that describes the relevant core processes as precisely as possible. Step 2 translates the process explanation into the formal rules – mathematical statements/algorithms – that transparently specify the process mechanisms. This is a key advantage of this approach to theorizing in terms of precision and transparency. Step 3 instantiates the process mechanisms in a computer simulation and conducts virtual exploration or experimentation to study the effect of the process mechanisms on the emergence of phenomena of

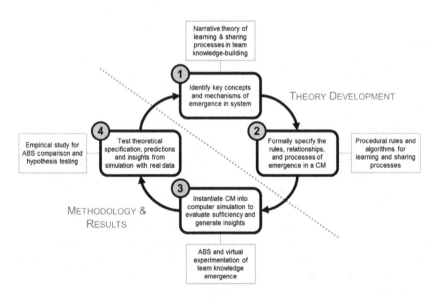

FIGURE 9.1 General framework for process-oriented computational theorizing.

Source: Adapted with permission from Grand (2016).

interest. Does the phenomenon behave as the theory suggests? This is essentially like varying the parameter values for the boid rules and observing the effects on flocking behavior (e.g., how quickly do boids flock?). Step 4 evaluates the insights from the virtual experiments in Step 3 against data – archival or generated. Step 4 then advances back to Step 1 to refine the process mechanisms or parameter values and the cycle continues. Our work employs an agent-based simulation, but there are a range of other simulation alternatives (Harrison et al., 2007).

This is a very different way to build theory. The typical theory paper in most journals would stop at Step 1 with the narrative description and some decontextualized propositions. Done. We know that most of those theories will never be tested, refined, or pruned (Halbesleben et al., 2004). Computational theorizing puts the theory in motion and establishes whether it is a plausible explanation for the process phenomenon of interest. Theorizing about process phenomena that unfold over time, interplay across levels of a system, and emerge as collective phenomena is complicated. It is exceptionally informative to put the theory in motion; to run the movie, rather than assume a snapshot captures one's reasoning. Having put the theory in motion to evaluate its plausibility, the theorist can gain additional insights through virtual experimentation or exploration, evaluating the theory against real-world data, and then refining the theoretical mechanisms and parameters to improve it. This is how a cumulative science functions.

It is also critical to appreciate that this form of process-oriented, computational theorizing is a fusion of theory building, methodology/data, and theory evaluation/refinement. It represents a direct interplay between theory and data; an interplay that appreciates the close coupling of theory building and data generation. One that can advance organizational science to be an informative and insightful form of scholarly inquiry in the midst of big data, the ongoing data revolution, and technological advances that characterize our evolving world.

Acknowledgment

I gratefully acknowledge my colleagues, students, and fellow learners – Michael T. Braun, Chu-Hsiang (Daisy) Chang, Georgia T. Chao, James A. Grand, Daniel J. Griffin, Goran Kuljanin, Jeffery Olenick, and Ajay Somaraju – for the many insights I have gained from our work focused on process-oriented computational theorizing. I also acknowledge support provided by the Army Research Institute for the Behavioral and Social Sciences (ARI; Grant W911NF-14-1-0026; S. W. J. Kozlowski and G. T. Chao, principal investigators) that contributed, in part, to the development of this chapter. Any opinions, findings, conclusions, and recommendations expressed are those of the author and do not necessarily reflect the views of ARI.

Notes

1 There have been prior efforts to organize theoretical concepts, but they are specific to a particular point (e.g., Bacharach, 1989; Colquitt & Zapata-Phelan, 2007); I could not locate one that endeavored to capture its evolution in the organizational sciences.

2 I also note that there is very little consensus on the modifiers used to describe different theory concepts. I have endeavored to use descriptive labels and to explain the nature of each concept with respect to the typology.

3 What exactly is meant by the term *process* is complicated. It is an issue unpacked in a subsequent section.

4 Obviously, there are cross-cultural and other such issues that can be problematic; however, these concerns are not germane to my argument.

References

Aldrich, J. (2005). Fisher and regression. *Statistical Science, 20*, 401–417.

Allen, T. D. (2015). Connections past and present: Bringing our scientific influence into focus. *The Industrial-Organizational Psychologist, 52*, 126–133.

Anthes, G. (2015). Data brokers are watching you. *Communications of the ACM, 58*(1), 28–30.

Arthur, W. B. (1994). On the evolution of complexity. In G. Cowan, D. Pines, & D. Meltzer (Eds.), *Complexity: Metaphors, models, and reality* (pp. 65–77). Addison-Wesley.

Bacharach, S. (1989). Organizational theories: Some criteria for evaluation. *Academy of Management Review, 14*, 496–515.

Bailey, K. D. (1994). *Typologies and taxonomies: An introduction to classification techniques*. Sage Publications.

Bales, R. F. (1950). *Interaction process analysis*. University of Chicago Press.

Bass, B. M., & Avolio, B. J. (1994). *Improving organizational effectiveness through transformational leadership*. Sage Publications.

Becker, K. A. (2003). *History of the Stanford-Binet intelligence scales: Content and psychometrics. Stanford-Binet intelligence scales*, Fifth Edition Assessment Service Bulletin Number 1. Riverside Publishing.

Binning, J. F., & Barrett, G. V. (1989). Validity of personnel decisions: A conceptual analysis of the inferential and evidential bases. *Journal of Applied Psychology, 74*, 478–494.

Bollen, K. A., & Pearl, J. (2013). Eight myths about causality and structural equation models. In S. L. Morgan (Ed.), *Handbook of causal analysis for social research* (pp. 301–328). Springer.

Braun, M. T., Kuljanin, G., & DeShon, R. P. (2018). Special considerations for the acquisition and wrangling of Big Data. *Organizational Research Methods, 21*, 633–659.

Brauner, E., Boos, M., & Kolbe, M. (2018). *The Cambridge handbook of group interaction analysis*. Cambridge University Press.

Buolamwini, J., & Gebru, T. (2018). Gender shades: Intersectional accuracy disparities in commercial gender classification. *Proceedings of Machine Learning Research, 81*, 77–91.

Chaffin, D., Heidl, R., Hollenbeck, J. R., Howe, M., Yu, A., Voorhees, C., & Calantone, R. (2015). The promise and perils of wearable sensors in organizational research. *Organizational Research Methods, 20*, 3–31.

Coen, C., & Maritan, C. A. (2011). Investing in capabilities: The dynamics of resource allocation. *Organization Science, 22*, 99–117.

Cohen, S. G., & Bailey, D. E. (1997). What makes teams work: Group effectiveness research from the shop floor to the executive suite. *Journal of Management, 23*, 239–290.

Colquitt, J., & Zapata-Phelan, C. (2007). Trends in theory building and theory testing: A five-decade study of *Academy of Management Journal*. *Academy of Management Journal, 50*, 281–303.

Corley, K., & Gioia, D. (2011). Building theory about theory building: What constitutes a theoretical contribution? *Academy of Management Review, 36*, 12–32.

Cronbach, L. J., & Meehl, P. E. (1955). Construct validity in psychological tests. *Psychological Bulletin, 52*(4), 281–302

Cronin, M. A., Weingart, L. R., & Todorova, G. (2011). Dynamics in groups: Are we there yet? *The Academy of Management Annals, 5*, 571–612.

Davis, M. S. (1971). That's interesting! Toward a phenomenology of sociology and a sociology of phenomenology. *Philosophy and Social Science, 1*, 309–344.

DeShon, R. P., Kozlowski, S. W. J., Schmidt, A. M., Milner, K. R., & Wiechmann, D. (2004). A multiple goal, multilevel model of feedback effects on the regulation of individual and team performance. *Journal of Applied Psychology, 89*, 1035–1056.

Dubin, R. (1978). *Theory development*. Free Press.

Feldman, J. (1975). Considerations in the use of causal-correlational technique in applied psychology. *Journal of Applied Psychology, 60*, 663–670.

Fernandez, R., Vozenilek, J., Hegarty, C., Motola, I., Reznek, M., Phrampus, P., & Kozlowski, S. W. J. (2008). Developing expert medical teams: Toward an evidence-based approach. *Academic Emergency Medicine, 15*, 1025–1036.

Ferris, G. R., Hochwarter, W. A., & Buckley, M. R. (2012). Theory in the organizational sciences: How will we know it when we see it? *Organizational Psychology Review, 2*, 94–106.

Gell-Mann, M. (1994). Complex adaptive systems. In G. Cowan, D. Pines, & D. Meltzer (Eds.), *Complexity: Metaphors, models, and reality* (pp. 17–29). Addison-Wesley

Gersick, C. J. G. (1988). Time and transition in work teams: Toward a new model of group development. *Academy of Management Journal, 31*, 9–41.

Gersick, C. J. G. (1989). Marking time: Predictable transitions in task groups. *Academy of Management Journal, 32*, 274–309.

Gladstein, D. L. (1984). Groups in context: A model of task group effectiveness. *Administrative Science Quarterly, 29*, 499–517.

Graen, G. B., & Scandura, T. (1987). Toward a psychology of dyadic organizing. In: B. Staw & L. L. Cumming (Eds.), *Research in organizational behavior* (Vol. 9, pp. 175–208). JAI Press.

Grand, J. A., Braun, M. T., Kuljanin, G., Kozlowski, S. W. J., & Chao, G. T. (2016). The dynamics of team cognition: A process-oriented theory of knowledge emergence in teams [monograph]. *Journal of Applied Psychology, 101*, 1353–1385.

Grand, J. A., Pearce, M., Rench, T., Fernandez, R., Chao, G. T., & Kozlowski, S. W. J. (2013). Going DEEP: Guidelines for building simulation-based team assessments. *BMJ Quality & Safety, 22*, 436–448.

Hackman, J. R., & Morris, C. G. (1975). A review and proposed integration. In L. Berkowitz (Ed.), *Advances in experimental social psychology* (Vol. 8, pp. 45–99). Academic Press.

Hackman J. R. & Oldham, G. R. (1975). Development of the job diagnostic survey. *Journal of Applied Psychology, 60*, 159–170.

Halbesleben, J., Wheeler, A., & Buckley, M. (2004). The influence of great theoretical works on subsequent empirical work. *Management Decision, 42*, 1210–1225.

Hambrick, D. (2007). The field of management's devotion to theory: Too much of a good thing? *Academy of Management Journal, 50*, 1346–1352.

Hanges, P. J., & Wang, M. (2012). Seeking the holy grail in organizational psychology: Establishing causality through research design. In S. W. J. Kozlowski (Ed.), *The Oxford handbook of organizational psychology* (pp. 79–116). Oxford University Press.

Harrison, J., Lin, Z., Carroll, G. R., & Carley, K. M. (2007). Simulation modeling in organizational and management research. *Academy of Management Review, 32,* 1229–1245.

Hollenbeck, J. R., Beersma, B., & Schouten, M. E. (2012). Beyond team types and taxonomies: A dimensional scaling conceptualization for team description. *The Academy of Management Review, 37*(1), 82–106

Hollenbeck, J. R., Ilgen, D. R., Sego, D., Hedlund, J., Major, D. A., & Phillips, J. (1995). The multi-level theory of team decision-making: Decision performance in teams incorporating distributed expertise. *Journal of Applied Psychology, 80,* 292–316.

Huang, J. L., Liu, M., & Bowling, N. A. (2015). Insufficient effort responding: Examining an insidious confound in survey data. *Journal of Applied Psychology, 100,* 828–845.

Hulin, C. L., & Ilgen, D. R. (2000). Introduction to computational modeling in organizations: The good that modeling does. In D. R. Ilgen, & C. L. Hulin (Eds.), *Computational modeling of behavior in organizations: The third scientific discipline* (pp. 3–18). American Psychological Association.

Ilgen, D. R., Hollenbeck, J. R., Johnson, M., & Jundt, D. (2005). Teams in organizations: From input-process-output models to IMOI models. *Annual Review of Psychology, 56,* 517–543.

James, L. R., Mulaik, S. A., & Brett, J. M. (1982). *Causal analysis: Assumptions, models, and data,* 1. Sage.

Jöreskog, K. G. (1970). A general method for analysis of covariance structures. *Biometrika, 57,* 239–251.

Judge, T. A., & Piccolo, R. F. (2004). Transformational and transactional leadership: A meta-analytic test of their relative validity. *Journal of Applied Psychology, 89,* 755–768.

Judge, T. A., Piccolo, R. F., & Ilies, R. (2004). The forgotten ones? The validity of consideration and initiating structure in leadership research. *Journal of Applied Psychology, 89,* 36–51.

Kaplan, R. M., & Saccuzzo, D. P. (2010). *Psychological testing: Principles, applications, and issues.* Wadsworth.

Katz, D., & Kahn, R. L. (1966). *The social psychology of organizations.* Wiley.

Kauffman, S. A. (1994). Whispers from Carnot: The origins of order and principles of adaptation in complex nonequilibrium systems. In G. Cowan, D. Pines, & D. Meltzer (Eds.), *Complexity: Metaphors, models, and reality* (pp. 83–136). Addison-Wesley.

Kozlowski, S. W. J. (2009). Editorial. *Journal of Applied Psychology, 94,* 1–4.

Kozlowski, S. W. J. (2012). On the horizon. In S. W. J. Kozlowski (Ed.), *The Oxford handbook of organizational psychology* (pp. 1385–1389). Oxford University Press.

Kozlowski, S. W. J. (2015). Advancing research on team process dynamics: Theoretical, methodological, and measurement considerations. *Organizational Psychology Review, 5,* 270–299.

Kozlowski, S. W. J., Biswas, S., & Chang, C.-H. (2018). *Measuring, monitoring, and regulating teamwork for long duration missions.* Final report (NNX13AM77G). National Aeronautics and Space Administration.

Kozlowski, S. W. J., Chang, C.-H., Biswas, S., Dishop, C., Olenick, J., Morrison, M., & Misisco, A. (2019, August). Capturing the dynamics of team interaction processes. In C. G. Collins & N. Quigley (Chairs), *Explorations of team dynamics: Advances in theory and methodology.* Symposium presented at the 79th Annual Convention of the Academy of Management Association, Boston, MA.

Kozlowski, S. W. J., & Chao, G. T. (2012). The dynamics of emergence: Cognition and cohesion in work teams. *Managerial and Decision Economics, 33*, 335–354.

Kozlowski, S. W. J., & Chao, G. T. (2018). Unpacking team process dynamics and emergent phenomena: Challenges, conceptual advances, and innovative methods. *American Psychologist, 73*, 576–592.

Kozlowski, S. W. J., Chao, G. T., Chang, C.-H., & Fernandez, R. (2015). Team dynamics: Using "Big Data" to advance the science of team effectiveness. In S. Tonidandel, E. King, & J. Cortina (Eds.), *Big data at work: The data science revolution and organizational psychology* (pp. 272–309). Routledge Academic.

Kozlowski, S. W. J., Chao, G. T., Grand, J. A., Braun, M. T., & Kuljanin, G. (2013). Advancing multilevel research design: Capturing the dynamics of emergence. *Organizational Research Methods, 16*, 581–615.

Kozlowski, S. W. J., Chen, G., & Salas, E. (2017). One hundred years of the *Journal of Applied Psychology:* Background, evolution, and scientific trends. *Journal of Applied Psychology, 102*, 237–253.

Kozlowski, S. W. J., & Farr, J. L. (1988). An integrative model of updating and performance. *Human Performance, 1*, 5–29.

Kozlowski, S. W. J., Gully, S. M., McHugh, P. P., Salas, E., & Cannon-Bowers, J. A. (1996). A dynamic theory of leadership and team effectiveness: Developmental and task contingent leader roles. In G. R. Ferris (Ed.), *Research in personnel and human resource management* (Vol. 14, pp. 253–305). JAI Press.

Kozlowski, S. W. J., Gully, S. M., Nason, E. R., & Smith, E. M. (1999). Developing adaptive teams: A theory of compilation and performance across levels and time. In D. R. Ilgen & E. D. Pulakos (Eds.), *The changing nature of work performance: Implications for staffing, personnel actions, and development* (pp. 240–292). Jossey-Bass

Kozlowski, S. W. J., & Klein, K. J. (2000). A multilevel approach to theory and research in organizations: Contextual, temporal, and emergent processes. In K. J. Klein & S. W. J. Kozlowski (Eds.), *Multilevel theory, research and methods in organizations: Foundations, extensions, and new directions* (pp. 3–90). Jossey-Bass

Kozlowski, S. W. J., Watola, D., Jensen, J. M., Kim, B., & Botero, I. (2009). Developing adaptive teams: A theory of dynamic team leadership. In E. Salas, G. F. Goodwin, & C. S. Burke (Eds.), *Team effectiveness in complex organizations: Cross-disciplinary perspectives and approaches* (pp. 113–155). Routledge Academic.

Landy, F. J. (1993). The concept of validity and the validation process. *Journal of Business and Psychology, 7*, 369–371.

Lazer, D., Pentland, A., Adamic, L., Aral, S., Barabasi, A. L., Brewer, D., Christakis, N., Contractor, N., Fowler, J., Gutmann, M., Jebara, T., King, G., Macy, M., Roy, D., & Van Alstyne, M. (2009). Life in the network: The coming age of computational social science. *Science, 323*(5915), 721–723.

Lehmann-Willenbrock, N., & Allen, J. A. (2018). Modeling temporal interaction dynamics in organizational settings. *Journal of Business and Psychology, 33*, 325–344.

Leonnig, C. D., Hamburger, T., & Helderman, R. S. (2017, September 6). Russian firm tied to pro-Kremlin propaganda advertised on Facebook during election. *The Washington Post.* https://www.washingtonpost.com/politics/facebook-says-it-sold-political-ads-to-russian-company-during-2016-election/2017/09/06/32f01fd2-931e-11e7-89fa-bb822a46da5b_story.html

March, J. G. (1991). Exploration and exploitation in organizational learning. *Organization Science, 2*, 71–87.

Marks, M. A., Mathieu, J. E., & Zaccaro, S. J. (2001). A temporally based framework and taxonomy of team processes. *Academy of Management Review, 26*, 356–376.

Mathieu, J. E., Cobb, M. G., Marks, M. A., Zaccaro, S. J., & Marsh, S. (2004). Multi-team ACES: A research platform for studying multi-team systems. In S. G. Schiflett, L. R. Elliot, E. Salas, & M. D. Coovert (Eds.), *Scaled worlds: Development, validation and application* (pp. 297–315). Ashgate Publishing.

Mathieu, J. E., Maynard, M. T., Rapp, T., & Gilson, L. (2008). Team effectiveness 1997–2007: A review of recent advancements and a glimpse into the future. *Journal of Management, 34*, 410–476.

Mayer-Schonberger, V., & Cukier, K. (2013). *Big data.* Houghton Mifflin.

McGrath, J. E. (1964). *Social psychology: A brief introduction.* Holt, Rinehart, & Winston.

McKinley, W. (2010). Organizational theory development: Displacement of ends? *Organization Studies, 31*, 47–68.

Merriam, S. B. (2002). *Qualitative research in practice: Examples for discussion and analysis.* Jossey-Bass.

Milinovich, G. J., Williams, G. M., Clements, A. C, & Hu, W. (2014). Internet-based surveillance systems for monitoring emerging infectious diseases. *Lancet Infectious Diseases, 14*, 160–168.

Moon, H., Hollenbeck, J. R., Humphrey, S. E., Ilgen, D. R., West, B., Ellis, A., & Porter, C. O. L. H. (2004). Asymmetrical adaptability: Dynamic structures as one-way streets. *Academy of Management Journal, 47*, 681–696.

Murphy, K. R. (2021). In praise of Table 1: The importance of making better use of descriptive statistics. *Industrial and Organizational Psychology: Perspectives on Science and Practice, 14*, 461–477.

Nicolis, G., & Prigogine, I. (1989). *Exploring complexity.* Freeman.

Nisbett, R. E., & Wilson, T. D. (1977). Telling more than we can know: Verbal reports on mental processes. *Psychological Review, 84*, 231–259.

Olguin, D. O., & Pentland, A. (2010, February). *Assessing group performance from collective behavior.* Paper presented at the CSCW-2010 Workshop on Collective Intelligence in Organizations: Towards a Research Agenda, Savannah, GA.

Olguin, D. O., Waber, B. N., Kim, T., Mohan, A., Ara, K., & Pentland, A. (2009). Sensible organizations: Technology and methodology for automatically measuring organizational behavior. *IEEE Transactions on Systems, Man, and Cybernetics: Part B, Cybernetics, 39*, 43–55.

Orbach, M., Demko, M., Doyle, J., Waber, B. N., & Pentland, A. (2015). Sensing informal networks in organizations. *American Behavioral Scientist, 59*, 508–524.

Oswald, F. L., Behrend, T. S., Putka, D. J., & Sinar, E. (2020). Big data in industrial-organizational psychology and human resource management: Forward progress for organizational research and practice. *Annual Review of Organizational Psychology and Organizational Behavior, 7*, 505–533.

Pentland, A. (2007). Automatic mapping and modeling of human networks. *Physica A.* https://doi.org/10.1016/j.physa.2006.11.046

Pentland, A. (2014). *Social physics: How good ideas spread-the lessons from a new science.* Penguin Press.

Pillutla, M. M., & Thau, S. (2013). Organizational sciences' obsession with "that's interesting!": Consequences and an alternative. *Organizational Psychology Review, 3*, 187–194.

Pinder, C. C., & Moore, L. F. (1980). *Middle range theory and the study of organizations*. Springer.

Ployhart, R. E., Schneider, B., & Schmitt, N. (2006). *Staffing organizations: Contemporary practice and theory*. Erlbaum.

Putka, D. J., & Oswald, F. L. (2016). Implications of the big data movement for the advancement i-o science and practice. In S. Tonidandel, E. King, & J. Cortina (Eds.), *Big data at work: The data science revolution and organizational psychology* (pp. 181–212). Routledge

Reynolds, C. W. (1987). Flocks, herds, and schools: A distributed behavioral model. *ACM SIGGRAPH Computer Graphics, 21*, 25–34.

Roberts, K. H., Hulin, C. L., & Rousseau, D. M. (1978). *Developing an interdisciplinary science of organizations*. Jossey-Bass.

Roethlisberger, F. J., & Dickson, W. J. (1939). *Management and the worker*. Harvard University Press.

Rohrer, J. M. (2018). Thinking clearly about correlations and causation: Graphical causal models for observational data. *Advances in Methods and Practices in Psychological Science, 1*, 27–42.

Rosen, M. A., Bedwell, W. L., Wildman, J. L., Fritzsche, B. A., Salas, E., & Burke, C. S. (2011). Managing adaptive performance in teams: Guiding principles and behavioral markers for measurement. *Human Resource Management Review, 21*, 107–122.

Russell, B. (1931). *The scientific outlook*. George Allen & Unwin.

Salas, E., Reyes, D. L., & Woods, A. L. (2017). The assessment of team performance: Observations and needs. In A. A. von Davier et al. (Eds.), *Innovative assessment of collaboration, methodology of educational measurement and assessment*. Springer.

Shane, S. (2017, September 7). The fake Americans Russia created to influence the election. *The New York Times*. https://www.nytimes.com/2017/09/07/us/politics/russia-facebook-twitter-election.html

Silverman, C. (2018, June 1). Facebook has finally put its controversial trending product out of its misery. *BuzzFeed News*. https://www.buzzfeednews.com/article/craigsilverman/facebook-killing-trending-an-obituary-for-a-controversial

Simon, H. A. (1973). The organization of complex systems. In H. H. Pattee (Ed.), *Hierarchy theory* (pp. 1–27). Braziller

Stanton, J. M. (2001). Galton, Pearson, and the peas: A brief history of linear regression for statistics instructors. *Journal of Statistics Education, 9*. http://jse.amstat.org/contents_2001.html

Steiner, I. D. (1972). *Group process and productivity*. Academic Press.

Student (1908). The probable error of a mean. *Biometrika, 4*, 1–24.

Sutton, R. I., & Staw, B. M. (1995). What theory is not. *Administrative Science Quarterly, 40*, 371–384.

Terman, L. M. (1916). *The measurement of intelligence: An explanation of and a complete guide for the use of the stanford revision and extension of the Binet-Simon Intelligence Scale*. Houghton Mifflin.

Thompson, J. D. (1967). *Organizations in action: Social science bases of administrative theory*. McGraw-Hill.

Tonidandel, S., King, E. B., & Cortina, J. M. (2018). Big data methods: Leveraging modern data analytic techniques to build organizational science. *Organizational Research Methods, 21*, 535–547.

Tweney, R. D. (2014). History of analysis of variance. In N. Balakrishnan, T. Colton, B. Everitt, W. Piegorsch, F. Ruggeri, & J. L. Teugels (Eds.), *Wiley StatsRef: Statistics reference online*. https://doi.org/10.1002/9781118445112.stat06304

Vancouver, J. B. (2008). Integrating self-regulation theories of work motivation into a dynamic process theory. *Human Resource Management Review, 18*, 1–18.

Vancouver, J. B., Putka, D. J., & Scherbaum, C. A. (2005). Testing a computational model of the goal-level effect: An example of a neglected methodology. *Organizational Research Methods, 8*, 100–127.

Vancouver, J. B., Weinhardt, J. M., & Schmidt, A. M. (2010). A formal, computational theory of multiple-goal pursuit: Integrating goal-choice and goal-striving processes. *Journal of Applied Psychology, 95*, 985–1008.

Van de Ven, A. H., Delbecq, A. L., & Koenig, R. (1976). Determinants of coordination modes within organizations. *American Sociological Review, 41*, 322–338.

van Knippenberg, D., & Sitkin, S. B. (2013). A critical assessment of charismatic—transformational leadership research: Back to the drawing board? *The Academy of Management Annals, 7*(1), 1–60.

Verma, M., Kishore, K., Kumar, M., Sondh, A. R., Aggarwal, G., & Kathirvel, S. (2018). Google search trends predicting disease outbreaks: An analysis from India. *Healthcare Informatics Research, 24*, 300–308.

von Bertalanffy, L. (1968). *General system theory: Foundations, development, applications.* George Braziller.

Vroom, V. H. (1964). *Work and motivation.* Wiley.

Weaver, S. J., Rosen, M. A., DiazGranados, D., Lazzara, E. H., Lyons, R., Salas, E., Knych, S. A., McKeever, M., Adler, A., Barker, B., & King, H. B. (2010). Does teamwork improve performance in the operating room? A multilevel evaluation. *The Joint Commission Journal on Quality and Patient Safety, 36*, 133–142.

Weinhardt, J. M., & Vancouver, J. B. (2012). Computational models and organizational psychology: Opportunities abound. *Organizational Psychology Review, 2*, 267–292.

Wenzel, R., & Van Quaaquebeke, N. (2017). The double-edged sword of big data in organizational and management research: A review of opportunities and risks. *Organizational Research Methods, 21*, 548–591.

Whetten, D. A. (1989). What constitutes a theoretical contribution? *Academy of Management Review, 14*, 490–505.

Williams, L. J., O'Boyle, E. H., & Yu, J. (2020). Condition 9 and 10 tests of model confirmation: A review of James, Mulaik, and Brett (1982) and contemporary alternatives. *Organizational Research Methods, 23*, 6–29.

Wright, S. (1921). Correlation and causation. *Journal of Agricultural Research, 20*, 557–585.

Zhang, Y., Olenick, J., Chang, C.-H., Kozlowski, S. W. J., & Hung, H. (2018a). The I in team: Mining personal social interaction routine with topic models from long-term team data. *Proceedings of the ACM 23rd International Conference on Intelligent User Interfaces* (pp. 421–426). https://doi.org/10.1145/3172944.3172997

Zhang, Y., Olenick, J., Chang, C.-H., Kozlowski, S. W. J., & Hung, H. (2018b). TeamSense: Assessing personal affect and group cohesion in small teams through dyadic interaction and behavior analysis with wearable sensors. *Proceedings of the ACM on Interactive, Mobile, Wearable and Ubiquitous Technologies, 2*(3). https://doi.org/10.1145/3264960

10

SCHOLARLY COURSE CORRECTIONS NEEDED TO ADVANCE ORGANIZATIONAL SCIENCE

Field Tests of Theory-Based Deductions are Long Overdue

Craig J. Russell

My goal in this chapter is to discuss the need for, and hopefully encourage organizational scientists to perform, tests of management theory that include more experimental/quasi-experimental field research demonstrating the value of theory-based interventions to managers. By definition, the latter will test organizational policies/practices directly deduced from organizational science theories and models. I first review evidence and trends suggesting organizational science has placed too much emphasis on inductive theory development at the expense of theory testing over the past 30+ years. I then review salient reasons why this imbalance exists and make suggestions about what might be done. My expectation is there will be healthy disagreement with many of my observations that, I hope, will energize more efforts to test organizational science theories.

Before beginning, recent suggestions that "theory is dead" must be addressed. Authors from multiple disciplines (e.g., Coveney, Dougherty & Highfield, 2016; Pigliucci, 2009) have written about this, though perhaps Chris Anderson's (2008) *Wired* magazine article presented it most simply in arguing the prediction accuracy of algorithms derived from "big data" precludes the need for understanding or insight provided by theory. Until the advent of big data and advances in analytics that accompanied it, organizational scholars developing theoretical models were arguably challenged only by the: 1) slow accumulation of evidence generated from "small data" studies, occasionally punctuated by meta-analytic syntheses and 2) rare tests of competing theoretical predictions in organization settings using fixed effect research designs. Scholars iteratively reformulated competing theories/models as this slow trickle of new evidence emerged, new theoretical models were developed, and occasional tests of policies/practices deduced from these theories were performed. For example,

DOI: 10.4324/9781003015000-13

a meta-analytic dataset first reported by Schmitt et al. (1984) and subsequently updated by Russell et al. (1994) and others through 2011 found median $N = 104$ for all criterion validity performance prediction studies in the *Journal of Applied Psychology* and *Personnel Psychology* between 1965 and 2011. This dataset captured the best cumulative evidence demonstrating our ability to predict and explain employee job performance as reported in two leading refereed journals dominating this literature.

In contrast, over the last 20 years findings derived from big data have overwhelmed cumulative evidence in this and many other organizational science arenas. Specifically, starting around 2000 firms like ePredix, PreVisor, and SHL started selling online personnel selection systems, generating archival data bases with individual predictor/criterion data on many millions of client employees. Total current sample sizes are many multiples of any meta-analytic sample accumulated from published performance prediction studies and growing larger. Elaborate cross validation strategies estimating optimized prediction algorithms consistently yield higher prediction accuracy than any traditional selection test developed from a job analysis performed on a single employer's $N \sim 104$ employees. As a result, organizational scholars are now challenged by powerful prediction algorithms that provide better prediction than "theory-based" applicant measures. When the goal is prediction accuracy and prediction algorithms provide a more useful (i.e., accurate) wrench, users do not have an immediate need for a "theory of the wrench." Unless theory suggests some previously unmeasured/undiscovered predictor model deficiency, scholarly models of how individual differences relate to subsequent outcomes of interest cannot be expected to contribute incremental prediction to cross validated, optimally scored tests. In this context, I use the term "scholarly" to refer to models based largely on theories, often accompanied by a handful of small sample studies applying those theories in operational contexts. Historically this argument parallels the expectation that theory-based "rational" biographical information scoring keys will asymptotically approach prediction accuracy achieved by empirically optimized scoring keys. Until the perfect "theory" comes along that captures all latent causal influences captured between a set of predictors and criterion, scoring keys optimized to predict the criterion should always be more accurate.[1]

This prediction versus explanation tension is not unique to organizational science. Growing up I saw neighbors in rural Iowa use sophisticated times series models to predict future agricultural commodity prices from past commodity prices. Every small farmer selling futures contracts knew these models shed no insight into what actually caused commodity prices, though insight into causal processes is exactly what Department of Agriculture regulators needed to make policy intervention decisions to help US agricultural markets survive and thrive. Another example is found cognitive psychologists' initial use of latent semantic analysis to find predictive and (less often) theoretical meaning from sparse matrices using singular value decomposition (Landauer & Dumas, 1997). Biographical information inventories, time series commodity prediction models, and latent semantic analysis all use empirical tools to harvest latent meaning from predictor measures that forecast future outcomes more accurately than competing theory-based predictions.

Unfortunately, the "theory is dead" authors' algorithms do not help guide management policies and practices requiring something more than a forecast. Theory necessarily retains its importance when one is interested in making interventions, i.e., using deductions derived from a theory or model to craft policies/practices that "manage" people, raw materials, and financial resources to maximize desired organizational outcomes. Intervention, as opposed to simple prediction, requires valid insights into latent causal processes, i.e., valid theory (Dubin, 1978). To put this in perspective, consider how silly it would be to use an optimized empirically keyed biographical information inventory to advise students who are preparing to make initial career path decisions. First, some life events are not "manageable" as students cannot go back in time and change the number of magazines their parents subscribed to during their high school years. Second, many life events will be correlates of some true but unknown causal influence. Russell et al. (1990, p. 571) found moderate levels of "breaking off steady dating relationships" in high school predicted subsequent performance of Naval Academy applicants as officers in the fleet. While making a useful contribution to prediction, no sane scholar would suggest high school students both form steady dating relationships and break them off with moderate frequency to prepare themselves for success as naval officers.

Unfortunately, rarely do developers of these empirically derived prediction tools take the next steps needed to shed substantive insight into latent causal processes. While big data business analytics yields welcome increases in management science predictive accuracy, it contributes only a first step in grounded theory building needed to guide interventions (Glaser & Strauss, 1967). Almost 30 years ago I described iterative theory-based processes for biographical inventory item generation encouraging simultaneous theory development and testing (Russell, 1994). I successfully pursued these tactics in proprietary commercial personnel selection applications, yielding large increased incremental criterion validity and detection and subsequent empirical support for alternate theoretical explanations of why prior life events predict future performance outcomes. Unfortunately, the emergence of business analytics and big data generally remains an unrealized opportunity for management theory testing and development. Successful intersection of these two domains would contain, for example, scholars authoring both empirical studies examining artificial intelligence applications to common management domains and *Academy of Management Review (AMR)* articles that expand theory in those domains. Unfortunately, this intersection is not currently densely populated. As a result, the balance between theory development and testing for most organizational scholars is seriously tilted.

The Problem

Evidence from the Academy of Management Review

I am going to use *AMR* as the target of criticism in what follows, but to be fair my arguments can be levelled against the whole journal publication system. I do so because *AMR* is arguably the premier scholarly journal devoted solely to developing organizational science theory, consistently yielding high citation counts and impact indices (ranked 6th of 152 "Business" category journals by the Web of Science Journal Citation Report, 2020). Disturbingly, Jose Cortina's 2015 SIOP conference presidential speech in Philadelphia and Kacmar and Whitfield's (2000) earlier empirical examination of *AMR* publications presented compelling evidence of organizational scientists' ongoing general failure to test these theories. Jose, citing unpublished work by Jeff Edwards, noted ~92% of all studies published in *AMR* are never subsequently subjected to empirical tests. Don Hambrick's (2007) editorial explicitly warned of excessive devotion to theory development, noting it was aggravated by the de facto *Academy of Management Journal (AMJ)* policy not to publish tests of theories first published in *AMR* unless they incrementally extend the theoretical model above and beyond the original *AMR* model.[2] My sincere hope is that some of the observations made in this chapter will result in more than 8% of *AMR* publications to be subjected to systematic tests by 2040.[3] I find it alarming that organizational scientists have been aware of the current state of affairs for over 20 years, i.e., since Kacmar and Whitfield (2000), and yet done nothing about it. I certainly enjoy scholars' theory development efforts that weave striking tapestries linking existing and attractive new construct "threads" in imaginative direct, mediated, and moderated relationships, i.e., the typical *AMR* publication. Unfortunately, these tapestries are ultimately pointless if never subjected to systematic tests – in Oklahoma we call this kind of scholarship "all hat, no cattle." It is past time for organizational scientists to start testing the pretty theoretical pictures they paint, which means they will need to become acquainted with emerging opportunities provided by big data and business analytics.

    AMR began publication the year I started graduate school with an original mission that included publication of methods-oriented studies – I cannot help but wonder how Kacmar and Whitfield's (2000) results might have differed if that focus had remained. Regardless, its focus quickly narrowed to exclusively serve as organizational science's leading intellectual petri dish. With ~92% of the theories never being subjected to systematic follow up research, it might be more accurately viewed as a theory development cesspool where ideas go to fester and spread decay through a combination of high citations and no subsequent empirical tests. Investigators are clearly not taking the next step in completing *AMR*'s mission as stated on its web site to "... extend theory in ways that develop *testable* knowledge-based claims" (emphasis added). Ironically, an unintended side effect of this state of affairs is that "failure to replicate" problems common elsewhere in social science research are not of current concern, since ~92% of *AMR* theory-based predictions are never tested to begin with.

Contributions to Chasing Our Theoretical Tails and Trends Away From Theory Testing

Teaching and performing organizational science research for the last ~45 years as well as rereading all *AMR* articles published since 1990 led to a number of observations that might explain why only ~8% were subject to subsequent empirical evaluation.

Unjustified Theory Veneration

Murphy and Russell (2017) noted a theory fetish dominating organizational science scholarship today, though I first noticed this bent as a doctoral student in 1977 while teaching a required undergraduate Management Principles survey course. After reading multiple failed empirical tests of Herzberg's 2-factor theory of motivation and Maslow's hierarchy of needs in my first Organizational Behavior doctoral seminar in 1976, I was surprised to see these theories uncritically presented in my Management Principles textbook. At the time I thought textbook authors were: 1) not current in their reading of organizational science research and/or 2) presenting these theories as recent stages of management history that newer students would need to be aware of if only to be able to converse with older graduates. I recently returned to the Management Principles survey course almost 40 years later and was shocked and dismayed to see all major texts continue to uncritically present Herzberg's 2-factor theory and Maslow's hierarchy of needs. I know the training these textbook authors received – some are personal friends and all are professional acquaintances. When asked, none could provide a justification for retention of these models in training virtually all undergraduate business majors nationwide.[4] Apparently some models are so attractive that scholars are loath to leave them even in the face of compelling invalidity evidence. In spite of Box (1976, 1979) and many others noting that all theories are just waiting to be discovered wrong, management scholars are so enamored with theory and "scholarship" that they insist on instilling theories into the future generations of managers in spite of compelling evidence that the theories are invalid. A member of another university's faculty recently gave an invited talk to my department (a former *AMR* editorial board member of my age/vintage), arguing that theory advancement was the only thing worth pursuing and stating "who cares about performance, theory is paramount." This colleague's position is not uncommon, though almost all such scholars spend their careers in academia, pursuing "academic" questions, i.e., those of trivial interest to all but a few like-minded scholars. Imagine publicly traded consulting firms were founded with strategic missions committing them to the sale of consulting products implementing specific management theories/models. I have to wonder what portion of my scholarly colleagues' retirement funds would be devoted to each "theory's" stocks? Nonetheless, *AMR*'s citation count and impact ratings suggest the field has "advanced" to the point where >92% of scholarly theories/models are so bedazzling that no one wants to even risk soiling them with dirty little tests.

Questionable Rodent Control

Of the *AMR* theories/models actually subjected to systematic examination, some motivate empirical research streams of extremely dubious value. Dunnette's (1966) classic article titled "Fads, Fashions, and Folderol" is still relevant today, with organizational scientists seduced by select constructs and attendant models they find attractive, cute, and otherwise intellectually stimulating in spite of evidence of the model's triviality. Box (1976, p. 792) noted "(s)ince all models are wrong the scientist must be alert to what is importantly wrong. It is inappropriate to be concerned about mice when there are tigers abroad." Decades of research suggests many management theories are populated with cute little rodent constructs/models that make little or no contribution in predicting any outcome of interest to anyone other than the scholars dominantly contributing to that literature stream (e.g., locus of control, organizational citizenship, negative affectivity, stereotypic threat), and certainly did not lead to evidence justifying targeted organizational interventions. Evidence showing mediocre to low relationships between organizational citizenship and virtually everything else has (appropriately) discouraged researchers from testing training or compensation interventions targeting extra-role job behaviors. Only our imaginations limit the theories/models that might explain why people/groups/organizations engage in any activity, and organizational scholars are very imaginative. Nonetheless, research efforts should be redirected once enough evidence accumulates suggesting the activity constitutes collective rodent tail chasing, i.e., is weakly related to important organizational outcomes. As with *AMR* theories/models that go untested, perhaps the long life of theories/models demonstrating weak relationships with anything of interest should not be surprising given the continued edification of Herzberg and Maslow's theories in the face of decades old invalidating evidence.

Search for the "Holy Grail"

Organizational scholars also exhibit long term infatuations with certain topics that, while generating lots of publications, simply reinvent slightly different conceptualizations drawn from some larger "seductive" construct domain. For example, concepts emerging from employee affective responses to work have attracted scholarly attention at least since the Hawthorne studies of the 1920s. To be sure, employee affect remains an important outcome of theoretical and practical concern. However, its usefulness as an antecedent variable in causal models of other organizational phenomena remains doubtful. I heard Bob Guion first address this at an invited talk in 1985, expressing amazement at all the research effort put into studying job satisfaction, organizational commitment, alienation, job involvement, job/organizational identity, embeddedness, and various alternate conceptualizations of employee affect. He noted that when he started graduate school in the early 1950s this was all called "morale" and it was not clear whether "advances" in morale's measurement model were really necessary to advancing our understanding of why people do what they do at work. Blizzards of publications mark the launch of new latent measurement models (e.g., behavioral intention commitment versus affective commitment), after which enthusiasm slowly declines years/decades later when evidence accumulates showing measures of the "new" constructs exhibit little or no incremental criterion validity (e.g., see my demonstration that "embeddedness" appears to be much ado about nothing in predicting voluntary turnover, Russell, 2013). Organizational scholars continue to extend great effort towards finding the (as yet) undiscovered employee affect construct/measure that will magically increase predictive power of models of job performance, job design, voluntary turnover, etc. (e.g., Rubenstein et al., 2019). History suggests this infatuation will be difficult to grow out of, but grow out of it we must, as it consumes far too many scarce organizational science research resources for trivial gains in understanding or prediction of important organizational outcomes.

Fatally Flawed Tests of Theory

Examination of the ~8% of *AMR* articles actually subjected to empirical test reveals some led to decades of fatally flawed research. Mitchel and Lee's (1994) *AMR* article articulating the "unfolding model of voluntary employee turnover" theoretically examined how cognitive processes underlying employees' decision to quit change over time, something I wholeheartedly agreed with then and now (Russell, 2013; Russell & Van Sell, 2011). This model basically recasts March and Simon's (1958) static model of employee voluntary turnover decisions as a trajectory of choices over time, with continuous and discrete course corrections due to changes in both decision inputs and how the inputs are weighed and combined, and suggesting homogeneous groups of employees will exhibit similar trajectories. The subsequent 25+ years of empirical research "testing" the unfolding model focused solely (with one exception) on codifying how former employees remembered the process by which they had decided to quit (excluding all current employees and former employees who decided to stay). Importantly, no studies led to estimates of how well the unfolding model actually predicted current employees' decisions to quit, let alone tools to help managers influence valuable employees' voluntary turnover decisions (Russell, 2013). These investigators seem to have forgotten the phenomena targeted by the theory is how *current* employees decide to quit, not how *former* employees remember why they quit. True tests of the unfolding model require tracking a cohort of current or newly hired employees, estimating decision models they use to decide whether to remain employed versus quit at multiple points over time, determining whether these models coincide with unfolding model predictions related to discrete change, and determining whether those decision models accurately predict subsequent decisions to stay/quit. Russell and Van Sell (2011) estimated turnover decision models for newly hired individuals once at time of hire. Results suggested homogeneous groups with similar models could be identified and these models resulted in high incremental validity in predicting job tenure relative to the competing Mobley et al. (1979) and Price and Mueller (1981) models. A true test of the unfolding model awaits a field study in which employees' individual turnover models are estimated at multiple points in time to determine decision process trajectories and the effects of shocks (discrete change), both of which are key deductions from the unfolding model that remain unexamined. Science advances through direct comparisons of competing theoretical predictions (Dubin, 1978), and the presence of just one criterion validity study that, while promising, only weakly tested unfolding model tenants prevents direct comparison to predictions made by the earlier Mobley et al. (1979) and Price and Mueller (1980) models. Scholars and practitioners find the larger body of unfolding model "empirical tests" yield findings that, while consistent with aspects of the unfolding model, fail in every important way to reveal its theoretical or practical value. As the subsequent unfolding turnover model research stream was counted as empirical tests of Lee and Mitchell's (1994) *AMR* article, I suspect the true percentage of *AMR* articles subjected to *appropriate* and *rigorous* subsequent tests is less than 8%.

In sum, review of the leading scholarly organizational science journal devoted to theory development suggests a disturbing imbalance in scholars' attempts to advance organizational science. Evidence of management scholars' systematic failures to test organizational theories advanced in the leading management journal should not have been ignored for the last 30+ years and must not be ignored going forward. The trends contributing to this imbalance described above constitute my view of the state of scholarly organizational science affairs.

This chapter will be successful if some scholars find them compelling enough to refocus their efforts toward more theory testing research.

Why Has this Happened?

Of course I will use a classic theory of human performance to portray what causes organizational scholars to perform tests of theory, where theory testing performance (P) is a function of scholars' motivations (M), abilities (A), and opportunities (O), or P = f(M,A,O) (Campbell et al., 1970). Trends involving scholarly infatuations with construct domains (job affect) and theories (Herzberg's 2-factor theory) suggest motivational main effects, though causal relationships likely exist between M, A, and O as well. Like any good AMR publication, some trends describe latent interactions reflecting Campbell et al.'s (1970) hypothesis that P = f(M x A x O). For example, scholarly motivation (M) to pursue rodent constructs/models that practitioners find unimportant are expected to limit access to real world research venues (O), and when opportunity or O = 0 and P = f(M x A x O), P = 0. This section describes some (but certainly not all) metaphorical motivation, ability, and opportunity "tigers" lying in the weeds that discourage tests of management theory. The final section offers suggestions on how these obstacles might be overcome.

Motivation

"Method" Bias

All methods must, by definition, be atheoretical, as methods are just tools needed to harvest evidence bearing on a theory's veracity. Organizational theories generally do not specify exactly how constructs should be measured or what evidence should be accumulated to support/refute expected relationships. Yet management scholars often display a distain for research methods needed to test theory. Colleagues routinely dismiss big data/business analytics as exercises in excessively elaborate, atheoretical quantitative methods. Assuming science advances best when theory development and testing receive equal emphasis, one would expect most Academy of Management member to join its Research Methods division. Similarly, one would expect most APA members interested in advancing psychological science would join its Division 5. Neither organization's membership profile has ever been close to this circumstance.

Unfortunately, these types of observations are not new or unique to big data/business analytics. For example, Owens and Schoenfeldt (1979) noted how empirically keyed biographical information inventories used to successfully forecast applicants' future performance as employees were often pejoratively dismissed as "dustbowl empiricism." This criticism was leveled in spite of the virtual universal use of cross validation of empirical keys (a procedure also universally found with big data/business analytics) to systematically address statistically optimized prediction models' optimization procedures' tendencies to capture sample-specific random associations as part of their prediction models. Attenuated cross validation estimates reflect prediction error expected from both the original sample and future samples a prediction model might be applied to, hopefully minimizing future "failure to replicate" problems. Estimates of strength of theory-based associations obtained from single samples are also expected to take advantage of chance associations within an initial sample and exhibit some "shrinkage" when cross validated in holdout samples (though not as severe a level of shrinkage as seen with empirically optimized keying). Yet I have never seen a published test of management theory-based expectations estimate cross validities, suggesting findings testing theory-based relationships are likely inflated due to capitalization on chance associations within their datasets and less likely to survive replication.

"Scholarly Construct" Bias

Holtom et al. (2008) recently stated "[g]iven that the study of turnover is a *phenomenon-driven* research domain (emphasis added), it seems reasonable to assume that this would be one area where the impact of research on managerial practice would be high. However, there is no evidence that this is the case." (p. 263). This quote reveals at least two latent values likely to influence the type of research management scholars pursue.[5] First, it suggests the study of observable organizational "phenomena" that impact organizational performance is somehow of lesser importance than studies of linkages between abstract constructs embedded in models of underlying causal mechanisms (e.g., employee "attachment," "engagement," or "embeddedness," which of course then leads to the observed voluntary turnover "phenomenon"). Muchinsky (1985) pilloried this bias when commenting on the distressing trend of dropping "phenomenon" measures in tests of voluntary turnover models altogether, substituting more theoretically proximate "intention to turnover" measures as the criterion (which conveniently yielded higher criterion validities). Muchinsky (1985) revealed the silliness of stopping at prediction of turnover intention by equating it to studying survey measures of employees' intentions to perform when testing theories/ models of job performance. Second, Holtom et al. (2008) suggested management practitioners were being unreasonable for not putting theories of voluntary turnover to use. An alternative explanation is that practitioners rightly view the theories as not very good and not predicting well. In the over 40 years since I first encountered research on employee voluntary turnover, managers rarely rush to solve their voluntary turnover problems using the best scholarly theoretical models of this era, that can be summarized as saying "unhappy people start to think about quitting, then quit" (e.g., Mobley et al., 1979; Price & Mueller, 1981). Barrick and Zimmerman (2005) noted most practitioners instead use personnel selection tools unrelated to any extant theories of voluntary turnover to address voluntary turnover problems. These "tools" may be atheoretical, but they work.

Management Scholars Grasping at "Might Be" Moderators

If I had any ambiguity about the primary motivation of management scholars studying voluntary turnover (i.e., weaving elaborate, intellectually stimulating theory), about 10 years ago an anonymous review received prior to publication of Russell and Van Sell (2011) set me straight. The reviewer noted our results showing high voluntary turnover prediction accuracy should be discounted because the sample/occupation exhibited high levels of voluntary turnover.[6] Russell and Van Sell (2011) used job tenure prior to quitting as the criterion measure in an 8-year study of nurses, during which time ~80% quit. Note, all organizations will sooner or later experience high turnover because all employees eventually leave their jobs (100 years from now all current employees will have voluntarily or involuntarily turned over). Absent any theoretical or evidence-based reason to believe time on the job moderates voluntary turnover decision processes, this criticism is revealed to be one of an almost infinite number of "might be moderator" speculations of the "… observed X-Y relationship reported might actually depend on Z …" variety, where in this case Z is an occupation's average job tenure. Moderator relationships are arguably at the heart of all organizational science theories – I could not find one *AMR* publication since 1990 (and most published earlier) that did not contain at least one hypothesized moderation effect. Importantly, "might be moderator" speculations may prove useful for future research directions when current research results fail to support a priori theory and/or exhibit no criterion validity. "Might be moderators" become a perverse theory fetish manifestation when used to dismiss findings showing a criterion was predicted meaningfully better than it had been from expected relationships drawn from prior theory (e.g., Russell & Van Sell, 2011, predicted voluntary turnover 80–190% better than existing models depending on how turnover was operationalized). Empirical examination of current employees' decisions to stay/quit often take years or decades to get enough observations, one of many nontrivial hurdles to tests of theories of voluntary turnover likely to have chilling effects on investigator motivation. Advocating investigators studying jobs/careers with low rates of voluntary turnover uses baseless speculation to further lengthen the time required to investigate this important organizational phenomenon. Managers facing average call center operator job tenure of $\bar{Y} = 30$ days need solutions that increase this figure now, not after some management scholar has tested some theory in a sample that takes $\bar{Y} = 5-6$ years to quit. I cannot imagine doctoral dissertation committees approving proposals that explicitly plan to study voluntary turnover in settings where it happens infrequently.

Career Success Regardless

Perhaps the most disheartening is the simple observation that very successful scholarly careers occur without testing organizational science theories. Authors of ~92% of *AMR* articles enjoyed the rewards and high regard associated with publishing in a top-tier refereed journal without ever testing the models they developed. *AMR*'s high impact ratings mean studies published in other highly regarded journals cite, but do not test, hypotheses from those same ~92% of *AMR* studies. Editors and reviewers of other leading journals must also favorably evaluate submissions that leverage untested theories published in *AMR* articles. Real scientific advancement requires scholars engage in more than de facto collusion to not test organizational science theory.

Opportunity

A number of circumstances likely limit scholars' access to organizational settings needed to test their theories/models.

Availability Bias and Overly Simplistic Theory

Faced with the absence of evidence bearing on the "unfolding model's" ability to predict voluntary turnover, the Mobley et al. (1979) and Price and Mueller (1981) models of voluntary turnover remain the models with the highest meta-analytic criterion validity estimates (Griffeth, Hom & Gaertner, 2000, reported best individual predictors yielded $\bar{r} \approx .30$). Practitioners might be forgiven for not embracing solutions suggested by these models, as no published tests of the Mobley et al. (1979) or Price and Mueller (1982) models report estimates of actual economic utility of subsequent management actions using Bourdreau and Berger's (1985) established estimation method. Equally unfortunately, these models also suffer from what Tversky and Kahneman (1974) called availability bias, i.e., scholars over emphasis on phenomenon or cues that are readily available. My granddaughter (then age 4) recently revealed this bias to me by spontaneously "inventing" the Price and Mueller (1981) and Mobley et al. (1979) models of voluntary turnover. When asked, she said she stopped playing with her friend Janey next door (i.e., voluntary turned over) because Janey made her unhappy and want to come home. Experience telling practitioners facing voluntary turnover problems that our best theoretical insight reveals "employees who quit first become unhappy, then decide to quit, then follow it up by actually quitting" has historically left me with at least three problems: 1) survey measures of job satisfaction and intention to turnover do not predict voluntary turnover particularly accurately, especially compared to models that directly estimate employee turnover decision models (Russell & Van Sell, 2011) and empirically keyed personnel selection systems; 2) the models do not reveal why employees became unhappy or what factors entered into their decisions to quit; which happens because 3) theories of voluntary employee turnover are so overly reliant on readily available explanatory constructs that my 4-year old granddaughter could have thought them up (and practicing managers give you the "that is obvious" look in dismissing your theory-based solution to their problem). Unfortunately, many organizational science theories find themselves seriously challenged by the "Janey test."

Lack of Access to Organizations

Grant and Wall (2009) and many others described the high expected value of quasi-experimental field research in organizational settings. Researchers with the greatest time available to do scholarly quasi-experimental organizational science research required to test and advance theory tend to hold academic appointments at leading universities.[7] It takes a great deal of time for faculty to grow and develop relationships with organizations needed to gain access for theory testing, and "growing/developing collaborations with organizations" is a topic missing from most doctoral program curriculum. Personally, I historically used a "guerilla research" approach in which I weaved my theory-testing agenda around some problem organizations needed solved, maintaining strict transparency so the client firm/government was aware of and permitted publication of subsequent research. While this has led to what I consider some of my best research (e.g., Russell, 2001; Russell et al., 1990; Russell & Van Sell, 2011), these projects took an average of eight years to complete (the longest 14 years). Typical 5–6 year tenure clocks at most universities mean untenured faculty cannot design and launch strong field tests of organizational theory. Scholars holding senior positions could design and execute research programs that both: 1) advance organizational science by testing competing theoretical predictions and 2) provide solutions to real organizational problems. Tenured faculty positions by definition provide the employment protection needed for such efforts. While I see a small number of scholars doing this (I will not name names for fear of leaving someone out), most simply continue doing what they did as untenured assistant professors, i.e., conducting observational research in convenience samples using one or two survey administrations and/or archival data collected elsewhere (or writing *AMR* articles). I have heard dozens of newly tenured and promoted faculty members describe how tenure will finally permit their research to address more important and serious scholarly questions. Their new enthusiasm for "important" research lasts 1–2 years post-tenure, as they realize: 1) the difficulty of developing relationships with organizations needed to perform tests of management theory and 2) the reality of facing annual performance reviews with meaningfully fewer or no publications. Carefully designed quasi-experimental field studies take years to come to fruition and most annual faculty performance review systems do not value ongoing programmatic research efforts absent published outcomes. Hence, most organizational scholars never have access to the opportunities needed to test organizational science theory in field settings.

Ability

Other chapters in this volume address specific research methodology issues and will not be addressed here. As captured by evidence and trends noted above, organizational scholars' theory fetish results in theoretical filigree made up of elaborately hypothesized moderating relationships (let alone mediated moderation and moderated mediation). Murphy and Russell (2017) noted many if not most moderator hypotheses are virtually impossible to test using random effects survey research designs and interval scaled measurements so common in organizational science research. Further, there is no simple way to state what constitutes appropriate evidence supporting/refuting moderation effects, as multiple research choices and circumstances determine the answer (Carte & Russell, 2003). The combination of random effects survey research designs using interval scaled measurement makes it possible to detect the presence of a true moderation effect, though not estimate its size using traditional OLS moderated regression procedures (Vancouver et al., 2021).

This might have been enough to advance occasional tests of management theory before the big data era, as some "small data" studies would align the moderator tea leaves just right to reveal statistically significant moderator effects. However, big data sample sizes overpower main and moderator effects making null hypothesis significance testing worthless. For example, analyzing criterion validity evidence for online personnel selection systems at ePredix ~20 years ago in multiple samples with $N > 100k$ revealed all main and interactive OLS parameter estimates were statistically significantly different from zero (significant incremental contributions to criterion validity occurred at the fifth decimal point). In spite of this, because OLS moderated regression used with interval scale measures cannot discriminate between pure interactive and combined linear and interactive models (see Schmidt, 1973, footnote 4), no estimates of moderator effect size were available with which to make judgements of "practical" significance.[8] Carte and Russell (2003) described nine different research design and measurement factors that can drastically influence both our ability to detect the presence of moderation effects and their size. As virtually all organizational science theories involve at least one hypothesized moderator effect, scholars are rapidly approaching a point at which traditional random effects survey research designs paired with OLS model estimation will yield no evidence of value in testing organizational science theory. OLS moderated regression estimates using interval scaled measurement and random effects designs constitute at best coarse, pilot test evidence that a moderator might be operating. Compelling evidence of moderator effect size, including guidance about what manipulations are likely to yield what outcomes, await experimental or quasi-experimental manipulations of predictor variables in relevant organizational settings (see Bobko, 1986, for an example of what this might look like using specific cell contrasts).

General Ignorance of How to Detect Moderation Effects

Results of a survey by Busenbark et al. (2022) suggested most organizational scientists have little or no idea what evidence should be gathered and how it should be analyzed to test hypothesized moderation effects. If Busenbark et al.'s sample was representative, their results may partially explain why some *AMR* publications are never empirically tested – scholars simply do not know how. Organizational scientists' abilities to conceive moderator relationships apparently far exceeds their ability to perform research that might yield evidence bearing on the hypothesized moderator relationships.

General Practitioner Ignorance of How to Estimate Utility of Theory-Based Interventions

This may be more appropriately labeled an "opportunity" issue, though it is placed here as precursor to the description of similar ignorance on the part of organizational scholars below. Readers should not be surprised to learn that CEOs do not scour each new issue of *AMR* for its practical insights. Famously, the CEO of a large corporation invited by Lyman Porter to attend an Academy of Management annual conference in the 1980s is said to have observed "you people talk funny." Human resource management executives often have seats at the table with top corporate strategic decision makers and make natural candidates for research collaboration. Long personal experience suggests at least three hurdles impede these collaborations. First, HR professionals as a group have very poor quantitative skills and are routinely intimidated by basic statistics, let alone the Greek symbols in the BCG model used to estimate the economic value of any organizational action (i.e., $\Delta U = r_{xy} SD_\$ \bar{Z}_s$, Cronbach & Gleser, 1965). Unfortunately, as anyone who teaches in US business schools knows, undergraduate BBA management majors (as opposed to finance, accounting, etc.) tend to attract students trying to avoid anything that looks like their required prerequisite quantitative methods courses. Majors offered by management departments at US accredited business schools constitute a prime source of training for a large portion of public and private sector HR professionals. If they can't understand how to show the economic value of organizational science interventions, they certainly aren't going routinely estimate it in deciding which organizational science theories/models to use. I encountered a second and unexpected hurdle the few times I interacted with HR executives who were quantitatively skilled. Specifically, the HR vice president of the *Fortune* 50 firm reported in Russell (2001) had the following reaction to a technical report I wrote using the BCG model to estimate expected value of the executive selection system we were developing (and I paraphrase from memory here).

> "This is wonderful, cutting edge stuff. I can't tell you how impressed I am with how far the field has come in showing how HR can add value. However, you have to promise me one thing – please never share this with or show it to any other employee here at XXXXXXX. As you know, our primary industries are engineering oriented, and if I show this to any members of our executive board (all of whom were trained as engineers or accountants), I will lose all credibility. They simply won't believe "soft" stuff like HR can ever be shown to impact "hard" stuff like production or accounting numbers."

I have helped a number of consulting firms develop BCG model-based online "utility calculators" to help clients see the economic value added of firm services. Experience suggests only clients large enough to employee Ph.D.-trained organizational scientists on staff use these tools.

Organizational Scholar Ignorance of How to Estimate Utility of Theory-Based Interventions

A third and most troubling hurdle is that many organizational scientists do not receive training in fundamental models of how organizational interventions (macro and micro) relate to financial performance outcomes (cf. Russell, 2009). This shortcoming is painfully captured when scholarly research routinely reports OLS analysis coefficient of determination (R^2) effect sizes. Every time an author dismisses a theoretical model that <u>only</u> predicted nine percent of variance in some economic outcome ($R^2 = .09$) I want to shout "but it also means $R = .30$, meaning 30% of the available economic utility has been predicted!" After balancing their check book, no one says "wow, variance in dollars spent was much higher than variance in dollars deposited last month." Variance is an important statistical concept for understanding and drawing inferences about organizational phenomena, but it is not the "currency of the realm" used by managers. Hence the common question "how big does a correlation have to be to be good?" asked by practitioners trying to read a criterion validity study. Basic understanding of the three key variables r_{xy} (not r_{xy}^2), $SD_\$$, and $\overline{Z}_s$ contributing to an organizational intervention's economic utility is required if organizational scholars hope to gain access to settings needed to test their theories, as most practitioners are less interested in testing organizational theory and more interested in solving their own problems.

What to Do About It

Lewin is often quoted as having said "there is nothing as useful as good theory." While scholarly management journals may publish innovative theory and models, we will never know how useful they might be absent evidence supporting/ refuting them. I argued above that the organizational science "theory development – theory testing" scale is tipped excessively towards theory development. This section will describe possible ways change in researcher abilities, opportunities, and motivations might restore balance.

Changing Ability

Members of my doctoral graduation cohort (1982) had difficulty establishing and maintaining research publication track records if we did not keep up with later methodological innovations in structural equation modeling, hierarchical linear modeling, meta-analysis, bootstrapping, item response theory, and more recently latent semantic analysis and machine learning/artificial intelligence. Newly minted organizational science Ph.D.'s graduate from good programs with cutting edge research methods skills have no excuse for not keeping these skills up to date. I would coarsely estimate newly minted organizational science Ph.D.'s statistical/research methods "half-life," i.e., the time it takes for half of their statistical research skills to be out of date without some continuing training/education, is about 12 years (at most), or about the time it takes to earn appointment as a full professor at a major US research university. Failure to keep research methods skills current condemns scholars to spend the last approximately 2/3rds (or more) of their careers severely deficient in their abilities to test advancing organizational science theories.

Relying on selective collaboration with junior coauthors with more current statistical/research methods skills is a crutch used by senior scholars in the past, though the discrete change captured by big data/business analytics might make this tactic less available now. Regardless, while coauthors often bring different, complimentary skill sets to a research project, collaboration presents opportunities for all researchers to expand their respective skill sets. When asked a methods question about study published in the past, no coauthor should have to say "you need to ask Dr. Smith, who was the methods person on this project." While

"Dr. Smith" may in fact have brought unique methodological expertise to the collaboration, all coauthors should have taken the opportunity to gain a working knowledge of that expertise before project completion.

Opportunities abound for continuing methodological education needed to test advances in organizational science theory. Most US research universities offer faculty sabbaticals every six years, so faculty have at least one sabbatical period during the first 12 years of their careers to refresh their research skills. Pre-conference workshops at national meetings of the Academy of Management and Society for Industrial/Organizational Psychology address a wide variety of emerging research tools. The Consortium for the Advancement of Research Methods and Analysis (CARMA) offers in-person and online short courses. I have served as both participant and presenter in sessions from all the above sources and can attest to their quality. However, I experienced perhaps the most useful and intense skill acquisition when colleagues at my university (or physically adjacent ones) let me audit research methods doctoral seminars on topics, including cognitive modeling, structural equation modeling (to learn more about learning curve models), graphic representation of data, and visual basic programming.[9] One lesson common to all these continuing education activities I can pass on involves computer resources – I strongly advocate using a "just in time" approach to acquiring computer skills, not bothering to learn anything related to computer software/programming today if I anticipate needing it tomorrow, because it will likely change between today and tomorrow and I will have wasted meaningful time. If my career was just starting, I would also not bother learning any commercial statistical packages, instead using free software available from the R Project for Statistical Computing.

Finally, contributions to organizational science will continue to be hindered if scholars remain unaware of the BCG model ($\Delta U = r_{xy}SD_\$\bar{Z}_s$). A required doctoral seminar using Cronbach and Gleser's (1965) classic textbook supplemented by work done to extend the BCG model (e.g., Boudreau & Berger, 1985) and measurement of its components (e.g., Bobko, Shetzer & Russell, 1991) would be a wonderful addition to any curriculum. Scholars seeking collaboration and access to organizational research sites must know how estimate a theory's expected utility to organizations.

Changing Opportunity

Practitioners Do the Right Thing

"C suite" executives could finally recognize the inherent value of organization science theories and start welcoming scholars into their organizations with open arms. The profusion of new journal titles published by the Academy of Management over the last 30 years was at least partially aimed at helping executives experience this epiphany. I suspect for the time being that scholars will benefit more from their own proactive efforts.

Change the Dominant Scholarly Institutional Model

Universities could adopt an agricultural college extension or medical school (Packer, 2018) business model for organizational science research. Psychology departments sometimes do this with members of their clinical psychology faculties who also have private practices. I know of one well-known and highly regarded I/O psychology professor who negotiated a change in his university employment status from full to half-time status (going from 2 to 1 course per semester) in order to commit the other half of his time to his consulting firm. The consulting firm provided paid internships for I/O graduate students and access to data for theses and dissertations in what (at least from the outside) looked like a very symbiotic relationship beneficial to everyone. While happening informally at the instigation of more entrepreneurial faculty members, an institutional shift is needed to monetize organizational science by building relationships with organizations through which faculty can simultaneously: 1) advance research, 2) solve organizational problems, and 3) capture the value added from that process in consulting fees. This is not taught in most organizational science graduate programs nor is it something most university administrators know how to do. Innovative partnerships between universities and public/private organizations would make opportunities for quasi-experimental field research much less like the random walk it currently is.

Changing Motivation

Scholars Do the Right Thing

Organizational scholars could finally recognize the shortcomings raised by Hambrick (2007) and above, rebalancing their efforts to more systematically test the theories they develop. Hambrick's (2007) call was at least as pointed and certainly more elegant than this chapter. Given scholars' nonresponse to his editorial, I suspect something more will be needed to motivate a rebalancing.

Change How AMR Articles Are Viewed

Scholars convinced by arguments raised here and earlier by Hambrick (2007) could start to raise concerns in P & T committees and with academic administrators about the status of *AMR* and other management theory development-oriented publications. Annual faculty performance reviews could initially consider all *AMR* articles as "B" journal publications. Reclassification of the *AMR* article as an "A" level publication could occur at some later time when an "A" journal publishes a subsequent test of that faculty member's *AMR* publication. Later annual faculty performance reviews could reference both the earlier *AMR* publication and citation of the empirical test of that publication's theory published that year in a different "A" level journal. *AMR*'s status could revert back to its current "A" level if/when more than 50% of its publications are subsequently subjected to empirical tests. Organizational science will likely progress faster if we stop rewarding faculty for writing imaginative fairytales that are never systematically tested. To this point, one *AMR* author I know pays for a publicist to ensure the author's highly stimulating scholarly writing gets favorably mentioned in business magazines, newspapers, and online forums. The author credited the publicist when a number of practitioner oriented "coffee table" management books of the author's made the *New York Times* best seller list. I cannot help but believe that advancing management science requires more tests of extant theory and fewer coffee table books.

Change Feedback/Rewards in the Scholarly Performance Management Process

It takes about 30% of one's career (~12 years) for a new Ph.D. to reach the pinnacle of resourced organizational science research employment positions (tenured full professor).[10] "A" level refereed journal publications dominate annual performance reviews throughout scholarly careers, though especially during this early period. Untenured scholars focus on "pipeline management," i.e., detecting and initiating some number of research projects through to completion of a manuscript ready for submission to a scholarly journal. Common heuristics include "never rest unless you have at least X manuscripts under review at all times," with X ranging from 3 to 6. The dichotomous nature of career outcomes in this period (granted/not granted tenure, promoted/not promoted) and the (typical) absence of other rewards[11] often leads to overwork, as new faculty don't know which projects might lead to the refereed journal publications and thus never say "no" to any research opportunity. Notably, maximizing likelihood of "A" journal publications (e.g., *AMR*) $\neq$ maximizing likelihood of advancing management theory and practice through iterations of theory development and testing. As noted above, newly tenured/promoted colleagues are often heard to say "now I can finally focus on research likely to make a bigger impact … I am so tired of being a dog chasing every "possible A publication" car that passes by." However, examination of curriculum vita of individuals nominated for promotion and tenure at leading schools over 30+ years suggests organizational scholars are not unique in how they respond to incentives – what gets rewarded gets done. Think in terms of a modified version of the title of Steve Kerr's classic

AMJ articles (Kerr, 1975, 1995) retitled "On the folly of hoping to advance science, while rewarding "A" journal publications." Unfortunately, those charged with allocating promotion/tenure rewards are rarely capable of evaluating how an organizational scholar's work contributed to scientific advancement beyond simply counting numbers of publications. "Nationally recognized scholars from peer institutions (or better)" evaluate these contributions at least twice early in scholarly careers, but rarely after promotion to full professor. Annual performance reviews by department chairs (sometimes advised by a faculty review committee) are typically the only form of evaluative feedback provided for remaining ~2/3rds of their careers. While I have heard of individuals granted promotion and tenure at prestigious research institutions based on a single publication (the economist I am thinking of won a Nobel Prize for ideas expressed in the single book he single authored before being awarded tenure), these are rare exceptions. Hence, if incentives in the first 1/3rd of scholarly careers are not necessarily the ones that will lead to theory testing and development in the latter 2/3rds, how should efforts/outcomes be rewarded differently during the 2nd 2/3rds of a career? As described above, some research streams can yield high "impact factors" while chasing Box' (1976) rodent concepts/models, yielding false peeks, loops, or dead ends described above characterized by lots of "A" publications and little or no theory advancement.

Changing the criterion and standards used to evaluate performance of senior organizational scholars would help, giving more weight to strong field tests of organizational theory that take more time to complete and, by definition, yield fewer publications. Currently departments often equate "A" level publications across faculty regardless of study content or co-authorship. For example, a faculty I served on once equated two "A" level journal publications, one a multiyear longitudinal quasi-experimental field study coauthored with a single research partner, the other a seventh co-authorship on a single survey research design examining student perceptions of recruiting experiences. Both publications counted equally in the respective annual faculty performance ratings and subsequent merit pay increases. At a minimum, university administrators need to distinguish between the contribution made by an *AMR* article that never gets tested versus the contribution made from appropriately designed, longitudinal empirical quasi-experimental field examinations of important organizational theories and practice.

Conclusion

Arguments made here reveal organizational science theory "emperor's" cloths for what they are, i.e., largely absent any threads constituting empirical support. While I sincerely hope this chapter helps initiate that change, the nonresponse to Hambrick's (2007) earlier warning suggests it will be easy for scholars to continue the status quo. The harsh light of decreasing budgets caused by discrete pandemic-related change in how universities deliver their teaching, research, and service products might reveal the imbalanced state of organizational science and force change upon us. Ultimately the process by which organizational scholars realize the pendulum has swung too far toward theory does not matter. Before I started elementary school a state legislator asked my university's president "what kind of university are you trying to have down there?" Our president's ironic response was "We strive to be a university our football team can be proud of" (Pittman, 2012). Organizational science faces just this kind of "tail wags dog" circumstance led by generations of scholars guided by Dubin's (1978) classic *Theory Building* textbook (among others). Future organizational scholars must rebalance their theory building efforts with evidence-based deductive tests and research. Organizational science theory without evidence is just self-indulgent intellectual entertainment for insular cohorts of organizational scholars.

Author Note

I would like to thank Paul Sparrow, Philip Bobko, Shaila Miranda, and Kevin Murphy for their comments and thoughts on an earlier draft of this chapter, though all errors and, importantly, possible offence readers might take to what I wrote remains my own.

Notes

1 I demonstrated in a number of proprietary technical reports for some of the consulting firms cited above as well as select high volume public and private sector employers that empirically keyed Big-5 personality inventories yield scores with higher cross validities than the original Big-5 personality scale scores in holdout samples.

2 Personal experience as well as those of a number of colleagues suggests this unwritten *AMJ* decision rule is still in effect in spite of its editor's insistence that it is not.

3 Note I am implicitly assuming theories published in *AMR* address phenomena important to organizational scientists and practitioners. If this assumption is incorrect, the only course correction needed is for organizational scientists to decrease their collective regard for *AMR* publications, lowering its impact ratings.

4 As I did in 1977, I currently spend 10 minutes describing these theories and subsequent evidence failing to support their measurement and/or structural models. Then I apologize for the continued presence of these theories in the text, ascribing it to organizational researchers' irrational exuberance for theory-based "scholarship," and indicate I will not hold them accountable for any of this information on my exams.

5 Please know I am not suggesting these values are embraced by Holtom or his coauthors, just that this observation captures these values. Many other authors use the term "phenomenon driven" in similar ways.

6 To which I had two knee jerk responses of: 1) "so we are supposed to study voluntary turnover where it doesn't happen?" and 2) "'high' turnover rates are relative, as most voluntary turnover research I do involves call centers exhibiting average job tenure of ~ 32 days." I did not share these thoughts in our written responses to the invitation to revise and resubmit.

7 Many well trained and capable researchers are also employed in industry and governments, though most must use personal time to go through the manuscript writing/submissions/revision process as it is not part of their job descriptions.

8 See Russell & Bobko (1992) for an example of data known a priori to have come from the model $Y = XZ$ in which the 1) combined linear and interactive model yielded $R^2 = .927$ and 2) incremental ΔR^2 due to the interaction term was .058. In other words, though the interaction term in fact caused <u>all</u> of explained variance in the criterion, OLS moderated regression's estimated interaction effect size was .058. If this data had come from a real piece of management research, investigators would not have known a priori which true latent model explained the data, and would have estimated the moderator effect as $\sim \Delta R^2 = .06$, when the true moderator effect would be closer to $R^2 = .93$.

9 Once again, "thank you" to the late Herb Simon and Robert Terry, Joe Rodgers, and Shaila Miranda.

10 More time is typically needed to be awarded an endowed position, with accompanying research support budgets.

11 Merit pay increases in higher education markets are typically tied to state budget increases, if only because so many top-tier universities are units of state governments. Given state budget increases have been below the rate of inflation for many years, faculty learn quickly that the fastest way high job performance leads to meaningful change in compensation is through job change.

References

Anderson, C. (2008). The end of theory: The data deluge makes the scientific method obsolete. *Wired Magazine, 16*(7), https://www.wired.com/2008/06/pb-theory/.

Barrick, M. R., & Zimmerman, R. D. (2005). Reducing voluntary, avoidable turnover through selection. *Journal of Applied Psychology, 90,* 159–166.

Bobko, P. (1986). A solution to some dilemmas when testing hypotheses about ordinal interactions. *Journal of Applied Psychology, 71,* 323–326.

Bobko, P., Shetzer, L., & Russell, C. J. (1991). On the robustness of judgments of SDy in utility analysis: Effects of frame and presentation order. *Journal of Occupational Psychology, 64,* 179–188.

Boudreau, J. W., & Berger, C. J. (1985). Decision-theoretic utility analysis applied to employee separations and acquisitions. *Journal of Applied Psychology, 70,* 581–612.

Box, G. E. P. (1976). Science and statistics. *Journal of the American Statistical Association, 71,* 791–799.

Box, G. E. P. (1979). Robustness in the strategy of scientific model building. In Launer, R. L., & Wilkinson, G. N. (Eds.), *Robustness in statistics* (201–236), Academic Press.

Busenbark, J. R., Graffin, S. D., Campbell, R. J., & Lee, E. Y. (2022). A marginal effects approach to interpreting main effects and moderation. *Organizational Research Methods, 25,* 147–169.

Campbell, J., Lawler, E. E., Dunnette, M. D., & Weick, K. E. (1970). Managerial behavior performance, and effectiveness. McGraw-Hill.

Carte, T. A., & Russell, C. J. (2003). In pursuit of moderation: Nine common errors and their solutions. *Management Information Systems Quarterly, 27,* 479–501.

Coveney, P. V., Dougherty, E. R., & Highfield, R. R. (2016). Big data need big theory too. Philosophical transactions. *Series A, Mathematical, Physical, and Engineering Sciences, 374*(2080), 20160153. https://doi.org/10.1098/rsta.2016.0153

Cronbach, L. J., & Gleser, G. (1965). Psychological tests and personnel decisions. Urbana, IL: University of Illinois Press.

Dubin, R. (1978). Theory Building (2nd ed.) Free Press, New York.

Dunnette, M. D. (1966). Fads, fashion, and folderol. *American Psychologist, 21*, 343–351.

Glaser, B. G., & Strauss, A. L. (1967). The discovery of grounded theory: Strategies for qualitative research. Aldine, New York.

Grant, A. M., & Wall, T. D. (2009). The neglected science and art of quasi-experimentation: Why-to, when-to, and how to advice for organizational researchers. *Organizational Research Methods, 12*, 653–685.

Griffeth, R. W., Hom, P. M., & Gaertner, S. (2000). A meta-analysis of antecedents and correlated of employee turnover: Update, moderator tests, and research implications for the next millennium. *Journal of Management, 26*, 463–488.

Hambrick, D. J. (2007). The field of management's devotion to theory: Too much of a good thing? *Academy of Management Journal, 50*, 1346–1352.

Holtom, B. C., Mitchell, T. R., Lee, T. W., & Eberly, M. B. (2008). Turnover and retention research: A glance at the past, a closer review of the present, and a venture into the future. *The Academy of Management Annals, 2*, 231–274.

Kacmar, K. M., & Whitfield, J. M. (2000). An additional rating method for journal articles in the field of management. *Organizational Research Methods, 3*, 392–406.

Kerr, S. (1975). On the folly of hoping for A while rewarding B. *Academy of Management Journal, 18*, 769–783.

Kerr, S. (1995). Academy of management classic: On the folly of hoping for A while rewarding B. *Academy of Management Perspectives, 9*, 7–14.

Landauer, T. K., & Dumas, S. T. (1997). A solution to Plato's problem: The latent semantic theory of acquisition, induction, and representation of knowledge. *Psychological Review, 104*, 111–140.

March, J. G., & Simon, H. A. (1958). *Organizations.* New York: Wiley.

Mobley, W. H., Griffeth, R. W., Hand, H. H., & Meglino, B. M. (1979). Review and conceptual analysis of the employee turnover process. *Psychological Bulletin, 86*, 493–522.

Muchinsky, P. M. (1985). Some new criterion variables for I/O psychology. *The Industrial/Organizational Psychologist, 23*(1), 9–11.

Murphy, K. R., & Russell, C. J. (2017). Mend it or end it: Redirecting the search for interactions in the organizational sciences. *Organizational Research Methods, 20*, 1–25.

Owens, W. A., & Schoenfeldt, L. F. (1979). Toward a classification of persons. Journal of Applied Psychology, 65, 569–607.

Packer, M. (2018). Med school's business model is officially dead. MedPage Today.

Pigliucci, M. (2009). The end of theory in science? *EMBO Reports, 10*, 534.

Pittman, K. (2012). Cross, George Lynn (1905–1998). *Encyclopedia of Oklahoma History and Culture.* Accessed April 1, 2021. http://digital.library.okstate.edu/encyclopedia

Price, J. L., & Mueller, C. W. (1981b). A causal model of turnover for nurses. *Academy of Management Journal, 24*, 543–565.

Rubenstein, A. L., Kammeyer-Mueller, J. D., Wang, M., & Thundiyil, T. G. (2019). "Embedded" at hire? Predicting the voluntary and involuntary turnover of new employees. *Journal of Organizational Behavior, 40*, 342–359.

Russell, C. J. (1994). Biodata item generation procedures: A point of departure. In G. Stokes, M. Mumford, and W. C. Owens (Eds.), *Biodata handbook: Theory, research and use of biographical information for selection and performance prediction* (pp. 18–38). Consulting Psychologist Press: Orlando, FL.

Russell, C. J. (2001). A longitudinal study of top-level executive performance. Journal of Applied Psychology, 6, 510–517.

Russell, C. J. (2009). Establishing the usefulness of strategic management research: On inverted Lewinians and naked strategy scholars. In D. Ketchen & D. Bergh (Eds.), *Research methodology in strategy and management, 5* (pp. 55–74). Bingley, UK: JAI Press.

Russell, C. J. (2013). Is it time to voluntarily turnover theories of voluntary turnover? *Industrial and Organizational Psychology: Perspectives on Science and Practice, 6,* 156–173.

Russell, C. J., Mattson, J., Devlin, S. E., & Atwater, D. (1990). Predictive validity of biodata items generated from retrospective life experience essays. *Journal of Applied Psychology, 75,* 511–520.

Russell, C. J., Settoon, R. P., McGrath, R., Blanton, A. E., Kidwell, R. E., Lohrke, F. T., Scifries, E. L., & Danforth, G. W. (1994). Investigator characteristics as moderators of selection research: A meta-analysis. *Journal of Applied Psychology, 79,* 163–170.

Russell, C. J. & Van Sell, M. (2011). A closer look at decisions to quit. *Organizational Behavior and Human Decision Processes, 117,* 125–137.

Schmidt, F. L. (1973). Implications of a measurement problem for expectancy theory research. *Organizational Behavior and Human Performance, 10,* 243–251.

Schmitt, N., Gooding, R. Z., Noe, R. A., & Kirsch, M. (1984). Meta-analysis of validity studies published between 964 and 1982 and the investigation of study characteristics. *Personnel Psychology, 10,* 407–422.

Tversky, A., & Kahneman, D. (1974, September 27). Judgment under uncertainty: Heuristics and biases. *Science, 185,* 1124–1131.

Van Iddekinge, C. H., Aguinis, H., Mackey, J. D., & DeOrtentiis, P. S. (2018). A meta-analysis of the interactive, additive, and relative effects of cognitive ability and motivation on performance. *Journal of Management, 44,* 249–279.

Vancouver, J. B., Carlson, B. W., Dhanani, L. Y., & Colton, C. E. (2021). Interpreting moderated multiple regression: A comment on Van Iddekinge, Aguinis, Mackey, and DeOrtentiis (2018). *Journal of Applied Psychology, 106,* 467–475.

Web of Science Journal Citation Report (2020). Academy of Management Review.

PART 4

Implications for Organizational Science

11

THE RESEARCH ENVIRONMENT

Opportunities and Obstacles for Advancing Organizational Science

Georgia T. Chao

Research in organizational science is shaped by environmental factors that can help or hinder how research ideas are developed, how projects are conducted, and how results influence our lives, our work, and subsequent research. Environmental factors range from more macro-environments that are external to a researcher's university (e.g., political or social environments), as well as more micro-environments that are internal to a university (e.g., resources or policies). This chapter describes these environmental factors and provides recommendations for building research environments that will promote new generations of researchers for organizational science. This chapter will focus on basic research conducted in university settings. Although many businesses support applied research and development projects, the environmental factors that influence this research are more varied, and industry scientists are less likely to publish their research (Kinney, Krebbers & Vollmer, 2004). Thus, a focus on basic research in university settings will allow a more in-depth examination of research environments that are most likely to advance organizational science.

The Macro-Environment

Aguilar (1967) developed a framework to analyze business environments. Four macro-environmental factors were identified: political, economic, social, and technological to help organizations develop strategic management plans to optimize their operations within these environments. These macro-environmental factors can also be used to describe research environments. Aguilar's framework has been revised and expanded several times (Sammut-Bonnici & Galea, 2015) and for this review, a fifth factor, international contexts, is included to recognize

DOI: 10.4324/9781003015000-15

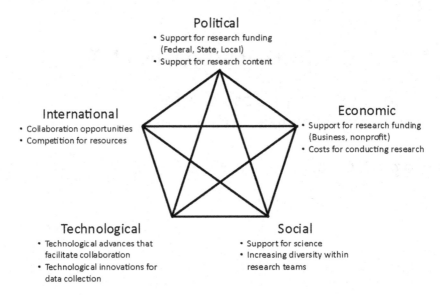

Political
- Support for research funding (Federal, State, Local)
- Support for research content

International
- Collaboration opportunities
- Competition for resources

Economic
- Support for research funding (Business, nonprofit)
- Costs for conducting research

Technological
- Technological advances that facilitate collaboration
- Technological innovations for data collection

Social
- Support for science
- Increasing diversity within research teams

FIGURE 11.1 Macro-environmental factors affecting research in organizational science.

multicultural impacts on organizational research. Each factor is described with regard to how it can shape organizational research.

Although each environmental factor will be presented in separate sections, their effects need to be considered as interdependent and dynamic influences on organizational science. Figure 11.1 displays these factors in an all-channel star model, with each factor connected to all others. For example, political actions often react to economic conditions, technological innovations, social crises, and/or international trends.

Political Environment

Political factors that impact organizational research include federal funding to support research, legislation that affects management and organizational behavior, and government policies that impact federal employees. Federal funding for basic research was about $40 billion for Fiscal Year 2019, with most of these funds allocated to the Department of Health and Human Services (47.7%, primarily to the National Institutes for Health [NIH]), the National Aero nautics and Space Administration (NASA, 14.2%), the National Science Foundation (NSF, 13.0%), and the Department of Energy (12.7%). Of these four agencies, NSF's funding is the most diversified, supporting research for all fields of science and engineering, except for medical sciences (funded by NIH). In FY 2021, NSF's budget was $8.5 billion and it supports about a quarter of all federally funded basic research in US colleges and universities (NSF, n.d.a). Federal funds for organizational science research are available from other departments and agencies (e.g., Department of Commerce, Department of Defense, U.S. Agency for International Development) with specific research areas identified to better serve their strategic objectives.

NSF's Directorate for Social, Behavioral, and Economic Sciences (SBE) houses the Science of Organizations (SoO) program, instituted to fund "research that advances our fundamental understanding of how organizations develop, form, and operate" (NSF, n.d.b). In addition to SoO, NSF has several foundation-wide programs that may support organizational research. For example, NSF actively promotes multidisciplinary or convergent research with the Future of Work at the Human-Technology Frontier program. Throughout the foundation, there is a push to fund "high-risk, high-payoff" research, multidisciplinary research, and to broaden the participation of underrepresented groups and diverse institutions. These strategic objectives can shape the content of research proposals submitted to NSF, and more importantly, those likely to be funded.

Although NSF and its governing board, the National Science Board (NSB), are apolitical independent federal agencies, the director of NSF and all members of the NSB are appointed by the President, and they serve as advisors to the President and to Congress. In recent years, some members of Congress have tried to restrict NSF's funding for social science in general, and for political science, in particular (Matthews, 2014). To date, these efforts have generally failed, but they have compelled NSF and the National Academies of Sciences, Engineering, and Medicine to devote time and resources to defend SBE sciences as a national priority (NASEM, 2017). Proposals for funding cuts for SBE have been speculated to be due to political influences (Diep, 2018). Furthermore, Figure 11.2 shows how funding for SBE has remained relatively flat and low compared to the other research directorates (American Association for the Advancement of Science [AAAS], 2020). Thus, despite the apolitical stance of federal science organizations, they may be affected by politically-driven initiatives from the President or Congress.

Political climates and legal factors often identify important research areas that can inform evidence-based management. For example, employment laws that define protected groups, such as Title VII of the 1964 Civil Rights Act, the Americans with Disabilities Act, and the Age Discrimination in Employment Act, make it unlawful for employers to discriminate against employees on the basis of race, color, religion, sex, national origin, disability, or age. Research on how and why unfair discrimination persists, and what interventions might reduce or eliminate such discrimination, can make substantial contributions to organizational science.

The political environment also includes recent and current legislation that can open new opportunities for research in organizational science. The

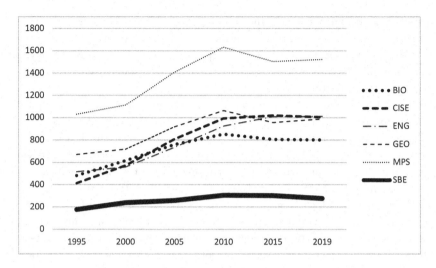

FIGURE 11.2 Funding across NSF research directorates: 1995–2019.

Note:
Funding is shown in millions. BIO = Biological Science; CISE = Computer and Information Science and Engineering; EHR = Education and Human Resources; ENG = Engineering; GEO = Geosciences; MPS = Mathematical and Physical Sciences; SBE = Social, Behavioral and Economic Sciences.

Source: Data for this table provided by American Association for the Advancement of Science (https://www.aaas.org/programs/r-d-budget-and-policy/historical-trends-federal-rd).

Coronavirus Aid, Relief, and Economic Security (CARES) Act of 2020 provided $76 million in supplemental appropriations to NSF to support research related to the COVID-19 pandemic. As the Program Officer for the SoO program at that time, I was able to fund several research projects related to the pandemic's effects on workplace disruptions, remote work, teamwork, and organizational strategic responses with CARES funds. The American Rescue Plan Act of 2021 provided $600 million in supplemental appropriations to NSF "to fund or extend new and existing research grants, cooperative agreements, scholarships, fellowships, and apprenticeships, and related administrative expenses to prevent, prepare for, and respond to coronavirus" (American Rescue Plan Act, 2021, p. 108). These Acts stimulate new directions and research projects for organizational science.

The Endless Frontiers Act (2021) proposed a new directorate for NSF dedicated to technology and innovation. The bill included research topics germane to organizational science: "to study questions that could affect the design (including human interfaces), safety, security, operation, deployment, or the social and ethical consequences of technologies in the key technology focus areas, including the development of technologies that complement or enhance the abilities of workers and impact of specific innovations on domestic jobs and equitable opportunity" (Endless Frontier Act, 2021, p. 181).

Lastly, Presidential executive orders can directly affect government agencies, federal contractors, and federal grant recipients with changes to workplace practices or priorities. Such changes and any controversies surrounding them can spark new calls for organizational research. For example, in 2020, President Donald Trump issued Executive Order 13950 on Combating Race and Sex Stereotyping that banned diversity and inclusion training programs that promoted certain topics such as implicit bias, race or sex stereotyping, or "divisive concepts" (Decot, 2020). A few months later, on his first day in office, President Joe Biden revoked Executive Order 13950 with Executive Order 13985: Advancing Racial Equity and Support for Underserved Communities Through the Federal Government. Confusion over how diversity and inclusion training programs should be designed and implemented continues to be addressed. Richardson (2021) describes how the Iowa State Senate passed a bill that is patterned after Executive Order 13950 to ban diversity and inclusion training programs at the state level. Certainly, the current literature on diversity training can inform local, state, and federal governments on policies to guide the development of a diverse workplace. Furthermore, the questions raised about workforce diversity and inclusion can initiate future research directions.

The political environment can change significantly with each election year. Funding for basic research may be shaped by political motives and/or perceived needs to protect the country. Governmental policies or practices at the federal level can also influence state and local policies. Furthermore, they may shape how private organizations and businesses develop management strategies that drive organizational objectives or human resource practices.

Economic Environment

General economic conditions can influence research opportunities in direct and indirect ways. Favorable economic conditions can provide additional resources for businesses and private foundations to support research. In 2018, businesses spent $441 billion on research and development; however, only 6.5% of that amount was allocated to basic research (Wolfe, 2020). Unfavorable economic conditions constrain funding for basic research. Economic recessions provoke states to cut education appropriations; furthermore, the effects of these cuts are cumulative across recessions. The State Higher Education Executive Officers Association (2021) reported four economic recessions between 1980 and 2020. Each subsequent recession saw deeper cuts in state and local education appropriations, with longer recovery times. The report noted that state funding for higher education never completely recovered from recessions that started in 2001 and 2008 further exacerbating problems in the 2020 economic recession.

Significant budget reductions, coupled with limited means to increase revenue, can force universities to reduce support for research and require more researchers to search for increasingly competitive grants. Researchers in business schools generally had access to internal research budgets with funds from healthy student enrollments and executive education programs; there were few rewards or incentives to seek external funding (Maurer, 2016). However, the current economic environment may require more researchers to apply for grants, exacerbating the competition for these scarce resources. Maurer (2016) posits that a greater alignment of national research resources and business school research activities could have long-term transformations that benefit worker well-being, partnerships between industries and universities, and US economic competitiveness.

Social Environment

Several aspects of the social environment can affect organizational science. They range from distal societal reactions to science in general, to proximal social reactions within a specific research area. These factors influence how the research is conducted, how it is perceived by the general public, and how it might be used, or misused, in organizational practice.

Various factions of society have refuted scientific claims throughout history, with notable examples including Galileo's trials to defend heliocentric theory (Zanatta et al., 2017), the Scopes Trial and human evolution (Moran, 2021), and current debates on the reality of climate change, or benefits versus risks of genetically-modified foods and vaccines (Otto, 2016). The skepticism on science may influence politicians and organizational leaders as they determine funding levels and support for science. With regard to organizational science, misinformation can be used to guide opinions and organizational practices. An example may be found in a recent documentary on personality tests. HBO Max released *Persona: The dark truth behind personality tests* in 2021. The film showcased the Myers-Briggs Type Indicator (MBTI) and big five personality tests and concluded these tests should not be used in personnel selection because they are discriminatory and not valid. Despite efforts to correct the misinformation (e.g., the MBTI was never designed to be used for personnel selection, Society for Industrial and Organizational Psychology [SIOP], 2021), articles in the popular press accept the film's conclusions. For example, Rozsa (2021) drew from his own workplace struggles to identify with the film's premise that personality tests are unfair. This example may be a reflection of how organizational science needs to better communicate with external audiences, and it also illustrates how personal work experiences may challenge the acceptance of scientific findings. Reactions to current research results by workers, organizations, and the general public can affect the implementation and acceptance of workplace interventions.

The social environments of organizational researchers have also changed dramatically over the past 50 years, with more research publications authored by teams that are increasing in size and that are more likely to be interdisciplinary and multinational (Hsiehchen, Espinoza & Hsieh, 2015; Porter & Rafols, 2009). These trends are attributed to the increasing complexity of research questions that span multiple disciplines and the availability of technologies that facilitate collaborations across borders and time zones. The prevalence of research teams across all science disciplines has resulted in the emergence of a "science of team science" (Stokols et al., 2009). This research area seeks to understanding a range of micro, meso, and macro factors on scientific teams, including how they are organized, how they conduct their research, how their members communicate and interact with one another, and how they interface with university structures, independent science traditions, and research funding contexts (Börner et al., 2010). The dominance of team research productivity has challenged universities as they evaluate the individual contributions of faculty members.

The research process has fundamentally changed from the model of an individual genius to a research team. Wuchty, Jones, and Uzzi (2007) reviewed millions of publications over a 50-year period and found clear trends in science and engineering. In social sciences, team-authored publications were more frequently cited and had higher impact than research from single authors. Whereas single authors were largely responsible for high-impact research in the 1950s, this distinction was clearly assumed by research teams by the 2000s.

Furthermore, the changing demographics of faculty members may also affect research teams. The PhD Project (n.d.) reported that the number of minority business professors has quintupled since its founding in 1994. In addition, Brown (2016) found a small increase in the percentage of full-time women faculty in business schools, from 26.9% in 2006–07 to 31.2% in 2015–16. A more diverse population of researchers in organizational science may require new skills to initiate, cultivate, and evaluate diversity and inclusion goals for research teams. These trends have changed the social environments of research teams to require researchers to work with more collaborators who are less likely to have the same demographic, geographic, or professional backgrounds as themselves.

Technological Environment

Technological innovations such as artificial intelligence, robotics, and digital platforms are more likely to change jobs, work processes, and organizations in ways that cannot be understood by current theories in organizational science (Bailey et al., 2019). Emerging technologies are more intelligent, able to work autonomously or with human teammates, with examples in machine learning, smart sensors, augmented reality, and data analytics. Bailey et al. (2019) note: "emerging technologies are transforming how, when, and where work gets done, as well as by whom and for whom, leading to the creation of new business models" (p. 643). NSF's Big Idea on the Future of Work at the Human-Technology Frontier recognizes the need for more research to better understand how new technologies will impact future work and workers. Thus, researchers in organizational science will be essential collaborators in research teams examining human-technology partnerships at work.

Technology not only drives new research directions, but also shapes how research is designed, conducted, and evaluated. Preliminary research ideas may be presented, exchanged, and developed electronically through a number of internet forums such as blogs, podcasts, online discussion forums, chat-based platforms, and social networks. Potential collaborators may also be found from internet connections. Computer literacy and information literacy, skills needed to use a computer to search and access information germane to a research project, are basic skills needed for researchers. Theory building can be advanced from traditional narratives by using computational modeling. This approach to theory specification and development compels researchers to be more transparent by specifying algorithms or mathematical equations to describe theoretical processes (Grand et al., 2016; Guest & Martin, 2021).

Similarly, researchers may require new skills to collect data or build new databases. The design of on-line surveys (e.g., Qualtrics, https://www.qualtrics.com/), and crowdsourcing participants for research studies (e.g., Amazon's Mechanical Turk, https://www.mturk.com) can facilitate organizational research. Additional methods of data collection include smart sensors that can track a number of physiological responses such as heart rate and galvanic skin response to detect stress, as well as eyewear that can track motion and detect level of concentration (Arakawa, 2019). Video communications platforms like Zoom (https://zoom.us/) can be used to collect qualitative data, hold virtual meetings of research teams, and present research results to target audiences. Although communication platforms can facilitate connections among research collaborators, Binz-Scharf, Kalish, and Paik (2015) note that the social aspects needed to conduct research have not changed. In the field of biology, they found that scientists were more likely to collaborate with others whom they have had face-to-face interactions and have built trust. Virtual technologies enable the development of working relationships, but preexisting professional ties (e.g., meetings at professional conferences) can serve as critical foundations for these relationships.

International Environment

As mentioned previously, scientific research is more likely to be conducted by research teams and these teams are likely to be multinational (Milliman & von Glinow, 1998a). The convenience of video conferencing platforms like Zoom has made it easier for multinational teams to meet virtually and to contact one another more frequently. Benefits from multinational research teams include the extension of research ideas to multiple cultures, process gains with the potential for more creative and innovative ideas to emerge from a diverse team, and the sharing of resources (e.g., high performance computing) that may not be available to all team members (Nason & Pillutla, 1998; Stahl et al., 2010). However, the challenges with language and cultural differences are likely to contribute to group process losses that can slow down progress and create conflict within the team (Stahl & Maznevski, 2021). Thus, cultural effects on a multinational team's performance can act like a double-edged sword, affecting advantages from process gains and disadvantages from process losses.

A single country may have multicultural teams, however, the legal, historical, and cultural differences across countries are likely to amplify cultural diversity in multinational teams. If these teams primarily interact in virtual contexts, it becomes unclear whether problems are traced back to technical communication difficulties, to cultural differences, or to both. Milliman and von Glinow (1998b) posit that these teams require a strong leader to establish the team's structure, project goals, and processes to guide teamwork. A shared understanding of who will do what, how resources will be shared, what and where results will be published, and how conflicts may be resolved, could help avoid some process losses and minimize uncertainties (Milliman & von Glinow, 1998a).

Although there are many successful international research teams, there is also competition among countries to claim innovations in science and technology. A recent report by the American Academy of Arts & Sciences (2020) identified China as outranking the US in its investment in research and development, as measured at purchasing power parity. Comparisons between the US and China show the US still leading on funding for basic research. However, China is closing the gap on expenditures for R&D and the numbers of doctorates in science and engineering that each country produces is about even. Furthermore, China now leads the US on numbers of patents granted, articles published in science and engineering, and in the numbers of researchers and baccalaureate degrees in science and engineering. The US also faces stiff competition from members of the European Union, the UK, and Japan. These trends have prompted Congress to pass the American Creating Opportunities to Meaningfully Promote Excellence in Technology, Education, and Science (COMPETES) Act of 2007, the American COMPETES Reauthorization Act of 2010, the American Innovation and Competitiveness Act of 2017, and current consideration of the National Strategy to Ensure American Leadership Act of 2021 (National SEAL Act, 2021). These laws increase resources for research and education in order to maintain a dominant role in science and technology. In addition, new policy goals may be needed to support a global knowledge system to advance science in open and ethical ways; yet still protect US intellectual rights, economic interests, and competitive edge (Working Group on Science and Technology in US – China Relations, 2020).

Summary of Macro-Environments

Five macro-environments can affect research projects in organizational science. Political environments provide government research funds and can create new research initiatives. Economic environments shape the latitude businesses and foundations have to support research. The social environment is becoming more diverse, increasing the likelihood for diverse research teams and research focused on diversity and inclusion in the workplace. Technological innovations can enable teams to work better and offer new ways to collect data. Finally, more research projects are operating in international environments that require additional considerations to form and manage multinational research teams.

These environments have direct impacts (e.g., laws are enacted that provide funding for research) as well as indirect impacts (e.g., economic recessions prompt university budget cuts that then affect research). Furthermore, each of these types of macro-environments can influence how other macro-environments may enable or constrain research. International collaborations may benefit from technological innovations and cultural diversity, but they may also suffer from political and/or economic constraints and social conflicts. In addition to these macro-environments, research in organizational science is influenced by meso- and micro-environmental factors that are more internal to the profession and to a researcher's university. Two of these factors are highlighted: the profession of organizational science and the university environment.

Meso- and Micro-Environments

Professional environments are described as meso-environments because they are bounded by the content of science and practice instead of macro boundaries of country borders or micro boundaries of organizational structures. Organizational science can be described by professional environments such as industrial and organizational psychology, human resource management, organizational behavior, organizational theory, and strategic management. In contrast, the university environment is a more micro-environment for researchers. It can be parsed into a number of levels (e.g., university, college, department, interest area) but this discussion will review different aspects of the university environment under a single micro-environment category.

Professional Environments in Organizational Science

Organizational science is multidisciplinary, with roots in traditional disciplines such as psychology, sociology, economics, and political science. Furthermore, research in organizational science ranges from topics at micro levels (e.g., performance assessment of individual workers) to macro levels (e.g., strategic management and globalization), with many levels in-between (e.g., leadership, teams, organizational learning, etc.). Professional organizations such as the Academy of Management (AoM), the International Association of Applied Psychology, and the SIOP bring together students, academics, and practitioners in conferences to showcase research, advance professional development, and build networks that promote career development. The conferences offer opportunities for researchers to share and develop their ideas and find new research partners. Conference themes can set criteria for which proposals and submissions are selected for the program. Keynote addresses and tutorial sessions can inspire researchers to pursue current "hot topics" with new methods. Hesli and Lee (2011) found that conference attendance was positively correlated with number of publications for 1,399 faculty in political science, and it is reasonable to expect similar relationships between conference attendance and publications in organizational science.

Professional organizations do more than offer conferences. Some offer research grants to promote research in particular areas. For example, the SIOP Foundation established a small grant program to fund anti-racism research in the wake of the 2020 George Floyd murder and Black Lives Matter movement (https://www.siop.org/Foundation/Anti-Racism-Grant). SIOP's Visionary Grant program supports research examining the future of work. In another example, the Strategic Management Society's Strategy Research Foundation offers research grants to support graduate student dissertations as well as grants that build partnerships with organizations, and grants that are germane to strategic management (https://www.strategicmanagement.net/srf/overview/overview).

In addition to professional organizations influencing research ideas and projects, journals can call for manuscripts for special issues. For example, the *Journal of Applied Psychology* issued a call for papers related to the COVID-19 pandemic. Manuscripts were evaluated using a rapid review process for quick publication in order to inform practitioners and researchers on the pandemic's effects at work. This example shows how a societal problem can initiate new research streams that can help organizations. The federal government can release new funds to support this research and journals can facilitate the publication and dissemination of the new knowledge. Focus on a particular topic for research can inspire others to conduct further investigations. Just as macro-environments can impact one another, so can they interact with meso- and micro-environments.

While efforts by professional organizations and journals can inspire new directions for research, their payoff can be difficult to predict. In a cautionary essay regarding faddishness in behavioral and social science research, Starbuck (2009) identified four constant causes for research fads. A mass production approach to publishing research has resulted in many publications with limited contributions to science. Starbuck found 20% of published articles are not cited at all and only 10% of articles in management claim 50% of citations. The "chaff" can bury research gems; worse yet, they may serve as models to new researchers who are motivated to succeed by publishing more of the same. Second, social science may be guided predominantly by mechanistic conceptions of behavior assumed to be regular and predictable. Research fads can bloom when scientists are caught up in the minutia of theoretical details while overlooking the dynamics of larger contexts. Third, searches for generalized phenomena in organizations may spawn a fad of research that explains various contingencies of organizational behavior. When universal processes are not found, research interest tapers off. Lastly, social sciences' reliance on statistical methods such as a normal (Gaussian) distribution or null-hypothesis significance tests can falsely identify meaningful relationships, motivating more researchers to explore them. Starbuck concludes that these causes for research fads are difficult to change. It may take a concerted effort from journal editors, prominent scientists in the field, and evaluations of organizational science research by outsiders to minimize the frequency and intensity of research fads.

University Environment

A scientist's ability to conduct research can be influenced by a number of university features. Resources for research projects include facilities, infrastructure, equipment, personnel, and funds to support data collection, analysis, and dissemination of results. Universities also offer training programs, workshops and support services to help scientists find funding sources for their research, as well as help with grant proposals, statistical analyses, and writing support. The extent to which these resources are readily available can define boundaries for research projects. From a resource-based perspective (Barney, 1991), the extent to which these resources are valued, rare, and cannot be imitated or substituted would define a university's competitive advantage for getting future grants to support research.

Expectations for research productivity for tenure and promotion considerations can communicate how a department or college values or prioritizes research against other faculty obligations such as teaching and service. Taylor, Fender, and Burke (2006) surveyed 715 academic economists and found their research productivity was negatively related to both teaching and service loads. Conversely, the economists' research productivity was positively related to whether the university had a doctoral program in economics (vs. only a baccalaureate degree program), the extent to which there were peers who also published, and the availability of summer stipends. A study by Long and McGinnis (1981) classified 557 biochemists into five work contexts: faculty in research-oriented universities, faculty in teaching-oriented colleges, scientists in academic, governmental or industrial laboratories that encouraged publication, scientists in industrial laboratories that did not encourage publication, and research administration.

Controlling for research productivity prior to starting a job in an organization, and tracking subsequent research productivity over a nine-year period, Long and McGinnis found an individual's research productivity conformed to the organizational context. Not surprisingly, the number of publications was highest for faculty in research-oriented universities and scientists in laboratories that encouraged research and lowest for research administrators.

The effects of institutional characteristics on an individual's research productivity might be evidence for the idea that "the place makes the people." Particularly for early-career researchers, the university environment and a department's values and research culture can help shape an individual's identity as a researcher (Ajjawi, Crampton & Rees, 2018). Bland and Ruffin (1992) identified 12 organizational environment factors that were correlated with research productivity: (1) clear organizational goals that complement the individual researcher's personal goals, (2) priority on research productivity for promotion and tenure decisions, (3) shared values that promote a culture for research, (4) positive relationships and acceptance of group members, (5) participative leadership and participative governance, (6) flat and decentralized organizational structures, (7) good communications within the research team and with external colleagues, (8) access to physical and human resources that can support research, (9) research team size, age, and diversity, (10) valued rewards for research productivity, (11) selection and socialization of new, talented researchers, and (12) good leaders who serve as role models for research expertise, structure tasks, and develop positive relationships among team members. These 12 factors are interrelated, and the synergy among individual, organizational, and leadership characteristics contribute to an organizational culture that can encourage research.

As noted earlier, economic recessions have triggered substantial budget cuts and reductions in state allocations to public universities (State Higher Education Executive Officers Association, 2021). One particular trend among these universities is the reduction of tenure-track faculty, in favor of more part-time and full-time nontenure-track faculty who are hired primarily to teach. Kezar and Maxey (2014) note that the US professoriate has changed radically over the past 40 years, from one where tenure-track faculty predominate, to a current one where nontenure-track faculty make up over 70% of the professoriate. This change has increased the number of faculty members who are not research-active, potentially constraining the number of research-active colleagues who can work together. This change also creates a three-tier faculty system (tenure-track, full-time nontenure-track, and part-time nontenure-track) with different expectations and rewards for research productivity. The traditional emphasis on research may not be sustained with these changes (Kezar & Maxey, 2014).

The university environment directly affects how research productivity is valued, supported, and rewarded. Researchers located in psychology departments are more likely to be rewarded for research grants than faculty members in business schools. Furthermore, the various disciplines in organizational science can facilitate meetings and networks of researchers, across universities and countries, to share ideas that advance research. These meso- and micro-environments interact with macro-environments, resulting in a wide variety of opportunities for, and threats against, productive research. In order to minimize the threats, several recommendations are presented to encourage more research.

Recommendations to Improve Environments for Research

Recommendations are categorized by the type of environment that is most likely to be the primary catalyst to support them; however, all recommendations are influenced by multiple macro-, meso-, or micro-environments. Summaries of these recommendations are in Table 11.1.

Political Environment

The federal government is primarily responsible for much of the funded basic research in US colleges and universities. In order to maintain US dominance in science and technology, the American Academy of Arts & Sciences (2020) highly recommended that funding for federally supported basic research be expanded

TABLE 11.1 Recommendations for improving environments for organizational science

Primary environment	Recommendation
Political	• Increase federal funding for organizational science research • Restore state funding of universities
Economic	• Strengthen university – industry partnerships
Social	• Improve STEM education in K-12 schools to improve quality of students • Counteract misinformation the public may have on organizational practices with good research
Technological	• Better integrate new technologies that connect people with supportive social interactions • Revise human subjects and data protections when new technologies impact rights to privacy and data confidentiality
International	• Facilitate international experiences for US researchers • Retain US-trained international scientists
Professional	• Improve practices to support a robust and open science • Promote organizational science to multiple audiences
University	• Improve tenure and/or promotion process to support methodological rigor, open science, high-risk/high payoff research, and communication of organizational science to multiple audiences • Evaluate current structure of tenure-track and nontenure-track faculty to ensure a healthy population of research-oriented faculty

from the current 0.2% of GDP to 0.3% of GDP. Moreover, these increases should not be drawn from funding allocated to applied R&D. Factors that may inhibit increased funding efforts include the country's overall economic health and public support for science that could influence political motivations from the President and Congress. Increased funding for basic research can be encouraged by professional societies. For example, SIOP has been active in government advocacy efforts to support increased funding for programs related to research in industrial and organizational psychology (https://www.siop.org/About-SIOP/Advocacy/Government-Relations). These advocacy efforts help communicate the benefits of organizational science research to policy makers and federal funding agencies.

At the state level, restoring funding to public universities could reinvigorate research initiatives. Funding for public universities in 36 states have not yet recovered from Great Recession budget cuts. Compounding this problem, the COVID-19 pandemic in 2019–2021 has triggered more cuts in at least 27 states (Jackson & Saenz, 2021). Additional revenue may be generated from more aggressive taxes on the wealthy, from federal funds (e.g., American Rescue Plan Act, 2021; National SEAL Act, 2021), and from cost savings in faculty and staff reductions. Generating additional revenue from increases in tuition are not likely to be feasible under current economic conditions. Past tuition hikes have already increased the students' share of public university finances from 20.9% of total revenue in 1980 to 44.0% in 2020 (State Higher Education Executive Officers Association, 2021). Jackson and Saenz (2021) caution that many students and their families are unlikely to afford additional tuition increases, particularly for low-income students and underrepresented minority students. Significant increases for state support to public universities will depend on good economic trends and public support.

Economic Environment

University – industry partnerships have initiated many research projects with mixed success (Cyert & Goodman, 1997). These alliances should benefit from complementary resources, teaming university researchers with industry experts. However, the two organizations often have different goals, timeframes, and expected outcomes, that can lead to conflict and failure. When both partners value organizational learning, as opposed to an instrumental focus of what one partner can do for the other, team-based partnerships can be created to achieve common research project goals.

University – industry partnerships that are focused on social science can be initiated when all parties are brought together to build a strong network and explore partnership opportunities. This may be accomplished in professional conferences or in specialized workshops. For example, nonprofit organizations like the

University Industry Demonstration Partnership, MITRE, and the Consortium of Social Science Associations will hold workshops to bring together academic researchers, government representatives, and industry leaders interested in social sciences (https://bsos.umd.edu/academics-research/university-industry). These workshops are supported by NSF and represent another example of how political, economic, and university environments can work together to identify new opportunities for research in organizational science.

Although university – industry partnerships are more likely to emerge when economic conditions can support them, the relationships can be facilitated by non-research partnerships that may not require substantial funding. Partnerships such as educational programs, internships, and recruitment of university graduates can build a foundation for future research partnerships. Benefits from these partnerships may also influence how the public views both parties.

Social Environments

Organizational science often involves work behaviors and issues that most employed people encounter. However, research results may not be accepted when contradicted by personal anecdotal information (Hart et al., 2009). Human resource practices that are not support by evidence-based management are often implemented because practitioners prefer to believe in them (Lawler, 2007). For example, van der Zee, Bakker, and Bakker (2002) found human resources managers preferred to use unstructured interviews in personnel selection, despite compelling research evidence that finds structured interviews to be more valid. Another example may be the belief that decision-making algorithms eliminate human biases, despite evidence that data mining and machine learning can replicate unfair patterns against protected groups (Barocas & Selbst, 2016). Misinformation should be corrected by effective and persistent science communicators (Lewandowsky et al., 2012).

Lupia (2017) identified three recommendations for social scientists to increase the impact, and future opportunities, of their research. First, researchers need to increase their competence to communicate their work to practitioners, policy makers, and the general public. Effective communication includes making research results easily available to nonacademic audiences and using language that accommodates an audience's motivation and capacity to learn. Second, social science disciplines need to be committed to transparent practices in the presentation of science. Current practices of hiding null results (e.g., file-drawer problem) or of capitalizing on statistical findings (e.g., p-hacking) can create misleading conclusions. Incentives and rewards for researchers to fully describe research designs, share data, and replicate studies can mitigate publication biases and help communicate a more complete picture of what science has found and not found. Finally, researchers need to be aware of potential stakeholder needs.

If potential end-users or societal segments understand how social science can benefit them, support for future research can be strengthened. This recommendation transcends communication of specific research results noted in Lupia's first recommendation. It focuses on how social science can appeal to the values of various stakeholders at a higher level. A good understanding of how social science can benefit government, organizational decision makers, students, and the general public can increase each stakeholder's interest, acceptance, and advocacy for social science.

In a different context, future researchers need to be grounded with a good education in science. It is recommended that education in Science, Technology, Engineering, and Math (STEM) is improved in K-12 schools and more students are encouraged to major in STEM fields (American Academy of Arts & Sciences, 2020). The OECD's Programme for International Student Assessment (PISA) regularly tests 15-year-old students on reading, math, and science comprehension. In 2018, the percentage of American top-performing students in at least one of these subject areas was not significantly different from the OECD average. In contrast, 21 of the 78 participating countries and economies had significantly higher percentages of top-performing students, compared to the OECD average (OECD, 2019). The recommendation to improve STEM education in K-12 schools should better prepare students to pursue research-focused careers and also improve the US's position as a leader in knowledge creation.

Technological Environment

New technologies will always stimulate research projects designed to better understand how technology can and should be used to improve work and organizations. It is recommended that researchers in organizational science find better ways to partner with researchers in other fields, particularly in technology and engineering. This may be achieved by federal grant programs, such as NSF's Future of Work at the Human-Technology Frontier, that specifically calls for multidisciplinary research that integrates technological and social aspects of future work.

As researchers use new technologies to design studies, collect data, and analyze and share results, there may be new ethical concerns and protections for human subjects. Organizational surveillance of employee email, social media, and computer usage can conflict with an individual's right to privacy (Chory, Vela & Avtgis, 2016). Current technological tools make it easy to collect unobtrusive data on people without their consent. Furthermore, computer hacking can compromise confidential information, regardless of a researcher's data management plan (Elhai, Levine & Hall, 2016). For data coding and analyses, machine learning algorithms can perform these tasks with little oversight from researchers. It is recommended that researchers in organizational science take a proactive role in responsible research design with new technologies. It is also recommended that organizational science exercise voice in forming new policies regarding ethical human subjects protections, data integrity, and Institutional Review Board (IRB) standards. Researchers in biomedical and health research have already noted a growing trend for more technology-enabled research (Dunseath et al., 2018). This growth is likely to generate complementary federal regulations and IRB protocols that could generalize to research in organizational science.

International Environment

Given the increase in international research teams, researchers need to be effective in these teams. The number of international scientists who were trained in the US has steadily increased over the past 20 years (NSB, 2020). In 2017, about a third of all US doctorates and master's degrees were earned by international students, with the majority coming from China and India. However, Widener (2019) reported the number of applications from international graduate students recently declined about 4% across all fields and tighter restrictions on work visas and US immigration policy may deter many foreign-born scientists from remaining in the US. Furthermore, the competition for scientists has increased worldwide, with attractive opportunities outside the US. The American Academy of Arts and Sciences (2020) recommended that the number of work visas (H1-B) is doubled for scientists and that accommodations for their immediate families are made to facilitate their stay in the US. The Department of Homeland Security (DHS) also manages the Optional Practical Training (OPT) program that allows graduates in STEM fields to work in the US for up to three years before requiring a H1-B work visa (Rosenthal, 2021). However, at this time, disciplinary fields such as industrial-organizational psychology, organizational behavior, or sociology are not recognized as STEM fields by DHS.

Professional societies such as SIOP can help their international members who were trained in the US to begin their careers in the US. When I was President of SIOP (2020–2021), the organization engaged in efforts to have DHS recognize industrial–organizational psychology as a STEM field. This recognition may help international I-O graduates pursue research careers in the US. Although this recognition has not been achieved to date, it remains as an active goal for SIOP's federal outreach and advocacy. In a similar fashion, many business schools such as Harvard, Stanford, and Duke have designated specialized STEM tracks in the MBA program to attract more international students and to qualify their graduates for STEM-related work visas (Ethier, 2020). With some MBA programs recognized as STEM, it may be feasible for doctoral programs in organizational behavior, strategic management, and management science to also provide this distinction and advantage to their graduates.

Professional Environment

Recently, there has been renewed attention for scientists to make their research more transparent, open, and reproducible (Nosek et al., 2015). Grand et al., (2018) note two environmental trends that call for the current focus on open science. First, the research community is rapidly growing, resulting in an exponential growth of scientific publications. Publishing norms that favor unique, statistically significant, and innovative results create incentives for researchers to find such results as opposed to a more robust science that includes replication studies, null results, and more transparency (Nosek et al., 2015). Second, the research environment has become highly dynamic with new technologies, globalization, and multiple disciplines collaborating to produce research with greater impact on organizational practice and public policy. Current journal standards and research practices may not be able to accommodate the growth and complexity of the scientific enterprise; hence, new calls for open science have generated updated recommendations and standards such as the Center for Open Science's Transparency and Openness Promotion Guidelines (TOP; Nosek et al., 2015) and the American Psychological Association's Journal Article Reporting Standards (JARS; Appelbaum et al., 2018; Levitt et al., 2018). Grand et al. (2018) present 22 recommendations for 12 stakeholders to promote robust science in I-O psychology. The recommendations to improve open science practices will necessitate collaboration among researchers, journals and publications, universities and organizations, and professional associations to align incentives to publish with incentives to practice good science (Nosek, Spies & Motyl, 2012).

Professional societies can also help promote organizational science by offering workshops or tutorials to help members better communicate their research to external audiences. The recommendation to inform employees, managers, funding sources, and the general public on research in social sciences can help these stakeholders better understand the value of organizational science, to promote it to others for shared appreciation, and to encourage future research to address stakeholder needs (Lupia, 2017). Improved communication of organizational research can also be aided by university resources and rewards discussed in the next section.

University Environment

Most research-oriented universities with tenure systems typically evaluate their faculty on their research, teaching, and service, with heavy emphasis on research productivity. These universities may need to expand their tenure and promotion policies beyond publication counts in top-tier journals to include evaluation of a researcher's methodological rigor, sharing information in online repositories (Grimes, Bauch & Ioannidis, 2017), communicating research to potential beneficiaries or supporters, or pursuing high-risk/high-payoff research (Lupia, 2017). Furthermore, the pressure to publish should be qualified to publish research that truly advances science as opposed to publications that lacked scientific integrity or were only possible with unethical research practices (Martinson et al., 2009).

In addition to aligning research incentives with open science goals, it is recommended that the hiring practices for faculty be designed to nurture a healthy population of research-oriented faculty. The current trend for universities to hire more nontenure-track faculty should be evaluated against a broader view of the future of the professoriate and its impact on research and science. The three-tier system of tenure track, full-time nontenure-track, and part-time nontenure-track is not working (Kezar & Maxey, 2014). This system developed from reactions to economic, political, and social environments that were not coordinated or considered with any strategic planning. There is some evidence that business school faculty under a tenure-track system were more productive in their research, compared to faculty under a rolling three-year contract system, even when both systems had similar expectations for faculty research, teaching, and service (Allen & Sweeney, 2017). The right mix of tenure and nontenure track, or research focused and non-research focused faculty, remains to be determined.

Conclusion

Otto (2016) estimated that science will create more new knowledge in the next forty years, than what has been created in the entire past. This rapid growth is attributed to the growth in the number of scientists and engineers in the world and their ability to learn from, and collaborate with one another, virtually, and in-person. Like all other scientific disciplines, organizational science is influenced by the interactions of macro-, meso-, and micro-environments. These environments will adjust to the unprecedented growth of research productivity in a variety of ways that can encourage or undermine future research.

Several recommendations to improve environments for organizational science were presented. Their implementations will require actions from individuals, universities, organizations, professional societies, publication outlets, and governing bodies as different groups work together to achieve common goals related to an open and robust science. The recommendations are not quick and easy. They will require course corrections to current educational practices, university structures, publishing standards, and government policies that may be resistant to change.

Organizational science has already made profound contributions to the quality of work lives and the effectiveness of organizations. These benefits are directly tied to US economic growth, national security, and societal health. A common understanding and appreciation of these benefits are likely to nurture environments for future research in organizational science.

References

Aguilar, F. J. (1967). *Scanning the business environment*. New York: Macmillan.

Ajjawi, R., Crampton, P. E. S., & Rees, C. E. (2018). What really matters for successful research environments? A realist synthesis. *Medical Education, 52*, 936–950.

Allen, M. T., & Sweeney, C. A. (2017). Faculty research productivity under alternative appointment types: Tenure vs non-tenure track. *Managerial Finance, 43*(12), 1348–1357.

American Academy of Arts & Sciences. (2020). The perils of complacence. America at a tipping point in science & engineering. Retrieved May 14, 2021, from https://www.amacad.org/publication/perils-of-complacency.

American Association for the Advancement of Science. (2020). Historical trends in Federal R&D. Retrieved June 3, 2021, from https://www.aaas.org/programs/r-d-budget-and-policy/historical-trends-federal-rd

American Rescue Plan Act, H.R. 1319, 117th Congress. (2021). https://www.congress.gov/117/bills/hr1319/BILLS-117hr1319enr.pdf

Appelbaum, M., Cooper, H., Kline, R. B., Mayo-Wilson, E., Nezu, A. M., Rao, S. M. (2018). Journal article reporting standards for quantitative research in psychology: The APA publications and communications board task force report. *American Psychologist, 73*(1), 3–25.

Arakawa, Y. (2019). Sensing and changing human behavior for workplace wellness. *Journal of Information Processing, 27*, 614–623.

Bailey, D., Faraj, S., Hinds, P., von Krogh, G., & Leonardi, P. (2019). Special issue of organization science: Emerging technologies and organizing. *Organization Science, 30*(3), 642–646.

Barney, J. (1991). Firm resources and sustained competitive advantage. *Journal of Management, 17*(1), 99–120.

Barocas, S., & Selbst, A. D. (2016). Big data's disparate impact. *California Law Review, 104*, 671–732.

Binz-Scharf, M. C., Kalish, Y., & Paik, L. (2015). Making science: New generations of collaborative knowledge production. *American Behavioral Scientist, 59*(5), 531–547.

Bland, C. J., & Ruffin, M. T. (1992). Characteristics of a productive Research Environment: Literature review. *Academic Medicine, 67*(6), 385–397.

Börner, K., Contractor, N., Falk-Krzesinski, H. J., Fiore, S. M., Hall, K. L., Keyton, J., Spring, B., Stokols, D., Trochim, W., & Uzzi, B. (2010). A multi-level systems perspective for the science of team science. *Science Translational Medicine, 2*(49), 49cm24.

Brown, J. (2016, February 24). The percentage of women as full-time faculty at U.S. Business School: Surging ahead, lagging behind or stalling out? *AACSB*. Retrieved June 9, 2021, from https://aacsbblogs.typepad.com/dataandresearch/2016/02/the-percentage-of-women-as-full-time-faculty-at-us-business-schools-surging-ahead-lagging-behind-or-.html

Chory, R. M., Vela, L. E., & Avtgis, T. A. (2016). Organizational surveillance of computer-mediated workplace communication: Employee privacy concerns and responses. *Employee Responsibilities & Rights Journal, 28*, 23–43.

Coronavirus Aid, Relief, and Economic Security (CARES) Act. H.R. 748, 116th Congress (2020). https://www.congress.gov/116/bills/hr748/BILLS-116hr748enr.pdf

Cyert, R. M., & Goodman, P. S. (1997). Creating effective university-industry alliances: An organizational learning perspective. *Organizational Dynamics, 25*(4), 45–57.

Diep, F. (2018, March 19). Why did the National Science Foundation propose slashing its own social science budget? Retrieved June 15, 2021, from https://psmag.com/news/national-science-foundation-social-science-budget

Decot, C. N. (2020, December 28). Federal court issues nationwide order enjoining enforcement of Trump executive order on diversity training. Retrieved June 10, 2021, from https://www.natlawreview.com/article/federal-court-issues-nationwide-order-enjoining-enforcement-trump-executive-order

Dunseath, S., Weibel, N., Bloss, C., & Nebeker, C. (2018). NIH support of mobile, imaging, pervasive sensing, social media and location tracking (MISST) research: Laying the foundation to examine research ethics in the digital age. *Digital Medicine, 1*, 20171. https://doi.org/10.1038/s41746-017-0001-5

Elhai, J. D., Levine, J. C., & Hall, B. J. (2016). Anxiety about electronic data hacking: Predictors and relations with digital privacy protection behavior. *Internet Research, 27*(3), 631–649.

Endless Frontier Act, S.1260, 117th Congress. (2021). https://www.congress.gov/bill/117th-congress/senate-bill/1260

Ethier, M. (2020). All the STEM programs at major U.S. business schools. *Poets & Quants*, retrieved June 28, 2021, from https://poetsandquants.com/2020/04/20/all-the-stem-programs-at-major-u-s-business-schools/

Grand, J. A., Braun, M. T., Kuljanin, G., Kozlowski, S. W. J., & Chao, G. T. (2016). The dynamics of team cognition: A process-oriented theory of knowledge emergence in teams [monograph]. *Journal of Applied Psychology, 101*(10), 1353–1385.

Grand, J. A., Rogelberg, S. G., Allen, T. D., Landis, R. S., Reynolds, D. H., Scott, J. C., Tonidandel, S., & Truxillo, D. M. (2018). A systems-based approach to fostering robust science in industrial-organizational psychology. *Industrial and Organizational Psychology, 11*(1), 4–42.

Grimes, D. R., Bauch, C. T., & Ioannidis J. P. A. (2017). Modelling science trustworthiness under publish or perish pressure. *Royal Society Open Science, 5*, 171511. http://dx.doi.org/10.1098/rsos.171511

Guest, O., & Martin, A. E. (2021). How computational modeling can force theory building in psychological science. *Perspectives on Psychological Science*. https://doi.org/10.1177/1745691620970585

Hart, W., Albarracín, D., Eagly, A. H., Brechan, I., Lindberg, M. J., & Merrill, L. (2009). Feeling validated versus being correct: A meta-analysis of selective exposure to information. *Psychological Bulletin, 135*(4), 555–588.

Hesli, V. L., & Lee, J. M. (2011). Faculty research productivity: Why do some of our colleagues publish more than others? *Political Science, 44*, 393–408.

Hotez, P. J. (2020). Combating antiscience: Are we preparing for the 2020s? *PLoS Biol* 18(3): e3000683. https://doi.org/10.1371/journal.pbio.3000683

Hsiehchen, D., Espinoza, M., & Hsieh, A. (2015). Multinational teams and diseconomies of scale in collaborative research. *Science Advances, 1*(8), e1500211. https://advances.sciencemag.org/content/1/8/e1500211?intcmp=trendmd-adv

Jackson, V., & Saenz, M. (2021). States can choose better path for higher education funding in COVID-19 recession. Retrieved June 22, 2021, from: https://www.cbpp.org/sites/default/files/2-17-21sfp.pdf

Kezar, A., & Maxey, D. (2014). Understanding key stakeholder belief systems or institutional logics related to non-tenure-track faculty and the changing professoriate. *Teachers College Record, 116*, 1–42.

Kinney, A. J., Krebbers, E., & Vollmer, S. J. (2004). Publications from industry. Personal and corporate incentives. *Plant Physiology, 134*, 11–15.

Lawler, E. E., III. (2007). Why HR practices are not evidence-based. *Academy of Management Journal, 50*(5), 1033–1036.

Levitt, H. M., Bamberg, M., Creswell, J. W., Frost, D. M. Josselsomm, R., & Suárez-Orozco, C. (2018). Journal article reporting standards for qualitative primary, qualitative meta-analytic, and mixed methods research in psychology: The APA publications and communications board task force report. *American Psychologist, 73*(1), 26–46.

Lewandowsky, S., Ecker, U. K. H., Seifert, C. M., Schwarz, N., & Cook, J. (2012). Misinformation and its correction: Continued influence and successful debiasing. *Psychological Science in the Public Interest, 13*(3), 106–131.

Long, J. S., & McGinnis, R. (1981). Organizational context and scientific productivity. *American Sociological Review, 46*(4), 422–442.

Lupia, A. (2017). Now is the time: How to increase the value of social science. *Social Research: An International Quarterly, 84*(3), 669–694.

Martinson, B. C., Crain, A. L., Anderson, M. S., & De Vries, R. (2009). Institutions' expectations for researchers' self-funding, Federal grant holding and private industry involvement: Manifold drivers of self-interest and researcher behavior. *Academic Medicine, 84*(11), 1491–1499.

Maurer, T. (2016). *Unique challenges and opportunities for business schools in pursuing federal research grants.* NSF Workshop Report for Grant # 1545303. Georgia State University.

Matthews, D. (2014, November 12). Why congressional republicans want to cut social science research funding. Retrieved May 24, 2021, from https://www.vox.com/2014/11/12/7201487/congress-social-science-nsf-funding

Milliman, J., & von Glinow M. A. (1998a). Research and publishing issues in large scale cross-national studies. *Journal of Managerial Psychology, 13*(3/4), 137–142.

Milliman, J., & von Glinow M. A. (1998b). The academic international research team: Small world after all. *Journal of Managerial Psychology, 13*(3/4), 150–155.

Moran, J. P. (2021). *The Scopes trial: A brief history with documents* (2nd ed.). Boston, MA: Bedford/St. Martin's.

Nason, S. W., & Pillutla, M. M. (1998). Towards a model of international research teams. *Journal of Managerial Psychology, 13*(3/4), 156–166.

National Academies of Sciences Engineering & Medicine (NASEM). (2017). The value of social, behavioral, and economic sciences to national priorities: A report for the National Science Foundation. Retrieved April 25, 2021, from http://nap.edu/24790.g

National Science Board. (2020). Foreign-born students and workers in the U.S. science and engineering enterprise. Retrieved June 28, 2021, from https://www.nsf.gov/nsb/sei/one-pagers/Foreign-Born.pdf

National Science Foundation. (n.d.a) *About the National Science Foundation.* Retrieved June 2, 2021, from https://www.nsf.gov/about/

National Science Foundation. (n.d.b) *Science of Organizations.* Retrieved June 2, 2021, from https://www.nsf.gov/funding/pgm_summ.jsp?pims_id=504696

National SEAL Act, S. 1213, 117th Congress. (2021). https://www.congress.gov/bill/117th-congress/senate-bill/1213

Nosek, B. A., Alter, G., Banks, G. C., Borsboom, D., Bowman, S. D., Breckler, S. J., ... Yarkoni, T. (2015). Promoting an open research culture. *Science, 348*, 1422–1425.

Nosek, B. A., Spies, J. R., & Motyl, M. (2012). Scientific utopia: II. Restructuring incentives and practices to promote truth over publishability. *Perspectives on Psychological Science, 7*(6), 615–631.

OECD. (2019). PISA 2018 results. Combined executive summaries. Retrieved June 28, 2021, from https://www.oecd.org/pisa/Combined_Executive_Summaries_PISA_2018.pdf

Otto, S. (2016). *The war on science. Who's waging it, why it matters, what we can do about it.* Minneapolis, MN: Milkweed Editions.

PhD Project. (n.d.) Milestones & achievements. Retrieved June 9, 2021, from https://www.phdproject.org/our-success/milestones-achievements/

Porter, A. L., & Rafols, I. (2009). Is science becoming more interdisciplinary? Measuring and mapping six research fields over time. *Scientometrics, 81*(3), 719–745.

Richardson, I. (2021, April 28). Iowa senate republicans approve limits on diversity trainings; democrat fears bill targets 1619 Project. Retrieved May 20, 2021, from https://www.desmoinesregister.com/story/news/politics/2021/04/28/iowa-senate-diversity-training-bill-banning-concepts-1619-project-sen-herman-quirmbach/4863185001/

Rosenthal, R. (2021, March 10). The STEM graduate system is broken. Here's how to fix it. Retrieved June 29, 2021, from https://www.bloomberg.com/graphics/2021-opinion-optional-practical-training-problems-stem-graduates-deserve-better-jobs-opportunities/

Rozsa, M. (2021). "Persona" argues convincingly that it's time to cancel personality tests. Retrieved June 8, 2021, from https://www.salon.com/2021/03/15/persona-argues-convincingly-that-its-time-to-cancel-personality-tests/

Sammut-Bonnici, T., & Galea, D. (2015). PEST analysis. In C. Cooper (Ed.), *Wiley encyclopedia of management, 12.* Retrieved April 20, 2021, from https://www.researchgate.net/publication/257303449_PEST_analysis

SIOP. (2021, April 6). HBO Max documentary on personality tests fails: SIOP responds. Retrieved June 8, 2021, from https://www.siop.org/Portals/84/PDFs/SIOP%20Response%20to%20HBO%20Max%20Persona%20Film.pdf?ver=NJZrkm6P5SK4KM142FC6Hw%3d%3d

Stahl, G. K., & Maznevski, M. L. (2021). Unraveling the effects of cultural diversity in teams: A retrospective of research on multicultural work groups and an agenda for future research. *Journal of International Business Studies, 52*, 4–22.

Stahl, G. K., Maznevski, M. L., Voigt, A., & Jonsen, K. (2010). Unraveling the effects of cultural diversity in teams: A meta-analysis of research on multicultural work groups. *Journal of International Business Studies, 41*, 690–709.

Starbuck, W. H. (2009). The constant causes of never-ending faddishness in the behavioral and social sciences. *Scandinavian Journal of Management, 25*, 108–116.

State Higher Education Executive Officers Association. (2021). *State Higher Education Finance: FY 2020.* Retrieved June 6, 2021, from https://shef.sheeo.org/wp-content/uploads/2021/05/SHEEO_SHEF_FY20_Report.pdf

Stokols, D., Hall, K. L., Taylor, B. K., & Moser, R. P. (2009). The science of team science: Overview of the field and introduction to the supplement. *American Journal of Preventive Medicine, 35*(2S), S77–S89.

Taylor, S. W., Fender, B. F., & Burke, K. G. (2006). Unraveling the academic productivity of economists: The opportunity costs of teaching and service. *Southern Economic Journal, 72*(4), 846–859.

van der Zee, K. I., Bakker, A. B., & Bakker, P. (2002). Why are structured interviews so rarely used in personnel selection? *Journal of Applied Psychology, 87*(1), 176–184.

Widener, A. (2019). Science in the US is built on immigrants. Will they keep coming? *Chemical & Engineering News, 97*(9), 35–40.

Wolfe, R. M., National Center for Science and Engineering Statistics. (2020). *U.S. businesses reported $441 billion for R&D performance in the United States during 2018, a 10.2% increase from 2017*. NSF 20-316. Alexandria, VA: National Science Foundation. Available at https://ncses.nsf.gov/pubs/nsf20316

Working Group on Science and Technology in US – China Relations. (2020). Meeting the China challenge: A new American strategy for technology competition. Retrieved June 2, 2021, from https://www.chinafile.com/library/reports/meeting-china-challenge-new-american-strategy-technology-competition

Wuchty, S., Jones, B. F., & Uzzi, B. (2007). The increasing dominance of teams in production of knowledge. *Science, 316*(5827), 1036–1039.

Zanatta, A., Zampieri, F., Basso, C., & Thiene, G. (2017). Galileo Galilei: Science vs. faith. *Global Cardiology Science and Practice*. Retrieved June 8, 2021, from http://dx.doi.org/10.21542/gcsp.2017.10

12

TRAINING (AND RETRAINING) IN DATA, METHODS, AND THEORY IN THE ORGANIZATIONAL SCIENCES

Frederick L. Oswald, Felix Y. Wu, and Karyssa A. Courey

Most I-O psychologists would agree that over its decades of maturity, organizational research has become increasingly complex in virtually all areas of data, methods, and theory. In terms of *data*, organizations produce an abundance of data – big data, even (McAbee, Landis & Burke, 2017; Oswald et al., 2020; Ryan & Herleman, 2015; Wenzel & Van Quaquebeke, 2018). Large and complex datasets are emerging in organizations as a function of sophisticated technologies for recording and storing data (e.g., social media scraping, logging website activities, recording employee card swipes, processing audio and video surveillance data, capturing the nature and timing of customer transactions), and I-O psychologists are scrambling to learn new methods of handling and analyzing these data. Therefore, in terms of *methods*, I-O psychologists are increasingly receiving training in areas new to the field, such as network analysis, Bayesian analysis, and machine learning, building on their traditional statistical foundations to better summarize and understand new sources of data. Overarching these areas of data and methods is *theory*, a term that is rife with surplus meaning, but is intended in this chapter to reflect any useful framework or rationale that informs how data are collected, analyzed, and interpreted. In other words, theory is intended to be a guide or a tool as a means to an end, not an intellectual end merely unto itself (Campbell & Wilmot, 2018). These three areas of data, methods, and theory are mutually informative; Figure 12.1 shows a simple Venn diagram to illustrate the point and let us also consider multilevel modeling as a prime example of these interrelationships in organizational research.

DOI: 10.4324/9781003015000-16

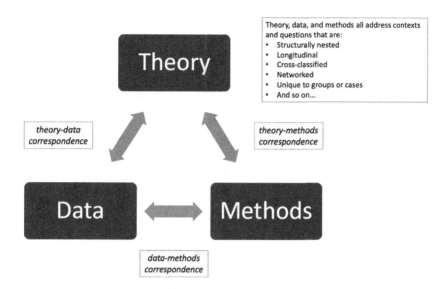

FIGURE 12.1 Correspondence between data, methods, and theory in I-O psychology.

Multilevel Modeling: Where Data, Methods, and Theory Have Come Together

The organizational data that I-O psychologists often collect are inherently multilevel in nature (e.g., time points within employees, employees within teams, teams within organizations). This type of data creates both challenges and opportunities for organizational researchers; the nesting of people within teams or organizations makes it possible to ask questions about individual and organizational effects and their interrelationships. The analysis of multilevel models and the interpretation of the results of these analyses can be complex, but there are potential payoffs that go well beyond the usual statistical rationale for these models (e.g., that the nesting of people within organizations or teams can distort error terms in regression analyses that ignore this nesting; Bliese & Hanges, 2004). Multilevel models ask researchers to consider questions that are at the heart of the organizational sciences, particularly how individual and organizational level factors influence behavior in complex organizational systems. Ignoring multilevel data structures inherent in a dataset (e.g., in visualization and machine learning, let alone ordinary least square [OLS] regression) might sacrifice interpretative value.

I-O psychologists have offered deep insights that address multilevel effects in the workplace, such as whether group- or team-level effects are due to environmental characteristics, aggregated group member effects, or some emergent combination or interaction of unique group member effects (e.g., see Chan, 1998; Kozlowski & Klein, 2000). In turn, group-level effects surely affect individual employees, such as when managers provide task-based and interpersonal guidance to their direct reports. At roughly the same rate that multilevel theories have matured, multilevel modeling as a statistical method has also matured in I-O psychology, with its early influence coming from educational psychology (e.g., Bryk & Raudenbush, 1992), then migrating over to I-O psychology (e.g., Hofmann, 1997), and today, multilevel analyses are omnipresent in virtually every well-known organizational psychology journal.

As a basic motivating example of a multilevel statistical analysis in organizations, consider the relationship between conscientiousness and job performance. We know that there is often a positive relationship between the two; yet how might this relationship vary across a large number of groups? This question has been addressed in various ways in the I-O psychology literature to date (e.g., see Liao & Chuang, 2004; Wallace & Chen, 2006; Yeo & Neal, 2004, for well-known examples) Let us say that we want to examine this relationship across numerous departments within an organization (many more than the small handful of departments that would be examined in an ANOVA). If the same type of data was collected across departments, then a multilevel regression analysis might proceed in increasing stages of complexity to determine whether (a) the same regression line best characterizes all departments, (b) slopes are the same but regression intercepts vary, (c) slopes are different (i.e., variance in the slopes across settings is nonzero after sampling error variance is accounted for), and then (d) intercept and slope differences are accounted for by departmental factors (e.g., differences in managerial styles and/or organizational cultures). A major reason such a wide range of organizational multilevel analyses are being conducted these days, in addition to compelling multilevel theory and available data, is the availability and accessibility of multilevel software and resources that are now widely used and discussed by the I-O psychology research community. For example, the R package multilevel (Bliese, 2016) is free to download and use; it contains extensive documentation and datasets relevant to organizations; and example code is provided that can be applied to these datasets, so that researchers and practitioners alike can learn through hands-on experience.

Thus, the growth and use of multilevel modeling in I-O psychology – due to the maturing and mutual influence of available data, methods, and theory (per Figure 12.1) – can teach us broader lessons about how other types of useful statistical analyses might be incorporated into the repertoire of current and future I-O psychologists. To that end, the next sections will discuss the prospects for Bayesian analyses and machine learning in I-O psychology research.

Bayesian Analysis: The Data and Theory Are Here, So Why Not the Method?

Bayesian methods have a 250-year history, but it is increased computing power that created a "Bayesian revolution," allowing researchers to investigate and make inferences about all sorts of models, both simple and complex. In I-O psychology and organizational research, however, Bayesian analysis has barely made a presence, despite several informative appeals to consider doing so (e.g., Kruschke, Aguinis & Joo, 2012; Krackhardt, Schwab & Starbuck, 2020; Zyphur & Oswald, 2015). Today, Bayesian software packages have become more freely accessible and usable (e.g., JASP Team, 2020) – so let us try again here, and outline several reasons why Bayesian analyses have their appeal over traditional frequentist analyses that you are used to conducting (e.g., null hypothesis significance testing [NHST]). In doing so, we hope you will appreciate how data, method, and theory can usefully come together under a Bayesian framework.

First and foremost, Bayesian results tend to have a much more natural interpretation that is consistent with its underlying mathematics. For example, in a Bayesian analysis, a statistical estimate (e.g., a correlation, a mean difference) has an associated 95% *credibility interval* (CrI), where it is both reasonable and completely accurate to say "there is a 95% chance that the true effect falls within this range." Such a statement would receive failing marks in the traditional frequentist paradigm, because a 95% *confidence interval* (CI) leads to statements such as, "95% of intervals created in this manner will contain the parameter of interest." These two statements are not merely different; the Bayesian statement is much less awkwardly worded, and much more aligned with the conclusions that researchers and practitioners actually want to reach in their work. In fact, whenever social scientists misinterpret traditional confidence intervals (and they usually do), they are often unknowingly using the language of Bayesian credibility intervals (Hoekstra et al., 2014), rather than the more convoluted language of the traditional frequentist approach! Although Bayesian approaches might seem complicated to new users, the natural and intuitive interpretation of Bayesian results makes these analyses easier to understand and easier to communicate to others. Although no statistical paradigm or model is perfect, the statement of Bayesian conclusion seems to strike a better balance between being more honest to the technical aspects of the analysis, while also more directly addressing organizational research questions of interest.

Second, Bayesian analyses have the option of formally incorporating prior knowledge into your analyses (base rates), whereas traditional frequentist analyses typically do not. For example, when I-O psychologists develop studies or projects involving the measurement of conscientiousness and job performance, they might do so because meta-analyses have found relatively consistent support for a positive correlation between these variables (e.g., Barrick & Mount, 1991;

Dudley et al., 2006). Meta-analytic results can provide an empirical range of relevant parameter estimates that are expected, versus those that would be highly unusual (Bosco et al., 2015). This prior information is known to the researcher, but in traditional analyses, meta-analytic results are not formally included in the model; it is effectively ignored. In Bayesian analyses, meta-analytic results can be explicitly incorporated into the Bayesian prior, which then is mathematically combined with the results from the study data (i.e., as a likelihood, using Bayes Theorem) to produce the final study results that balance the two (in the form of a posterior distribution).

You can think of the Bayesian prior as a representation of what you knew about the conscientiousness-performance relationship before you started analyzing data from your own study. It was not nothing. Researchers almost always have at least some ideas about the strength and nature of the effects they are studying before they even collect data for their own studies, and Bayesian analyses allow them to incorporate this knowledge formally into their analyses. Conceptually, this approach is useful because when a particular study reports an unusual finding (e.g., if conscientiousness was negatively correlated with job performance), then in the Bayesian framework, that study must also come with a great deal of data associated with that finding to challenge or override all prior knowledge that has accumulated. In other words, extraordinary claims require extraordinary evidence (as attributed to astronomer Carl Sagan; see Kaufman, 2011, p. 124). Alternatively, a Bayesian analysis can specify default priors that contain very little information, meaning that data and resulting statistics are essentially allowed to speak for themselves (similar to the frequentist approach, yet with a more intuitive interpretation of results, as noted above). Of course, prior information should neither be overweighted nor underweighted, and Bayes Theorem provides the appropriate calibration.

Third, Bayes Factors (BF) can be used as an effective alternative to p-values. In short, BF reflect how much the data is supported by one model relative to another being compared (e.g., null vs. alternative hypothesis). Practically speaking, Bayesian analyses often yield similar outcomes to traditional hypothesis tests. For example, Wetzels et al. (2011) reanalyzed 855 t-tests and compared p-values versus BF, finding that the two were highly correlated, but also that the BF approach was generally more conservative in concluding the presence of an effect. Overall, the Bayesian approach is favored here because, it carries all the other advantages listed, and the BF tend to be more flexible in making model comparisons. Any summary statistic to which cutoffs can be applied – p-value, BF, or confidence intervals – runs the risk of oversimplifying the statistical problem and underemphasizing the critical need to investigate a research problem from multiple perspectives and sources of information (McShane et al., 2019). By focusing on the strength of evidence in favor of alternative explanations rather than the significant-not significant dichotomy, Bayesian analyses bring more information and better information to bear in making decisions about what the data means.

Fourth, a Bayesian analysis allows the researcher to gather evidence in support of the null hypothesis directly. This stands in contrast with traditional NHST where you cannot technically support the null hypothesis but (awkwardly) you can only conclude that you failed to reject it. That said, there exist frequentist solutions that test whether the smallest effect size of interest is both statistically and practically significant (Lakens, Scheel & Isager, 2018). A very practical solution is found in an integrative framework for power and significance tests for minimal effects has been developed (Murphy, Myors & Wolach, 2014) that incorporates traditional F tests and all related tests used for evaluating the significance of correlations, comparisons among groups, regressions and other applications of the general linear model (GLM). Related to this work, recent organizational simulations have compared frequentist and Bayesian attempts to support the null hypothesis (Stanton, 2021). Currently, the Bayesian approach seems to more naturally approach how evidential weight favoring the null hypothesis can best be assessed and communicated.

Fifth, Bayesian analyses generally do not require statistical corrections for family-wise error when making subgroup estimates (e.g., in a Bayesian ANOVA, Bayesian multilevel models). Instead, Bayesian analysis borrows strength from the overall estimate whenever subgroups are small. This borrowing strength tends to shrink parameter estimates to prevent overfitting, which also makes significance tests appropriately more stringent (thus, no need to control for multiple testing; Gelman, Hill & Yajima, 2012).

And if all these points supporting Bayesian analyses were not compelling enough to I-O psychologists, there are even more. For example, Bayesian analyses can kick-start the estimation of complex models that cannot be run in traditional approaches, by incorporating reasonable Bayesian priors. Many excellent and current Bayesian resources are available in terms of tutorials (e.g., McElreath, 2020) and reporting standards (e.g., DePaoli & van de Schoot, 2017; Kruschke, 2021; van de Schoot, 2021). Furthermore, I-O psychologists can learn from substantive examples of Bayesian analyses that are increasingly appearing across areas of organizational research (e.g., goal setting, Ballard, Vancouver & Neal, 2018; personality and turnover, Woo et al., 2016; training, Grand, 2017; assessment centers, Jackson et al., 2016). Although traditional null hypothesis significance testing has been criticized for decades, its disfavor only continues to grow (Amrhein, Greenland & McShane, 2019; Wasserstein & Lazar, 2016; Wasserstein, Schirm & Lazar, 2019); Although not without its own set of statistical assumptions, the Bayesian approach directly addresses many of the shortcomings of significance testing of the sort so commonly found in current organizational research.

Machine Learning: The Excitement of (Big) Data and Methods ... but No Theory?

The traditional and Bayesian statistical models covered up to this point are strongly model-driven. Even when an analytic approach is exploratory, an underlying model is usually driving the exploration. For example, a basic exploratory factor analysis (EFA) usually assumes that all variables will load to varying degrees on the factors that are extracted, that factor scores are uncorrelated with the variables' unique (error) variances, and these unique variances are themselves uncorrelated with each other (DeVellis, 2016). In contrast with a strong model-driven approach, the algorithms underlying machine learning approaches are much more flexible and seek to *mine* the data for relationships that exist, meaning that these methods often do not restrict themselves to linearity or even the types of nonlinearities that we commonly examine in I-O psychology (e.g., interactions and quadratic effects).

Generally speaking, machine learning attempts to search large and varied datasets for complex relationships wherever they exist (to avoid underfitting the data), yet *cross-validate* those relationships in independent samples (to avoid overfitting the data). In an excellent example and tutorial from I-O psychology, Putka, Beatty & Reeder (2018) used 83 biodata items to predict job performance in a large US Army sample ($N = 9,257$). Six different machine learning algorithms were implemented; they largely outperformed traditional OLS regression analysis at the item level, yet at the level of 12 scale composites, prediction was similar (and lower). The predictive benefits of machine learning, like those found here, depend on the nature of the prediction problem, the variables and measures involved, where the predictive superiority of machine learning is often an advantage but obviously not always a guarantee (e.g., see Allen, Affourtit & Reddock, 2020).

Literally hundreds of machine learning algorithms are available, and the number seems to be growing by the day (see https://cran.r-project.org/web/views/MachineLearning.html). Roughly speaking, machine learning algorithms can be divided into *supervised methods,* where prediction of an organizational outcome is accomplished via their relationships with a large number of predictors, and *unsupervised methods*, where the goal is to cluster people based on profile similarities across a large number of variables, without any outcome to be predicted (hence, the term unsupervised; Bouveyron et al., 2019). Both supervised and unsupervised methods have their traditional counterparts, such as multiple regression and k-means clustering, respectively. But the additional *potential* benefits of mining organizational data for greater complexity are found in machine learning (Oswald & Putka, 2016).

To explain one popular machine learning method (also used in the Putka et al., 2018, example above), consider the *random forests* algorithm (Breiman, 2001), and although the technical details would be distracting in this chapter (e.g., see James et al., 2021, for those), the general description is worth making here. Random forests are made of a large number of *decision trees* (say 1,000 of them). One predictor is selected and gets situated at the top node of the tree, and a cutoff is created, so that people higher than the cutoff travel down one branch of the tree toward one node, and people lower than the cutoff travel down the other branch toward a different node. Then, at these new nodes, other predictors are selected, each with their own separate cutoffs. This process keeps repeating until the specified depth of the tree is reached (e.g., 4 layers).

Importantly, at each node of the tree just described, only a small random sample of the available predictors is considered. This restriction forces each decision tree to make diverse predictions (after all, if they made the same prediction, one would only need one decision tree). The one predictor that is chosen for a given node, out of the set of candidates available, is the one that maximizes the mean difference (creates the largest Cohen's *d*) on the outcome between those above vs. below a cutoff, where any cutoff is allowed to be used. Hundreds of decision trees of this nature are generated, thus creating the random forest, where out-of-sample predictions are then made across these hundreds of trees and then averaged. This creates a wisdom-of-the-crowds (or trees) approach, where no one tree dominates, but rather they all contribute to prediction together. All decision trees in a random forest are set to be similar in terms of the number of variables considered at each node (e.g., the square root of the number of variables), the depth of the tree (e.g., a shallow tree, such as 3–5 levels), and the number of trees generated (e.g., several hundred). Several different random forests can be generated by varying these *hyperparameters*, ultimately choosing the random forest that maximizes out-of-sample prediction.

A few general lessons can be learned from this and other machine learning approaches. First, the number of variables can far exceed the number of cases, thus addressing the "$p \gg N$ problem" of big data (also called the "curse of dimensionality," Domingos, 2012). Note that traditional OLS linear regressions simply cannot be conducted when this problem is encountered (namely, the covariance matrix of predictors will simply not invert). This makes big data methods almost essential for prediction problems to proceed, without reducing the number of variables in some way (e.g., via item composites; so-called feature engineering that combines data that are not items; or dimension reduction such as principal components analysis). Second, it is hopefully appreciated how random forests model an immense amount of complexity: each decision tree represents a type of interaction, and then out-of-sample predictions based on these interactions are then averaged across the random forest comprising a large number of these trees. Arguably, this mining for complexity, while cross-validating any complexity that is detected, is why random forests often outperform traditional linear regression models in terms of prediction.

Third, perhaps the most important and obvious point to keep in mind is that improvements in prediction via machine learning are not the same as improvements in understanding. Random forests (the model) may well improve prediction (the data), but without the researcher knowing exactly why it is doing so (the theory). We might want to know which variables were responsible for good prediction, in what combination across the decision trees, for which people in the dataset, but that is often not the point of machine learning. The point is that it is all of these things in combination; attempting to disentangle them is to take away the benefits of machine learning. Note that psychometric methods and experimental designs have each been developed in psychology *precisely* in the attempt to disentangle (a) construct-relevant phenomena that we would like to understand and predict (e.g., job knowledge, job satisfaction, training effectiveness, and other organizational phenomena) from (b) construct-irrelevant sources of error that we would like to minimize and/or statistically account for (e.g., as social desirability, anxiety, or unnecessary vision or language requirements when taking a test). With their statistical knowledge of psychometrics and their substantive knowledge about the workforce, I-O psychologists provide essential expertise in teasing apart construct-relevant variance from construct-irrelevant variance or bias, thus serving as an important input (and occasional antidote) to machine learning and big data approaches.

With their potential limitations in mind, machine learning stands in the service of effective prediction or clustering in complex and messy datasets, dealing with a combination of data, analyses, and solutions that might be literally impossible to address via traditional statistical methods. Traditional statistical and psychometric approaches lean toward interpretability, but they are becoming increasingly complex and dynamic in ways that have been noted above and in other new ways (e.g., multilevel modeling with streaming data for prediction, Ippel et al., 2019; network psychometrics for clustering, Epskamp, Rhemtulla & Borsboom, 2017). Conversely, machine learning leans toward complexity, yet some algorithms provide more interpretability than others (e.g., lasso regression provides coefficients for the predictors chosen). But on this latter point, the fact that "explainable" and "interpretable" machine learning and AI are very popular topics suggests the typical opaqueness of the algorithms (Molnar, Casalicchio & Bischl, 2020).

Algorithmic bias is a pressing topic that is tied to this opaqueness because machine learning algorithms may discriminate quickly and on a large scale, and without knowing why that is the case, one cannot isolate and address the source of bias. Interpretable statistical approaches therefore help address algorithmic bias, as does understanding organizational data and context based on one's professional, legal, and ethical knowledge, as found in professional standards for I-O psychology (Society for Industrial and Organizational Psychology, 2018; Tippins, Oswald & McPhail, 2021). Merely predicting organizational outcomes effectively for its own sake – without understanding relationships between relevant data, methods, and theory – is clearly to be avoided. Thus, there are vast opportunities for partnerships between I-O psychology and the machine learning and AI communities, and those partnerships are now starting to emerge.

It is worth noting in this context that I-O researchers and practitioners have long been analyzing data to examine differences between job-relevant subgroupings (e.g., job type), job-irrelevant subgroupings (e.g., demographics), and subgroupings whose differences might be relevant and/or irrelevant (e.g., multisource data from supervisors, peers, and subordinates). Typically, they will use methods such as differential prediction, measurement invariance, and multitrait-multimethod matrices (e.g., see Nye et al., 2020, for differential prediction; Feeney et al., 2020, for measurement invariance; and for an interesting machine learning application that incorporates multitrait-multimethod analyses, see Mathieu et al., 2021). The connection between this research on seeking biasing sources of subgroup differences in measurement and prediction, and the nature of algorithmic bias in machine learning, seems to go vastly underappreciated. Of course, relative to machine learning applications, this type of work has been conducted with fewer variables, smaller sample sizes, and simpler models that may have weaker predictions. But to the extent these organizational research questions are more strongly aligned with model-based analyses, and the attendant measures are more theory-driven and psychologically relevant, then there is likely much for I-O psychologists to offer those who have been invested in machine learning applications in organizations.

As an analytical tool, machine learning does not require the skills and knowledge of an I-O psychologist, but to actually understand how data are identified and combined, interpret what machine learning algorithms might actually be doing, and consider the implications of the predictive algorithm almost certainly does require the expertise of an I-O psychologist. For example, our field contains a vast literature concerned about whether different types or combinations of predictors will lead to biases in assessment or hiring (e.g., Hattrup, Rock & Scalia, 1997; Murphy & Shiarella, 1997; Ryan, Ployhart & Friedel, 1998). Without some form of guidance from the I-O psychology literature, then the blind application of machine learning will not benefit from prediction systems that can reduce existing biases and barriers to equal employment; in fact, given that similar data and samples were used, machine learning with a sole focus on prediction could magnify biases and barriers.

Back to Basics

This chapter has barely scratched the surface with regard to the types of sophisticated analyses that can be conducted to inform organizational research questions of interest. For example, models of dynamic phenomena have been developed that innovate on and integrate past methods, moving the field forward in building its toolbox of methodological approaches (e.g., Wang, Zhou & Zhang, 2016; Zyphur, Allison, et al., 2020a; Zyphur, Voelkle, et al., 2020b). When used appropriately, such methods can not only offer additional meaningful insights for a particular research question; they can stimulate a larger community of interest and use among I-O psychologists, to the point that what was once viewed as an advanced method becomes relatively commonplace. We had mentioned multilevel modeling previously as an example, but now also consider the related and extremely popular method of meta-analysis. For decades following their seminal article, Schmidt and Hunter (1977) continuously encouraged I-O psychologists to gain better statistical estimates within organizational research domains by accounting for variation in effect sizes (such as correlation coefficients and d-values) by statistical artifacts, such as sampling error variance, measurement error variance, and range restriction (Schmidt & Hunter, 2014). Historically, these statistical artifacts were virtually ignored for their deleterious effects on research findings, but now thanks to Schmidt and Hunter, attempts to account for them are routine in I-O psychology meta-analyses.

In this section, we want to contrast the sophistication in data analyses reviewed above by emphasizing that taking initial "back to basics" approaches are essential toward understanding one's data better and otherwise informing the analyses one conducts. This is old news, and in fact, one can still gain great value by reading the 1999 APA report on fundamental research considerations, such as study design, sampling and assignment strategies, measurement, effect sizes and confidence intervals, statistical power, and data visualization (Wilkinson, L. & Task Force on Statistical Significance, 1999). The subsequent APA Journal Article Reporting Standards (JARS) for quantitative, qualitative, and mixed-methods research provides a set of related reminders that all I-O psychology researchers can benefit from reading and rereading (see https://apastyle.apa.org/jars).

At the very least, some back-to-the-basics data management should make I-O psychologists feel more confident in their analyses, such as knowing that variables were coded correctly (e.g., reverse coding, coding data for missingness), extreme univariate outliers were addressed, and missing data are dealt with appropriately. Additionally, basic data analyses might provide important and interesting information or context around the central theory and analytic methods that will follow (similar to Figure 12.1). Murphy (2021) documented a typical problem, where authors ritualistically report descriptive statistics in Table 12.1 of their manuscripts (e.g., means, standard deviations, correlations, group means), but they do not use them to inform the more complex models and analyses they run.

TABLE 12.1 I-O psychology training: Enhancing data, methods, and theory

Below are components offered to enhance or restructure an existing I-O psychology curriculum at the Master's or PhD level, or for one's own retraining once out of school. No single I-O psychology curriculum, nor any one I-O psychologist's training, would ever be expected to reflect all these components.

First Year (Master's, PhD)
Psychological Statistics I: Data Management, Descriptive Statistics

- R and RStudio
- Data management
- Descriptive statistics
- Exploratory data analysis
- Data visualization

Psychological Statistics II: Inferential Statistics
The following would be taught under the integrated general linear model framework (GLM):

- ANOVA
- Regression
- Multilevel analysis
- Mixed-effects models

Second Year (Master's, PhD)
Psychometrics and Psychological Measurement
Experimental Design
Qualitative and Mixed-Methods Research
Third Year (PhD, or elective for master's students)
Take at least one of the below
Bayesian Modeling and Statistics
Machine Learning: Prediction and Clustering
Concurrent Courses
Open Science Methodologies
Philosophy of Science
(e.g., induction, deduction, testing and falsification, scientific and professional ethics)
Elective Course Examples (based on faculty expertise and student interests)

- *Network Modeling and Group Dynamics*
- *Natural Language Processing with Machine Learning*
- *Longitudinal Modeling and Intensive Sampling Methods*

For illustration, we will consider a very simple example, where a measure of job performance is being predicted by a measure of conscientiousness. Figure 12.2 provides a range of different prediction scenarios, where correlation and regression are used to summarize the linear relationships (related code that you are free to modify and use is at https://osf.io/6bv9h). In each of the left four panels, we see that the correlation is exactly the same value ($R^2 = .13$), and yet the regression slopes vary greatly (a one-unit change in conscientiousness predicts anywhere from .12 to 2 units of change in job performance). In each of the right four panels illustrate the opposite situation, where the correlation takes on different values

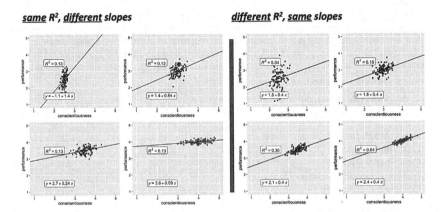

FIGURE 12.2 Different prediction scenarios: Conscientiousness predicting job performance.

(R^2 ranges widely, from .04 to .64), yet the regression coefficient indicates that a one-unit change in conscientiousness always predicts a .4 unit change in job performance. Likewise, notice across all panels that the location and spread (means and standard deviations) of both conscientiousness and job performance also vary greatly, but this gets completely ignored if one only focuses on correlations and regression coefficients. Ostroff and Harrison (1999) make a similar point in the context of the meta-analysis of correlations.

Altogether, this illustration reminds us that focusing on correlation or regression coefficients alone will not provide all the value that our research could offer. The same point applies to d-values, where raw means and standard deviations can also be an informative supplement. It also applies to more complex statistical models. For example, it is easy for many I-O psychologists to imagine another common ritual, where researchers conduct structural equation models (SEM) and then report a litany of common indices of global model fit as they relate to rule-of-thumb cutoffs for acceptable fit (e.g., chi-square, CFI, TLI, RMSEA, RMSR). This ritual might provide some benefit, but it often does little to illuminate whether models, or model comparisons, are truly meaningful for their substantive implications.

Just to point out one fundamental issue with this ritual: the measurement model (estimating reliability) and the structural model (estimating hypothesized pathways) both contribute to overall model fit statistics, so therefore, this means fit statistics confound these two sources of fit. Some work in I-O psychology has sought to unconfound them (see O'Boyle & Williams, 2011; more broadly, see McDonald, 2010), and beyond that, the "back-to-the-basics" mentality suggests examining the model components that contribute to model fit and model fit comparisons. For example, a structural model can show excellent overall model fit, yet still have some weak factor loadings suggesting poorly measured indicators. Similarly, a single reliability coefficient alone does not tell you about the variability of factor loadings or even whether the measure is unidimensional (Cortina et al., 2020). To reiterate, it is generally worthwhile to examine fundamental descriptive statistics and data distributions in the first place, before conducting any further modeling.

The importance of developing a clear understanding of the implications of simple descriptive statistics (e.g., means, standard deviations, outliers) seems to be *more* important as the complexity of our analyses increases because those implications can be so easily hidden. As Figure 12.2 illustrates, it can be hard enough to get a clear understanding of precisely what the correlation and the simple regression equations connecting only two variables means. In more complex models – those incorporating many more variables, multilevel structure, temporal dynamics, mediated moderation, moderated mediation, and the like – the interpretation of coefficients can become very complex indeed. If you do not understand what your data mean before you submit them to a complex data analysis intended to answer an important question, then it is a very good bet that you will not entirely understand your results once the analysis is completed.

Training (and Retraining): Tensions to Navigate in I-O Psychology

Just as the world of work does not remain static, neither does I-O psychology as a field in studying that world. The profession keeps evolving in its ecosystem: for example, in the United States, the number of online and on-campus terminal I-O master's programs is growing rapidly, while Ph.D. programs remain cautiously stable. This state of affairs has future implications for the number and nature of I-O psychologists working in university psychology departments, business schools, and in various roles within industry, consulting, and government. Keeping this diversity of I-O psychology in mind, we suggest many arenas of common training in this concluding section of the chapter: i.e., data management, data visualization, traditional statistical analyses within an integrative framework, research design, and more modern statistical analyses, all guided by philosophy of science that covers issues around the purpose of statistical testing experimental design, and the scientific and professional ethics that should guide them.

Driving these training recommendations is to facilitate and strengthen clear and useful communication by I-O psychologists. Effective communication – whether written or verbal, statistical or interpersonal – is a highly valued skill in I-O psychology and virtually any scientifically-oriented profession. For example, when the ever-despised Reviewer 2 complains vacuously that "more theory is needed," perhaps the real issue is the "back to basics" approach and the need to achieve and better communicate your true understanding of the underlying data, methods, and theory, and how they are related (Figure 12.1) – and not the ill-defined and unproductive need to "build theory" for its own sake (Tourish, 2020).

The field of I-O psychology has long embraced the scientist-practitioner model, and our graduate training has been uniquely well-positioned to carry out solid science while communicating the results of that science to organizational stakeholders. These strengths remain steady, while the important specifics change as we continue working with a diverse range of partners and stakeholders (e.g., executive decision-makers, clerical staff, HR and IT professionals, economists, policy-makers, to name several). In fact, these ongoing science-practice interactions are arguably what force I-O psychologists to develop new skills, tools, and methods that facilitate communications and progress with respect to joint projects of interest. For example, data visualization can communicate inductively through relationships or patterns found in the data, and it can communicate deductively, such as through providing model-based predictions or forecasts with their associated uncertainty (Sinar, 2015; Tay et al., 2016, 2018).

Visualization has emerged as an increasingly critical tool for understanding and communicating the meaning of data. To this end, scientists across a range of disciplines have adopted R as a platform for data manipulation, examination, analysis, and visualization, because of the wide range of tools and the equally wide and strong base of community support. Visualization capabilities in R range from simple tools, such as histograms and boxplots, to complex, interactive, and visually arresting graphic presentations, using packages such as ggplot2 (Wickham, 2016). The learning curve for I-O psychologists accustomed to commercial data analysis programs, such as SPSS and Excel, can appear forbidding and even unnecessary, but investment in R pays off richly, and with practice, data visualization in R becomes natural and simple, yet powerfully flexible.

Whereas a picture can be worth a thousand words when communicating across disciplinary boundaries, so can interactive statistical tools. In the area of meta-analysis, for instance, the metaBUS platform allows users to visualize and navigate organizational constructs arranged in a hierarchical taxonomy; to select correlations between any pair of those constructs within its massive database (over a million correlations and 14,000 articles); to conduct instant meta-analyses and visualize the effect sizes and study results; and to filter the set of effects further and reanalyze them in real-time (Bosco et al., 2020). Additionally, as two selfish examples, our lab has created free open-science tools related to adverse impact (Alexander & Oswald, 2019) and utility analysis (Alexander, Mulfinger & Oswald, 2019), where users can go to online to enter data and/or manipulate relevant characteristics to see how resulting statistics change. The point of these examples is to excite you about developing, using, and sharing useful online statistical tools, because they can give you and other users a literal feel and deeper understanding of how statistics and organizational phenomena work – also providing answers in a faster and more engaging way than typical approaches such as look-up tables and spreadsheets.

Other approaches to effective communication are valuable but require more effort. For example, an I-O psychologist might traditionally conduct an exploratory or confirmatory factor analysis (EFA or CFA) to determine how strongly items on a measure are interrelated, yet as an important alternative approach, a network-oriented analysis might also indicate how strongly items are clustered together via network connections (instead of factor loadings). Which analysis to use, then? If either analysis provides similar results, yet network analyses allow an I-O psychologist to communicate more effectively with applied statisticians and computer scientists who have that training, then perhaps this is the preferred analysis.

I-O psychology is increasingly embracing open science activities that encourage greater transparency in the research process (Banks et al., 2019; Grand et al., 2018). Transparency is an umbrella term that relates to sharing one's research design, data and materials, and methodology and code, which in turn is hoped to improve various forms of research communication, collaboration, education, and creativity within the I-O psychology community. Earlier, we had noted that the code used to create Figure 12.2 was publicly available through the Open Science Framework (OSF), a gold mine for sharing information. The current book editor (Dr. Kevin Murphy) informs us that he has provided OSF access to graduate-level statistics courses that use R for conducting a range of simple and complex data analyses (in the form of narrated PowerPoint presentations, broken down into modules) at https://osf.io/2gksq. Dr. Richard Landers provides a full course on data science using R, at https://datascience.tntlab.org/. These are just two examples; there are many others, but we encourage even more I-O psychologists to provide similar open access to offerings that improve the research and practice of I-O psychology (on OSF or otherwise).

A Curriculum for the Future

In conclusion, we will offer the types of I-O psychology training that tie together the three aforementioned points: going back to basics, using more visualization and interactive tools in our work, and learning more about statistical methods that span other disciplines and stakeholders. Walking through Table 12.1, we suggest what we have witnessed ourselves that involving R and RStudio in the early training of graduate students, or the retraining of one's skills as an I-O psychologist, will pay high dividends (e.g., the software and its thousands of packages are free, meaning that code can be easily used by others as a result; also the R user community is vast in size, support, and collaboration). One way to gain familiarity with this software is to engage in skills shown in this table:

managing datasets, visualizing them, and conducting descriptive statistics on them to summarize them intelligibly (e.g., Braun, Kuljanin & DeShon, 2018). We believe that the spirit and specifics of the course sequence laid out below will motivate the next generation of I-O psychologists to obtain the essential training and tools for navigating an increasingly complex landscape of data types and research questions in the world of work.

In Table 12.1, the section on inferential statistics contains the traditional ANOVA and regression approaches, both taught in the same semester, along with an introduction to multilevel analysis and the mixed-effects modeling that subsumes it. All of these models are related and fit within the GLM framework, meaning these methods are much easier to teach, to learn – and to enhance effective communication. A chart that nicely shows how these models are related, along with R code snippets, can be found online in Lindeløv (2019). Following this training in inferential statistics, we also view psychometrics and psychological measurement, qualitative and mixed-methods research, and philosophy of science as essential, further providing I-O psychologists with skills that add greater meaning to multidisciplinary groups working on organizational research problems.

Some of the other forms of I-O psychology education are on the more sophisticated side of the statistical training continuum (e.g., Bayesian analysis, machine learning, and specialized methodology courses), have complementary forms of analytic and multidisciplinary value. We recommend these while fully well appreciating an important chicken-and-egg problem: organizational researchers and practitioners are constantly catching up on current methods because those who train them must also train themselves. We can break this cycle by committing to, investing in, and collaborating with I-O psychologists and other quantitative experts trained in these educational areas, with the goal of advancing I-O psychology, both the research and the professionals involved in it. Remembering that a cornerstone of the I-O psychology skill set is recruitment, selection and training, we should be able to do that if we have our hearts and minds set on it.

But even with that said, we are not naive. The challenges to building and sustaining even a subset of curriculum elements outlined in Table 12.1 are clear. First, our field and many others in the social sciences that are even more quantitatively oriented (e.g., psychometrics; see Aiken, West & Millsap, 2008), it is becoming increasingly difficult to find enough qualified faculty to provide training, especially in advanced research and statistical methods. Although many of the courses outlined above would be very valuable, many and perhaps most I-O programs would be hard-pressed to staff these courses. Valuable online resources aligned with Table 12.1 that are open-science based (and free) should continue to be developed, identified – and importantly, curated – to supplement the graduate training of I-O psychologists across the board. Such online resources would also help address the growing need for continuous learning by I-O access to expert guidance and materials at our professional conferences, but continuous learning can still remain very challenging in terms of access, where the risk/reward ratio self-training versus calling in a consultant can be unknown. Or it can be very well known: the many job responsibilities of an I-O psychologist often place severe practical limits on how much can be reasonably expected when learning completely new methods and analytic platforms. So, we are offering a hopeful educational template here that we hope some I/O psychologists pursue as they weigh an evolving range of options.

For many I-O psychologists, the most realistic approach to mastering the range of analytic skills that are increasingly in demand is to work in multidisciplinary teams, where such skills are distributed across many members. Not every I-O psychologist needs to be a Bayesian or machine learner, but every I-O psychologist might at least learn enough about those methods to communicate better in a multidisciplinary team. A National Research Council report (2015) summarizes the science behind creating effective multidisciplinary research teams, but once again, our scientist-practitioner model also gives us a leg up in this sort of effort. Many I-O psychologists have deep experience working with people whose training, expertise, and knowledge is very different from ours, and one can imagine how this experience is likely to transfer to working with multidisciplinary teams. This type of work might help I-O psychologists keep up with evolving relationships among data, methods, and theory – and maybe sometimes keep ahead of them.

References

Allen, K. S., Affourtit, M., & Reddock, C. M. (2020). The machines aren't taking over (yet): An empirical comparison of traditional, profiling, and machine learning approaches to criterion-related validation. *Personnel Assessment and Decisions, 6*(3), 4–12. https://doi.org/10.25035/pad.2020.03.002

Alexander, L., III, Mulfinger, E., & Oswald, F. L. (2019). *Investing in people online (Version 2.0) [Software]*, Rice University, Houston, Texas. Available from https://orgtools.shinyapps.io/IIP3/

Alexander, L., III., & Oswald, F. L. (2019). *Free adverse impact resource (FAIR)*. Retrieved from https://orgtools.shinyapps.io/FAIR/

Aiken, L. S., West, S. G., & Millsap, R. E. (2008). Doctoral training in statistics, measurement, and methodology in psychology: Replication and extension of Aiken, West, Sechrest, and Reno's (1990) survey of PhD programs in North America. *American Psychologist, 63*(1), 32–50. https://doi.org/10.1037/0003-066X.63.1.32

Amrhein, V., Greenland, S., & McShane, B. (2019). Scientists rise up against statistical significance. *Nature, 567*, 305–307. https://doi.org/10.1038/d41586-019-00857-9

Ballard, T., Vancouver, J. B., & Neal, A. (2018). On the pursuit of multiple goals with different deadlines. *Journal of Applied Psychology, 103*(11), 1242–1264. https://doi.org/10.1037/apl0000304

Banks, G. C., Field, J. G., Oswald, F. L., O'Boyle, E. H., Landis, R. S., Rupp, D. E., & Rogelberg, S. G. (2019). Answers to 18 questions about open science practices. *Journal of Business and Psychology, 34*(3), 257–270. https://doi.org/10.1007/s10869-018-9547-8

Barrick, M. R., & Mount, M. K. (1991). The Big Five personality dimensions and job performance: A meta-analysis. *Personnel Psychology, 44*(1), 1–26. https://doi.org/10.1111/j.1744-6570.1991.tb00688.x

Bliese P. (2016). Multilevel: Multilevel Functions (R package Version 2.6). Available: http://cran.R-project.org/package=multilevel.

Bliese, P. D., & Hanges, P. J. (2004). Being both too liberal and too conservative: The perils of treating grouped data as though they were independent. *Organizational Research Methods, 7*(4), 400–417. https://doi.org/10.1177/1094428104268542

Bosco, F. A., Aguinis, H., Singh, K., Field, J. G., & Pierce, C. A. (2015). Correlational effect size benchmarks. *Journal of Applied Psychology, 100*(2), 431–449. https://doi.org/10.1037/a0038047

Bosco, F. A., Field, J. G., Larsen, K. R., Chang, Y., & Uggerslev, K. L. (2020). Advancing meta-analysis with knowledge-management platforms: Using metaBUS in psychology. *Advances in Methods and Practices in Psychological Science, 3*(1), 124–137.

Bouveyron, C., Celeux, G., Murphy, T. B., & Raftery, A. E. (2019). *Model-based clustering and classification for data science: With applications in R* (Vol. 50). Cambridge University Press. https://doi.org/10.1017/9781108644181

Braun, M. T., Kuljanin, G., & DeShon, R. P. (2018). Special considerations for the acquisition and wrangling of big data. *Organizational Research Methods, 21*(3), 633–659. https://doi.org/10.1177/1094428117690235

Breiman, L. (2001). Random forests. *Machine Learning, 45*(1), 5–32. https://doi.org/10.1023/A:1010933404324

Bryk, A. S., & Raudenbush, S. W. (1992). *Hierarchical linear models: Applications and data analysis methods.* Sage Publications, Inc.

Campbell, J. P., & Wilmot, M. P. (2018). The functioning of theory in industrial, work and organizational psychology (IWOP). In D. S. Ones, N. Anderson, C. Viswesvaran, & H. K. Sinangil (Eds.), *The SAGE handbook of industrial, work & organizational psychology: Personnel psychology and employee performance* (pp. 3–38). Sage. https://doi.org/10.4135/9781473914940.n2

Chan, D. (1998). Functional relations among constructs in the same content domain at different levels of analysis: A typology of composition models. *Journal of Applied Psychology, 83*(2), 234–246. https://doi.org/10.1037/0021-9010.83.2.234

Cortina, J. M., Sheng, Z., Keener, S. K., Keeler, K. R., Grubb, L. K., Schmitt, N., … Banks, G. C. (2020). From alpha to omega and beyond! A look at the past, present, and (possible) future of psychometric soundness in the *Journal of Applied Psychology. Journal of Applied Psychology, 105*(12), 1351–1381. https://doi.org/10.1037/apl0000815

Depaoli, S., & van de Schoot, R. (2017). Improving transparency and replication in Bayesian statistics: The WAMBS-Checklist. *Psychological Methods, 22*(2), 240–261. https://doi-org.ezproxy.rice.edu/10.1037/met0000065

DeVellis, R. F. (2016). *Scale development: Theory and applications.* Sage Publications.

Domingos, P. (2012). A few useful things to know about machine learning. *Communications of the ACM, 55*(10), 78–87. https://doi.org/10.1145/2347736.2347755

Dudley, N. M., Orvis, K. A., Lebiecki, J. E., & Cortina, J. M. (2006). A meta-analytic investigation of conscientiousness in the prediction of job performance: Examining the intercorrelations and the incremental validity of narrow traits. *Journal of Applied Psychology, 91*(1), 40–57. https://doi.org/10.1037/0021-9010.91.1.40

Epskamp, S., Rhemtulla, M., & Borsboom, D. (2017). Generalized network psychometrics: Combining network and latent variable models. *Psychometrika, 82*(4), 904–927. https://doi.org/10.1007/s11336-017-9557-x

Feeney, J. R., Gellatly, I. R., Goffin, R. D., & Inness, M. (2020). Organizational attachment: Conceptualization, measurement, and incremental prediction of work attitudes and outcomes. *Journal of Personnel Psychology*. https://doi.org/10.1027/1866-5888/a000252

Grand, J. A. (2017). Brain drain? An examination of stereotype threat effects during training on knowledge acquisition and organizational effectiveness. *Journal of Applied Psychology, 102*(2), 115–150. https://doi.org/10.1037/apl0000171

Gelman, A., Hill, J., & Yajima, M. (2012). Why we (usually) don't have to worry about multiple comparisons. *Journal of Research on Educational Effectiveness, 5*(2), 189–211. https://doi.org/10.1080/19345747.2011.618213

Grand, J. A., Rogelberg, S. G., Allen, T. D., Landis, R. S., Reynolds, D. H., Scott, J. C., … Truxillo, D. M. (2018). A systems-based approach to fostering robust science in industrial-organizational psychology. *Industrial and Organizational Psychology, 11*(1), 4–42.

Hattrup, K., Rock, J., & Scalia, C. (1997). The effects of varying conceptualizations of job performance on adverse impact, minority hiring, and predicted performance. *Journal of Applied Psychology, 82*(5), 656–664. https://doi.org/10.1037/0021-9010.82.5.656

Hoekstra, R., Morey, R. D., Rouder, J. N., & Wagenmakers, E. J. (2014). Robust misinterpretation of confidence intervals. *Psychonomic Bulletin & Review, 21*(5), 1157–1164. https://doi.org/10.3758/s13423-013-0572-3

Hofmann, D. A. (1997). An overview of the logic and rationale of hierarchical linear models. *Journal of Management, 23*(6), 723–744. https://doi.org/10.1177/014920639702300602

Ippel, L., Kaptein, M. C., & Vermunt, J. K. (2019). Estimating multilevel models on data streams. *Psychometrika, 84*(1), 41–64. https://doi.org/10.1007/s11336-018-09656-z

Jackson, D. J., Michaelides, G., Dewberry, C., & Kim, Y. J. (2016). Everything that you have ever been told about assessment center ratings is confounded. *Journal of Applied Psychology, 101*(7), 976–994. https://doi.org/10.1037/apl0000102

James, G., Witten, D., Hastie, T., & Tibshirani, R. (2021). *An introduction to statistical learning.* Springer. https://doi.org/10.1007/978-1-0716-1418-1

JASP Team. (2020). *JASP (Version 0.14.1).* https://jasp-stats.org/

Kaufman, M. (2011). *First contact: Scientific breakthroughs in the hunt for life beyond Earth.* Simon and Schuster.

Kozlowski, S. W., & Klein, K. J. (2000). A multilevel approach to theory and research in organizations: Contextual, temporal, and emergent processes In K. J. Klein & S. W. J. Kozlowski (Eds.), *Multilevel theory, research and methods in organizations: Foundations, extensions, and new directions* (pp. 3–90). Jossey-Bass.

Krackhardt, D., Schwab, A., & Starbuck, W. H. (2020). Why we all should be Bayesians: An introduction to Bayesian studies. In *Academy of Management Proceedings* (Vol. 2020, No. 1, p. 14550). Academy of Management. https://doi.org/10.5465/AMBPP.2020.14550symposium

Kruschke, J. K., Aguinis, H., & Joo, H. (2012). The time has come: Bayesian methods for data analysis in the organizational sciences. *Organizational Research Methods, 15*(4), 722–752. https://doi.org/10.1177/1094428112457829

Kruschke, J. (2021). Bayesian analysis reporting guidelines. *Nature Human Behavior.* https://doi.org/10.1038/s41562-021-01177-7

Lakens, D., Scheel, A. M., & Isager, P. M. (2018). Equivalence testing for psychological research: A tutorial. *Advances in Methods and Practices in Psychological Science, 1*(2), 259–269. https://doi.org/10.1177/2515245918770963

Liao, H., & Chuang, A. (2004). A multilevel investigation of factors influencing employee service performance and customer outcomes. *Academy of Management Journal, 47*(1), 41–58. https://doi.org/10.2307/20159559

Lindeløv, J. K. (2019). Common statistical tests are linear models (or: how to teach stats). Available from https://lindeloev.github.io/tests-as-linear/

Mathieu, J. E., Wolfson, M. A., Park, S., Luciano, M. M., Bedwell-Torres, W. L., Ramsay, P. S., Klock, E. A., & Tannenbaum, S. I. (2021). Indexing dynamic collective constructs using computer-aided text analysis: Construct validity evidence and illustrations featuring team processes. *Journal of Applied Psychology.* Advance online publication. https://doi.org/10.1037/apl0000856

McAbee, S. T., Landis, R. S., & Burke, M. I. (2017). Inductive reasoning: The promise of big data. *Human Resource Management Review, 27*(2), 277–290. https://doi.org/10.1016/j.hrmr.2016.08.005

McDonald, R. P. (2010). Structural models and the art of approximation. *Perspectives on Psychological Science, 5*(6), 675–686. https://doi.org/10.1177/1745691610388766

McElreath, R. (2020). *Statistical rethinking: A Bayesian course with examples in R and Stan.* (2nd ed.). CRC Press. https://doi.org/10.1201/9780429029608

McShane, B. B., Gal, D., Gelman, A., Robert, C., & Tackett, J. L. (2019). Abandon statistical significance. *The American Statistician, 73*(sup1), 235–245. https://doi.org/10.1080/00031305.2018.1527253

Molnar C., Casalicchio G., & Bischl B. (2020) Interpretable machine learning – A brief history, state-of-the-art and challenges. In I. Koprinska et al. (Eds.) ECML PKDD 2020 Workshops. ECML PKDD 2020. *Communications in Computer and Information Science,* Vol. 1323. Springer, Cham. https://doi.org/10.1007/978-3-030-65965-3_28

Murphy, K. R. (2021). In praise of Table 1: The importance of making better use of descriptive statistics. *Industrial and Organizational Psychology: Perspectives on Science and Practice, 14*(4).

Murphy, K., Myors, B. & Wolach, A. (2014). *Statistical power analysis: A simple and general model for traditional and modern hypothesis tests* (4th ed.). Taylor & Francis.

Murphy, K. R., & Shiarella, A. H. (1997). Implications of the multidimensional nature of job performance for the validity of selection tests: Multivariate frameworks for studying test validity. *Personnel Psychology, 50*(4), 823–854. https://doi.org/10.1111/j.1744-6570.1997.tb01484.x

National Research Council. (2015). *Enhancing the effectiveness of team science.* The National Academies Press. https://doi.org/10.17226/19007

Nye, C. D., White, L. A., Drasgow, F., Prasad, J., Chernyshenko, O. S., & Stark, S. (2020). Examining personality for the selection and classification of soldiers: Validity and differential validity across jobs. *Military Psychology, 32*(1), 60–70. https://doi.org/10.1080/08995605.2019.1652482

O'Boyle, E. H., Jr., & Williams, L. J. (2011). Decomposing model fit: Measurement vs. theory in organizational research using latent variables. *Journal of Applied Psychology, 96*(1), 1–12. https://doi.org/10.1037/a002053

Ostroff, C., & Harrison, D. A. (1999). Meta-analysis, level of analysis, and best estimates of population correlations: Cautions for interpreting meta-analytic results in organizational behavior. *Journal of Applied Psychology, 84*(2), 260–270. https://doi.org/10.1037/0021-9010.84.2.260

Oswald, F. L., Behrend, T. S., Putka, D. J., & Sinar, E. (2020). Big data in industrial-organizational psychology and human resource management: Forward progress for organizational research and practice. *Annual Review of Organizational Psychology and Organizational Behavior, 7*, 505–533. https://doi.org/10.1146/annurev-orgpsych-032117-104553

Oswald, F. L., & Putka, D. J. (2016). Statistical methods for big data: A scenic tour. In S. Tonidandel, E. King, & J. Cortina (Eds.), *Big data at work: The data science revolution and organizational psychology* (pp. 43–63). Routledge.

Putka, D. J., Beatty, A. S., & Reeder, M. C. (2018). Modern prediction methods: New perspectives on a common problem. *Organizational Research Methods, 21*(3), 689–732. https://doi.org/10.1177/1094428117697041

Ryan, A. M., Ployhart, R. E., & Friedel, L. A. (1998). Using personality testing to reduce adverse impact: A cautionary note. *Journal of Applied Psychology, 83*(2), 298–307. https://doi.org/10.1037/0021-9010.83.2.298

Ryan, J., & Herleman, H. (2015). A Big Data platform for workforce analytics. In S. Tonidandel, E. King, & J. Cortina (Eds.), *Big data at work: The data science revolution and organizational psychology* (pp. 19–42). Routledge.

Schmidt, F. L., & Hunter, J. E. (1977). Development of a general solution to the problem of validity generalization. *Journal of Applied Psychology, 62*(5), 529–540. https://doi.org/10.1037/0021-9010.62.5.529

Schmidt, F. L., & Hunter, J. E. (2014). *Methods of meta-analysis: Correcting Error and Bias in Research Findings* (3rd ed.). Sage. https://doi.org/10.4135/9781483398105

Sinar, E. F. (2015). Data visualization. In S. Tonidandel, E. King, & J. Cortina (Eds.), *Big data at work: The data science revolution and organizational psychology* (pp. 115–157). Taylor & Francis.

Society for Industrial and Organizational Psychology (SIOP). (2018). *Principles for the validation and use of personnel selection procedures* (5th ed.). Retrieved from https://www.apa.org/ed/accreditation/about/policies/personnel-selection-procedures.pdf

Stanton, J. M. (2021). Evaluating equivalence and confirming the null in the organizational sciences. *Organizational Research Methods, 24*(3), 491–512. https://doi.org/10.1177/1094428120921934

Tay, L., Parrigon, S., Huang, Q., & LeBreton, J. M. (2016). Graphical descriptives: A way to improve data transparency and methodological rigor in psychology. *Perspectives on Psychological Science, 11*(5), 692–701. https://doi.org/10.1177/1745691616663875

Tay, L., Ng, V., Malik, A., Zhang, J., Chae, J., Ebert, D. S., … Kern, M. (2018). Big data visualizations in organizational science. *Organizational Research Methods, 21*(3), 660–688. https://doi.org/10.1177/1094428117720014

Tippins, N. T., Oswald, F. L., & McPhail, S. M. (2021). Scientific, legal, and ethical concerns about AI-based personnel selection tools: A call to action. *Personnel Assessment and Decisions, 7*(2).

Tourish, D. (2020). The triumph of nonsense in management studies. *Academy of Management Learning & Education, 19*(1), 99–109.

van de Schoot, R., Depaoli, S., King, R., Kramer, B., Märtens, K., Tadesse, M. G., … Yau, C. (2021). Bayesian statistics and modelling. *Nature Reviews Methods Primers, 1*(1), 1–26. https://doi.org/10.1038/s43586-020-00001-2

Wallace, C., & Chen, G. (2006). A multilevel integration of personality, climate, self-regulation, and performance. *Personnel Psychology, 59*(3), 529–557. https://doi.org/10.1111/j.1744-6570.2006.00046.x

Wang, M., Zhou, L., & Zhang, Z. (2016). Dynamic modeling. *Annual Review of Organizational Psychology and Organizational Behavior, 3*, 241–266. https://doi.org/10.1146/annurev-orgpsych-041015-062553

Wasserstein, R. L., & Lazar, N. A. (2016) The ASA's statement on *p*-values: Context, process, and purpose. *The American Statistician, 70* (2), 129–133. https://doi.org/10.1080/00031305.2016.1154108

Wasserstein, R. L., Schirm, A. L., & Lazar, N. A. (2019). Moving to a world beyond "p < 0.05". *The American Statistician, 73* (sup1), 1–19. https://doi.org/10.1080/000313 05.2019.1583913

Wenzel, R., & Van Quaquebeke, N. (2018). The double-edged sword of big data in organizational and management research: A review of opportunities and risks. *Organizational Research Methods, 21*(3), 548–591. https://doi.org/10.1177/1094428117718627

Wetzels, R., Matzke, D., Lee, M. D., Rouder, J. N., Iverson, G. J., & Wagenmakers, E. J. (2011). Statistical evidence in experimental psychology: An empirical comparison using 855 *t* tests. *Perspectives on Psychological Science, 6*(3), 291–298. https://doi.org/10.1177/1745691611406923

Wickham, H. (2016). *ggplot2: Elegant graphics for data analysis*. Springer-Verlag. https://doi.org/10.1007/978-3-319-24277-4

Wilkinson, L., & Task Force on Statistical Significance (1999). Statistical methods in psychology journals: Guidelines and explanations. *American Psychologist, 54*(8), 594–604. https://doi.org/10.1037/0003-066X.54.8.594

Woo, S. E., Chae, M., Jebb, A. T., & Kim, Y. (2016). A closer look at the personality-turnover relationship: Criterion expansion, dark traits, and time. *Journal of Management, 42*(2), 357–385. https://doi.org/10.1177/0149206315622985

Yeo, G. B., & Neal, A. (2004). A multilevel analysis of effort, practice, and performance: effects; of ability, conscientiousness, and goal orientation. *Journal of Applied Psychology, 89*(2), 231–247. https://doi.org/10.1037/0021-9010.89.2.231

Zyphur, M. J., & Oswald, F. L. (2015). Bayesian estimation and inference: A user's guide. *Journal of Management, 41*(2), 390–420. https://doi.org/10.1177/0149206313501200

Zyphur, M. J., Allison, P. D., Tay, L., Voelkle, M. C., Preacher, K. J., Zhang, Z., . . . & Diener, E. (2020). From data to causes I: Building a general cross-lagged panel model (GCLM). *Organizational Research Methods, 23*(4), 651–687. https://doi.org/10.1177/1094428119847278

Zyphur, M. J., Voelkle, M. C., Tay, L., Allison, P. D., Preacher, K. J., Zhang, Z., . . . & Diener, E. (2020). From data to causes II: Comparing approaches to panel data analysis. *Organizational Research Methods, 23*(4), 688–716. https://doi.org/10.1177/1094428119847280

13

REBUILDING RELATIONSHIPS BETWEEN DATA, METHOD, AND THEORIES

How the Scientific Method Can Help

Jeffrey M. Cucina and Mary Anne Nester

When authors write manuscripts for industrial-organizational (I-O) psychology and management literatures, they are strongly encouraged to make a new theoretical contribution if they want their work to be published in the premiere outlets. This is a relatively recent trend in I-O psychology, as documented by Cucina and Moriarty (2015) who showed a dramatic increase in the use of words beginning with "theor" over the history of the *Journal of Applied Psychology* (*JAP*) and *Personnel Psychology* (*PPsych*). Editorial statements and manuscript criteria also changed over time and authors have responded by proposing lengthy theoretical models and discourse in their manuscripts. Many I-O psychologists have noted and debated the rise of "theory" in the field (Aguinis, Bradley & Broderson, 2014; Campbell & Wilmot, 2018; Cortina, 2014; Cucina et al., 2015; Kepes & McDaniel, 2013; Köhler, DeSimone & Schoen, 2020; Ryan & Ployhart, 2014). In the past, theoretical work in I-O psychology was considered the exception rather than the rule, with a greater focus on empirical data.

The emphasis on theory has a longer history within the management literature. Indeed, there is speculation that the increased role of theory in I-O psychology stems from the management literature (Aguinis et al., 2014). Journals in management, such as the *Academy of Management Journal* (*AMJ*), often require manuscripts to make a theoretical contribution and will even desk reject manuscripts that do not emphasize theory. Note that Sutton and Staw (1995) specifically singled out I-O psychology's *JAP* and *PPsych* as being at the "most empirical end of the spectrum" of management-related journals (p. 379). These journals have changed and now are more in line with management journals, such as *AMJ*, which require strong theoretical contributions to accompany empirical research.

DOI: 10.4324/9781003015000-17

At the same time that journals have increased emphasis on theory, data scientists and some I-O psychologists have begun using machine learning in applied settings, which is a methodology that largely relies on what was once known as "dustbowl empiricism." This has a resulted in a disjointed relationship between data, methods, and theory, with some I-O psychologists overemphasizing theory, others focusing on data at the expense of building scientific knowledge, and a gap between statistical advances and research practice.

There is a need in I-O psychology to rebuild the relationships between data, methods, and theory, and the aim of this chapter is to explain how these concepts should be related. We use the scientific method as a framework for this discussion. In the remainder of this chapter, we review the scientific method, describe how data, methods, and theory are related within the framework of the scientific method, and discuss two other configurations and research approaches.

Overview of the Scientific Method

Organizational researchers are no doubt familiar with the spirit and conduct of science. However, we view it as instructive to review the scientific method as it is defined and implemented in other fields of science because the recent emphasis on theory building and theoretical contributions in I-O psychology represents a significant philosophical departure from the scientific method. For instance, authors of scientific papers in I-O psychology are often expected to start a paper or research project by developing theory, often devoting significant journal space to theory exposition. There is also an expectation that the proposed theory will be supported, which results in theory-reaffirming data and results. As a result, there is less emphasis on important empirical work, studies that report interesting and practically useful results (but that lack theory development), and research in areas that do not have extensive and complex theories. In contrast, the scientific method and research practices in other disciplines often do not begin with theory but instead with an observation. The scientific method also allows for research designs that can disconfirm (as well as confirm) proposed hypotheses and theories; in fact, there is an emphasis on designing studies that would disconfirm a theory.

Many other areas of science have a formally described approach to conducting scientific research. This approach consists of an iterative seven-step process, which Cucina et al. (2014) observed to recur in their review of textbooks and coursework from various scientific fields (e.g., astronomy, physics, biology, chemistry). A depiction of the scientific method is provided in Figure 13.1. In the following sections, we describe each step in detail and explain how data, methods, and theory relate to the activities within each step.

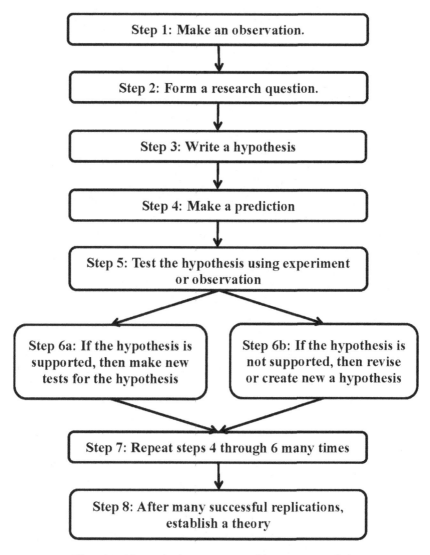

FIGURE 13.1 The scientific method as summarized by Cucina et al. (2014).

Step 1: Make an Observation

The scientific method begins with an observation about the natural world (including organizations and employees). An observation could be an anecdote, a casual observance of the everyday world, the results of previous scientific research, a case study, or information gleaned when providing consulting services to organizations. For example, a researcher could simply observe that individuals in a certain village have a lower incidence of a certain disease. Alternately, a researcher with access to a large dataset might observe a correlation between two variables. An organizational researcher might make an observation by watching the interaction between a leader and a subordinate. An observation could even be the results of a previously published study.

Although observations are most often based on data, observations based on methods and theory could serve as the basis for step 1 of the scientific method. The observations mentioned in the previous paragraph are essentially data-based observations. In some cases, the quality of the data is not robust, with small samples, uncontrolled environments, and measures with questionable construct validity limiting the conclusions that can be drawn from the study. However, this is not a problem as more robust testing of the hypothesis will occur in the subsequent steps. The observation in step 1 could also be based on more robust data (even published data and meta-analyses). For instance, a researcher might notice the correlation between two variables in a meta-analysis and build follow-up hypotheses. Observations can also be made about methods used in previous studies and a researcher could create hypotheses about using other methodologies to study an issue. Observations can also be based on existing theories, including conflicts between competing theories, or the applicability of existing theories to new areas. Observations about a stream of research can also be made. For instance, problematization (e.g., identifying incompleteness, inadequacy, and incommensurability in existing research as described by Locke & Golden-Biddle, 1997) can also serve as the basis for observations. An observation could also be based on issues facing organizations.

There are also circumstances in which a combination of data, methods, and theory can serve as the basis for an observation. For instance, Schmidt and Hunter's (2003) development of validity generalization and meta-analysis was initially built on data-based observations that showed differing validity coefficients for different industry jobs versus military data that showed consistent validity coefficients, a method-based observation that industrial studies often had much smaller sample sizes and much larger sampling error versus military studies, and a theoretical observation concerning the theory of situational specificity. This led to a hypothesis that the industrial data was inconsistent across studies due to sampling error. This was followed by the subsequent development of meta-analytic techniques, which in turn led to the theory of validity generalization and the disconfirmation of situational specificity theory.

Step 2: Form a Research Question

Most research questions in the organizational sciences focus on the relationship (e.g., correlation, regression, mean differences) between two (or more) naturally occurring variables. The research question should be concise and easily understood. Some examples include "does spatial reasoning correlate with job performance for pilots?" "are job satisfaction and turnover correlated?" and "which tasks and competencies are important for a particular job?" At this point in the process, it can be helpful to consider how meaningful and important the research question is for the field of study (e.g., the potential relevance to organizations).

Step 3: Write a Hypothesis

A hypothesis is a broad statement that aims to answer the research question. It need not be elaborately thought out; an "educated guess" (Cucina et al., 2014, pp. 358–359), conjecture, or even a hunch can serve as a hypothesis. As we will discuss later, the hypothesis could very well be revised or discarded in later steps. The hypothesis should be written so that it can apply to multiple studies, not just the study at hand. In some ways, the new theory that many I/O psychology and management journals ask authors to create in an introduction section is similar to a hypothesis. However, hypotheses are different in several regards. A hypothesis should be clear, concise, and elegant. It should not be lengthy with a large number of variables and many proposed relationships. In principle, it should be fully testable in one paper. A hypothesis could be based on existing theory, but it could also be based on an entirely new development.

At this point in the scientific method, it is beneficial to evaluate the hypothesis and potentially revise it before proceeding further. A hypothesis should make a testable proposition and it should be falsifiable (Popper, 1934, 1959). The prediction can be predicated on the logic that if the hypothesis is true, then the prediction must be true. However, Platt (1964) also makes a case for "strong inference" whereby a prediction is made such that if the prediction is true, then the hypothesis must be false. Ideally, effort should be given to the development of competing hypotheses for the research question, which would allow use of Platt's (1964) strong inference, which will be mentioned in the subsequent steps. Some elements of problematization (Locke & Golden-Biddle, 1997), especially incommensurability problematization (in which alternate theses are explored and assumptions underlying a particular area of research are examined and challenged) are also relevant here.

Step 4: Make a Prediction

A prediction is more specific in scope than a hypothesis because it is written to apply to a single study, not multiple studies. It focuses more on what is expected in the specific context of a study in terms of the methodology (e.g., participant population, organizational context, measures) rather being a general statement, such as the hypothesis. It also specifies the expected results of the data analysis. A prediction can often be portrayed formulaically (e.g., Mean$_{\text{Group A}}$ > Mean$_{\text{Group B}}$, with a Cohen's, 1992, d near 1.0). The prediction is written to apply to the methodology of the study, including the measures used, the experimental manipulations, and the operational definitions of the variables.

Step 5: Test the Hypothesis Using Experiment or Observation

In this step, an empirical study is conducted to test the hypothesis. Although there are aspects of theory that relate to this step (e.g., psychometric and statistical theory are employed), data and methods play the key roles. The researcher must first design an empirical study and some thought needs to be given to the type of data that will be collected, the suitability of the data for testing the hypothesis, and the data analysis strategy. The methods used in the study are crucial in yielding suitable data for hypothesis testing. If competing hypotheses were generated in step 3, the methodology of the empirical study should yield data that could rule out one or more of the hypotheses, allowing for a "crucial experiment" (Platt, 1964, p. 347).

It can be helpful to review data from previous studies concerning the methods and data quality. If there are flaws in the research methods or the data is of poor quality, then the experiment or observational study may not adequately test the hypothesis. For psychologists, issues such as construct validity and scale reliability are critical. Many psychological measures, especially behavioral ones, are inherently unreliable. For instance, supervisory ratings of job performance have interrater reliabilities of about .52 (Shen et al., 2014; Viswesvaran, Ones & Schmidt, 1996). Many of the behavioral outcome variables used to study the relationship between personality and behavior were based on unreliable single instances of behavior. This led Mischel (1968) to question the importance of personality (vs. situational variables) in determining behavior, which had theoretical implications for personality and social psychology. However, a rebuttal by Epstein (1979) demonstrated that personality predicts behavior when more reliable behavioral outcome variables based on multiple instances of behavior are created. Thus, when designing a study, the potential validity and reliability of the measures used should be considered, lest a researcher could erroneously conclude that they have discovered a new construct or that their construct does not predict behavior.

In addition, there are other methodological considerations. For example, a power analysis should determine the sample size; however, consideration of the accuracy of effect size point estimates should also be considered. For instance, suppose a researcher anticipates a correlation of .30 between two variables. A total of 115 cases will yield 95% power for detecting the correlation; however, the 95% confidence interval about a correlation of .3 with 115 cases ranges from .12 to .46 (which is a large interval). The situation becomes worse when artifacts such as measurement error and range restriction are taken into account (Schmidt et al., 1976). Unfortunately, in our experience as reviewers of many I-O psychology manuscripts and presentations, empirical studies are too often conducted with measures having questionable construct validity, poor reliability, insufficient power[1], and insufficient precision in effect size estimates. This is unfortunate given the researcher and participant time and effort involved in conducting many empirical studies.

Once the empirical study is completed, the data are analyzed to determine if the hypothesis was supported. Obviously, quantitative and qualitative methods play an important role in this phase. Sometimes, data analysis can shed new insight on the research question and hypothesis, leading to further refinements of the hypothesis or development of *post hoc* hypotheses, as will be discussed in step 6b.

Step 6a: If the Hypothesis Is Supported, Then Make New Tests for the Hypothesis

This step is quite similar to step 5; however, researchers should attempt to test the hypothesis using additional empirical studies. Step 6a, can be implemented with multi-study articles or with separate follow-up studies (although we would recommend avoiding piecemeal publication). The new studies could be conducted by different research teams (e.g., a second research team might design a new test of a hypothesis that another team studied previously). The use of additional studies is important because Type I and II errors, unknown confounds, and experimenter error can lead to incorrect conclusions about hypotheses.

Direct replication is one approach to additional testing (Open Science Collaboration, 2015); however, modified conceptual replication often provides a better test of the hypothesis (Cucina & Hayes, 2015). In fact, modified conceptual replications are more consistent with the spirit of the scientific method since these allow for more robust testing of the hypothesis using different methodologies, types of data, measures, manipulations, populations, and so forth. For instance, directly replicating a criterion-related validation study of a scale measuring a new construct which predicted cashier job performance in a second sample of cashiers does not yield as much scientific information as a conceptual replication would. A conceptual replication might compare other approaches for measuring the construct, how well the construct adds incremental validity over other tests, whether the construct predicts performance for other jobs and for other domains of performance. Thus, in our view, parts of the recent "replication crisis" in psychology have been misguided given that an important goal for science is to develop a database of existing studies containing many different types of tests for a hypothesis. This allows for an evaluation of the external and ecological validity of the initial study's conclusion and a better determination of whether moderators exist.

Step 6b: If the Hypothesis Is Not Supported, Then Revise or Create a New Hypothesis

When a hypothesis is not supported, the best approach is to change the hypothesis, provided that the methodology and data used to test it were sufficient. This can be accomplished by revising the hypothesis or discarding it in favor of a new hypothesis. This is an instance in which data, and to some extent methods (e.g., if use of a particular methodology suggests that the hypothesis is not supported) inform a hypothesis.

In many fields, including I-O psychology, researchers are expected to predict the outcome of their studies correctly before collecting and analyzing their data. Publishing a study that does not support an initial hypothesis is discouraged and, in some cases, forbidden by the policies of academic journals (Cortina, 2016). Additionally researchers cannot revise their hypotheses (step 6b), unless they resort to hypothesizing after the results are known (HARKing, Kerr, 1998) or collecting additional data and running statistical tests multiple times to achieve significance (Simmons, Nelson & Simonsohn, 2011). There is evidence that organizational researchers sometimes alter their hypotheses after the data is collected (O'Boyle, Banks & Gonzalez-Mulé, 2017). When unreported in manuscripts, both practices are disingenuous and create statistical issues.

A much better approach is to simply allow researchers to admit their hypotheses are wrong in their papers' discussion sections and to propose (and possibly test in follow-up studies) new *post hoc* hypotheses in an open and transparent manner. Results-blind manuscript reviews and registered reports (which some I-O psychology outlets such as the *Journal of Business and Psychology* are now supporting) can serve as a foundation for this practice. Giving authors allowances (perhaps in supplemental materials) to describe additional exploratory analyses they conducted on the data can also assist in increasing transparency and providing better documentation of the research study. Additionally, the practice of maintaining a laboratory notebook[2] (Pain, 2019) often seen in the natural sciences, and open notebook science (Bradley, 2006, 2007; Schapira et al., 2019) could encourage researchers to be more transparent and provide more valuable information about their data analyses.

Many of science's greatest discoveries began with a researcher who first made a hypothesis that turned out to be flatly incorrect but later made and tested a new hypothesis that turned out to be correct. As described in Watson's (1997) firsthand account, Watson and Crick (1953) went through multiple iterations of hypotheses for the structure of DNA. They hypothesized that DNA consisted of 1, 2, 3, or 4 chains, that the chains were held together by Magnesium or Calcium ions (in fact they are held together by hydrogen bonds), that DNA's helix had rotations of different lengths (e.g., 28 or 68 Angstroms), and so forth. Their work led to so many disproven hypotheses that their laboratory director, Sir Francis

Bragg (a Nobel Laureate), attempted to ban them from continuing work on the topic. Efforts by other researchers, including Linus Pauling (Pauling & Corey, 1953), also consisted of multiple tests of disproven hypotheses. The scientific method allows for this research strategy and has led to Nobel Prize winning discoveries like Watson and Crick.

Step 7: Repeat Steps 4–6 Many Times

The seventh step in the scientific method involves repeated testing of the hypothesis in different settings, using different methodologies, and often involving multiple teams of researchers. Independent verification of findings and conceptual variations of the methodology are important practices for hypothesis testing. This helps to avoid situations in which a researcher is motivated to marshal support for a hypothesis that is credited to him or her, even if a specific study does not demonstrate support for the hypothesis.

Step 8: After Many Successful Replications, Establish a Theory

A hypothesis can only become a theory if it is supported after multiple replications (or if it can be shown to be true using logical or mathematical proofs). Whether a hypothesis rises to the level of a theory depends on the amount and quality of data from the studies that are used to test it as well as an evaluation of the adequacy of the methodology used to test it.

Establishing a theory is a group effort undertaken by an entire scientific community. It requires multiple replications in different settings to yield enough studies for a thorough meta-analysis. Even researchers who established theories without collecting their own data (e.g., Einstein's work on general relativity, meta-analysts showing the validity generalization of conscientiousness and general mental ability) make use of data from multiple studies conducted by other researchers.

Note that a single researcher would likely not follow all of the steps of the scientific method in a single study. Instead, he or she could begin with conjectures, observations, general conclusions, and other ideas and conduct and publish research on different steps of the process. For instance, a researcher could develop hypotheses or publish observations that could later be followed up and tested empirically by other research teams. Further note that abduction (i.e., proposing and testing hypotheses that explain a phenomenon) can also be implemented using the scientific method. Essentially, a researcher could use abduction to generate explanatory hypotheses which are then tested using the steps in the scientific method.

As we will discuss later in this chapter, we believe that the current state of theory development in I-O psychology and management has diverged from how theories are developed in other fields of science. I-O psychology and management researchers often start directly with creating a theory, ignoring the earlier steps in the scientific method that should lead to theory development. In addition, I-O psychology and management researchers are often encouraged to develop new theories in each paper they write as top journals often will not publish papers that do not develop new theory or that seek to test existing theories and hypotheses (Hambrick, 2007).

Designing Studies to Produce Quality Evidence and Evaluating the Quality of Evidence

When designing tests of a hypothesis, a researcher should consider the quality of evidence that will be generated by the study and how that relates to the hypothesis. Researchers should also consider the quality of evidence in support (or not in support) of a hypothesis when deciding whether to revise it or create a new hypothesis and whether the hypothesis can become a theory. As many researchers are aware, there are inherent issues with research practices and the literature, including lack of replications, fallacies (e.g., the jingle-jangle fallacy, the fallacy that correlation implies causation), and insufficient testing of hypotheses. Thus, it is important to consider the quality of evidence for a hypothesis or theory. Medical researchers have devised a pyramid or hierarchy of evidence used to evaluate evidence for medical hypotheses and theories as part of evidence-based medicine. This framework, although not without its critics (e.g., Blunt, 2015), can be used by I-O psychologists when following the steps in the scientific method. Indeed, I-O psychologists have begun to incorporate aspects of evidence-based medicine into I-O psychology and management research (Pfeffer & Sutton, 2006; Reay, Berta & Kohn, 2009).

The pyramid of evidence can be traced to a report by the Canadian Task Force on the Periodic Health Examination (1979). Since that time, different adaptations of the pyramid have been developed. Blunt (2020) has catalogued 195 versions as of August 2020, almost all of which appear in medical outlets. Reay et al. (2019) presented an adaptation of the pyramid for management research. Using many of the pyramids that Blunt (2020) catalogued, as well as the one by Reay et al. (2019), we compiled the pyramid of evidence shown in Figure 13.2. We added a few sources of evidence that are more germane to I-O psychology using asterisks.

As one progresses from the bottom of the pyramid of evidence to the top, the quality of evidence increases. At the very bottom of the pyramid are untested hypotheses and at the top of the pyramid are theories and solid empirical findings, often demonstrating evidence of causality. The pyramid shown in Figure 13.2 contains some methodologies that are not widely used in I-O psychology (e.g., case control studies) but that perhaps could be useful approaches to

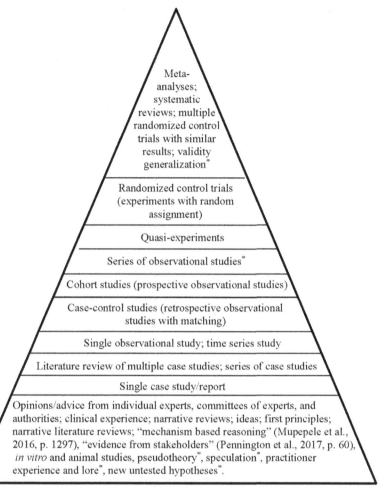

Meta-
analyses;
systematic
reviews; multiple
randomized control
trials with similar
results; validity
generalization[*]

Randomized control trials
(experiments with random
assignment)

Quasi-experiments

Series of observational studies[*]

Cohort studies (prospective observational studies)

Case-control studies (retrospective observational
studies with matching)

Single observational study; time series study

Literature review of multiple case studies; series of case studies

Single case study/report

Opinions/advice from individual experts, committees of experts, and
authorities; clinical experience; narrative reviews; ideas; first principles;
narrative literature reviews; "mechanism based reasoning" (Mupepele et al.,
2016, p. 1297), "evidence from stakeholders" (Pennington et al., 2017, p. 60),
in vitro and animal studies, pseudotheory[*], speculation[*], practitioner
experience and lore[*], new untested hypotheses[*].

Note: *Additions we made ourselves are denoted with asterisks.*

FIGURE 13.2 The pyramid of evidence as summarized from multiple sources.

studying the effects of organizational interventions when experiments are not feasible. We also should note that in some contexts (e.g., personnel selection), the ultimate goal is to establish valid prediction rather than causality and thus some forms of evidence are not always applicable.

The Role of Pseudotheorizing Within the Pyramid of Evidence

It is worth noting that the pseudotheorizing (i.e., creating an elaborate untested hypothesis; Cucina et al., 2014) that has become popular in I-O psychology and management journals is not explicitly included in the medical versions of the pyramid of evidence. It is most closely related to "mechanism-based reasoning" and "mechanistic reasoning" which Mupepele et al. (2016) included in the bottom layer of the pyramid. They define this type of reasoning as a statement that is not based on empirical data but instead is based on an inferential chain of mechanisms. Howick, Glasziou & Aronson, (2010) provide more insight on mechanistic reasoning in the medical field, where it is defined as an inferential link between mechanisms and an outcome for a patient. A mechanism is a hypothesis, theory (Howick et al., 2010), or "nomological machine" (Cartwright, 1999, p. 50) involving features or systems that have regular inputs and outputs, such as the heart. Essentially, mechanistic reasoning is conjecture that uses established findings and concepts to predict the outcome associated with an intervention. Howick et al. (2010) pointed out several examples of cases in which mechanistic reasoning led to incorrect conclusions (e.g., the famous author of childrearing advice books, Dr. Spock, used mechanistic reasoning to recommend that parents place their babies on their stomachs when sleeping to reduce the risk of babies choking on vomit and dying of sudden infant death syndrome). In our field, pseudotheorizing is not always used to justify organizational interventions; however, we do note several parallels between the quality of resulting evidence and thinking processes of mechanistic reasoning and pseudotheorizing. Both involve using the literature to make inferential leaps and create new propositions. This is not to say that mechanistic reasoning and hypothesizing should be discounted, as Howick et al. (2010) point out. It can serve as the basis for hypotheses that are later tested empirically and that ascend the pyramid of evidence. Mechanistic reasoning can also be more valid when each link in the inferential chain is tied to robust empirical evidence.

Howick et al. (2010) also noted an issue with lengthier inferential chains that has parallels with a fact that is based on path analysis. They give an example of an input having five intermediate steps, each with an effect of .90 probability leading to an outcome. On the surface, one might expect that the input will lead to the outcome with high certainty; however, the final effect of the intervention on the outcome is $.90^5$, which equals only .59. A similar situation can occur with path analysis and organizational pseudotheorizing. Suppose that an organizational intervention has a standardized path analysis coefficient of .50 with construct A, which in turn has a .50 coefficient with construct B, which in turn has a .50 coefficient with job performance and that there are no significant unmodeled paths (e.g., a direct path from A to job performance) in the model (see Figure 13.3). We might conclude that the intervention has a sizable effect on job performance because the standardized coefficients in each path are all large effect sizes (per Cohen, 1992). However, the path analysis tracing rule (Kenny, 1979, 2004) tells us that the correlation between the intervention and job performance is only .5 × .5 × .5, which equals .125, a small effect. Unfortunately, authors often

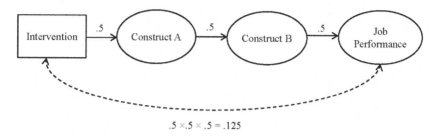

FIGURE 13.3   Path analysis model showing the diminishing effect from an intervention to job performance when it passes through two mediating constructs.

create hypotheses and pseudotheories involving these types of paths between constructs without realizing that the underlying multiplicative effect leads to small outcomes.

How the Pyramid of Evidence Informs the Scientific Method

The pyramid of evidence can inform the scientific method and there is an inherent reciprocal relationship between the two. Much of the evidence at the base of the pyramid (e.g., opinions, advice, experience, a case study) can serve as the observations in step 1 of the scientific method and can inspire the research questions and hypotheses in steps 2 and 3. Steps 4 and 5 are represented in the middle of the pyramid of evidence where single observational or experimental studies appear. As additional studies testing the hypothesis are conducted (i.e., steps 6 and 7), the evidence for a hypothesis is closer to the top. Only when the hypothesis has been supported by repeated testing can it be considered a theory.

The quality of evidence for testing a hypothesis and establishing a theory depends on the methodology used to collect data in empirical studies. Poorer quality methodologies (e.g., case studies) appear at the bottom of the pyramid of evidence. Methodologies that show a correlation between a potential cause and outcome appear in the middle, with statistical control methods (e.g., case-control studies, cohort studies) bolstering the quality of evidence. Experimental methods are required for demonstrating causality and these methods appear at the top of the pyramid. One of goals of evidence-based medicine is to identify which treatments have a causal effect on a patient's outcome, thus experiments (i.e., randomized control trials) are often considered the best type of primary study. However, issues of Type I and II errors and replicability, and other methodological issues (Cook & Campbell, 1979) can impact the results of experiments and observational studies. This is why the pyramid of evidence places repeated studies with similar results (which can include meta-analyses of those studies) at its pinnacle and the scientific method defines theory (its pinnacle finding) as a hypothesis that has received support from multiple studies using different methodologies. Thus, in most fields of science, a meta-analytic review would form the basis of theoretical establishment, whereas some I-O psychologists have written that "a review or meta-analysis does not constitute good theory" (Klein & Zedeck, 2004, p. 932).

The pyramid of evidence also adds systematic reviews, which are common in the medical literature, to its pinnacle. Uman (2011) provides an overview of medical systematic reviews, which we summarize here. Unlike a traditional narrative literature review, when conducting a systematic review, the authors search and locate articles that meet certain criteria (e.g., a specific population, specific key terms). This is similar to the literature search strategy that is used in meta-analyses. In contrast, traditional narrative reviews often do not include a detailed list of search criteria, but instead might include literature that an author is familiar with. Typically, two coders separately review each study and extract data (e.g., sample size, methodology, results) and a measure of inter-rater reliability is computed. A meta-analysis is then typically conducted with supplemental analyses (e.g., forest and funnel plots) to assist in examining heterogeneity of results and publication bias. In some cases, a meta-analysis is not appropriate due to differing methodologies or outcome variables used in the studies (Cochrane Library, n.d.). Many medical systematic reviews are conducted as part of the Cochrane Collaboration (which includes a peer review and publication of the research protocol) and often included detailed information on the methodology including separate 1–2 page tables describing characteristics of each study (e.g., methods, participants, setting, potential sources of bias, outcomes; see, e.g., Merry et al., 2012). Thus, these reviews not only provide the overall meta-analytic results but also compile summaries of individual articles in one place that could be useful to researchers and practitioners. This is one practice that I-O psychology could consider following.

Systematic reviews also consider the methodologies and limitations of the studies being reviewed, which could address some limitations of meta-analysis. For instance, if the database of studies for a meta-analysis omitted certain potential moderators, populations, or other key variables, then the authors of a systematic review could highlight those limitations for further research and to caution researchers and practitioners about potential boundary conditions for the findings. Additionally, systematic reviews are regularly updated. The Cochrane Collaboration recommends that its medical reviews be examined periodically to determine if an update is warranted and provides guidance for doing so (Cumpston & Chandler, 2020). A survival analysis of 100 completed meta-analytic systematic reviews determined that median survival time of a review (i.e., the time at which the results had a meaningful change since the previous review was conducted) was 5.5 years (Shojania et al., 2007). This speaks to the importance of (a) authors of meta-analyses examining whether their meta-analytic findings have changed since publication and (b) journals being open to publishing updated meta-analyses.

Other Configurations between Data, Methods, and Theory

The scientific method described earlier in this chapter is the predominant approach for empirical research used in nearly all fields of science (Cucina et al., 2014). I-O psychology has shifted in its approach in recent years, placing a much greater emphasis on theory (Cucina & Moriarty, 2015). However, there has also been discussion of how induction and deduction can inform scientific research. In our opinion, both approaches (i.e., focus on making a theoretical contribution and distinguishing between induction and deduction) have been misguided. In the next two sections, we discuss these two approaches in detail, pointing out how they relate to and conflict with the scientific method and how the scientific method should be the preferred approach in I-O psychology.

The Myth of the "Theoretical Contribution"

Earlier we mentioned the rise of "theory" in I-O psychology and management, which has been well documented (e.g., Aguinis et al., 2014; Cortina, 2014; Nicklin & Spector, 2016). In this section, we provide a clear definition of what theory should and should not be in science and explain how it is nearly impossible for authors to make a true theoretical contribution in their manuscripts. We make the case that by conducting research with the primary intent to make a theoretical contribution in our manuscripts; we are actually making our work less scientific. Our motivation is not to cast blame, but instead to steer I-O and management research onto the road of the scientific method and off of the road of pseudotheory.

How Do We Define Theory? The first author began with an informal review of the I-O psychology and management textbooks, editorial statements, and chapters to find a definition of "theory." It proved difficult to find a clear, concise, and agreed-upon definition of what a theory is in the I-O psychology and management literatures. Similar observations have been made by Corley and Gioia (2011) and Sutton & Staw (1995). Some of the common characteristics of what a "theory" is include long passages of text containing what Cortina (2016 p. 1143) termed "revelatory originality" rather than summaries of well-replicated empirical findings. Cortina, Aguinis, and DeShon (2017) traced the history of publications in the *Journal of Applied Psychology* and noted that in the early 1960s, introduction sections were often a couple of paragraphs. By the 1980s, a couple of pages were devoted to theory, and since the 1990s introduction sections have continued to grow in order to more fully develop it.

New "theories" are often based on case studies, common-sense, or tangentially related research. Incorporating a previously stated hypothesis or well-established theory is frowned upon and criticized as being "nothing new" and "argumentation by citation" (Ketchen, 2002, p. 586). Thus, new constructs are proposed and "surprising" statements are awarded the distinction of good theory, whereas previously supported hypotheses are not regarded as making a theoretical contribution (Corley & Gioia, 2011; Mintzberg, 2005). Figures showing complex causal models with independent, dependent, mediating, and moderating variables are common in theoretical work. This is despite the fact that the less parsimonious a causal model is the less likely it is to be true as pointed out recently by Saylors and Trafimow (2021) in the context of organizational research and by Aristotle, St. Thomas Aquinas, and William of Ockham hundreds of years ago in the context of science in general (Kaye, n.d.).

How Do Other Sciences Define Theory? Other scientific fields have much more clear and concise definitions of theory. A survey of college textbooks and interdisciplinary literature from other fields of sciences (e.g., astronomy, physics, biology) by Cucina et al. (2014) revealed a clear consensus: a theory is a well-replicated and strongly supported hypothesis. A similar survey was conducted for this paper using updated sources, and the definitions of hypothesis and theory quoted in Table 13.1 largely confirm Cucina et al.'s (2014) findings.

In I-O psychology and management, some leading journals (e.g., *Academy of Management Review*) publish only articles which essentially propose new hypotheses and models (rather than establishing that a hypothesis is well-replicated and strongly supported). Leading journals in other fields of science rarely publish articles that contain only hypotheses. For example, *Nature* (2015) publishes articles that are hypotheses "rarely, only about once a year." Moreover, it is rare for a journal to publish only speculative work. We found few analogues to the theoretical outlets of the organizational sciences in other areas of science. One exception is the journal *Medical Hypotheses* (n.d.), which publishes "interesting theoretical papers." The criteria for publication are whether or not a manuscript presents ideas that "are radical, interesting, and well-argued" (Corbyn, 2010). However, *Medical Hypotheses* has a controversial track record and is largely looked down upon by the scientific community (Corbyn, 2010).

How We Are Misdefining Theory. The theories we develop often fail to meet the definition of theory used in other sciences and many theories are only tested once, if at all (Edwards et al., 2014; Kacmar & Whitfield, 2000). Consider that theories in other fields of science are most often based on numerous empirical studies that have provided considerable support for a hypothesis. Yet much of the pseudotheory produced in the I-O psychology and management literatures lacks empirical support (Edwards et al., 2014). Modern theories in I-O psychology and management literatures often reflect the personal viewpoints of the authors rather than the very empirical evidence that should be reported. This is

TABLE 13.1 Definition of "hypothesis" and "theory" in different fields of science

Field	Hypothesis	Theory	Source
Astronomy	"One possible explanation of the observed facts."	"One or more 'well-tested' hypotheses [that have been] elevated to the stature of a physical law and come to form the basis of a theory of even broader applicability .... Scientific theories share several important defining characteristics: they must be testable, ... tested, ... simple, ... [and] elegant."	Chaisson and McMillan (2017, p. 22)
	"an idea that leads to testable predictions. The scientific method consists of observation or ideas, followed by hypothesis, followed by prediction, followed by further observation or experiments to test the prediction, and ending with a tested theory."	"If continuing tests fail to disprove a hypothesis, the scientific community will come to accept it as a theory and, after enough confirmation, eventually treat it as a law of nature. Scientific theories are only accepted as long as their predictions are borne out ... Science is sometimes misunderstood because of the ways that scientists use everyday words. An example is the word *theory*. In everyday language, theory may mean a conjecture or a guess .... In everyday parlance a theory is something worthy of little serious regard. "After all," people say, "it's only a theory. " In stark contrast, a *scientific* **theory** is a carefully constructed proposition that takes into account all the relevant data and all our understanding of how the world works. ... A successful and well-corroborated theory is the pinnacle of human knowledge about the world."	Kay et al. (2013, p. 9)
Physics	"an educated guess"	"a synthesis of a large body of information that encompasses well-tested and verified hypotheses about certain aspects of the natural world."	Hewitt (2015, pp. 8–9)
	"any statement of interest that can be empirically tested. That the moon is made of cheese is a hypothesis, which was empirically tested, for example, by the Apollo astronauts."	"theories[1] are created to explain the results of experiments that were created under certain conditions ...." [1]"The term 'theory' in science does not just mean 'what someone thinks,' or even 'what a lot of scientists think.' It means an interrelated set of statements that have predictive value, and that have survived a broad set of empirical tests."	Crowell (2020, p. 16)

(Continued)

TABLE 13.1 Definition of "hypothesis" and "theory" in different fields of science *(Continued)*

Field	Hypothesis	Theory	Source
Biology	"… [a] potential explanation… After making careful observations, scientists construct a **hypothesis**, which is suggested explanation that accounts for … observations. A hypothesis is a proposition that might be true."	"Scientists use the word **theory** in two main ways. The first meaning of theory is a proposed explanation for some natural phenomenon, often based on some general principle…Such theories often bring together concepts that were previously thought to be unrelated …. The second meaning of theory is the body of interconnected concepts, supported by scientific reasoning and experimental evidence, that explains the facts in some area of study …. To a scientist, theories are the solid ground of science, expressing ideas of which we are most certain. In contrast, to the general public, the word theory usually implies the opposite – a *lack* of knowledge, or a guess. Not surprisingly, this difference often results in confusion. In this text, theory will always be used in its scientific sense, in reference to an accepted general principle or body of knowledge ….Some critics outside of science attempt to discredit evolution by saying it is 'just a theory.' The hypothesis that evolution has occurred, however, is an accepted scientific fact – it is supported by overwhelming evidence."	Mason, Losos, Singer, Raven, and Johnson (2020, pp. 5–7)
	"a testable statement to explain a phenomenon or a set of observations"	"an explanation for a very general class of phenomena or observations that are supported by a wide body of evidence."	Freeman et al. (2017, pp. 2–3)
	"a proposed explanation for a natural phenomenon. It is a proposition based on previous observations or experimental studies ….A useful hypothesis must make **predictions** – expected outcomes that can be shown to be correct or incorrected…a useful hypothesis is testable"	"a broad explanation of some aspect of the natural world that is substantiated by a large body of evidence. Biological theories incorporate observations, hypothesis testing, and the laws of other disciplines such as chemistry and physics…In everyday language, a theory is often viewed as little more than a guess.… However, in biology, a theory is much more than a guess. A theory is an established set of ideas that explains a vast amount of data and offers valid predictions that can be tested."	Brooker et al., (2020 pp. 14–15)

(Continued)

TABLE 13.1 Definition of "hypothesis" and "theory" in different fields of science (*Continued*)

Field	Hypothesis	Theory	Source
	"A tentative, falsifiable explanation for one or more observations. If tests support a hypothesis, it may be incorporated into broader theories. Outside of science, *hypothesis* is used interchangeably with *theory*." "a proposed explanation for a phenomenon .... Commonly, when non-scientists use the word 'theory' – as in 'I've got a theory about why there's less traffic on Friday mornings than on Thursday mornings' – they actually mean that they have a hypothesis."	"Outside of science, the word *theory* is often used to describe an opinion or a hunch .... These tentative explanations are really untested hypotheses ....A falsifiable, comprehensive explanation for a natural phenomenon, typically backed with many lines of evidence. Nonscientists often use the term as a synonym for *opinion or hunch* ..." "an explanatory hypothesis for natural phenomena that is exceptionally well supported by the empirical data. A theory can be thought of as a hypothesis that has withstood the test of time and is unlikely to be altered by any new evidence.... it has ... been repeatedly tested and no observations or experimental results have contradicted it, a theory is viewed by the scientific community with nearly the same confidence as a fact. For this reason, it is inappropriate to describe something as 'just a theory' as a way of asserting that it is not likely to be true. Theories in science also tend to be broader in scope than hypotheses ... Scientific theories do not represent speculation or guesses ... Rather, they are hypotheses – proposed explanations for natural phenomena – that have been so strongly and persuasively supported by empirical observation that the scientific community views them as very unlikely to be altered by new evidence."	Hoefnagels (2019, pp. 13–14) Phelan (2015, p. 22)
Chemistry	"*a tentative explanation for a set of observations.*"	"*a unifying principle that explains a body of facts and/or those laws that are based on them* .... Proving or disproving a theory can take years, even centuries, in part because the necessary technology may not be available."	Chang & Goldsby (2019, p. 5)

(*Continued*)

TABLE 13.1 Definition of "hypothesis" and "theory" in different fields of science (*Continued*)

Field	Hypothesis	Theory	Source
	"Whether derived from observation or from a 'spark of intuition,' a hypothesis is a proposal made to explain an observation. A sound hypothesis need not be correct, but it must be *testable by experiment*."	"Set of conceptual assumptions that explains data from accumulated experiments; predicts related phenomena … **theories**, based on *experiments* that test *hypotheses* about *observations* distinguishes scientific thinking from speculation ….As hypotheses are revised according to experimental results, a model emerges to explain how the phenomenon occurs …. If reproducible data support a hypothesis, a model (theory) can be developed to explain the observed phenomenon"	Silberberg & Amateis (2018, pp. 12–13)
	"a tentative and testable explanation for an observation or a series of observations"	"a general explanation of widely observed phenomena that has been extensively tested ….Theories usually start out as tentative explanations of why a set of experiments results was obtained, or why a particular phenomenon is consistently observed. Such a tentative explanation is called a **hypothesis** ….A hypothesis that withstands the tests of many experiments and accurately predicts the results of further observations and experimentation may be elevated to the rank of a scientific theory."	Gilbert et al., (2014, p. 14)
Geology	" … a tentative (untested) explanation …"	"When a hypothesis has survived extensive scrutiny and when competing hypotheses have been eliminated, a hypothesis may be elevated to the status of scientific **theory**. In everyday speech, we frequently hear people say 'that's only a theory,' implying that a theory is an educated guess or hypothesis. But to a scientist, a theory is a well-tested and widely accepted view that the scientific community agrees best explains certain observable facts."	Lutgens, Tarbuck and Tasa (2014, pp. 10)

(*Continued*)

TABLE 13.1 Definition of "hypothesis" and "theory" in different fields of science (*Continued*)

Field	Hypothesis	Theory	Source
	"A provisional explanation for observations that is subject to continual testing. If well-supported by evidence, a hypothesis may be called a theory ... Tentative explanations, or hypotheses, are then formulated to explain the observed phenomenon."	"An explanation for some natural phenomenon that has a large body of supporting evidence. To be scientific, a theory must be testable (e.g., plate tectonic theory) .... Finally, if one of the hypotheses is found, after repeated tests, to explain the phenomena, then that hypothesis is proposed as a theory .... The term theory has various meanings. In colloquial usage, it means a speculative or conjectural view of something – hence, the widespread belief that scientific theories are little more than unsubstantiated wild guesses. In scientific usage, however, a theory is a coherent explanation for one or several related natural phenomena supported by a large body of objective evidence."	Wicander and Monroe (2013, p. 5)
	"tentative explanations ... formulated to explain the observed phenomena."	"Finally, if one of the hypotheses is found, after repeated tests, to explain the phenomena, then the hypothesis is proposed as a theory."	Monroe and Wicander (2015, p. 6)
Psychology	"... the predicted outcome of an experiment or an educated guess about the relationship between two variables. In common terms, a hypothesis is a *testable* hunch about behavior."	"A **theory** is a system of ideas designed to interrelate concepts and facts in a way that summarizes existing data and predicts future observations."	Coon & Mitterer (2018, pp. 20–21)
	"a statement that can be used to test a prediction."	"**Theories** synthesize observations in order to explain phenomena, and they can be used to make predictions that can be tested through research. Many people believe that scientific theories are nothing more than unverified guesses or hunches, but they are mistaken (Stanovich, 2010). A theory is a well-established body of principles that often rests on a sturdy foundation of scientific evidence."	Licht and Hull (2014, pp. 20–21)

(Continued)

TABLE 13.1 Definition of "hypothesis" and "theory" in different fields of science (Continued)

Field	Hypothesis	Theory	Source
	"a tentative statement that describes the relationship between two or more *variables*. A hypothesis is often stated as a specific prediction that can be empirically tested…a testable prediction or question."	"a tentative explanation that tries to account for diverse findings on the same topic … a theory integrates and summarizes numerous research findings and observations on a particular topic."	Hockenbury, Nolan and Hockenbury (2015, p. 20)
Interdisciplinary	"A tentative explanation for an observation, phenomenon, or scientific problem that can be tested by further investigation. Scientific hypotheses must be posed in a form that allows them to be rejected."	"A plausible or scientifically acceptable, well-substantiated explanation of some aspect of the natural world; an organized system of accepted knowledge that applies in a variety of circumstances to explain a specific set of phenomena and predict the characteristics of as yet unobserved phenomena."	National Academy of Sciences (n.d.)
		"In everyday usage, 'theory' often refers to a hunch or a speculation. When people say, 'I have a theory about why that happened', they are often drawing a conclusion based on fragmentary or inconclusive evidence. The formal scientific definition of theory is quite different from the everyday meaning of the word. It refers to a comprehensive explanation of some aspect of nature that is supported by a vast body of evidence. Many scientific theories are so well-established that no new evidence is likely to alter them substantially."	National Academy of Sciences and Institute of Medicine (2008, p. 11)
	"A tentative statement about the natural world leading to deductions that can be tested. If the deductions are verified, the hypothesis is provisionally corroborated. If the deductions are incorrect, the original hypothesis is proved false and must be abandoned or modified. Hypotheses can be used to build more complex inferences and explanations."	"In science, a well-substantiated explanation of some aspect of the natural world that can incorporate facts, laws, inferences, and tested hypotheses." Note that a Law is defined as "a descriptive generalization about how some aspect of the natural world behaves under stated circumstances."	National Center for Science Education (2016)

(Continued)

TABLE 13.1 Definition of "hypothesis" and "theory" in different fields of science (*Continued*)

Field	Hypothesis	Theory	Source
	"a possible (tentative) scientific explanation or prediction of an observation or set of observations…A hypothesis must be testable through a scientific investigation."	"A theory is a comprehensive explanation of some aspect of nature that is supported by a vast body of evidence. A theory is used to explain many different hypotheses about the same phenomenon or a closely related class of phenomena. Scientific theories are well-established and highly-reliable explanations that have been verified multiple times by repeated testing and have a great deal of empirical evidence that confirm them as valid."	Texas Gateway/ Texas Education Agency (n.d.)
	"an idea that proposes a tentative explanation about a phenomenon or a narrow set of phenomena observed in the natural world. The two primary features of a scientific hypothesis are falsifiability and testability, which are reflected in an 'If … then' statement summarizing the idea and in the ability to be supported or refuted through observation and experimentation."	"a broad general explanation that incorporates data from many different scientific investigations undertaken to explore hypotheses."	Rogers (2016)

Note: In all cases, emphasis appears in the original texts.

problematic as human beings have an amazing ability to create hypotheses that are flat out wrong. Examples exist in psychology (Lilienfeld et al., 2009), statistics (Lance & Vandenberg, 2015), logic (illogical fallacies such as assuming that if all S are P, then all P must be S), physics (even Albert Einstein was not infallible as he incorrectly hypothesized the existence of a cosmological constant; Harvey & Schucking, 2000; Siegel, 2013), and prescience (e.g., noting that birds did not succumb to the plague, medieval doctors assumed that wearing beak-shaped masks would make them immune to disease).

Additionally, elegance and parsimony are considered hallmarks of true scientific theories, yet much of our pseudotheories contain multiple hypotheses, paths, mediators, moderators, moderated mediators, and so forth. In some cases, prior works (e.g., previously published hypotheses or true scientific theories) are cited (and miscited) with only cursory attention to how these relate to, or can be tested in, the current study. The typical theory produced today is unclear, unconcise, untested, and often untestable. Contrast this with the true scientific theories that exist in our field such as goal-setting theory (Locke & Latham, 2002), validity generalization of general mental ability (Schmidt & Hunter, 2004), classical test theory (Nunnally & Bernstein, 1994), and item–response theory (Hambleton, Swaminathan & Rogers, 1991).

Sometimes researchers define "theory" as the "how" behind a particular process or phenomenon. In other fields of science, this is known as the mechanism of a process. Although the mechanism of how a particular medication works or selection procedure works may not be critical for practical purposes, from a basic science perspective these are questions that are important. However, simply proposing a mechanism is not an adequate approach to understanding the "how" behind a process. Empirical work would need to be conducted to test the hypothesized mechanism. Thus, the "how" behind a process is a hypothesis in and of itself.

How Do Many Management/I-O Psychology Researchers Define Theoretical Contributions? Authors today strive to make a theoretical contribution in their manuscripts. But what is a theoretical contribution? In I-O psychology and management journals, a theoretical contribution is viewed as "new and innovative ideas and insights" and "meaningfully exten[sion of] existing theory" (*Journal of Applied Psychology, 89*(1), 178). It involves hypotheses, conjecture, stories, and imagination. Making a theoretical contribution is not viewed as an empirical process (in contrast to the scientific method). For example, consider the recommendations and inspirational messages for creating theory quoted in Table 13.2. These statements show that creating theory is much more art than science.

Unfortunately, the theoretical statements that most often appear in the recent I-O psychology and management literature are not really theories from a scientific standpoint. These statements are often poorly constructed hypotheses involving

TABLE 13.2 Quotations showing an unscientific definition of theory by OB and management theorists

Author (Year)	Quote	Page
Mintzberg (2005)	"We don't discover theory; we create it"	4
	"We get interesting theory when we let go of all this scientific correctness ... and allow our minds to roam freely and creatively – to muse like mad ..."	10
	"stories and anecdotes are better than measures on seven point scales and the like"	10
Davis (1971)	Good theorists are "*imaginative*" (italics appear in original)	344
	"Qualitative correlations" form better theories and are more "interesting than quantitative correlations"	323
	Too much focus on the scientific method results in "the 'Mediocre'"	328
	"'the creative spark'"	328
Sutton & Staw (1995)	Those who are "good at theoretical" work are "dreamy"	380
Klein & Zedeck (2004)	"Assertion and even evidence are no substitute for explanation and interpretation"	932
Shepherd & Suddaby (2017)	"compelling theories are at their core compelling stories." "theory building [can be centered] around the five key elements that inform every great story: conflict, character, setting, sequence, and plot and arc."	60 60

models that are too complex[3] to test in a single study, regardless of how well designed the study may be. Future researchers are discouraged from testing these hypotheses further because in doing so they fail to make their own new "theoretical contribution" by proposing new hypotheses. Thus, hypotheses are often only tested partially in the paper that proposes them (and some are not tested at all). As a result, we are creating new hypotheses and not allowing them to become falsifiable (one of the hallmarks of well-constructed hypotheses in science). These hypotheses often take up considerable journal page space, which is a limited resource. Highhouse (2014) has noted a substantial increase in the length of articles in I-O journals. This raises a question about the value of journal pages that present ideas lacking evidence of support or disconfirmation. If the goal of I-O psychology and management research is to improve the functioning of the workplace, shouldn't our journals strive to focus on publishing text that has an empirical basis? A better approach, as will be described below, would be to remove much of the hypothesizing and theoretical conjecture in favor of more concise and factual articles. The remaining pages could then be replaced with additional articles, especially conceptual replications of earlier works (Kepes & McDaniel, 2013).

What Is a True "Theoretical Contribution"? I-O psychologists' and management researchers' definition of a theoretical contribution differs greatly from that used in other sciences. In other fields, a theoretical contribution would include the results of a multi-study empirical research program that follows the scientific method. Locke & Latham's (2002) goal-setting theory is an excellent example of a theoretical contribution, yet making this contribution involved a "35-year odyssey" (p. 705) with over 400 studies by many scientists (Locke, 2007). Other examples of a theoretical contribution would include a meta-analysis showing a robust effect size (with small credibility intervals and no publication bias) or a review that convincingly shows support for a hypothesis. Occasionally, a crucial study that disconfirms an existing theory arises. This also could lead to a theoretical contribution; however, it might need to be replicated before rising to the level of a theoretical contribution. Thus, according to the scientific definition of theory and the scientific method, it would be extremely difficult for an author to make a theoretical contribution in a single paper.

In fact, in other fields of science, the term "theoretical contribution" rarely appears in individual articles. A search of two premiere multidisciplinary scientific journals (i.e., *Nature* and *Science*) was conducted for the phrase "theoretical contribution" through 2020. In *Nature*, this phrase appeared in only 101 of 422,374 articles. The term was almost always used to commend the work of someone else. Most of the hits, (i.e., 83) bestowed the term "theoretical contribution" on someone else, often in obituaries and stories of individuals receiving awards. Nine articles stated that based on existing theory, something can make a "theoretical" contribution to a process (e.g., there might be a "theoretical contribution of the three amino-acids" [Burgus et al., 1970] in a particular reaction). Seven articles mentioned the phrase in announcements for other (often new) journals. One article complained about untested theoretical contributions and the last mentioned it in terms of determining authorship credit.

The term was less commonly used in *Science*. Out of 297,556 articles, only 13 included the term. Again, the phrase "theoretical contribution" was most often used (in 11 of the 13 hits) to commend work of someone else, especially in obituaries and announcements of awards that have been given to certain individuals. Only two articles actually stated that the authors made a theoretical contribution. In an article about the planet Jupiter, Trafton and Wildey (1970) wrote that "The primary theoretical contribution of the study reported here has been the incorporation of the ammonia bands at 10 and 16 A into the model...." More recently, Lacour and Green (2014) authored an article on transmission of gay equality and stated "Our theoretical contribution is to introduce the distinction between active and passive contact, which are posited to produce different..." As an aside, this article was later retracted from *Science*.

Why Making a True Theoretical Contribution in One Paper Is Almost Mythical Authors are encouraged to write papers that make a theoretical contribution. As described above, this involves proposing a theory that is new and surprising, one that has not been presented in the literature previously. However, from a scientific standpoint, a paper that truly makes a theoretical contribution is almost mythical. Science is an incremental process, and few papers really can establish a brand new scientific theory that other scientists did not anticipate. Scientific theories evolve over many years and involve multiple published and presented studies, followed by a meta-analysis or review. In contrast with other fields of science, our field does not view this type of evidence as theory (Klein & Zedeck, 2004).

Clearly, we need to (re)embrace meta-analytic methods and other forms of credible evidence (e.g., systematic reviews) as a path toward establishing a theory. However, we also need to reconsider the notion that a theoretical contribution must be something completely new. This expectation has led to a proliferation of untested theories in I-O psychology and management (Edwards et al., 2004). Given the multiple steps involved in the scientific method for replication and designing new studies to test a hypothesis, it is often not logistically feasible for a researcher to create a novel hypothesis and establish it as a theory in a single paper, especially a primary study. Indeed, it is quite rare for a researcher to create a hypothesis and then find multiple existing studies showing enough support to establish it as a theory. Some possible exceptions exist. For example, Schmidt & Hunter's (1977) validity generalization of general mental ability tests and Einstein's theory of special relativity are possible exceptions. Yet, these theoretical contributions, although later shown to be strongly supported, underwent extensive empirical testing after being introduced. Schmidt and Hunter encountered substantial resistance to validity generalization, but after many follow-up articles (e.g., Schmidt et al., 1985) it was eventually accepted by most of the scientific community (Schmidt, 2015). Einstein's work also received initial skepticism and follow-up testing (Brush, 1999; Goldberg, 1987), but now is widely accepted. Both theories were also based on existing experimental evidence. Validity generalization was initially based on observations that small sample industrial validity coefficients varied widely, whereas large sample validity coefficients from military studies were more consistent (Schmidt, 2015).

It also might be possible for a researcher to spend years iterating through the steps of the scientific method to turn his or her new hypothesis into a theory and then publish all of the results at once. However, this is not a wise career move; the researcher's *CV* would have a huge hole, funding institutions and employers would wonder what progress is being made, and so forth. Additionally, other researchers would not be able to conduct independent tests and provide evidence that the results replicate in other contexts. Thus, this is not a viable approach.

The Best That Can Be Done. So what is the best that can be done in a single paper with respect to theory? A researcher can create a hypothesis that is new to the literature and either test it or propose that others test it (e.g., in an outlet such as *AMR*). After extensive testing this hypothesis could become recognized as a theory and the researcher could be noted for making a theoretical contribution. Additionally, a researcher could revise an existing hypothesis (and optionally test it). Researchers can also continue testing previously published hypotheses, which may one day become theory. Hypotheses can become theories when there is a large body of empirical evidence providing their support. Meta-analyses and literature reviews summarize the results of multiple studies testing a hypothesis. These types of reviews (quantitative and qualitative) provide the strongest basis for establishing a new theory, although many in our field would incorrectly view them as not making a theoretical contribution. Essentially, making a theoretical contribution, as defined in the sciences, is most often an effort of the scientific community rather than an effort of one person or one paper.

How to Use Theory Correctly. Currently, many authors develop a new theory to generate hypotheses for I-O psychology and management empirical research. However, there is another way to incorporate theory when designing research studies. There are many well-supported truly scientific theories in the basic research literature. Our field is sitting next to a scientific theory goldmine in other psychology journals, yet we neglect it in favor of creating our own untested theories. Originally, the goal of applied psychology was to apply theories and findings from basic psychology to the real world. However, we have drifted away from this goal.

Some examples of how to incorporate theory from other disciplines exist in the I-O related literature. For example, there is strong evidence for the theory of the self-serving bias in the social psychology and personality literatures (e.g., Dunning, Perie & Story, 1991). The essence of this theory is that when asked which traits are important for success, individuals have a tendency to report that the traits they perceive themselves as having are more important than other traits. Three studies have tested the theory of the self-serving bias in a new context, job analysis ratings, and have found that it exists in job analysis data (Aguinis, Mazurkiewicz & Heggestad, 2009; Cucina et al., 2012; Cucina, Vasilopoulos & Sehgal, 2005). In another example, based on empirical work encompassing over 460 datasets, Carroll (1993) developed the Three-Stratum Theory of mental abilities. One of these abilities, Meaningful Memory, bares a strong resemblance to the process of learning material in a training environment. It involves the ability to recall, after a study period, material that involves meaningful interrelations (e.g., a story, a concept, a biography of an individual). Recent work applying this ability from Carroll's theory shows that it is one of the few specific abilities that uniquely predicts training performance beyond general mental ability (Cucina et al., 2014). A third example resides in work by Carter et al. (2014) who applied the item response theory generalized graded unfolding model (GGUM; Roberts, Donoghue & Laughlin, 2000) from the psychometrics literature to scoring personality tests.

The Scientific Method as an Alternative to "Inductive" and "Deductive" Research

In recent years, there have been calls for renewed interest in inductive research within I/O psychology and OB (Locke, 2007; Locke, Williams & Masuda, 2015; Ones et al. 2017; Spector et al, 2014; Woo, O'Boyle & Spector, 2017). This can be contrasted with the heavy focus on deduction and theory building in many academic journals (Aguinis et al., 2014; Campbell & Wilmot, 2018; Cortina, 2014; Dilchert, 2017; Hambrick, 2007; Highhouse, 2014; Kepes & McDaniel, 2013; Olenick et al., 2018; Ones et al., 2017; Schneider, 2018). In this context, induction is often viewed as making an observation that is based on empirical data and then developing a general conclusion or a theory. Deduction is often viewed as developing general conclusions or theory and testing those empirically. In brief, induction is viewed as going from the particular to the general and deduction is viewed as going from the general to the particular.

In this section, we briefly review existing conceptualizations of inductive and deductive research often used in I/O psychology and OB. We then present alternative conceptualizations of induction and deduction that are more closely aligned with those appearing in the philosophical and logical literatures. We then describe how the different conceptualizations fit into the scientific method. We go further by suggesting that researchers can avoid having to make distinctions between induction and deduction by simply following the scientific method. Aspects of both conceptualizations of induction and deduction are folded into and encompassed in the scientific method. Later, we explain how our work relates to the recent debate concerning the role of and emphasis on theory in I/O psychology and OB research. (See the four articles in the point/counterpoint section of the *Journal of Organizational Behavior* edited by Nicklin and Spector, 2016, for an example of the debate). We conclude with recommendations for researchers.

Deductive and Inductive Reasoning

The roots of inductive and deductive reasoning lie in formal logic and the philosophy of science. Both induction and deduction involve using premises (e.g., statements, principles, evidence, observations) to reach a conclusion. In deductive reasoning, provided that the premises are true, a valid conclusion is necessarily true with 100% certainty. For example, suppose that we are given two premises: "All nonprofit organizations are groups organized for a purpose other than generating a profit" and "G Group is a nonprofit organization." Assuming the premises are true, we can validly conclude (with complete certainty) that G Group was organized for a purpose other than generating a profit. Logicians define induction as using evidence to reach a conclusion that may be true but that is not guaranteed to be true (Hawthorne, 2017; Skyrms, 2000). The conclusions in inductive reasoning are valid but not completely certain; instead there is a level of probability or confirmation associated with each conclusion. For example, suppose that we are given two premises: "67% of nonprofit organizations are public charities" and "G Group is a nonprofit organization." Based on the premises, we can validly conclude that there is a .67 probability that G Group is a public charity; thus, although it is likely that G Group is a public charity, we are left uncertain.

In their comprehensive discussion of the relationship between deduction and induction, Colberg, Nester and Trattner (1985) showed that these two types of reasoning converge in terms of their forms but differ with respect to the certainty of their conclusions. The examples from the preceding paragraph are presented below to show both the convergence of the reasoning forms and the difference in the certainty of the conclusion. (They are presented in conditional form rather than in set form.)

If an entity is a nonprofit organization, then it was organized for purposes other than generating a profit.

G Group is a nonprofit organization.

Therefore, G Group was (necessarily) organized for purposes other than generating a profit. (deductive)

If an entity is a nonprofit organization, then there is a .67 probability that it is a public charity.

G Group is a nonprofit organization.

Therefore (with a probability of .67), G Group is a public charity. (inductive)

In the first example above, G Group must have been organized for purposes other than generating a profit because of its membership in the set of nonprofit organizations, all of which were organized for purposes other than generating a profit. This example represents a basic form in deductive logic, called "modus ponens," in which a necessary conclusion is drawn about an individual based on information in a universal premise. It begins with the premise "if p then q." If it is affirmed that p is true, then it follows that q is true. In this example, a necessary conclusion is drawn about an individual based on information in a universal premise. In the second example, there is no universal premise. Instead, the first premise says that if an entity is a nonprofit organization, then there is a .67 probability that it is a public charity.

The valid conclusion is stated with a probability of .67, which means that it is possible but not certain that G Group is a public charity. As Colberg et al. (1985) explain:

> When logicians state that an inductive conclusion is never certain, they mean that there is no identity between the premises and the conclusion. In a deductive conclusion there is such an identity. This is the same as saying that in a deductive conclusion, if the premises are true and the schema

is correctly constructed, then the conclusion cannot be false, whereas in an inductive conclusion, even if the premises are true and the schema is correctly constructed, the conclusion can still be false. The falsity of the conclusion in an inductive schema is compatible with the premises and with the schema. Thus, a deductive conclusion is always necessary, never probabilistic, and an inductive conclusion is always probabilistic, never necessary.

(p. 682)

As a consequence of the identity between premises and conclusion in deductive arguments, they "... are usually limited to inferences that follow from definitions, mathematics, and rules of formal logic" (*Internet Encyclopedia of Philosophy*, 2016). By contrast, scientific research tries to go beyond deductive argument by observing natural phenomena. When these observations are about sets that cannot be known in their entirety, observations are usually made about a sample from the phenomenon being investigated. Any general conclusion drawn from such samples is an inductive, probabilistic conclusion. The statistical tools that enable scientists to estimate, for example, a population value from sample statistics have been developed mathematically, that is to say deductively. The use of these estimates to describe the population in question, however, represents an inductive exercise because the estimates are based on incomplete information about the population.

In the organizational science and I/O psychology literatures, deduction is often defined as applying a general principle or rule to a specific case, and induction is often described as observing a series of specific cases and inferring and formulating a general principle from the specific cases. Colberg et al. (1985) traced this misconception of inductive reasoning to early psychometric research by Thurstone (1938), who defined the term as "find[ing] a rule or principle for each item in the test."[4] It has also made its way into the research methods literature, whereby the process of first observing data and then making a general statement (e.g., a hypothesis or theory) is defined as inductive research and the process of first making a general statement (especially a hypothesis) and then observing data is defined as deductive research. This way of defining inductive and deductive research is incompatible with definitions used in logic and the philosophy of science, and it obscures the fact that all scientific research involves both induction and deduction.

The Scientific Method Incorporates the Process of Going From Particular to General and Vice Versa

The previously described distinction between inductive and deductive research in terms of general to particular and particular to general research can be rendered moot by adoption of the scientific method, which incorporates both processes.

The process of going from particular to general appears in several steps in the scientific method. A researcher could observe a particular phenomenon in step 1 (i.e., make an observation) and then construct a research question and hypothesis in steps 2 and 3 which later lead to a general conclusion in step 8 (i.e., form a theory). For instance, a researcher might begin with the observation that scores on certain measures in a battery she administered are related to leadership success. The finding could be used to form more general research questions and hypotheses concerning the constructs measured in the battery. The working hypothesis could then be tested in a new study. After repeated replication and meta-analysis, it might be possible to establish a general conclusion and theory about the constructs in question and leadership success. Unless the conclusion is true with deductive certainty, it is considered an inductive conclusion.

The process of going from general to particular is also incorporated in the scientific method, especially in steps 3 to 6 (i.e., hypothesizing, predicting, and testing). A researcher with a conjectural statement could begin at step 3 of the scientific method and design empirical studies to test that conjecture and make predictions about the findings for particular datasets and studies.

It is also possible to start with a general corroborated scientific theory and then ask research questions and create hypotheses extending the theory to particular new settings. For example, a researcher might start with a theory that is established in the basic psychological research literature (e.g., social psychology) and see if it applies to a particular organizational issue. Alternatively, a researcher might begin with a theory that applies to a certain population and then test its validity in another population (e.g., examining whether the five-factor model of personality seen in Western samples applies to a newly studied applicant pool in a different country).

Overall, we believe that organizational researchers do not necessarily need to make the distinction between going to and from particular to general when conducting research. Instead, they can simply adopt the scientific method as it is used in other fields. Full adoption of the definition of the scientific method used in other fields would allow organizational researchers to make and publish research going from the particular to the general, without special calls for inductive research. It would also simplify the instruction of students. Learning the distinction between general and particular or inductive and deductive would no longer be needed. In addition, there would be greater consistency in how the scientific methods are taught in organizational sciences courses and courses in other areas of science.

The Scientific Method Incorporates the Philosophical Definitions of Induction and Deduction

In this section, we describe how the philosophical definitions of induction and deduction are incorporated in the scientific method. Induction deals with probabilities and it appears clearly between steps 5 and 6, during which a researcher makes a probabilistic determination (based on statistical significance and effect size) as to whether the hypothesis is supported. It also appears clearly in step 7, when a field of scientific researchers makes a determination as to whether there is a high enough probability that a hypothesis is true for it to be considered a theory. Bayesian statistics, whose creator was one of the principal contributors to the field of inductive logic (Fitelson, 2006), can play a key role in these determinations. Indeed, validity generalization (a scientific theory) uses Bayesian statistics (Schmidt & Hunter, 1977; Schmidt & Raju, 2007; Schmidt et al., 1979), and some authors have noted the ability of Bayesian statistics to synthesize prior knowledge, accept null hypotheses, and state theories (Jebb & Woo, 2015; Kruschke, Aguinis & Joo, 2012).

There are also some striking similarities between the outcomes of Bayesian statistical analyses (e.g., a probability) and the results of expectancy table analyses used in the personnel selection literature. For instance, given the meta-analytic operational validity of .66 for general mental ability tests in medium–complexity jobs, an individual in the top 25% of scores on this test has a 57.6% probability of being in the top 25% on the criterion (compared to 3.1% for individuals with a test score in the bottom 25%).[5] These types of probabilities are commonly used to predict risk in actuarial and medical settings, to create weather forecasts, and even predict earthquakes. However, in all instances, the conclusions involve a probability; even if the probability can be stated with extreme precision (e.g., the 95% confidence interval for the probability of 57.6% in the above example is 55.7% to 59.6%)[6], the conclusions about an individual case are still uncertain and involve a probability. Essentially, at a global level, all empirical research is inductive and none is exclusively deductive because the researcher is always making an inference based on incomplete information and the conclusion can only be probabilistic.

Although all empirical research in psychology is inductive, there are examples of truly deductive research in these fields. Mathematics is a field that makes extensive use of deduction, especially in mathematical proofs and theorems (which are essentially theories based on deduction). Consider the mathematical proof for the correction of a correlation coefficient between a predictor (p) and a criterion (c) for criterion unreliability. Using a deductive process, it is possible to go from the equations for a partial correlation coefficient and a variance decomposition to the equation for the correction for criterion unreliability. Assuming that the premises are true (e.g., the formulas for partial correlation and variance decomposition are correct, the algebraic manipulations used in the derivation are correct, measurement error is random and uncorrelated with the predictor and criterion), the conclusion (i.e., the formula for correction for unreliability is $r_{PC}/\sqrt{rel_C}$) must be true. This type of reasoning is prominent in the psychometric literature. In many ways, psychometricians could be called theoretical psychologists and the derivations and proofs for classical test theory, item-response theory, and generalizability theory are examples of deductive reasoning.

There are also instances in which either of the philosophical definitions of induction and deduction can appear in the scientific method. Consider step 1 of the scientific method (making an observation). Whether induction or deduction is involved depends on the nature of the observation itself. An observation that entails complete information on the population of interest could be the basis for a deductive conclusion. For instance, an organizational scientist might observe that all of the employees in an organization who were rated unsuccessful were trained at training center X. If the entire population was studied here, a valid deductive conclusion would be that if employee Y was rated unsuccessful, then employee Y was trained at training center X. An observation that would be the basis for an inductive conclusion would be one in which the organizational scientist observed that 80% of the employees rated unsuccessful were trained at training center X. A valid inductive inference would be that if employee Y was rated unsuccessful, then there is a .8 probability that employee Y was trained at training center X.

Conclusion

The scientific methodology of I-O psychology and management research is currently drifting away from the scientific method and toward an embrace of pseudotheory. Our research culture is impeding adoption of the scientific method. Researchers are motivated to make theoretical contributions in their papers, yet by doing so they have adopted an incorrect viewpoint of what theory is. According to the scientific method, making a theoretical contribution in a single primary study is impractical if not impossible. If the research literatures of I-O psychology and management are to truly make a contribution to scientific knowledge, major changes are needed. (Re)Adopting the scientific method provides a sound and established basis for further advancing I-O and management research and making better contributions to organizations. It also provides a framework for how data, methods, and theory are necessarily related in scientific research.

Authors' Note

The views expressed in this chapter are those of the authors and do not necessarily reflect the views of U.S. Customs and Border Protection or the U.S. Federal Government. The authors would like to thank Magda Colberg, Kevin Murphy, and Paul Sparrow for their valuable comments and suggestions on this chapter. Portions of this chapter are based on an invited Distinguished Early Career Contributions Award address given by the first author at the 31st meeting of the Society for Industrial and Organizational Psychology, Anaheim, CA.

Notes

1 The low level of statistical power in many psychological studies is also unfortunate. Thirty years ago, Cohen (1992) lamented that there was little increase in statistical power of psychology studies since the first edition of his power handbook (Cohen, 1969) was published. Low statistical power continues to be an issue in the literature as the Open Science Collaboration (2015) reported a median sample size of 54 cases for the 97 original psychological studies it replicated. The mean replication effect size was a correlation of .197. Thus, on average, the authors of the original studies were attempting to detect a correlation of .197 with only 54 cases, which equates to a power of .30 according to G*POWER (Faul et al., 2007; Faul et al., 2009).

2 Traditionally, a laboratory notebook consists of a bound book with blank pages in which a researcher documents their empirical research and analyses. Writing is often done by hand in ink and the pages cannot be removed inconspicuously. This allows for a diary or journal of the researcher's activities and can be made available to other researchers for inspection. Computer-based versions of laboratory notebooks are also used.

3 This might be due to the perceived complexity of human behavior. Oftentimes we hear that organizational behavior is the study of people (in organizations) and that an individual human's behavior is complex, thus requiring complicated psychological models. However, psychology is not all that different from the other sciences in regard to the magnitude of empirical findings, the precision of measurements, the consistency of results, and the accuracy in predicting individual-level outcomes (Hedges, 1987; Meyer et al., 2001). Indeed, very few sciences can predict individual-level outcomes with complete accuracy. Consider the difficulty a meteorologist faces predicting the weather on any given day with complete accuracy. Actuaries predicting whether or not an individual will file an insurance claim and credit bureaus predicting individuals' creditworthiness also have difficulty predicting future events with complete certainty. Even in the laboratory sciences, difficulties exist. Most chemical reactions do not result in all molecules/atoms reacting (i.e., the "actual yield" of a most chemical reactions is less than the "theoretical yield"). Although there are many causes of an individual's behavior, there are also many causes of the behavior of an individual molecule, the weather, the economy, and so forth. In other fields, it is often helpful to study the effects of an independent variable on a dependent variable using parsimonious models and theories. We suggest that the same process be used by organizational researchers. Attempting to create a model that explains everything using every possible independent variable leads to a model that is difficult to test and to validate. It also introduces the possibility of redundancy and overlap in the independent variables (e.g., does the second independent variable relate to the dependent variable because it is a proxy for the first independent variable or are both measures of the same construct?).

4 This incorrect definition persists in the psychometric literature and appears in Carroll's (1993) treatise and McGrew's (2009; McGrew & Evans, 2004) reviews. Although using the incorrect definition of induction, Carroll (p. 238) noted the work of Colberg and her colleagues on general-to-particular inductive tasks.

5 These values were obtained using Hunter et al.'s (2006) reanalysis of Hunter's (1980) meta-analysis analysis and syntax for computing expectancies from Cucina, Berger & Busciglio, (2017).

6 This is based on the expectancies (obtained using Cucina et al.'s, 2017, R syntax) for the 95% confidence interval about the point estimate of .66 (.63 to .69 using the sample size of 12,933 reported by Hunter, 1986, and applying the corrections for unreliability and range restriction to the uncorrected upper and lower bounds of the confidence interval).

References

Aguinis, H., Bradley, K. J., & Broderson, A. (2014). Industrial-organizational psychologists in business schools: Brain drain or eye opener? *Industrial and Organizational Psychology, 7*(3), 284–303.

Aguinis, H., Mazurkiewicz, M. D., & Heggestad, E. D. (2009). Using web-based frame-of-reference training to decrease biases in personality-based job analysis: An experimental field study. *Personnel Psychology, 62*(2), 405–438.

Blunt, C. J. (2015). Hierarchies of evidence in evidence-based medicine (Unpublished doctoral dissertation). London, UK: London School of Economics.

Blunt, C. J. (2020, August 10). *Hiearchies of evidence.* London, UK: London School of Economics. Retrieved December 12, 2020, from http://cjblunt.com/hierarchies-evidence/

Bradley, J. C. (2007). Open notebook science using blogs and wikis. *Nature Precedings.* https://doi.org/10.1038/npre.2007.39.1

Bradley, J. C. (September 26, 2006). Open notebook science. *Drexel CoAS E-Learning.* Retrieved August 11, 2021, from http://drexel-coas-elearning.blogspot.com/2006/09/open-notebook-science.html

Brooker, R. J., Widmaier, E. P., Graham, L. E., & Stiling, P. D. (2020). *Biology.* (5th ed.). New York, NY: McGraw-Hill.

Brush, S. G. (1999). Why was relativity accepted? *Physics in Perspective, 1*, 184–214.

Burgus, R., Dunn, T. F., Desiderio, D., Ward, D. N., Vale, W., & Guillemin, R. (1970). Characterization of ovine hypothalamic hypophysiotropic TSH-releasing factor. *Nature, 226*(5243), 321–325.

Campbell, J. P., & Wilmot, M. P. (2018). The functioning of theory in industrial, work and organizational psychology (IWOP). *The SAGE handbook of industrial, work & organizational psychology, 3v: Personnel psychology and employee performance; organizational psychology; managerial psychology and organizational approaches, 1.*

Canadian Task Force on the Periodic Health Examination. (1979). The periodic health examination. *Canadian Medical Association Journal, 121*, 1193–1254.

Carroll, J. B. (1993). *Human cognitive abilities: A survey of factor analytic studies.* New York: Cambridge University Press.

Carter, N. T., Dalal, D. K., Boyce, A. S., O'Connell, M. S., Kung, M. C., & Delgado, K. M. (2014). Uncovering curvilinear relationships between conscientiousness and job performance: How theoretically appropriate measurement makes an empirical difference. *Journal of Applied Psychology, 99*(4), 564–586.

Cartwright, N. (1999). *The dappled world: A study of the boundaries of science.* New York, NY: Cambridge University Press.

Chaisson, E., & McMillan, S. (2017). *Astronomy: A beginner's guide to the universe* (8th ed.). London, UK: Pearson Education, Inc.

Chang, R., & Goldsby, K. A. (2019). *Chemistry* (13th ed.). New York, NY: McGraw-Gill.

Cochrane Library. (n.d.). *About Cochrane reviews.* John Wiley & Sons, Inc. Retrieved December 22, 2020, from https://www.cochranelibrary.com/about/about-cochrane-reviews.

Cohen, J. (1992). A power primer. *Psychological Bulletin, 112*(1), 155–159.

Colberg, M., Nester, M. A., & Trattner, M. H. (1985). Convergence of the inductive and deductive models in the measurement of reasoning abilities. *Journal of Applied Psychology, 70*(4), 681.

Cook, T. D., & D. T. Campbell (1979). *Quasi experimentation: Design and analytical issues for field settings.* Chicago, IL: Rand McNally.

Coon, D., & Mitterer, J.O. (2018). *Psychology: Modules for active learning* (14th ed.). Stamford, CT: Cengage Learning.

Corbyn, Z. (2010, January 23). Publisher attempts to rein in radical medical journal: Editor rejects proposal to have submissions peer reviewed. *Times Higher Education*. Retrieved June 8, 2015, from https://www.timeshighereducation.co.uk/news/publisher-attempts-to-rein-in-radical-medical-journal/410113.article.

Corley, K. G., & Gioia, D. A. (2011). Building theory about theory building: What constitutes a theoretical contribution? *Academy of Management Review, 36*(1), 12–32.

Cortina, J. M. (2016). Defining and operationalizing theory. *Journal of Organizational Behavior, 37*(8), 1142–1149.

Cortina, J. M. (2014). In Z. Sheng (Interviewer). An interview with SIOP's newly elected President, Dr. Jose Cortina. *The I/ON: The official newsletter of the industrial/organizational psychology program at George Mason University*. Fairfax, VA: George Mason University. Retrieved February 7, 2014, from http://www.gmu.edu/org/iopsa/Fall2013ION_updatedFINALpdf.pdf.

Cortina, J. M., Aguinis, H., & DeShon, R. P. (2017). Twilight of dawn or evening? A century of research methods. *Journal of Applied Psychology, 102*(3), 274–290.

Crowell, B. (2020). *Light and Matter*. Fullerton, CA: Fullerton College.

Cucina, J. M., Nicklin, J. M., Ashkanasy, N., Cortina, J. M., Mathieu, J. E., & McDaniel, M. A. (2015). *The role of theory in industrial/organizational psychology research and practice*. Debate presented at the 30th meeting of the Society for Industrial and Organizational Psychology, Philadelphia, PA.

Cucina, J. M., Berger, J. L., & Busciglio, H. H. (2017). Creating expectancy charts: A new approach. *Personnel Assessment and Decisions, 3*(1), 1.

Cucina, J. M., & Hayes, T. L. (2015). Comment on estimating the reproducibility of psychological science. *Science*.

Cucina, J. M., & Moriarty, K. O. (2015). A historical look at theory in industrial-organizational psychology journals. *The Industrial-Organizational Psychologist, 53*(1), 57–70.

Cucina, J. M., Hayes, T. L., Walmsley, P. T., & Martin, N. R. (2014). It is time to get medieval on the overproduction of pseudotheory: How Bacon (1267) and Alhazen (1021) can save I/O psychology. *Industrial and Organizational Psychology: Perspectives on Science and Practice, 7*(3), 356–364.

Cucina, J. M., Martin, N. R., Vasilopoulos, N. L., & Thibodeaux, H. F. (2012). Self-serving bias effects on job analysis ratings. *The Journal of Psychology: Interdisciplinary and Applied, 146*(5), 1–21.

Cucina, J. M., Su, C., Busciglio, H. H., & Thompson Peyton, S. (2015). Something more than *g*: Meaningful Memory uniquely predicts training performance. *Intelligence, 49*, 192–206.

Cucina, J. M., Vasilopoulos, N. L., & Sehgal, K. (2005). Personality-based job analysis and the self-serving bias. *Journal of Business and Psychology, 20*(2), 275–290.

Cumpston, M., & Chandler J. (2020). Chapter IV: Updating a review. In J. P. T. Higgins, J. Thomas, J. Chandler, M. Cumpston, T. Li, T. M. J. Page, & V. A. Welch (Eds.). *Cochrane handbook for systematic reviews of interventions (Version 6.1; updated September 2020)*. Hoboken, NJ: John Wiley & Sons & London, UK: Cochrane Collaboration. Available from www.training.cochrane.org/handbook.

Davis, M. S. (1971). That's interesting! Towards a phenomenology of sociology and a sociology of phenomenology. *Philosophy of the social sciences, 1*(2), 309–344.

Dilchert, S. (2017). Future of research published in the International Journal of Selection and Assessment: Incoming editor's perspective. *International Journal of Selection and Assessment, 25*(4), 416–418.

Dunning, D., Perie, M., & Story, A. L. (1991). Self-serving prototypes of social categories. *Journal of Personality and Social Psychology, 61*(6), 957–968.

Edwards, J. R., Berry, J., & Kay, V. S. (2014, January). Bridging the great divide between theoretical and empirical management research. In *Academy of management proceedings* (Vol. 2014, No. 1, p. 17696). Academy of Management.

Epstein, S. (1979). The stability of behavior: I. On predicting most of the people much of the time. *Journal of Personality and Social Psychology, 37*(7), 1097–1126.

Faul, F., Erdfelder, E., Buchner, A., & Lang, A. G. (2009). Statistical power analyses using G★Power 3.1: Tests for correlation and regression analyses. *Behavior Research Methods, 41*, 1149–1160.

Faul, F., Erdfelder, E., Lang, A.-G., & Buchner, A. (2007). G★Power 3: A flexible statistical power analysis program for the social, behavioral, and biomedical sciences. *Behavior Research Methods, 39*, 175–191.

Fitelson, B. (2006). Inductive Logic. In J. Pfeifer & S. Sarkar (Eds.). *Philosophy of science: An encyclopedia*. London, UK: Routledge Press.

Freeman, S., Quillin, K., Allison, L., Black, M., Podgorski, G., Taylor, E., & Carmichael, J. (2017). *Biological science* (6th ed.). Boston, MA: Pearson Education, Inc.

Gilbert, T. R., Kirss, R. V., Foster, N., & Davies, G. (2014). *Chemistry: An atoms-focused approach*. New York, NY: W.W. Norton & Company, Inc.

Goldberg, S. (1987). Putting new wine in old bottles: The assimilation of relativity in America. (pp. 1–26). In T. F. Glick. (Ed.). *The comparative reception of relativity*. Boston, MA: D. Reidel Publishing Company.

Hambleton, R. K., Swaminathan, H., & Rogers, H. J. (1991). *Fundamentals of item response theory*. Newbury Park, CA: SAGE Publications, Inc.

Hambrick, D. C. (2007). The field of management's devotion to theory: Too much of a good thing? *Academy of Management Journal, 50*(6), 1346–1352.

Harvey, A., & Schucking, E. (2000). Einstein's mistake and the cosmological constant. *American Journal of Physics, 68*(8), 723–727.

Hawthorne, J. (2017). Inductive Logic. *The Stanford Encyclopedia of Philosophy*. (Spring 2017 ed.), In E.N. Zalta (Ed.). https://plato.stanford.edu/archives/spr2017/entries/logic-inductive

Hedges, L.V. (1987). How hard is hard science, how soft is soft science? The empirical cumulativeness of research. *American Psychologist, 42*(2), 443–455.

Hewitt, P. G. (2015). *Conceptual physics* (12th ed.). Boston, MA: Pearson.

Highhouse, S. (2014). Do we need all these words? The need for new publishing norms in I-O psychology. *The Industrial-Organizational Psychologist, 51*(3), 83–84.

Hockenbury, S. E., Nolan, S., & Hockenbury, D. H. (2015). *Psychology* (7th ed.). New York, NY: Worth Publishers.

Hoefnagels, M. (2019). *Biology: The essentials* (3rd ed.). New York, NY: McGraw-Hill Education.

Howick, J., Glasziou, P., & Aronson, J. K. (2010). Evidence-based mechanistic reasoning. *Journal of the Royal Society of Medicine, 103*, 433–441.

Hunter, J. E. (1980). *Validity generalization for 12,000 jobs: An application of synthetic validity and validity generalization to the General Aptitude Test Battery (GATB)*. Washington, DC: U.S. Department of Labor, Employment Service.

Internet Encyclopedia of Philosophy. (2016). *Deductive and Inductive Arguments*. Retrieved July 17, 2016, from http://www.iep.utm.edu/ded-ind/.

Jebb, A. T., & Woo, S. E. (2015). A Bayesian primer for the organizational sciences: The "two sources" and an introduction to BugsXLA. *Organizational Research Methods, 18*(1), 92–132.

Journal of Applied Psychology. (2004). Instructions to authors. [Editorial]. *Journal of Applied Psychology, 89*(1), 178.

Kacmar, K. M., & Whitfield, J. M. (2000). An additional rating method for journal articles in the field of management. *Organizational Research Methods, 3*(4), 392–406.

Kay, L., Palen, S., Smith, B., & Blumenthal, G. (2013). *21st century astronomy* (4th ed.) New York, NY: W. W. Norton & Company, Inc.

Kaye, S. (n.d.). William of Ockham (Occam, c. 1280—c. 1349). *Internet Encyclopedia of Philosophy*. Retrieved January 4, 2021, from https://iep.utm.edu/ockham/#H2.

Kenny, D. A. (1979). *Correlation and causality*. New York: Wiley.

Kenny, D. A. (2004). *Correlation and causality* (Revised ed.). Storrs, CT: Author.

Kepes, S., & McDaniel, M. A. (2013). How trustworthy is the scientific literature in I-O psychology? *Industrial and Organizational Psychology: Perspectives on Science and Practice, 6*, 252–268.

Kerr, N. L. (1998). HARKing: Hypothesizing after the results are known. *Personality and Social Psychology Review, 2*(3), 196–217.

Ketchen, D. J. (2002). Some candid thoughts on the publication process. *Journal of Management, 28*, 585–590.

Klein, K. J., & Zedeck, S. (2004). Introduction to the special section on theoretical models and conceptual analyses – Theory in applied psychology: Lessons (re)learned. *Journal of Applied Psychology, 89*(6), 931–933.

Köhler, T., DeSimone, J. A., & Schoen, J. L. (2020). Prestige does not equal quality: Lack of research quality in high-prestige journals. *Industrial and Organizational Psychology, 13*, 321–327.

Kruschke, J. K., Aguinis, H., & Joo, H. (2012). The time has come: Bayesian methods for data analysis in the organizational sciences. *Organizational Research Methods, 15*, 722–752.

LaCour, M. J., & Green, D. P. (2014). When contact changes minds: An experiment on transmission of support for gay equality. *Science, 346*(6215), 1366–1369.

Lance, C. E., & Vandenberg, R. J. (2015). *More statistical and methodological myths and urban legends*. New York, NY: Routledge.

Licht, D., & Hull, M. (2014). *Scientific American: Psychology*. New York, NY: Worth Publishers.

Lilienfeld, S. O., Lynn, S. J., Ruscio, J., & Beyerstein, B. L. (2009). *50 great myths of popular psychology: Shattering widespread misconceptions about human behavior*. Malden, MA: Wiley-Blackwell.

Locke, E. A. (2007). The case for inductive theory building. *Journal of Management, 33*(6), 867–890.

Locke, E. A., & Latham, G. P. (2002). Building a practically useful theory of goal setting and task motivation: A 35-year odyssey. *American Psychologist, 57*(9), 705–717.

Locke, K., & Golden-Biddle, K. (1997). Constructing opportunities for contribution: Structuring intertextual coherence and "problematizing" in organizational studies. *Academy of Management Journal, 40*(5), 1023–1062.

Locke, E. A., Williams, K. J., & Masuda, A. (2015). The virtue of persistence. *The Industrial-Organizational Psychologist, 52*(4), 104–5.

Lutgens, F. K., Tarbuck, E. J., & Tasa, D.G. (2014). *Essentials of Geology* (13th ed.). New York NY: Pearson.

Mason, K. A., Losos, J. B., Duncan, T. Welsh, C. J., Raven, P. H., & Johnson, G. B. (2020). *Biology.* (12th ed.). New York, NY: McGraw-Hill.

McGrew, K. S. (2009). CHC theory and the human cognitive abilities project: Standing on the shoulders of the giants of psychometric intelligence research. *Intelligence, 37,* 1–10.

McGrew, K. S., & Evans, J. J. (2004). *Internal and external factorial extensions to the Cattell-Horn-Carroll (CHC) theory of cognitive abilities: A review of factor analytic research since Carroll's seminal 1993 treatise.* (Carroll Human Cognitive Abilities Project Research Report No. 2). Institute for Applied Psychometrics.

Medical Hypotheses. (n.d.). Guide for authors. Retrieved December 22, 2020, from https://www.elsevier.com/journals/medical-hypotheses/0306-9877/guide-for-authors.

Merry, S. N., Hetrick, S. E., Cox, G. R., Brudevold-Iversen, T., Bir, J. J., & McDowell, H. (2012). Cochrane Review: Psychological and educational interventions for preventing depression in children and adolescents. *Evidence-Based Child Health: A Cochrane Review Journal, 7*(5), 1409–1685.

Meyer, G. J., Finn, S. E., Eyde, L. D., Kay, G. G., Moreland, K. L., Dies, R. R., & Reed, G. M. (2001). Psychological testing and psychological assessment: A review of evidence and issues. *American psychologist, 56*(2), 128–165.

Mintzberg, H. (2005). Developing theory about the development of theory. *Great minds in management: The process of theory development,* 355–372.

Mischel, W. (1968). *Personality and Assessment.* New York, NY: John Wiley & Sons, Inc.

Monroe, J. S., & Wicander, R. (2015). *The changing earth: Exploring geology and evolution* (7th ed.). Stamford, CT: Cengage Learning.

Mupepele, A. C., Walsh, J. C., Sutherland, W. J., & Dormann, C. F. (2016). An evidence assessment tool for ecosystem services and conservation studies. *Ecological Applications, 26*(5), 1295–1301.

National Academy of Sciences and Institute of Medicine. (2008). *Science, evolution, and creationism.* Washington, DC: The National Academies Press.

National Academy of Sciences. (n.d.). *Evolution resources at the National Academies: Definitions of evolutionary terms.* Washington, DC: Author. Retrieved March 6, 2021, from https://www.nationalacademies.org/evolution/definitions.

National Center for Science Education. (2016). *Definitions of fact, theory, and law in scientific work.* Oakland, CA: Author. Retrieved March 6, 2021 from https://ncse.com/library-resource/definitions-fact-theory-law-scientific-work.

Nature. (2015). For authors: Other material published in *Nature.* Retrieved September 21, 2015, from http://www.nature.com/nature/authors/gta/others.html.

Nicklin, J. M., & Spector, P. E. (2016). Point/Counterpoint introduction: The future of theory in organizational behavior research. *Journal of Organizational Behavior, 37*(8), 1113–1115.

Nunnally, J. C., & Bernstein, I. H. (1994). *Psychometric theory* (3rd ed.). New York: McGraw Hill.

O'Boyle Jr., E. H., Banks, G. C., & Gonzalez-Mulé, E. (2017). The chrysalis effect: How ugly initial results metamorphosize into beautiful articles. *Journal of Management, 43*(2), 376–399.

Olenick, J., Walker, R., Bradburn, J., & DeShon, R. P. (2018). A systems view of the scientist–practitioner gap. *Industrial and Organizational Psychology, 11*(2), 220–227.

Ones, D. S., Kaiser, R. B., Chamorro-Premuzic, T., & Svensson, C. (2017). Has industrial-organizational psychology lost its way? *The Industrial-Organizational Psychologist, 54*(4). Retrieved from http://www.siop.org/tip/april17/lostio.aspx.

Open Science Collaboration. (2015). Estimating the reproducibility of psychological science. *Science*, *349*(6251), aac4716.

Pain, E. (2019, September 3). How to keep a lab notebook. *Science*. Retrieved August 11, 2021, from https://www.sciencemag.org/careers/2019/09/how-keep-lab-notebook.

Pauling, L., & Corey, R. B. (1953). Structure of the nucleic acids. *Nature*, *171*(4347), 346.

Pfeffer, J., & Sutton, R. I. (2006). Evidence-based management. *Harvard Business Review*, *84*(1), 62–74.

Phelan, J. (2015). *What is life? A guide to biology* (3rd ed.). New York, NY: W.H. Freeman and Company.

Platt, J. R. (1964). Strong inference: Certain systematic methods of scientific thinking may produce much more rapid progress than others. *Science*, *146*, 347–353.

Popper, K. (1934). *Logik der forschung: Zur erkenntnistheorie der modernen naturwissenschaft*. Vienna, Austria: Verlag von Julius Springer.

Popper, K. (1959). *The logic of scientific discovery*. London, UK: Hutchinson and Company.

Reay, T., Berta, W., & Kohn, M. K. (2009). What's the evidence on evidence-based management? *Academy of Management Perspectives*, *23*(4), 5–18.

Reay, T., Zafar, A., Monteiro, P. & Glaser, V. (2019). Presenting findings from qualitative research: One size does not fit all!. In T. Zilber, J. Amis and J. Mair. *The Production of Managerial Knowledge and Organizational Theory: New Approaches to Writing, Producing and Consuming Theory*. Emerald Publishing Limited.

Roberts, J. S., Donoghue, J. R., & Laughlin, J. E. (2000). A general item response theory model for unfolding unidimensional polytomous responses. *Applied Psychological Measurement*, *24*, 3–32.

Rogers, K. (2016, November 22). Scientific hypothesis. *Encyclopaedia Britannica*. Chicago, IL: Encyclopaedia Britannica, Inc. Retrieved January 24, 2017, from: https://www.britannica.com/topic/scientific-hypothesis.

Ryan, A. M., & Ployhart, R. E. (2014). A century of selection. *Annual Review of Psychology*, *65*, 693–717.

Saylors, R., & Trafimow, D. (2021). Why the increasing use of complex causal models is a problem: On the danger sophisticated theoretical narratives pose to truth. *Organizational Research Methods*, 24(3), 616–629.

Schapira, M., The Open Lab Notebook Consortium, Harding, R., J. (2019). Open laboratory notebooks: Good for science, good for society, good for scientists. [Version 2; peer review: 2 approved, 1 approved with reservations]. *F1000Research*, *8*, 87. pmid:31448096.

Schmidt, F. L. (2015). History and development of the Schmidt–Hunter meta-analysis methods. *Research synthesis methods*, *6*(3), 232–239.

Schmidt, F. L., & Hunter, J. E. (1977). Development of a general solution to the problem validity generalization. *Journal of Applied Psychology*, *62*, 529–540.

Schmidt, F. L., & Hunter, J. E. (2004). General mental ability in the world of work: Occupational attainment and job performance. *Journal of Personality and Social Psychology*, *86*(1), 162–173.

Schmidt, F. L., & Raju, N. S. (2007). Updating meta-analytic research findings: Bayesian approaches versus the medical model. *Journal of Applied Psychology*, *92*(2), 297.

Schmidt, F. L., Hunter, J. E., Pearlman, K., & Shane, G. S. (1979). Further tests of the Schmidt-Hunter Bayesian validity generalization model. *Personnel Psychology*, *32*, 257–281.

Schmidt, F., & Hunter, J. (2003). History, development, evolution, and impact of validity generalization and meta-analysis methods, 1975–2001. In K.R. Murphy (Ed.). *Validity generalization: A critical review*. (pp. 42–76). Mahwah, NJ: Lawrence Erlbaum Associates, Inc.

Schmidt, F.L., Hunter, J. E., Pearlman, K., & Hirsh, H. R. (1985). Forty questions about validity generalization and meta-analysis. *Personnel Psychology, 38*, 697–798.

Schmidt, F. L., Hunter, J. E., & Urry, V. W. (1976). Statistical power in criterion-related validation studies. *Journal of Applied Psychology, 61*(4), 473–485.

Schneider, B. (2018). Being competitive in the talent management space. *Industrial and Organizational Psychology, 11*(2), 231–236.

Shen, W., Cucina, J. M., Walmsley, P., & Seltzer, B. (2014). When correcting for unreliability of job performance ratings, the best estimate is still .52. *Industrial and Organizational Psychology: Perspectives on Science and Practice, 7*, 519–524.

Shepherd, D. A., & Suddaby, R. (2017). Theory building: A review and integration. *Journal of Management, 43*(1), 59–86.

Shojania, K. G., Sampson, M., Ansari, M. T., Ji, J., Doucette, S., & Moher, D. (2007). How quickly do systematic reviews go out of date? A survival analysis. *Annals of Internal Medicine, 147*(4), 224–233.

Siegel, E. (2013, May 17). "Einstein's greatest blunder" was REALLY a blunder! *ScienceBlogs*. Retrieved December 23, 2020, from https://scienceblogs.com/startswithabang/2013/05/17/einsteins-greatest-blunder-was-really-a-blunder.

Silberberg, M., & Amateis, P. (2018). *Chemistry: The molecular nature of matter and change* (8th ed.). New York, NY: McGraw-Hill Education.

Simmons, J. P., Nelson, L. D., & Simonsohn, U. (2011). False-positive psychology: Undisclosed flexibility in data collection and analysis allows presenting anything as significant. *Psychological Science, 22*(11), 1359–1366.

Skyrms, B. (2000). *Choice and chance: An introduction to inductive logic* (4th ed.). Wadsworth, Inc.

Spector, P. E., Rogelberg, S. G., Ryan, A. M., Schmitt, N., & Zedeck, S. (2014). Moving the pendulum back to the middle: Reflections on and introduction to the inductive research special issue. *Journal of Business and Psychology, 29*(4), 499–502.

Stanovich, K. E. (2010). *How to think straight about psychology* (9th ed.). Boston, MA: Allyn & Bacon

Sutton, R. I., & Staw, B. M. (1995). What theory is *not*. *Administrative Science Quarterly, 40*, 371–384.

Texas Gateway/Texas Education Agency. (n.d.). Theories. *Texas Gateway for online resources*. Austin, TX: Texas Education Agency. Retrieved March 6, 2021, from https://www.texasgateway.org/resource/theories.

Thurstone, L. L. (1938). Primary mental abilities. *Psychometric Monographs*, (No. 1).

Trafton, L. M., & Wildey, R. L. (1970). Jupiter: His limb darkening and the magnitude of his internal energy source. *Science, 168*(3936), 1214–1215.

U. S. Department of Labor. (1958). *Guide to the use of General Aptitude Test Battery – Section III: Development*. Washington, DC.

Uman, L. S. (2011). Systematic reviews and meta-analyses. *Journal of the Canadian Academy of Child and Adolescent Psychiatry, 20*(1), 57–59.

Viswesvaran, C., Ones, D. S., & Schmidt, F. L. (1996). Comparative analysis of the reliability of job performance ratings. *Journal of Applied Psychology, 81*(5), 557–574.

Watson, J. D. (1997). *The double helix. London: Weidenfeld & Nicholson*.

Watson, J. D., & Crick, F. H. (1953). Molecular structure of nucleic acids. *Nature, 171*(4356), 737–738.

Wicander, R., & Monroe, J. S. (2013). *GEOL2*. Belmont, CA: Brooks/Cole.

Woo, S. E., O'Boyle, E. H., & Spector, P. E. (2017). Best practices in developing, conducting, and evaluating inductive research. *Human Resources Management Review, 27*, 255–264.

INDEX

Note: Page references in *italics* indicate figures, **bold** indicates tables and "n" indicates footnotes.

Printed in the United States
by Baker & Taylor Publisher Services